THE FUTURE OF MARKET TRANSITION

RESEARCH IN SOCIAL STRATIFICATION AND MOBILITY

Series Editor: Kevin T. Leicht

Volumes 1–3:	Edited by Donald J. Treiman and Robert V. Robinson
Volumes 4–6:	Edited by Robert V. Robinson
Volumes 7–9:	Edited by Arne L. Kalleberg
Volumes 10–13:	Edited by Robert Althauser and Michael Wallace
Volumes 14 & 15:	Edited by Michael Wallace
Volume 16:	Edited by Kevin T. Leicht
Volume 17:	The Future of Affirmative Action – Edited by Kevin T. Leicht
Volume 18:	Edited by Kevin T. Leicht

RESEARCH IN SOCIAL STRATIFICATION AND
MOBILITY VOLUME 19

THE FUTURE OF MARKET TRANSITION

EDITED BY

KEVIN T. LEICHT
Department of Sociology, The University of Iowa, Iowa, USA

2002

JAI
An Imprint of Elsevier Science

Amsterdam – Boston – London – New York – Oxford – Paris
San Diego – San Francisco – Singapore – Sydney – Tokyo

ELSEVIER SCIENCE Ltd
The Boulevard, Langford Lane
Kidlington, Oxford OX5 1GB, UK

First edition 2002

Library of Congress Cataloging in Publication Data
A catalog record from the Library of Congress has been applied for.

British Library Cataloguing in Publication Data
A catalogue record from the British Library has been applied for.

ISBN: 0-7623-0835-4
ISSN: 0276-5624 (Series)

♾ The paper used in this publication meets the requirements of ANSI/NISO Z39.48-1992 (Permanence of Paper).
Printed in The Netherlands.

CONTENTS

PART III: ANALYSES OF OCCUPATIONAL ATTAINMENT AND GENDER INEQUALITY

PART IV: THEORETICAL AND EMPIRICAL EXPLICATIONS OF MARKET TRANSITION THEORY

LIST OF CONTRIBUTORS

Yanjie Bian	Division of Social Science, Hong Kong University of Science and Technology, Kowloon, Hong Kong
Michael Burawoy	Department of Sociology, University of California at Berkeley, USA
Yang Cao	Department of Sociology, Louisiana State University, Louisiana, USA
Doug Guthrie	Department of Sociology, New York University, New York, USA
Zsuzsa Hanto	Institute of Law and Government, Debrecen, Hungary
Ruyin Hu	Research Center, Shanghai Stock Exchange, Shanghai, PRC
Lisa A. Keister	The Ohio State University, Columbus, OH, USA
Victor Nee	Department of Sociology, Cornell University, Ithaca, New York, USA
Anthony Oberschall	Sociology Department, University of North Carolina at Chapel Hill, NC, USA
Sonja Opper	Economic Faculty, Tübingen University, Tübingen, Germany
Rachel A. Rosenfeld	Department of Sociology, University of North Carolina at Chapel Hill, NC, USA
Xiaoling Shu	Department of Sociology, University of California Davis, CA, USA

Ivan Szelenyi	Department of Sociology, Yale University, New Haven, CT, USA
Heike Trappe	Max Planck Institute for Human Development, Berlin, Germany
Sonia M. L. Wong	School of Business, The University of Hong Kong, Hong Kong
Raymond Sin-Kwok Wong	Department of Sociology, University of California, Santa Barbara, CA, USA
Zhanxin Zhang	Division of Social Science, Hong Kong University of Science and Technology, Kowloon, Hong Kong
Litao Zhao	Department of Sociology, Stanford University, Stanford, CA, USA
Wei Zhao	Department of Sociology, Duke University, NC, USA
Xueguang Zhou	Department of Sociology, Duke University, NC, USA

INTRODUCTION

In volume 19 of *Research in Social Stratification and Mobility*, we address one of the most important social and economic changes to come along in several centuries and perhaps ever (given the number of people affected). The collapse of state socialism in Russia and the satellite republics of the Soviet Union and Eastern Europe will almost certainly change the way the global economy works, who is counted as a member of the economic elite, and who is ruled "irrelevant". The rapid economic transformation of China, albeit under the direction of a state socialist political hierarchy, will almost certainly change the economic lives of billions of people, changing the fabric of Chinese society in ways that are still not well understood. As with *RSSM's* foray into the sensitive subject of affirmative action in Volume 17, the complexity, importance, and sensitivity of a topic should not drive stratification researchers *from* studying market transition, it should draw students and researchers *toward* it. I hope that the readers of this volume will be as stimulated by the research here as I was when I first read it and that new research ideas will result from the omissions and commissions of this excellent set of scholars.

Many of the participants in this special issue were participants in an earlier exchange in a 1996 issue of the *American Journal of Sociology*. These authors (Nee, Obershall and Szelenyi) take their analyses in important and new directions that I think readers will find interesting. Obershall offers a new analysis (and the only analysis in this volume) of the effects of market transition on the agricultural sector of a transition economy (Hungary). These authors are joined by Michael Burawoy, perhaps the most widely read and cited observer of the labor process under state socialism and capitalism. Burawoy has researched and commented on issues involving the development of market economies in other contexts and his participation in this collection of essays is a welcome addition to the original symposium group. The combined analyses and reflections of these scholars prove that there is still much to learn from the "old masters" that have studied this important institutional change from its beginnings. (That we can call scholars in the prime of their careers "old masters" in the study of market transition gives us some idea how rapidly things have changed.)

The remaining essays are from researchers who are relative newcomers to research on former state socialist economies. Opper, Wong and Hu provide an interesting and important analysis of the types of firms that are listed on

China's stock exchanges, who owns these firms, and what implications this has for the likely course of market transition. Guthrie and Keister (in separate contributions) document the extensive changes that are occurring in labor market institutions as these are enacted inside of firms, in the functioning of employment law, and in the behavior of employers and workers in labor markets. Wong offers our only comparative analysis of changes in the relative value of human and social capital in the stratification systems of Eastern European countries. Rosenfeld and Trappe examine changes in gender stratification in East and West Germany before and after German unification, one of the many places where rare but interesting "natural experiments" are possible in the study of market transition. Shu and Bian's research comparing the relationship between gender inequality and market penetration suggests that there is no straightforward relationship between gender inequality and growing capitalist markets. Finally, Zhao, Zhau and Zhou, and Bian and Zhang re-examine important tenets of market transition theory and debate in different contexts throughout China, leading readers toward a nuanced and complex interpretation of the effects of markets and political capital on social stratification.

If I assume that the submissions I've received for this issue are representative of market transition research overall, the thoughtful scholars who have contributed to this issue have produced research that highlights new and interesting questions that should keep researchers busy for years. But the questions are not merely academic; they affect most of the world's population covering about two-thirds of the earth's surface. This is one area of social science where the answers (and the policies that result from them) do matter. What would a future research agenda look like?

First, *the contributions to this volume point to the need for more systematic, cross-national comparisons between not only former state socialist economies but also between traditionally capitalist and former state socialist economies.* In fact, this new line of research should make systematic comparisons with various types of "capitalisms" rather than assuming that (say) all the G7 or OECD countries represent a "capitalist block" that can serve as an aggregate comparison group. The types of comparisons should begin simply and build up from there, and the measurement issues involved are far from trivial. But this work is necessary to answer some very important questions in the market transition debate.

As an example, most market transition research suggests that the spread of markets and market institutions should reduce the relative importance of political capital and increases the relative importance of human capital for securing rewards from the stratification system. This statement implies two comparisons. The first is a same-country comparison between a state socialist labor market at and earlier time and a capitalist labor market at some later time. While this comparison seems obvious, it has been difficult to execute in practice and the authors in this volume take significant steps in that direction.

But the need for this comparison, and the role that market transition research has played in highlighting it, brings to mind another comparison that is necessary if we are really going to make the comparisons that market transition theories require. That comparison would examine the role of human and political capital in the stratification systems of established market economies. Every time I look at a coefficient that translates the effect of a political cadre position into income, a question that pops into my mind is whether such political resources are worth anything in a "traditional" market economy and (if so) what. The question sounds stupid until you think about it; what is the value of coming from a family in the United States that belongs to the Republican Party? Or from a family of Christian Democrats in Germany? The comparisons could go on from there. How are we supposed to tell whether the effect of political capital is declining in a former state socialist economy that is moving toward a market economy if we don't know what value political capital has in the stratification systems of established market economies? As I write this, George W. Bush is promoting legislation that would end most inheritance taxes in the United States. This is just the latest of series of actions, large and small, that suggest that the market transition assumptions and predictions about the changing role of political capital need to be supported by research on political capital in established market economies.

A second and related research issue involves an "entrepreneurial failure" of sorts. It seems obvious that those who are relatively privileged in a social stratification hierarchy are going to attempt to maintain their positions using almost any means at their disposal. But we also know that the ability of elites to stay on top of the social stratification system is a variable – if it was not, there would be no point in doing market transition research at all and no reason to do most social stratification research anywhere else. As Charles Tilly (1998) suggests, there are plenty of niches for opportunity hoarding, emulation, mimicry and exploitation in the market transition context. However, instead of studying why former political elites stay on top, I would suggest focusing on a separate issue – *downward mobility among former political elites in market transition regimes*. Like research on the transition from feudalism to capitalism in the west and elsewhere, there is an historic opportunity here to study the decline and economic elimination of former economic elites that mirrors the disappearance of the feudal landlord of a prior age. But we can witness this new transition and interview directly those involved, something we've never been able to do with former feudal elites who were mysteriously swept away by waves of market capitalism. These new downwardly mobile elites almost certainly tried to do something to save themselves and their economic positions; what strategies did they use and why didn't they work?

A third component of a future research agenda should be to *incorporate more countries into market transition research and theory.* Like most research in this area outside of RSSM, a vast majority of work is done with data from China. While China may be a most interesting case in many respects (and certainly wins the population prize for the largest number of people affected), the conditions driving economic reform in China are unique and the results are likely to be unique as well. Far less work has dealt with Eastern Europe and Russia, areas that are at least as geopolitically important as China if not more so. Because communist political elites in Eastern Europe and Russia have surrendered political power as well as economic control, the consequences of the inability to develop stable economic institutions are far graver than the situation in China appears to be (at least at this point in the early 21st Century). In China, a failed market economy can be replaced by a state socialist economy (albeit with a great deal of political turmoil and at a serious human cost). In Eastern Europe and Russia the only alternative to stable economic institutions is a dangerous political abyss that promises to be a humanitarian disaster as well as a geopolitical nightmare. Further, it is a bit difficult to see how some versions of market transition theory can be adequately tested in a society where the leading political party hasn't surrendered its political monopoly.

Fourth, *market transition research needs to incorporate more institutions into its preview in addition to conditions in the labor market that produce social stratification at the individual level.* While it is doubtful that the workings of economic institutions can be understood by a total reliance on the study of individual-level social stratification, there are a whole series of institutions that market economies produce that (presumably) transition economies will need (if they don't have them already). Most of these institutions are under-researched. Among the institutions I'm thinking of are markets for agricultural commodities (a project started by the Obershall/Hanto contribution to this volume), commodity futures and other futures markets (the work by Opper, Wong & Hu is a good start on this), natural resource markets, real estate markets (both commercial and residential), insurance schemes, taxation, entertainment, and mass communications. Banking and credit have already received some attention and should receive more. I suspect that these markets affect the wide array of market signals that average people attempt to interpret as they work their way through a changing and unstable stratification system, but that leads me to the fifth component of a future research agenda.

Market transition research needs to collect data on and pay close attention to changes in the individual lifecourse. Much of our understanding of stratification in the market transition context is pretty wooden; cadre status + human capital + a regression residual = some measure of income in the here and now. We have a much poorer grasp of how individuals navigate their way through the stratification system to maximize their opportunities and buffer themselves from unpredictable turmoil beyond their control. Human capital theory and most theories of the lifecourse take seriously the timing and sequence of life events as these accumulate into multiple patterns of advantage and disadvantage. At this point (13 years after 1989) we still don't have any clear biographical information or life histories of average people in transition economies. This research needs to focus on people at different stages of the lifecourse, including young adults and teenagers who are still in school. Even if this research yielded little more than the recognition that the institutionalized lifecourse has fragmented in the market transition context much as it has fragmented in advanced capitalist economies, this would be a serious advance over the information we have now.

Sixth, *market transition research needs to address the ways that post-socialist economies are interfacing with the increasingly globalized market economy.* Eventually any economy calling itself "capitalist" in the 21st century will have to integrate itself into the globalized marketplace or world system. But what, exactly, do transition economies have to sell and how will they go about doing it? The scenarios here are as diverse as the cultures, languages and nations involved. The workforce in many of these nations is highly educated and skilled. But most of the basics of an economic infrastructure are weak. There undoubtedly are as many good scenarios possible here as nightmarish ones, but right now many of the nightmarish ones seem more plausible (economic stagnation, poverty, political instability, massive out-migration, ethnic conflict, organized crime, and international terrorism). China's ability to market itself as a low wage producer with a highly compliant workforce is only one of many options available. What will Poland, Hungary and Russia bring to the global marketplace?

Finally, *market transition research needs to expand its focus to local communities, networks, and the development of civil society and social capital.* Part of this involves a systematic and far reaching interrogation of the global, radical neoliberal social experiment. For political and economic elites in the West, state socialism provided a ready political and economic foil for a series of radical experiments in the promotion of "free markets". The consequences of these experiments are readily obvious to most observers – serious increases in income and wealth inequality, increases in child poverty, growing environmental destruction, a non-existent social contract, and an economic elite that believes that their very existence is the only contribution to human good they are required to provide. That these ideas are labeled "conservative" in the United States would be laughable if the consequences weren't so grave. That the same political elites who promote market anarchy favor "family values", oppose abortion, pornography, divorce, and rights for women and racial minorities while failing to see the role that free markets play in perpetuating these problems is simply a sign that postmodern manure-spreading is not confined to humanities scholars in cultural studies departments. In short, the historic recognition that markets are superior to centrally planned economies does not constitute proof that neoliberalism is right, economically or otherwise. The political failure to actively engage neoliberal ideologies will affect all of us, not just the citizens of transition economies.

I would be remiss if I didn't thank a few people for helping to put this volume together. Victor Nee approached me about doing a special issue of RSSM on market transition and his session at the 2001 ASA meetings in Anaheim, California helped to galvanize some of the ideas that our authors develop in these pages. Beth Lyman and Wang Jin, my research assistants, reviewed many of the papers and provided helpful suggestions that I incorporated into the reviews. Ann Marie Davenport has been a helpful and friendly face representing a large publishing corporation and she has been a continual advocate for *Research in Social Stratification and Mobility* within Elsevier and outside of it. Without Elsevier's generous support and patience RSSM would not be the growing enterprise it is today.

Finally, I would like to thank the Social Stratification Research Group (RC-28) of the International Sociological Association for adopting *RSSM* as its official journal. Michael Hout, Tom DiPrete, and Yossi Shavit have been especially helpful in cementing this relationship. This relationship should bring RSSM to more readers at lower prices (one of the localized virtues of wedding markets to a vibrant civil society). You'll be hearing more about the consequences of this intellectual marriage in the near future.

As usual, if you like what you read, please contact the authors and tell them how much you like their work. If you don't like what you read, contact the editor. Either way it is a privilege to be the editor of *Research in Social Stratification and Mobility* and to be exposed to world-class researchers from every part of the globe.

Kevin T. Leicht
June 10, 2002
Iowa City, Iowa

PART I:
MARKET TRANSITION AND LESSONS FOR SOCIAL SCIENCE

POSTSOCIALIST INEQUALITIES: THE CAUSES OF CONTINUITY AND DISCONTINUITY

Victor Nee and Yang Cao

INTRODUCTION

That change in the coordinating mechanism of an economy causes a change in the structure of social stratification is widely recognized by students of the twentieth century's experience with state socialism. Following the victories of communist parties in Russia, China and Eastern Europe, state-directed efforts to institute and consolidate centrally planned economies caused predictable changes in the stratification order. Wherever communist parties carried out the same set of institutional changes aimed at sharply diminishing and even eradicating markets and private ownership of productive assets, the stratification order that emerged was remarkably homogenous, despite significant differences in history and culture. The stratification order bore striking similarities with other state socialisms. Djilas's (1957) "new class" theory claimed applicability across a diverse set of national societies. As targets of state-directed class struggle, not only were capitalists and landowners expropriated of their ownership of the means of production, but the elimination of markets severely constrained regeneration of a new capitalist class. In the absence of markets, entrepreneurs lacked the economic institution essential for private capital accumulation.

In light of the remarkable regularity with which the earlier wave of institutional change brought about corresponding changes in the mechanisms shaping the stratification order, why has there been so much controversy

The Future of Market Transition, Volume 19, pages 3–39.

ISBN: 0-7623-0835-4

generated around market transition theory? The theory claims that in the course of the departures from state socialism, the growth of markets and the expansion of private property give rise to multiple bases of power and privilege. This diminishes the political elite's control over the sources of power and privilege, compelling it instead to compete with market-based power – whether through global market penetration, private entrepreneurship, or domestic labor markets – for the preferred pathway to social mobility. The expected increase in returns to human capital and corresponding decline in the relative advantage of the political elite are explained by reference to self-reinforcing mechanisms intrinsic to markets and state interventions directed at supporting the expansion of a market economy (Nee, 1989, 2000). Just as the elimination of markets curtailed opportunities not controlled by the redistributive elite in state socialism, so the growth of markets – domestic and global – can be expected to give rise to new structures of opportunities in which education and work experience, as opposed to political capital, provide the primary sources of advantage. In light of the effects on stratification of the earlier experience of suppressing markets, this proposition ought not be controversial.

Why has market transition theory stimulated persistent skepticism? Not only has its theoretical logic been challenged as a tautology, but its empirical claims have generated skepticism to the extent that positive findings are often dismissed, while purportedly negative findings gain ready acceptance. In this paper, we identify the type of disagreement the debate has generated, conceptually and empirically. We report a meta-analysis of current findings on the effect of state-crafted market transitions on the post-socialist stratification order. We suggest that the discrepant results reported by scholars can be explained by reference to processes sustaining equilibrium conditions leading to path dependence within the structure of social inequality established under state socialism. Discontinuity stemming from market forces most frequently commences from small beginnings through changes at the margins, which are often difficult to discern in empirical studies, especially in the early stages of transitions from state socialism. By contrast, continuity is more readily apparent since the processes that sustain equilibrium conditions embedded in long-standing formal and informal institutional structures are more resilient than many assume. Not until a tipping point is reached do changes at the margins move the stratification order towards a more decisive shift in the direction of discontinuous transformation. Both endogenous and exogenous factors, often in complex, interactive sequence of events, can trigger a tipping point.

The ongoing transitions from state socialism provide rare natural experiments that allow the social sciences the opportunity to study the nature of stratification orders as they adapt to institutional change on the scale of the Industrial Revolution in the West. The processes promoting continuity in the stratification order are persistent forces in any period of discontinuous societal change. We confirm continuity of the pre-existing stratification order through an analysis of occupational attainment in urban China at an early stage of far-reaching institutional change using World Bank data, which highlights jobs in the public sector of the urban economy. This finding, however, need not imply that the explanation of discontinuous change is erroneous or thereby disconfirmed in light of evidence supporting continuity. Because change induced by decentralized markets is an emergent property arising from small beginnings, confirmation of discontinuous change is difficult to obtain especially during the early stages of institutional change. Fundamentally, the causes of continuity and discontinuity are intertwined and coexist in mixed or hybrid institutional orders for relatively long periods, producing path dependence in the postsocialist stratification order. This is why evidence supporting continuity and evidence supporting discontinuity are likely to be embedded in the same data set, and the strong confirmation needed to decisively resolve conflicting claims is difficult to attain in empirical tests.

The problem of confirmation in the market transition debate, we maintain, is general to the social sciences. Confirmation is intrinsically difficult because analysts have yet to take into account the view that powerful forces reinforcing continuity can be expected to be coterminous and interact with causal mechanisms giving rise to discontinuous change. A theory explaining discontinuous change must specify the scope conditions – e.g. sectors in the transition economy – in which mechanisms promoting continuity and discontinuity are likely to concentrate. Hence, we also aim to address a general problem confronting the social sciences in explanations of large-scale institutional change.

WHY MARKET TRANSITION THEORY IS NOT TAUTOLOGICAL

Critics have charged that market transition theory is a tautology (Rona-Tas, 1994; Walder, 1996). However, if the declining-significance-of-redistributive-power hypothesis were truly tautological, then there would not have been so much debate and interest in the empirical claims advanced by market transition theory's propositions. A tautology does not require empirical confirmation since it is true by definition.

In state socialism, the privileges and advantages of the political elite were enormous in relative terms, but *their privileges were the perquisites of office.*

Bureaucrats in state socialism enjoyed their perquisites so long as they were office-holders, but as members of a status group, they could not efficiently convert their political capital into private wealth. The expansion of markets, however, enables the redistributive elite to *monetize* their political capital. Furthermore, diminished state control over the disposition of public assets stemming from the dismantling central planning opens the way for those closest to state power to wrest public resources into private hands through network ties with the political elite. Under the guise of privatization, vast wealth in natural resources was passed from the public coffer to cronies of the new Russian political elite, made up disproportionately of former communist party bureaucrats. Hence, economic marketization and dismantling central planning can plausibly augment, and even exacerbate, the social inequalities that characterized state socialist redistributive regimes (Nee, 1991; Nee & Lian, 1994; Rona-Tas, 1994; Parish & Michelson, 1996; Walder, 1996). Does the apparent anomaly of persistent and even augmented advantage of the political elite lead to the verdict that market transition theory is false? Not necessarily, for if the relative earnings and wealth of entrepreneurs, managers and professionals increase at a more rapid rate than that of the political elite as the market economy expands in scale, then the declining-significance-of-redistributive power hypothesis is confirmed. Cao and Nee (2000) elaborated a model that takes into account the increased earnings advantage of the political elite based on Rona-Tas's (1994) findings for Hungary, and yet demonstrates the predicted relative decline in power and advantage.

CAUSAL CHECKLIST, DATA SHIFTING AND FAIR CAUSAL COMPARISON

The validity of conflicting claims about winners and losers in the transitions from state socialism has been rigorously examined in the "market transition debate." Though the debate at times appears contentious, it involves what Miller has labeled as Level I disagreement, in which scholars actually agree on broad issues of conceptual framework but argue sharply over competing hypotheses (1987, pp. 200–219). Unlike Level II disagreement in which rival paradigms fight in zero-sum fashion over which approach should prevail, Level I disputes typically are resolved through conceptual clarification and empirical confirmation. Scholars produce "a causal checklist" in which alternative factors are specified by competing hypotheses. By means of a "shifting of data" from different case studies, false causes can be eliminated from the checklist, to arrive at "an adequate description of underlying causes" of the phenomenon to be explained which satisfies the requirement of causal depth (Miller, 1987,

p. 202). Confirmation is reached through "fair causal comparison" in assessing how rival sets of hypotheses account for the known facts. The crucial question a research program seeks to adjudicate is whether failures stem from the basic falsehood of hypotheses, as compared to rival hypotheses, or to technical or quantitative considerations. Since, as Miller points out, "causes do not typically leave their footprints in . . . neat ways," to resolve Level I disagreement requires multiple tests of competing hypotheses, which accounts in part for such debates giving rise to a rapid discovery program of research, as in the market transition debate.

Causal Checklist: Causes of Continuity and Discontinuity

To date, the market transition debate has been largely framed as a binary set of opposing claims about whether the shift to market coordination in departures from central planning augments or diminishes the advantages of the political elite, which formerly held monopoly control over the allocation of surplus. This framing of the debate is evident in the interest in empirical results showing the direction and statistical significance of earnings returns to political capital, measured by communist party membership and high rank in the party hierarchy, in tests to confirm or disconfirm market transition theory. The problem with this simple binary approach to testing the theory becomes apparent in reflecting on the path dependent nature of large-scale institutional change. Path dependent societal transformation gives rise to mixed institutional orders in which continuity with the preceding institutional framework is part and parcel of discontinuous change (Nee & Cao, 1999). In local stratification orders, the interests and group identity embedded in elite networks combine to reproduce established patterns of social inequality even in the context of rapid structural change in the coordinating mechanism of the economy (Rona-Tas, 1994; Walder, 1995; Nee, 1996; Parish & Michelson, 1996). Thus, it is entirely possible that the pre-existing pattern of inequality continues to be evident, coexisting with newly emergent patterns of social inequality stemming from market processes.

Because the postsocialist stratification is a hybrid social order, in which opposing tendencies in the mechanisms of stratification combine and interact in complex patterns, a simple binary approach to testing the declining-significance-of-redistributive power hypothesis is likely to yield mixed results. Moreover, any confirmatory test is highly sensitive to the manner in which key variables are operationalized and to model specification. The reason is obvious. *Core features of the state socialist redistributive order persist, while discontinuous change is modest in scope in the early stages of transition to a market economy.* Elsewhere we provide a detailed discussion of this problem with respect to Parish and Michelson's confirmatory test (1996), showing just how sensitive results are to model specification and research design (Nee & Cao, 1999, pp. 825–829). Only after a tipping point has been reached will the market-based stratification order as a whole begin to assume the dominant form in the postsocialist stratification order; until then it is subordinate to the preexisting state socialist stratification order.

We think the debate can be better resolved by developing a causal checklist which conceives of distinct but intertwined processes contributing to the formation of the postsocialist stratification order: the causes of continuity and the causes of discontinuity. Viewed in this light, an approach to confirmation that focuses on a binary positive or negative statistical result on the effect of political capital or position on earnings is less than satisfactory. We maintain that confirmatory tests must explicitly build into the research design and model specification the idea that the different causal mechanisms reproducing continuity and giving rise to discontinuity are likely to simultaneously produce conflicting and opposing tendencies within the same hybrid stratification order. In contrast to competing hypotheses, market transition theory specifies the institutional environments within which causal forces promoting continuity and discontinuity concentrate in the transition economy (i.e. Nee, 1989, pp. 667–668; 1992, pp. 4–18; 1996, pp. 911–916).

Models thus need to enable the researcher to account for a complex set of causal processes, some promoting continuity and others discontinuity. For example, research designs tailored for the urban context must specify economic sectors – hybrid/private economy, for-profit state-owned firms, and non-profit public organizations – in order to allow one to examine the effect of different causal processes in the labor market sectors in which they are most likely to concentrate. Causal mechanisms reproducing continuity are likely to be concentrated in the public sectors of the transition economy, while mechanisms giving rise to discontinuity will concentrate in the hybrid/private economy. Clearly, confirmatory tests that fail to build into models careful specifications of sectoral differences will not obtain results that differentiate the causes of continuity and of discontinuity. Nor, as we shall see, will data sets that undersample entrepreneurs and employees in the private economy enable one to study discontinuity in the postsocialist stratification order.

Continuity

Continuity in the stratification order, like discontinuity, should not be assumed, but instead needs to be explained by reference to mechanisms that reproduce the stratification order of state socialism in the postsocialist society. The processes that sustain continuity are powerful to the extent that state socialism sustained a stable institutional order.

We argue that continuity is spontaneously reproduced through self-reinforcing processes of interest and identity rooted in the informal rules of the game under state socialism and long-standing networks of the communist political elite. Despite changes in the formal institutional rules and arrangements stemming from regime change and reform of the economy, the informal rules embedded in long-standing elite social networks comprise the basis of an equilibrium in which interests and identity at the group and individual levels are locked in and difficult to dislodge. Whether in postsocialist societies that have undergone regime change or in reforming state socialism such as China and Vietnam, networks and norms of the state socialist political elite combine to sustain powerful oppositional forces to change in the formal rules of the game. Operating in the shadows of new institutional arrangements, the old state socialist redistributive elite, even when it is deposed from formal power, constitutes a powerful basis of opposition to the workings of free markets (Staniszkis, 1991; Rona-Tas, 1994). Both within the state bureaucracy and extending downward into firms and public organizations, long-standing clientelist ties provide a ready-made mechanism to coordinate interests through collusion and other forms of informal illicit transactions. This is the underpinning of the political markets that Parish and Michelson (1996) pointed to in which cronyism is the by-product of an institutional order that organized the allocation of resources by non-market means.

Numerous anecdotal stories, passed on during field research or reported in newspaper accounts, illustrate how clientelist networks operate in the postsocialist stratification order. These narratives include familiar stories of rent seeking by party officials who routinely accept bribes and detailing the uses of political power to transfer property rights from public to private ownership endemic in transition economies. The underlying analytical point of such narratives emphasizes the importance of network mechanisms in maintaining the power and privileges of the political elite in the postsocialist stratification order.

Discontinuity

The causes of discontinuous change have been outlined in detail by market transition theory. The transition to a market economy from an economy in which markets were suppressed and eradicated by the state necessarily means that market processes that were very weak, if not non-existent, expand as institutionalized forces that shape incentives and social relationships. The growth of a market economy gives rise to improved returns to individual performance, evidenced in increases in returns to investments in human capital, new opportunity structures that are beyond the reach of the state, and economic mobility through private entrepreneurship and labor market. *All three processes are discontinuous with the core mechanisms of stratification in centrally planned economies, and are the proximate causes of decline in relative power and advantage of political elite.*

Because market transition theory has been controversial, and critics have challenged its causal logic, we will provide in detail an illustration of its causal mechanisms through the device of an analytic narrative. Our story follows the career of Li Guangxiang, who started out as an engineer in a state-owned chemical factory in Hunan province where he finished his day's work only after a couple of hours of effort, and "spent most of his first year sipping tea and reading newspapers." He daydreamed about being a real engineer with a challenging job. "I couldn't stand the thought of another 20 years there," he told the *Wall Street Journal* (*WSJ*) correspondent (Wonacott, 2002). Li quit his state-sector job and left for Shenzhen after working only a year at his first job. There he found a job as a beginning engineer paying $240 a month. He shifted through three jobs in quick order until he gained the work experience that enabled him to land a job at a computer-parts plant near Zhuhai, which later was acquired by Flextronics International, a large multi-national. At 30 he is a senior engineer and an assistant manager at the plant, supervising five production lines, with an annual salary of $10,000. Last year, Li encouraged his brother to join him at the Zhuhai plant.

The *WSJ* correspondent reports that "all over the factories along this stretch of China's southeastern coast, the same extraordinary scenario is unfolding: workers move into more and more sophisticated jobs" through labor markets that connect China's inland provinces to the rapidly growing market economy along the southeastern coastal provinces. Li Gongxiang's pay may not be high by international standards for engineers, but by Chinese standards, $10,000 (U.S.) is many times higher than the annual salary paid to employees in state-owned enterprises and government offices with a comparable stock of human capital. It is also substantially higher than the annual salary of high-ranking party and government officials in the public sector of the transition economy.

China's still largely untapped work force in the hinterland provides a huge reserve of cheap labor for the emergent market economy concentrated in the coastal provinces. Unskilled labor costs 60 cents an hour in China, compared to $2.50 in Malaysia, $5 in Singapore and $25 in Japan. Skilled labor likewise is very cheap by international standards. Foreign firms and investors expect to benefit from China's cheap skilled labor force for some time to come. Drawn by the plentiful supply of cheap skilled and unskilled labor, Flextronics

International is starting construction of a $100 million new plant in Shanghai in April 2002. The cheapness of China's skilled and unskilled labor has led to a boom in high-tech exports from China, which accounted in 2001 for 17.5% of the country's total export, compared to just 5% in 1985. According to the World Bank, China's high-technology exports grew at 43% annually from 1985 to 1998, outpacing other East Asian economies, whose growth ranged from 18% to 28% per annum, by a wide margin.

At the same Flextronics plant outside Zhuhai, Wu Liying, a 20-year-old unmarried female migrant worker from rural China, works a four-to-midnight shift on the production line as a machine operator. Ms. Wu earns about the same $60 a month she did when she started three years ago. For unskilled workers, a nearly flat salary is typical in the emerging market economy of the southeastern coastal provinces. According to the *WSJ* correspondent, "Ms. Wu has no thought of returning to her village in Jiangxi, one of China's poorest provinces. 'What would I do back home?' she asks, sitting in the dormitory room she shares with three other women. At the factory, Ms. Wu has friends and feels in touch with the modern world. At night, crowds gather at the Flextronics recreation center for table tennis, pool and dancing." For her as "for many, the opportunities in coastal areas favored by foreign investors and bolstered by economic reforms are a step up no matter how low the wages." Indeed, Ms. Wu's wages as an unskilled worker, though low by global standards, is higher than the highest paid village-level government official (Matthews & Nee, 2001). Describing the transformation brought about by the penetration of global capitalism in the region near Zhuhai, the correspondent writes, "The odysseys of Mr. Li and Ms. Wu, repeated by countless others, have transformed the cities along the southern coast. Ten years ago, sugarcane fields surrounded Zhuhai. Hong Kong and Taiwanese companies vied to make toys and garments. Today, the focus is consumer electronics, and the city is ablaze in neon signs for companies such as Canon Inc. and Panasonic."

This narrative highlights the core mechanisms specified by market transition theory to explain discontinuous change: (1) that markets favor direct producers relative to their terms of exchange under state socialism; (2) that markets provide powerful incentives for direct producers evident in higher returns to investments in human capital; and (3) that new opportunity structures stemming from an emergent market economy open up avenues for social mobility beyond the control of the state, diminishing its power in shaping the postsocialist stratification order (Nee, 1989). We see in this narrative just how new market-based opportunity structures in the more marketized southeastern coastal provinces offer direct producers rewards not available in the inland provinces where markets are less developed and in the state socialist sectors of the transition economy, whether in government bureaus or in state-owned enterprises. Workers secure higher returns to human capital – education and work experience – through expanding labor markets that link China's emergent market economy with global capitalism. We also see in the story a demonstration of the tipping point principle (albeit at the regional level), which we elaborate below.

Tipping Point and the Acceleration of Discontinuous Change

The interplay among the various causal mechanisms reinforcing continuity and generating discontinuous change gives rise to a trajectory of societal transformation where qualitative breaks are often preceded by long periods of incremental change. While similar patterns have been the topics of numerous writings in economics, sociology, and political science, the underlying logic is perhaps best captured and elaborated by Thomas Schelling in what he calls critical-mass models (1978, pp. 91–110). A ready example of these models is that people are much more likely to double-park on a street where there already exist double-parked cars sufficient in number to create a sense of immunity. In essence, Schelling argues that transition from one state of stable equilibrium to another requires an initial departure beyond a certain minimum threshold. The initial departure can be built up by either internal efforts or external shock, although upon its achievement no additional propellant is needed to sustain the movement toward the destination state. Also referred to by many as the tipping point, this minimum threshold is an intrinsic property of the system which, like a watershed, marks both a change in the inherent tendency of movement and a decisive progression into a different terrain of existence.

For our purpose of understanding the postsocialist stratification the critical mass models and tipping point idea are heuristic. If socialist redistribution represents one equilibrium state and market represents another, then market transition necessitates an initial period of painstaking groundwork to accumulate momentum and/or to foster market growth before it evolves into a stage of self-sustained perpetuation. Such counter-conventional groundwork can result from internal causes, e.g. competition among factions, although in many cases it is the political and economic challenges in the global arena that prompt the communist party leadership to launch the reform campaign (Nee & Lian, 1994; Rona-Tas, 1997). In early stages of the market reform, formal redistributive institutions and longstanding clientelist networks centered on the state remain the principal mechanisms of resource allocation. Their impact reaches far beyond the redistributive sector, as economic actors still face a limited set of opportunities in the nascent market economy and are often forced to submit to, if not collude with, political interests. Transactions that are intended to be coordinated by emerging markets are inevitably embedded in such powerful socialist institutional legacies (Wank, 1995).

As power continues to center on the political domain, so do opportunities. Hence, a market economy in its early emergence does not automatically deprive the old redistributive elite and reduce them to pedestrians. Instead, there exist a variety of possibilities for those with political capital to derive even greater benefits from it. Market, on the other hand, attracts participation mainly from people who have limited career prospects under the redistributive regime (Zhou, Tuma & Moen, 1997). Even within the market sector reward distribution may be distorted by the strong presence of political networks and the state. Only when the market economy reaches a certain scale and degree of maturity will it be able to stand as an independent source of socioeconomic mobility. This can be construed as the tipping point where market-based stratification mechanisms assume momentum and discontinuous change becomes the dominant trend. Continuities will still be found (Rona-Tas, 1994), as long as the state has yet to completely reduce its role to a third-party regulator, but their significance becomes limited (S. Szelenyi, 1998; Cao & Nee, 2000).

The image of a change trajectory punctuated by tipping points does not suggest that change never occurs in an abrupt manner. Logically, a system can depart from its original state at any pace or speed, and it is the *size* of the departure that determines whether or not it passes the tipping point. However, once we take into account the complexity and the various intertwining components of a social system, it is not surprising that successful transformation tends to be incremental, especially given the huge initial setup costs entailed in remaking economic institutions in post-communist economies (Sachs & Pistor, 1997; North, 1990, p. 95). Radical reform approaches run an even greater risk of failing to accomplish the original purpose (Kornai, 1990). This is partly evidenced in the Russian experience, where advocates of the shock therapy overestimated the determinism of formal institutions and did not fully recognize the resiliency of the informal arrangements buttressing the Soviet socialism. State planning apparatus was dismantled before market mechanisms were ready to take over, and resource allocation remains dominated by non-market means, resulting in the so-called "merchant capitalism" (Burawoy, 1997).[1] A new order of stratification did appear, but it is based as much on the ruin of the Soviet regime as on markets. Thus, "supply and barter networks, access to locally scarce goods, connections with customs officials and local politicians, skill in the military and pleasure-providing arts – these, not education, are the most important forms of capital in the new

Russian market" (Gerber & Hout, 1998, p. 37). In our assessment, although the Russian reform did cause a sudden abruption, the departure was not comprehensive enough to produce a market society instantly. Instead the emergence of a market economy has been more gradual, accelerating after the financial crisis of the late 1990s, and less an immediate outgrowth of the shock therapy approach that relied on formal institutional changes.

China provides a sharp contrast to the big-bang approach to market transition. On the one hand, China's incremental reform strategy represents a much less drastic measure in eliminating the formal institutional basis of political advantages. As a result, researchers have documented systematic evidence for continuities in the stratification order (e.g. Nee, 1991; Bian & Logan, 1996; Parish & Michelson, 1996; Zhou, Tuma & Moen, 1997; Zhou, 2000). On the other hand, the central government's responsive yet steady implementation of its reform plan has not only proved effective in promoting economic performance, but also allowed various market elements to develop and mature in tandem. For example, recent studies find that despite the partiality of the Chinese reform, market exchange and networks are on the rise, whereas the significance of social and redistributive ties declines (Guthrie, 1998). Although it is still doubtful that China as a whole has made a decisive progress toward market, we think at least in certain geographic regions, e.g. the southeast coastal provinces, entrepreneurship and market capital have already become the most important determinants of success.

In summary, we suggest that changes in post-socialist stratification order are both complex and nonlinear. Decades of socialist experience created powerful inertial forces that help to reproduce features of the pre-existing structure of inequality. These forces may be highly resilient and tend to co-exist with newly introduced market mechanisms over an extended period of time. Only when a certain tipping point is reached does discontinuous change assume dominance.

Data Shifting: Meta-Analysis of Confirmatory Tests

Meta-analysis of empirical studies in the market transition literature in light of the causes of continuity and discontinuity shows highly consistent empirical support for hypotheses predicting change in the mechanisms of stratification stemming from the expansion of economic markets, as shown in Table 1. The data shifting shows near unanimous support for three of the four major hypotheses derived from market transition theory: increasing returns to human capital, economic mobility of private entrepreneurs, and new opportunity structure associated with the growing private sector. In other words, despite

Table 1. Summary of Empirical Studies Relevant to Market Transition Theory.

Data					Findings (if consistent with market transition theory)			
Study	Nation	Population	Year	Dependent variable	Political capital	Human capital	Entrepreneurs	Private sector
I. Szelenyi, 1988	Hungary	Rural, whole nation	1982–1983	Agricultural goods	Mixed	Yes	–	–
Nee, 1989	China	Rural, Fujian Province	1985	Income	Yes	Yes	Yes	–
Nee, 1991	China	Rural, Fujian Province	1985	Income	Yes	–	Yes	–
Peng, 1992	China	Urban & rural, selected areas	1986	Income	–	Yes	–	Yes
Rona-Tas, 1994	Hungary	Urban & rural, whole nation	1989, 1991	Employment	No	Yes	–	–
				Income	No	Yes	Yes	–
Domanski & Heyns, 1995	Poland	Urban & rural, whole nation	1987, 1991	Income	Yes	Yes	–	Inconclusive
Parish, Zhe & Li, 1995	China	Rural, eastern 2/3 of China	1993	Employment	Mixed	Yes	–	–
				Income	Yes	Yes	–	Yes
Nee, 1996	China	Rural, whole nation	1989–1990	Employment	Mixed	Yes	–	–
				Income	Yes	No	Yes	–
Parish & Michelson, 1996	China	Rural, whole nation	1988	Employment	No	–	–	–
				Income	No	–	–	–

Table 1. Continued.

	Data				Findings (if consistent with market transition theory)			
Study	Nation	Population	Year	Dependent variable	Political capital	Human capital	Entrepreneurs	Private sector
Xie & Hannum, 1996	China	Urban, whole nation	1988	Income	No	No	–	–
Bian & Logan, 1996	China	Urban, northern city Tianjin	1988, 1993	Income	No	Yes	–	Yes
Gerber & Hout, 1998	Russia	Urban & rural, whole nation	1991–1995	Income	–	No	Yes	–
Brainerd, 1998	Russia	Urban & rural, whole nation	1991–1994	Income	–	Yes	–	–
Nee & Cao, 1999	China	Rural, whole nation	1988	Employment Income	Yes Mixed	Yes Mixed	– Yes	– –
Zhou, 2000	China	Urban, whole nation	1995	Income	No	Yes	–	Yes
Matthews & Nee, 2000	China	Rural, whole nation, and Fujian Province	1989–1990 1985	Employment Gender inequality	–	Yes	–	Yes
Keister & Nee, 2001	China	Rural, whole nation	1989–1990	Employment	Mixed	Yes	Yes	Yes
Cao, 2001	China	Urban, two southern cities	1994–1995	Promotion	Inconclusive	Yes	–	–
Cao forthcoming	China	Urban, one southern city	2000	Income	Yes	Yes	Yes	Yes

significant differences in the historical context, human capital, entrepreneurship, and the private economy are key to understanding changes in the stratification order in post-socialist countries. These findings clearly testify to the profound impact of market forces.

By contrast, existing research provides only mixed confirmation for the hypothesis that predicts decline in relative earnings advantage for political capital. Given the rising opportunities for economic actors, as evidenced in the story about employees in the computer-part plant near Zhuhai, it would seem only logical that one would find a corresponding relative earnings decline for political capital. This is also suggested by the high consensus finding of increased returns to human capital, advantages of private-sector employment, and high financial returns to private entrepreneurs. How can this apparent contradiction be accounted for? We think there are two reasons behind it, one methodological and one substantive.

Methodologically, we observe in several studies a subtle discrepancy between research design and interpretation of results with regard to market transition theory's prediction of a relative decline of the significance of political capital. The idea of a relative decline requires that the magnitude of political advantages be evaluated in comparison to the increasing returns to human capital and private entrepreneurship. *The critical test thus lies in the extent to which cadres' monopolistic elite status is now being challenged by groups with market power.* By contrast, studies reporting negative findings have focused mostly on the redistributive elite's advantages *over unskilled workers*, a group that stand out in neither political capital nor market power (e.g. Rona-Tas, 1994; Bian & Logan, 1996; Zhou, 2000). Elsewhere, we discuss our disagreements with Xie and Hannum (1996) and Parish and Michelson (1996) in research design and model specification (Nee & Cao, 1999; Cao & Nee, 2000). Still, a healthy skepticism in the scholarly community remains about the validity of the hypotheses predicting relative decline in the earnings return to political capital (Bian, forthcoming).

Substantively, as our previous discussion indicates, there exist powerful inertial forces that continue to reward political capital, especially evident in the early stages of market transition. These inertial forces and the emerging markets represent alternative sources of upward mobility in a hybrid mixed economy. In early phases of the transition when labor markets have yet to develop and the emerging private economy still faces various bureaucratic barriers, it is even possible that returns to political capital rise faster than rewards gained through market power and private property. The studies reported in our meta-analysis are based on survey data collected in the late 1980s up through the mid-1990s. Hence, most findings for the persistence and augmentation of political advantage are likely to be accurate reflections of the continuity features of the post-socialist stratification system. Those with political capital and those with market power can *both* benefit from the market reform, and it is only when market reaches a certain degree of dominance and maturity that the latter overshadow the former in terms of economic advantages.

Overall, our meta-analysis confirms the co-presence of multiple institutional logic and stratification principles. Though plausible, this also raises the issue of causal indeterminacy in two senses. First, if market transition, like all other large-scale social changes, should be construed as a multi-faceted process involving divergent causal forces, then neither its trajectory nor its outcome can be accounted for by a deterministic theory. Second, insofar as different causal forces could produce similar outcomes, it may be impossible to adjudicate rival arguments with empirical evidence. We consider the causal indeterminacy in the first sense to be something that most, if not all, scientific undertakings have to live with.[2] The second, however, in our view, mainly reflects an inadequacy in research design. It can be reduced through careful specification of the scope conditions for different casual forces. For instance, recent studies of income inequality in urban China emphasize the distinction between organizations that remain dependent on the state and relatively autonomous economic sectors (Cao & Nee, 2001). By examining income determination in each sector separately, researchers gain additional leverage that allows them to better sort out the impacts of markets vis-à-vis those of the communist party/state. More specifically, these studies find higher returns to human capital in private/hybrid ownership firms as well as in relatively autonomous public enterprises. In their study of Chinese firms, Opper, Wong, and Hu further report direct evidence that the interaction between markets and private ownership serves as the most significant constraint on party interference in organizational decision making, and that party control appears to be perpetuated by the party committee's continued involvement in managerial recruitment (2002).

MARKET TRANSITION AND OCCUPATIONAL ATTAINMENT IN URBAN CHINA

In the rest of this paper we examine patterns of occupational attainment in reforming urban China. The aim of this analysis is to demonstrate our point that continuity, rather than discontinuity, is the central tendency during the earlier stages of rapid institutional change. By contrast, discontinuity is difficult to discern because the relevant changes occur at the margins of a stratification order and are hard to pinpoint, especially in a study of occupational attainment, which is less sensitive than income to changing mechanisms of stratification.

Data and Dependent Variable

The data we use were collected in 1995 by a World Bank study titled Chinese Household Income Project (CHIP hereafter) (Khan & Riskin, 1998). This study consisted of a rural survey and an urban survey. Our analysis employs data from the urban survey. The original sample includes 6,931 urban households randomly selected through a stratified sampling scheme from 69 counties[3] and municipalities in 11 of China's 30 provinces. Information on employment, income, and other demographic characteristics was collected for all 21,698 household members. After excluding people outside the labor force and those with missing values, we obtain a sample of 11,470 workers.

This World Bank survey of urban households appears to have systematically under-sampled self-employed entrepreneurs and also employees who had jobs in the private/hybrid sector of the economy. Private entrepreneurs accounted for only 1.7% of the entire CHIP sample (Table 2). All together only 4% of the

Table 2. Definition and Frequency Distribution of the Dependent Variable.

Occupational Status	Definition	Frequency
Government/Party Cadres	– Cadres in govt., party, & mass org. – Ranked *ke* or higher	329 (2.87%)
Administrators	– Directors in non-profit organizations – Ranked *ke* or higher	259 (2.26%)
Managers	– Managers in public & private firms – Ranked *ke* or higher if in public firms	391 (3.41%)
Professionals	– Professionals & technical workers – With mid- to senior professional rank	1,259 (10.98%)
Entrepreneurs	– Owners & co-owners of private businesses	190 (1.66%)
Ordinary White-collar Workers	– All other administrative/managerial, professional/technical, & office workers	5,058 (35.38%)
Manual Workers	– All manual workers, including both skilled & unskilled	4,984 (43.47%)
Total	– All sampled individuals that were employed or self-employed in 1995	11,470 (100%)

CHIP 1995 sample were employed in the private/hybrid sector, compared to the state's own tally of 14.8% for urban China in 1995 (State Statistical Bureau of China, 1996, Table 4-1). Ninety-six percent of the CHIP sample were employed in state-owned or collective-owned organizations. Twenty-five percent of the sample reported that they were members of the communist party, which reveals an over-sampling of those politically loyal to the regime. Consequently, our analysis of occupational attainment should be viewed mainly as a study of urban China's stratification order as it existed at the outset of discontinuous change since respondents who worked in the emergent urban market economy were largely omitted from the sample.

Our dependent variable is the person's current occupation at the time of the survey. We classify all occupations into seven categories (see Table 2). The first, *government and party cadres*, includes all officials in governmental agencies, party branches, and mass organizations with the administrative rank of *ke* – the Chinese equivalent of sectional chief – or higher. The second category consists of *administrators* in nonprofit organizations, also with rank of *ke* or higher. Public enterprise managers ranked *ke* or higher and all managers in private firms, joint ventures, and foreign companies are grouped into the third category – *managers*. Together these three groups constitute the power elite, accounting for 8.5% of our sample. The fourth occupational category is *professionals*, defined as professional and technical workers with mid-level to senior professional ranks. About 11% of our sample fall into this category. The fifth, *entrepreneurs*, includes owners and co-owners of private businesses, the majority (52.1%) of which were small self-employment undertakings (*getihu*). This group is less than 1.7% of the sample. The last two categories include ordinary *white-collar workers* and *manual workers*. Their respective percentages are 35.4 and 43.5.

The CHIP data does not provide information about the times when respondents got their current jobs, which poses a problem given our interest in understanding continuity and change. As a means to address this limitation, we use age cohorts to examine the effect of party membership on current occupation. This however must be viewed as a less than satisfactory proxy for a control on time of the shift to current job. Clearly, a longitudinal data set with control on the timing of shift to current job would have provided us with a better handle on the question of continuity and discontinuity. But as a study of occupational attainment after a decade of gradual reform and at the start of more sweeping institutional changes in the urban economy, the CHIP data provides a useful cross-sectional view of the public sector of China's urban economy. If change were instantaneous, and not concentrated at the margins of the urban stratification order, then even a small percentage of private entrepreneurs and workers in the private/hybrid economy would provide evidence of discontinuous change.

Between-Occupation Earning Inequality

To better convey a sense of what these occupational categories mean in urban Chinese societies, we examine income inequality between occupations throughout the first half of the 1990s. Specifically, we first use the CHIP data to find out the average annual incomes for each of the seven occupational categories from 1990 to 1995. We then calculate the ratios between these averages and the grand mean for the entire sample in the respective year. These ratios provide a measure of the relative standings of these occupations in terms of monetary compensation.

Figure 1 shows considerable income inequality among occupations (although compared to advanced capitalist societies in the West, it is nonetheless modest). Between 1990 and 1995, average annual incomes for cadres, administrators, managers, and professionals consistently surpassed the grand average by 15–40%, making these four groups the elite income-wise. Entrepreneurs also exceeded the average, though by a smaller margin (~ 10%), while ordinary white-collar workers barely reached it. The largest occupational group – manual workers – averaged only 85–90% of an equal share.

Figure 1 also reveals some interesting trends over time. The most noticeable is the growing inequality among these occupational categories during the five-year period. In particular, the earning gap between manual and non-manual occupations widened considerably, as average incomes for cadres, administrators, managers, professionals, and ordinary white-collar workers all experienced a relative increase at the expense of manual workers.[4] Administrators and managers registered the largest gain, with a magnitude of 12% and 15%, respectively. Ordinary white-collar workers improved from earning 98% of the overall average to 102%, while manual workers dropped from 90% to 85%. The combined result is a net increase of 9% in the income gap between these two largest occupational categories. Meanwhile, entrepreneurs also experienced an 8% decline in earning advantage, although partly due to the small size of this group in our sample we are unable to rule out the possibility that the observed decline is simply a result of random sampling errors.[5]

Overall, these trends suggest that occupational attainment in urban China had become ever more important for individuals' economic wellbeing. Though perhaps still modest by international standards, there appeared to be a widening income gap between manual and non-manual occupations, with occupations

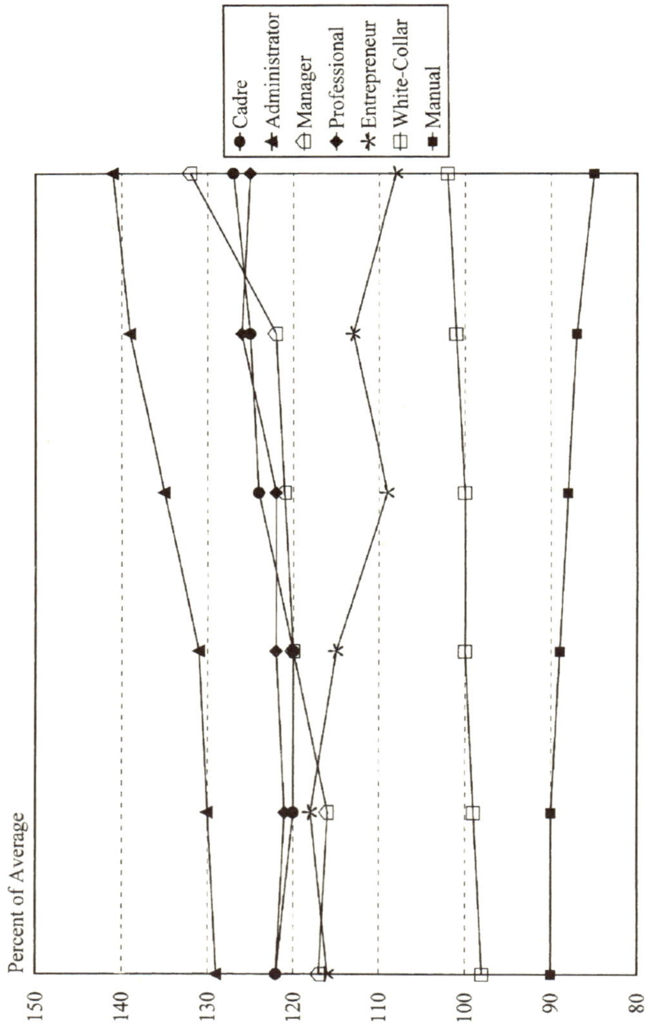

Fig. 1. Relative Annual Income in Urban China, by Occupation.

Source: 1995 Chinese Household Income Project.

with direct executive power leading the way in achieving material affluence. As the communist party's promise of an egalitarian utopia continues to fade, landing on the right career track becomes increasingly crucial for the Chinese urbanites.

Model and Independent Variables

Given the categorical nature of our dependent variable, we estimate multinomial logistic regression models to examine the effects of various individual attributes and contextual variables. We use manual workers as the reference category for the dependent variable. Logistic regression coefficients thus are estimates of the effects of the independent variables on the log-odds of entering a certain occupational category, as opposed to becoming a manual worker.

We use *CCP membership* as an indicator of political credential, and more importantly, affiliation in a closed but extensive network which monopolizes political power and hence control over resources allocated by the state. *Education* measures the stock of human capital acquired through schooling. In addition to *sex* and *age*, we control for two other demographic characteristics: *ethnic minority* and *birth cohort*. The former is a dummy variable taking the value of 1 if the person is an ethnic minority. This variable is included mainly because the CHIP survey sampled from several provinces with relatively high percentages of ethnic minorities, e.g. Gansu and Yunan, although it is also of substantive interest to gauge the extent of potential ethnic disparity. *Birth cohort* is based on the historical time period during which the person reached adulthood. In particular, those born before 1948 turned 18 before the political turmoil started in 1966; those born between 1948 and 1959 turned 18 during the Cultural Revolution and many of them were sent to countryside; and those born after 1959 turned 18 in the post-Cultural Revolution era.

In addition to these individual characteristics, we include a contextual variable *labor market* to measure the labor market development in each of the 69 counties and municipalities. The value of this variable is calculated as the percentage of sampled individuals who acquired their current jobs via labor market means, instead of via state allocation or job inheritance (*dingti*).[6] We also control for the geographic location by including in our regression models 10 dummy variables for provinces. The province of Gansu is chosen randomly as the omitted category. Descriptive statistics for these independent variables are reported in Table 3.

Table 3. Means and Standard Deviations of the Independent Variables.

Variable name	Mean	S.D.
Sex (male = 1)	0.53	0.50
Ethnic Minority	0.04	0.20
Age	38.41	9.43
CCP Membership	0.25	0.43
Education	10.81	2.79
Labor Market	0.21	0.10
Cohort		
Born after 1959	0.37	0.48
Born 1948–1959	0.46	0.50
Born before 1948	0.17	0.38
Province		
11 Provinces (omitted)	(omitted)	(omitted)
N	11,470	

Hypotheses

The most salient aspect of continuity in the postsocialist stratification order in China is the persistent advantage associated with the communist party, an extensive network that offers both strategic connections and legitimacy for its members. Under state socialism, political criteria are systematically enforced in the allocation of career opportunities (Walder, 1985). The communist party/state creates a variety of institutional and organizational devices that constantly monitor and sanction individuals' political conformity (Schurmann, 1968), and only those deemed trustworthy can be considered for positions with significant power and privilege. Patron-client ties between local party officials and activists also come into play (Walder, 1986). Members of the communist party thus enjoy better chances to enter elite occupations, owing to both their formal political credentials and their access to powerful networks and sponsorship. In the reform era, the political screening process remains largely intact in governmental agencies, while preexisting networks provide the informal basis to sustain political advantage in publicly owned enterprises and nonprofit organizations. Hence, we predict that in contemporary urban China:

> *Hypothesis 1*: CCP membership remains a significant determinant of attaining high occupations in the public sectors of the urban economy.

Another classic feature of mobility under state socialism is the so-called dual elite structure (I. Szelenyi, 1978; Walder, 1995). That is, in addition to the political elite, there exists a second elite group constituted by senior professionals. These two groups of elite are sometimes referred to as the "red" and the "experts." Both groups enjoy considerable prestige and privileges, although it is only the former that exercises redistributive power. Advancement to the two types of elite status tends to follow distinctive career paths. In particular, party membership is indispensable for recruitment into the political elite. Entry into the professional elite, on the other hand, requires high educational qualification; and though still favored, party membership is no longer a must. This leads us to predict that

> *Hypothesis 2a*: CCP membership plays a more dominant role in acquiring cadre, administrative, and managerial positions than in entering professional occupations in the public sectors of the urban economy.

> *Hypothesis 2b*: Formal education plays a more dominant role in entering professional occupations than acquiring cadre, administrative, and managerial positions in the urban economy.

Given the small number of the private/hybrid sector employees in our sample (about 4%), we expect discontinuity to be mainly associated with the emergence of a labor market. In contrast to the bureaucratic allocation of labor in a redistributive economy where employment is dictated by the state, a labor market allows mutual choices between potential employers and employees. The development of a labor market thus affords competent workers greater freedom to search for better alternatives, resulting in more meritocratic matching of persons to jobs. This implies a positive interactive effect between labor market growth and human capital factors, e.g. education, on the chance of entering elite occupations. However, we expect this interaction effect to vary with employer type, since organizations stressing efficiency are more likely to incorporate more meritocratic standards into their selection process (Cao, 2001; Cao & Nee, 2001). On the other hand, personnel recruitment in government agencies and state-controlled organizations still prioritizes political credential even when it takes place on the labor market and rarely, if ever, is CCP membership a liability. Hence, we predict that

> *Hypothesis 3a*: The development of a labor market does not undermine the advantages to CCP membership in occupational attainment in the public sector of the urban economy.

Hypothesis 3b: The development of a labor market enhances the importance of formal education mainly in acquiring high occupations in for-profit organizations in the urban economy.

A more direct way to discover discontinuity is to examine changes over time. Since our data is cross-sectional and does not allow comparison over time, we instead rely on age/birth cohort to approximate the timing of job acquisition. As explained earlier, our *cohort* variable distinguishes three groups of people according to the historical time period during which they reached adulthood. Certain differences between the two older cohorts and the youngest one – people who were born after 1959 and thus reached adulthood during the reform era – may constitute evidence for discontinuities in the mobility process. This is certainly not to say that people in the older cohorts could not change occupation in the reform period. But it seems reasonable that for the majority of them occupation had already been determined before the reform began. Other things being equal, we expect that

Hypothesis 4a: There is no difference in the effect of CCP membership between the older cohorts and the youngest one in the public sector of the urban economy.

Hypothesis 4b: Formal education has a greater effect on the attainment of high occupations for the youngest cohort than for the older two in the urban economy.

Results

Table 4 reports logistic regression coefficients from our baseline model. To better illustrate the effects of party membership and education, we also calculate the predicted probabilities of being in each of the seven occupational categories for party members and non-members at various educational levels. All imagined individuals are assumed to be male, non-ethnic minority, 38 years old (sample average), and 0.21 for the labor market variable (sample average). These probabilities are presented in Fig. 2.

The most striking finding here, in our view, is the persistence of political advantage. As predicted by Hypothesis 1, CCP membership remains a major determinant of occupational attainment in urban China, increasing the odds of entering all but one non-manual occupations by at least 58%.[7] These results clearly demonstrate the continuing significance of membership in the party as a network conferring strategic connections and legitimacy for career advancement in formal employment settings in urban China. Such persistent political

Table 4. Multinomial Logistic Regression of Occupational Attainment in Urban China: Baseline Model.

	Gov./party Cadre	Administrator	Manager	Professional	Entrepreneur	White-collar
Intercept	–15.35**	–17.64**	–14.01**	–17.66**	–7.54**	–6.05**
Sex (male = 1)	0.20**	0.04	0.25**	–0.23**	0.04	–0.15**
Ethnic Minority	–0.45*	–0.38#	–0.22	–0.00	–0.14	0.06
Age	0.12**	0.16**	0.14**	0.18**	0.04*	0.05**
CCP Membership	1.70**	1.44**	1.24**	0.46**	0.15	0.55**
Education	0.69**	0.72**	0.56**	0.84**	0.15**	0.42**
Labor Market	–1.55	0.42	–0.86	0.97#	4.44**	0.23
Cohort[a]						
Born 1948–1959	0.12	0.26#	0.22#	0.18*	–0.03	0.05
Born after 1959	0.10	0.10	0.19	0.30*	–0.01	0.19*
Province[b]	–	–	–	–	–	–

#, $p < 0.10$; *, $p < 0.05$; **, $p < 0.01$ (2–tailed tests).

Note: [a] Reference is those born before 1948.
[b] Coefficients not presented. Reference category is Gansu Province.

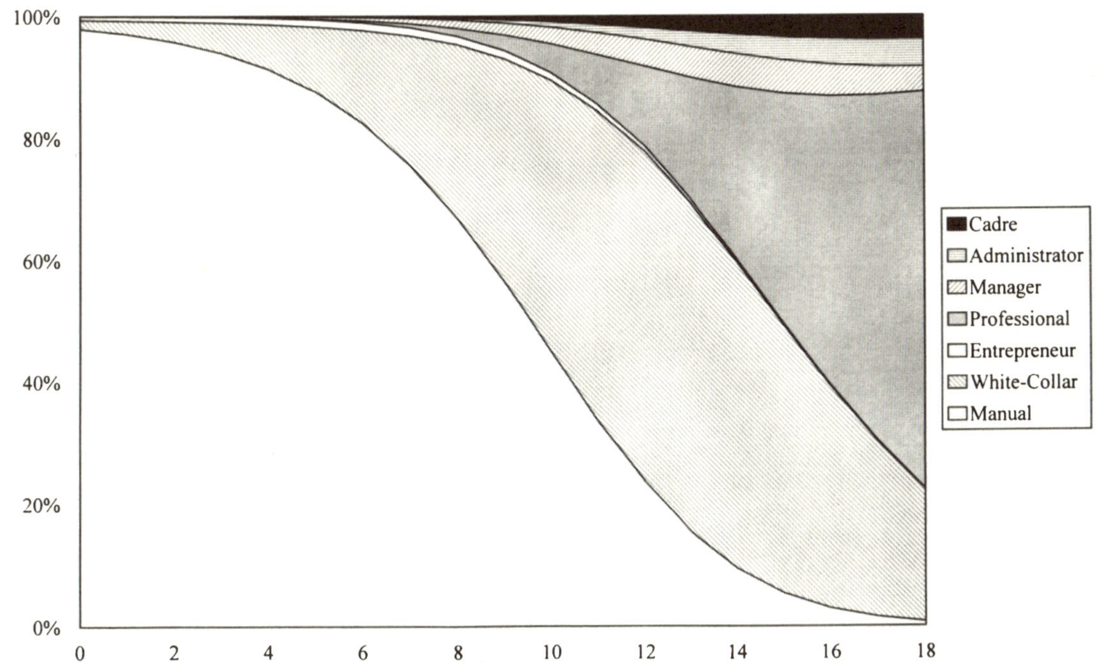

Fig. 2. Predicted Probabilities of Occupational Attainment for Non-Party Members, by Education.

Note: Probabilities calculated from Table 4. Assuming male, non-minority, and sample averages for continuous variables.

advantage is rooted deeply in China's socialist regime, and not until the CCP concedes its one-party dictatorship will we begin to observe its decline.

With regard to private entrepreneurship, we find that CCP members are no more likely than others to undertake it. While this is certainly consistent with the absence of political screening in the recruitment into entrepreneurship, it seems more plausible that entrepreneurship has yet to become a most attractive career choice. As we mentioned previously, over half of the entrepreneurs in our sample are in fact self-employed. Entry into self-employment in urban China has been virtually free. Self-employment also tends to entail risk and long and irregular working hours, with no benefits and only slightly above-average income (8% above the mean in 1995). Thus, it should not be surprising if most party members chose to pursue a career in either the state bureaucracy or other organizations.

Our analysis also renders strong support to both Hypotheses 2a and 2b. Specifically, we find that party membership confers much greater advantage in competing for cadre, administrative, and managerial positions than for professional positions. For instance, in Figs 2 and 3, the predicted probability of being a cadre, administrator, or manager for party members is more than twice that for non-party members, and this holds at all educational levels. The size of the effect is the largest for becoming political cadres, weaker for administrators in nonprofit organizations, and the weakest for managers. In contrast, once education exceeds 11 years, party members are in fact *less likely* than non-party members to become professionals. Meanwhile, although both statistically significant and positive, the effect of education on entering cadre/administrative/managerial occupations is considerably smaller than that on becoming a high professional.[8] This difference can be seen in Figs 2 and 3, where the probability of becoming a professional increases sharply with education, while the increased likelihood of becoming a cadre, administrator, or manager is relatively modest.

Two other findings shown in Table 4 are noteworthy. First, there is a strong positive relationship between the locality's labor market growth and private entrepreneurship. This is hardly surprising since entrepreneurship is almost by definition a job placement via labor market. Labor market growth also appears to be positively associated with entry into professional occupations. We have no plausible explanation for this result except a suspicion that our labor market variable might be correlated with the regional variation in economic industrialization and the geographic distribution of research/educational institutions. Second, we find fairly strong evidence for ethnic discrimination. Ethnic minorities are more likely to work in manual occupations and less likely to acquire administrative positions in government agencies, party branches, and

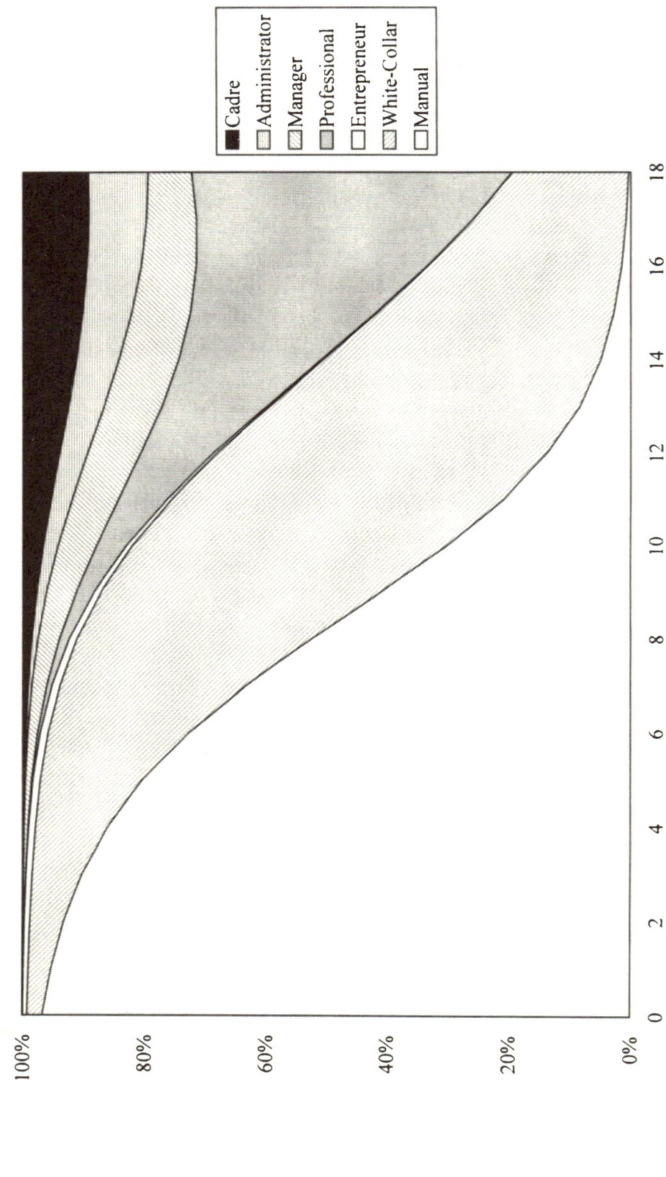

Fig. 3. Predicted Probabilities of Occupational Attainment for Party Members, by Education.

Note: Probabilities calculated from Table 4. Assuming male, non-minority, and sample averages for continuous variables.

non-profit organizations. While this may reflect the Chinese government's distrust in ethnic minorities, it could also be partly the outcome of more spontaneous social and political interactions on the grass-root level.

To better examine the impact of labor market, we expand the baseline model by adding in interaction terms between *CCP membership*, *education*, and *labor market*. Results from the expanded model are presented in Table 5.

We find no interactive effect between *CCP membership* and *labor market*. Individually or collectively, the six coefficients for the interaction term do not achieve statistical significance by any standard. In other words, there is no evidence that emerging labor markets in the public sector of the economy in urban China undermine the career advantage among party members. This finding is consistent with previous research as well as our Hypothesis 3a. Meanwhile, it should also be noted that though not against CCP members, the emergence of labor market does not appear to benefit them particularly either.

As expected, a labor market does not enhance the chance for more educated people to become either government/party cadres or administrators in nonprofit organizations. However, although the development of a labor market does not increase the size of the manager group (see Table 4 and the negative coefficient for *labor market* in Table 5), it does improve the chance that people with higher education become managers. This finding lends support to Hypothesis 3b. Our interpretation is that due to their market orientation, firms are more likely than state agencies and other organizations to rely on labor market mechanisms to search for qualified personnel, hence leading to more meritocratic manager recruitment.

Our final model, presented in Table 6, examines potential differences in the patterns of occupational attainment between age/birth cohorts. Overall, this model provides support to Hypothesis 4a and shows little statistical evidence for varying effect of CCP membership across cohorts. The only exception is that compared to their older counterparts, CCP members among those born after 1959 appeared to enjoy a greater edge in obtaining cadre status in governmental agencies and party organizations. This may indeed reflect a change in the party/state's screening process, but it may have also resulted from the CCP's aggressive recruitment among eligible youths who have already been admitted into the cadre echelon (Walder, 1995). Unfortunately our cross-sectional data does not allow us to distinguish these two possibilities.

There are considerable differences in the effect of education between cohorts. In particular, we find an increase in the importance of education in obtaining cadre positions, which we attribute to the party/state's effort to improve its political capacity in a modern era. Among the youngest birth cohort, education also confers greater advantage in becoming professionals and

Table 5. Multinomial Logistic Regression of Occupational Attainment in Urban China: Testing the Impact of Labor Market.

	Gov./party Cadre	Administrator	Manager	Professional	Entrepreneur	White-collar
Intercept	–15.26**	–18.29**	–13.03**	–17.59**	–8.42**	–6.19**
Sex (male = 1)	0.20**	0.03	0.25**	–0.23**	0.04	–0.15**
Ethnic Minority	–0.45*	–0.38#	–0.22	–0.01	–0.13	0.07
Age	0.13**	0.16**	0.14**	0.18**	0.04*	0.05**
CCP Membership	1.97**	1.33**	1.30**	0.53**	0.47*	0.55**
EDU × Labor Market	–1.36	0.57	–0.33	–0.37	–1.27	0.02
Education	0.67**	0.79**	0.48**	0.83**	0.28**	0.44**
EDU × Labor Market	0.12	–0.31	0.45#	0.02	–0.47*	–0.07
Labor Market	–2.36	3.65	–6.31*	0.48	7.58**	0.91
Cohort [a]						
Born 1948–1959	0.13	0.26#	0.23*	0.19*	–0.03	0.05
Born after 1959	0.11	0.09	0.19	0.31*	–0.02	0.19*
Province[b]	–	–	–	–	–	–

#, $p < 0.10$; *, $p < 0.05$; **, $p < 0.01$ (2-tailed tests).

Note: [a] Reference is those born before 1948.
[b] Coefficients not presented. Reference category is Gansu Province.

Table 6. Multinomial Logistic Regression of Occupational Attainment in Urban China: Testing Cohort Difference.

	Gov./party Cadre	Administrator	Manager	Professional	Entrepreneur	White-collar
Intercept	–15.59**	–16.41**	–13.80**	–18.18**	–7.54**	–6.31**
Sex (male = 1)	0.20*	0.03	0.25**	–0.23**	0.04	–0.15**
Ethnic Minority	–0.46*	–0.39#	–0.22	–0.01	–0.14	0.06
Age	0.12**	0.16**	0.14**	0.18**	0.05*	0.05**
CCP Membership	1.85**	1.43**	1.30**	0.49**	0.07	0.58**
× Born after 1959	0.26*	0.00	0.10	0.05	–0.12	0.04
Education	0.71**	0.63**	0.55**	0.88**	0.14**	0.44**
× Born after 1959	0.07#	–0.05	0.03	0.10**	–0.01	0.08**
Labor Market	–1.54	0.47	–0.84	1.01#	4.42**	0.28
Cohort[a]						
Born 1948–1959	0.12	0.28*	0.23*	0.20*	–0.02	0.06
Born after 1959	–0.82	1.00	–0.06	–0.75*	0.04	–0.64**
Province[b]	–	–	–	–	–	–

#, $p < 0.10$; *, $p < 0.05$; **, $p < 0.01$ (2-tailed tests).

Note: [a] Reference is those born before 1948.
[b] Coefficients not presented. Reference category is Gansu Province.

ordinary white-collar workers. While this is certainly consistent with our Hypothesis 4b, one could also argue for alternative causes such as the recent growth in the population's educational level (Walder, Li & Treiman, 2000), changes in state personnel policy (Zhou, 2000), and so on.

DISCUSSION AND CONCLUSION

Overall, our analysis of occupational attainment in urban China shows significant continuity from the pre-reform era but provides little definitive evidence for discontinuous change induced by markets. In particular, we find that party membership remains a major predictor of landing in high occupations and virtually a must-have for securing cadre, administrative, and managerial positions. How do these findings fit with market transition theory as well as previous studies documenting extensive changes in the income distribution?

First, there are reasons to question that the CHIP data could adequately reflect discontinuous changes taking place in urban China. As we mentioned earlier, only 4% of the CHIP sample were employed in the private/hybrid sector, where economic activities and career mobility are the most autonomous from the communist party/state. With 96% of the sample drawn from state-owned and collective-owned organizations, the CHIP data should be regarded as representative only of the public sector. Public sector is surely not static, but for urban China as a whole, apart from the southeastern coastal provinces, changes are still not as dramatic as many observers have thought. For instance, a labor market has grown rapidly in coastal and large metropolitan areas (Matthews, 1998), but in an average Chinese county/city only one in every five public sector employees acquired his/her job via labor market means (Table 3). Hence, without adequate representations of those in the private/hybrid sector, a national sample is likely to miss out changes at the margin. Moreover, that 25% in the CHIP sample were CCP members appears to be another telltale sign suggesting non-random selections even with the public sector. If, as we suspect, the CHIP survey was somehow biased toward people subject to direct political influence, it should not be surprising that analyses based on its data find a greater extent of continuity.

Second, methodological limitations obviously affect our empirical analysis. It is no doubt problematic that we use current occupation as the dependent variable without controlling for the time when the job was acquired. Because the question of continuity and discontinuity turns on the question of whether the job was acquired before or after institutional change, this limitation is in fact quite serious. We attempted to address the problem with the use of age cohorts, but this does not really provide a substitute for an adequate control of the time when the current job was secured. Our usage of the party membership variable suffers a similar limitation since we do not have control for the date of joining the party. Most people join the party after getting their first job, and many are recruited into the party on their current job (Bian, 1994; Bian, Shu & Logan, 2001). Hence, party membership is limited in its utility as an exogenous variable predicting current job. Moreover, joining the CCP in the 1990s does not mean the same as having joined the party 20 years ago, since today the Party actively recruits private entrepreneurs and others who can be expected to lack the same political commitments as Party members in the past (Nee & Lian, 1994).

A third consideration is that the 1995 CHIP data set was collected at an early stage of urban reforms, which had all but stalled in China until after the suppression of the Tiananmen pro-democracy movement. The major institutional changes accelerating the transition to an urban market economy did not take place until 1994 with the promulgation of China's Company Law and Labor Law, which together opened the way for the corporatization/privatization of for-profit state-owned enterprises and implementation of liberal labor market policies. Both laws were modeled after the company and labor laws of the advanced capitalist countries, especially the United States. Substantial change in urban occupational attainment would need to follow with a substantial lag compared to changes in the determinants of earnings, which as we discussed previously has proven to be a more sensitive barometer of the effects of transition to a market economy.

Clearly, what is needed are new studies of occupational attainment that use data collected since 2000 which control for the timing of job changes and is more representative of the emergent private/hybrid sectors of the transition economy. The next generation of confirmatory studies moreover needs to specify better than previous research jobs that are more dependent on state allocation mechanism and those that are more exposed to market competition, both with respect to labor markets and in the determination of rewards.

Explanations of institutional change need to take into account the causes of continuity and discontinuity arising from complex nonlinear processes driven by different sets of causal mechanisms. Our data shifting confirms that the causes of continuity and discontinuity co-exist in the postsocialist stratification. Overall, the analyses of income inequality confirm that discontinuous change in the stratification order is in progress. Although our analysis of occupational analysis highlights continuity, it does not rule out discontinuous change in the stratification order, especially at the early stages of large-scale institutional change, prior to a tipping point. The analytic narrative of the experiences of workers in the computer-parts plant near Zhuhai is suggestive of just how important tipping points can be in changing the mechanisms of stratification. Market transition theory is not a theory of radical change; instead it turns on the cumulative causation of decentralized market processes in promoting discontinuous change at the margins of the preexisting stratification order.

NOTES

1. The Russian experience raises the possibility of multiple equilibria in which a rather unique conjunction of historical conditions locks the economy into a state that is neither redistributive nor market. Such a scenario points to the limits of a simple critical-mass model for transition between two states. Elsewhere we discuss in detail the issues of multiple equilibria and path dependent transformation in postsocialist countries (Nee & Cao, 1999).

2. Since middle-range theories only focus on a limited set of parameters among all relevant ones, it is crucial to spell out the interplay between causal processes advocated by seemingly contradictory explanations in order to better understand social reality. This is exactly the main conceptual thrust of this paper.

3. Counties in the Chinese administrative system are essentially small cities. Compared to China's officially designated cities and municipalities, counties have a lower administrative rank and also tend to be less populous and less industrialized.

4. To ascertain the statistical significance of the changes in relative earning between 1990 and 1995, we conduct t-tests in two ways, one assuming independent samples from the two years and another treating observations from the two years as paired samples. Results from the two sets of t-tests are largely the same. Change in relative earning is not statistically significant for either cadres or professionals.

5. The number of entrepreneurs with income is 160 for 1990 and 190 in 1995. The p-value for the null hypothesis of no change over time is greater than 42%. Elsewhere we discuss the potential issue of under-representation of entrepreneurs, and private-hybrid sector employees in general.

6. The number of observations from each of the 55 counties/municipalities has a mean of 178 and a minimum of 80.

7. The smallest regression coefficient of 0.46 is for ordinary white-collar occupations. *Exp*. $(0.46) = 1.58$, or 158%.

8. The differences in the size of the coefficient are statistically significant.

ACKNOWLEDGMENTS

We wish to acknowledge with appreciation the helpful comments we received from Yianjie Bian, Mary Brinton, Theodore Gerber, David Grusky, Lisa Keister, Larry King, Sonja Opper, Yusheng Peng, Akos Rona-Tas, Rachel Rosenfeld, Andrew Walder, Martin Whyte, Xueguang Zhou and Wubiao Zhou.

REFERENCES

Bian, Y. (1994). *Work and Inequality in Urban China*. Albany, NY: SUNY Press.

Bian, Y. (2002). Chinese Social Stratification and Social Mobility. *Annual Review of Sociology, 28*, 91–116.

Bian, Y., & Logan, J. R. (1996). Market Transition and Income Inequality in Urban China. *American Sociological Review, 61*, 759–778.

Bian, Y., Shu, X, & Logan, J. R. (2001). Communist Party Membership and Regime Dynamics in China. *Social Forces, 79*, 805–842.

Brainerd, E. (1998). Winners and Losers in Russia's Economic Transition. *American Economic Review, 88*, 1094–1116.

Burawoy, M. (1997). The Soviet Descent into Capitalism. *American Journal of Sociology, 102*, 1430–1444.

Cao, Y. (2001). Careers Inside Organizations: A Comparative Analysis of Promotion Determination in Reforming China. *Social Forces, 80*, 683–712.

Cao, Y., & Nee, V. (2000). Comment: Controversies and Evidence in the Market Transition Debate. *American Journal of Sociology, 105*, 1175–1189.

Cao, Y., & Nee, V. (2001). Remaking Inequality: Market Expansion and Income Stratification in Reforming State Socialism. Working paper.

Djilas, M. (1957). *The New Class*. New York: Holt, Rinehart and Winston.

Domanski, H., & Heyns, B. (1995). Toward a Theory of the Role of State in Market Transition: From Bargaining to Markets in Post-Communism. *European Journal of Sociology, 36*, 317–351.

Gerber, T., & Hout, M. (1998). More Shock than Therapy: Market Transition, Employment, and Income in Russia, 1991–1995. *American Journal of Sociology, 104*, 1–50.

Guthrie, D. (1998). The Declining Significance of *Guanxi* in China's Economic Transition. *The China Quarterly, 154*, 31–62.

Keister, L., & Nee, V. (2001). The Rational Peasant in China: Flexible Adaptation, Risk Diversification, and Opportunity. *Rationality and Society, 13*, 33–69.

Khan, A. R., & Riskin, C. (1998). Income Inequality in China: Composition, Distribution, and Growth of Household Income, 1988 to 1995. *China Quarterly, 154*, 221–253.

Kornai, J. (1990). *The Road to a Free Economy*. New York: W. W. Norton.

Matthew, R. (1998). What Do Labor Markets Come from? The Emergence of Urban Labor Markets in the People's Republic of China. Ph.D. Dissertation, Department of Sociology, Cornell University, Ithaca, NY.

Matthews, R., & Nee, V. (2000). Gender Inequality and Economic Growth in Rural China. *Social Science Research, 29*, 606–632.

Miller, R. (1987). *Fact and Method: Explanation, Confirmation and Reality in the Natural and Social Sciences*. Princeton: Princeton University Press.

Nee, V. (1989). A Theory of Market Transition: From Redistribution to Markets in State Socialism. *American Sociological Review, 54*, 663–681.

Nee, V. (1991). Social Inequalities in Reforming State Socialism: Between Redistribution and Markets in China. *American Sociological Review, 56*, 267–282.

Nee, V. (1992). Organizational Dynamics of Market Transitions: Hybrid Forms, Property Rights, and Mixed Economy in China. *Administrative Science Quarterly, 37*, 1–27.

Nee, V. (1996). The Emergence of a Market Society: Changing Mechanisms of Stratification in China. *American Journal of Sociology, 101*, 908–949.

Nee, V. (2000). The Role of the State in Making a Market Economy. *Journal of Institutional and Theoretical Economics*, *156*, 64–88.

Nee, V., & Peng, L. (1994). Sleeping with the Enemy: A Dynamic Model of Declining Political Commitment in State Socialism. *Theory and Society*, *23*, 253–296.

Nee, V., & Cao, Y. (1999). Path Dependent Societal Transformation: Stratification in Hybrid Mixed Economies. *Theory and Society*, *28*, 799–834.

North, D. (1990). *Institutions, Institutional Change, and Economic Performance*. Cambridge, England and New York, NY: Cambridge University Press.

Opper, S., Wong, S., & Hu, R. (2002). Local Party Power in China's Listed Companies: Evidence on CCP Persistence. *Research on Social Stratification and Mobility* (this issue).

Parish, W., & Michelson, E. (1996). Politics and Markets: Dual Transformations. *American Journal of Sociology*, *101*, 1042–1059.

Parish, W., Zhe, X., & Li, F. (1995). Nonfarm Job and the Marketization of Chinese Countryside. *China Quarterly*, *143*, 697–730.

Peng, Y. (1992). Wage Determination in Rural and Urban China: A Comparison of Public and Private Industrial Sectors. *American Sociological Review*, *57*, 198–213.

Rona-Tas, A. (1994). The First Shall Be Last? Entrepreneurship and Communist Cadres in the Transition from Socialism. *American Journal of Sociology*, *100*, 40–69.

Sachs, J. D., & Pistor, K. (Eds) (1997). *The Rule of Law and Economic Reform in Russia*. Boulder, Colorado: Westview Press.

Schelling, T. (1978). *Micromotives and Macrobehavior*. New York: Norton.

Schurmann, F. (1968). *Ideology and Organization in Communist China*. Berkeley, CA: University of California Press.

Staniszkis, J. (1991). Political Capitalism in Poland. *East European Politics and Societies*, *5*, 127–141.

State Statistical Bureau of China (1996). *Zhongguo Tongji Nianjian (Chinese Statistical Yearbook)*. Beijing, China: Chinese Statistical Press.

Szelenyi, I. (1978). Social Inequalities in State Socialist Redistributive Economies. *International Journal of Comparative Sociology*, *19*, 63–87.

Szelenyi, I. (1988). *Socialist Entrepreneurs: Embourgeoisement in Rural Hungary*. Madison, WI: University of Wisconsin Press.

Szelenyi, S. (1998). *Equality by Design: The Grand Experiment in Destratification in Socialist Hungary*. Stanford, CA: Stanford University Press.

Walder, A. (1985). The Political Dimension of Social Mobility in Communist States: Reflections on the Soviet and China. *Research in Political Sociology*, *1*, 101–117. 1995.

Walder, A. (1986). *Communist Neo-Traditionalism: Work and Authority in Chinese Industry*. Berkeley, Los Angeles, CA, and London, England: University of California Press.

Walder, A. (1995). Career Mobility and the Communist Political Order. *American Sociological Review*, *60*, 309–328.

Walder, A. (1996). Markets and Inequality in Transitional Economies: Toward Testable Theories. *American Journal of Sociology*, *101*, 1060–1073.

Walder, A., Li, B., & Treiman, D. (2000). Politics and Life Chances in a State Socialist Regime: Dual Career Paths into the Urban Chinese Elite, 1949–1996. *American Sociological Review*, *65*, 191–209.

Wank, D. (1995). Private Business, Bureaucracy, and Political Alliances in a Chinese City. *Australia Journal of Chinese Affairs*, *33*, 55–71.

Wonacott, P. (2002). China's Secret Weapon: Smart, Cheap Labor for High-Tech Goods. *Wall Street Journal*, March 14, p. 1.

Xie, Y., & Hannum, E. (1996). Regional Variation in Earning Inequality in Reform-Era Urban China. *American Journal of Sociology, 101*, 950–992.

Zang, X. W. (2002). Labor Market Segmentation and Income Inequality in Urban China. *Sociological Quarterly, 43*, 27–44.

Zhou, X. (2000). Economic Transition and Income Inequality in Urban China: Evidence from a Panel Data. *American Journal of Sociology, 105*, 1135–1174.

Zhou, X., Tuma, N., & Moen P. (1997). Institutional Change and Job-Shift Patterns in Urban China, 1949 to 1994. *American Sociological Review, 62*, 339–365.

AN OUTLINE OF THE SOCIAL HISTORY OF SOCIALISM OR AN AUTO-CRITIQUE OF AN AUTO-CRITIQUE

Ivan Szelenyi

ABSTRACT

The purpose of this paper is to offer an outline of the history of changes in social structure during socialism and after the fall of communism. This 'history' is presented as an open one, which may have been pregnant at various time points with opportunities, which were not realized. I try to capture this 'openness' of the social history of socialism by presenting in an auto-critical way how I in my own work was compelled to reframe my analysis, and not necessarily because my analysis was wrong, but even more so because history did not deliver on some of its promises and offered surprises – some pleasant ones and some unpleasant ones – on other occasions. Thus Stalinism is presented here as a society ruled by a bureaucratic estate. Mature socialism was the Golden Age, in which the bureaucracy entertained to idea of compromise with the intellectuals and it was not unconceivable that socialism may turn into rational redistribution rule by the 'new class' of intellectuals. During late socialism, the alliance between the bureaucracy and intellectuals broke down and reform communist societies were on a 'third way', moved between socialism and liberal market economy and made concessions to the

The Future of Market Transition, Volume 19, pages 41–67.

ISBN: 0-7623-0835-4

working class and to the emergent new petty bourgeoisie. In post-communism, intellectuals did attain power, but not as a class of redistributors. They constituted a modernizing elite, a cultural bourgeoisie, which regards as its historic mission to 'build capitalism.' I end the paper with a methodological note. With the fall of communism the 'futuristic' or 'utopian' critique Marxism offers becomes increasingly problematic. Nevertheless, critical social science is still possible if it adopts the 'ironic' method, what retains the critical perspective for neo-classical sociology, or for the comparative sociology of capitalisms.

INTRODUCTION

Over the past 25 years I published three major books. Each one was an attempt to explain the dynamics of social change in socialist and post-communist societies and evaluate the potentialities these societies were pregnant with.

The three books, *Intellectuals on the Road to Class Power* (completed in 1974 and appeared in print in 1979), *Socialist Entrepreneurs* (completed in 1986 and printed in 1988) and finally *Making Capitalism without Capitalists* (published in 1998), in my mind, constitute a trilogy of a somewhat unusual sort. I was writing one book in three volumes over a span of 25 years, but the world around me changed fast and in many ways dramatically, and the three volumes of the book reflect those changes. Between the mid-1960s and 2000 I published other volumes too, but they were side-stories to what I intended to offer as the Grand Narrative of social structure and social change under socialism and post-communism.

In this paper I would like to subject the three volumes to auto-critical scrutiny. I hope I will be able to avoid being narcissistic in carrying out this task. My aim is to offer a sociology of knowledge of these texts as if they were foreign to me. The point is certainly not to claim that I knew it all along (what quite a few social scientists did claim after the fall of communism). Rather, I want to show that I got wrong every time. The first draft of this paper was in fact written for the panel convened by Victor Nee under the title "Market Transition in Post-Communist Societies" at the 2001 Annual Convention of the American Sociological Association. The purpose of the panel was to explore where analysts of socialist and transitional societies made the wrong predictions, and Michael Burawoy, Victor Nee and myself indeed wrote papers in this spirit (the other panelists were too young to have enough time to make erroneous predictions). Burawoy, in an eloquent paper, conceded he over-estimated the capacities of the working class to shape the future of socialist societies in his work on actually existing socialism. He believed during the

1980s that a genuine workers state was within the realm of possibilities. While Victor Nee speculated in his seminal article on the theory of market transition that cadre privilege will decline and the direct producers will benefit from more markets, he now concedes that he under-estimated the persistence of cadre power. Many cadres – even in China, Nee's "case study" – managed to preserve a great deal of their power and gained even more privileges than they ever had before.

I had more sins to confess than my distinguished colleagues did, in part since I practised this trade – the art of auto-critique – for a longer time. Already *Socialist Entrepreneurs* was the auto-critique of *Intellectuals on the Road to Class Power. Making Capitalism without Capitalists* is the "negation of negation," a critical analysis of *Socialist Entrepreneurs*. Since it is the negation of negation, in some ways it inevitably "rehabilitates" *Intellectuals on the Road to Class Power.*

Intellectuals on the Road to Class Power entertained the idea that a "new dominant class" may be in the making from the merger of the former bureaucratic estate, the technocracy and the humanistic intelligentsia in order to establish a goal-rational system of socialism (a system I called "rational redistribution").

Socialist Entrepreneurs acknowledged that this class project – if it ever had a shot at success – failed, and instead the bureaucratic estate retained its power monopoly by creating spaces for a new petty bourgeoisie, for the "socialist entrepreneurs." Instead of "rationalizing" socialism, the bureaucratic estate was rescuing its power monopoly by making concessions to petty capitalism, finding a "third way" between the socialist redistributive economy and market capitalism in a "socialist mixed economy."

In *Making Capitalism without Capitalists* I conceded that the "third way" failed – at least in European socialist societies, the story of China being a more complicated one – and as a result state socialism broke down. "Socialist entrepreneurs," the late socialist new petty bourgeoisie, was not the main winner of the transition from socialism to capitalism (in fact, most of them lost in big ways, since they proved to be non-competitive in liberalized markets with the massive privatization of the formerly state owned corporate sector).

According to this last volume, the *Intellectuals on the Road to Class Power* was more on target, therefore, than *Socialist Entrepreneurs*. The project of rational redistribution was abandoned and no new class was formed around the figure of the "teleological planner." The intellectuals, however, played a formidable role in the fall of socialism as advocates first of "civil society," then later as true believers of neo-liberal market capitalism. From the "intellectual vanguard" of a rational social order they turned into a new "cultural bourgeoisie," a second "Bildungsbürgertum." Their task and even their historic mission is similar to the social role played by the first "Bildungsbürgertum, the intelligentsia of the eighteenth and early nineteenth century in Central and Eastern Europe. The post-communist cultural bourgeoisie is not only promoting modernity but also "building" capitalism. It is in the business of creating capitalism without capitalists, and acts as a "substitute" for a propertied bourgeoisie. In other words, the possession of cultural capital did indeed become important as predicted by *Intellectuals on the Road to Class Power,* but it could not lay the foundation of lasting class power. Cultural capital – and its possessor, the cultural bourgeoisie – is the real "revolutionary force," not "charisma" as Weber argued. But power and privilege gained by the possession of cultural capital, just like charisma in Weber's sociology, is primarily a mechanism of transition. So while Burawoy and Nee turned their coats once, with my repeated auto-critique I turned it twice.

To put it rather immodestly these three "volumes" follow the logic of Hegelian dialectics, although not by design, but by default. (I would have loved to be always right!) The first volume proposes a "thesis," the second counters it with an "anti-thesis" and the third arrives as some sort of "synthesis" which "transcends" the initial thesis, negating it while preserving it at the same time. An orthodox Hegelian would call this movement Aufhebung. The idea of the intellectuals constituting themselves as a cultural bourgeoisie in order to "build market capitalism from above, or by design" is the "Aufgehebt" version of the thesis of the intellectual vanguard that sees its historic mission as the creation of a society of rational order.

There is, therefore, a dialectical negation of negation as far as the substance of the three volumes is concerned, and, I suppose what is more interesting, in the dynamics of social change from mature to late socialism and then from socialism to capitalism. In the methodology that I applied over the past quarter of a century there is, however, more continuity. All three volumes were "comparative," even though the nature of comparative framing changes over time. In *Intellectuals on the Road to Class Power* – and in work done well before this book was written – I adopted a method that David Stark later labeled the "method of mirrored comparisons"[1] (Stark, 1986). I began to develop this new methodology as I developed my theory of social inequality in market economies and under the conditions of what initially I called "administrative allocation" and what later I renamed – inspired by the work of Polanyi – the "redistributive economy."[2] In the empirical research I conducted with George Konrad during the late 1960s we found that in socialist redistributive economies, housing – and other important goods – were allocated in an inegalitarian way. However, these inequalities – contrary to the expectations of researchers before us, who suspected that socialist inequalities are inherited from the market capitalist past (Trotsky, 1972) – were the results of the redistributive intervention by governments. Furthermore – much to our surprise – we found that those who are "negatively privileged" by redistribution – to put it simplistically the workers and the peasants – had little choice but to try to help themselves on the secondary "coordinating mechanism," on the emergent, though still embryonic, markets.[3] We proposed a new comparative theory of social inequality. According to this new theory, in every system the dominant "economic mechanism" creates the privileges, serves those on the top of social hierarchies and generates inequalities. We did not use the term, which later was coined by David Stark, but we meant that capitalism and socialism were "mirror images" of each other: in capitalism the dominant market mechanism creates inequalities, which is counteracted to some extent by the redistributive intervention of the welfare state. In state socialism the dominant redistributive mechanism created the basic inequalities, which were "softened" by the engagement of negatively privileged groups in informal, market activities. To put it with Stark: comparing capitalism and socialism is like looking into a mirror, what is on your right side is on the left side of the mirror and vice versa.

Our new theory of social inequality was of course quite radically different from what it was turned into by Victor Nee, in his otherwise brilliant "market transition theory" in 1989. Nee's position is a version of "neo-liberal theory" – more market means more equality. Not all neo-liberals would necessarily agree with this (see Lal & Myint, 1996), since they may argue that economic dynamism requires inequality, but they will tend to believe that in a well functioning market at least "all boats rise," the effects of economic growth will trickle down and therefore those at the bottom of the social hierarchy will also benefit from more markets. Nee's later position (Nee, 1992, 1996; Nee & Lian, 1994) is more consistent with this neo-liberal theory, which may not anticipate necessarily more equality from more markets, but would expect benefits for all from market expansion. My theory was radically different. In my writings during the 1960s and 1970s I did not consider the possibility that a socialist redistributive economy can make a transition to a market capitalist one. Would I have done so – would I have had a theory of "transition" – it would have followed from my mirrored comparison that as market will replace redistribution as the dominant mechanism, market will also become the major source of inequality (we develop this idea in Kostello & Szelenyi, 1996).

I believed that this new method enabled me to offer a new type of critical analysis of socialism. I was convinced I did not need the vision of some idealized capitalism to be able to offer a critical analysis of actually existing socialism. The cross-systemic comparison is not necessary to show that one system is better than the other, but to show that they have different mechanisms, which create inequalities and domination in each one of them.[4]

At that time I was not familiar with the works of Michele Foucault. Even when I wrote *Intellectuals on the Road to Class Power*, a rather foucauldian book in more ways than one, I had not read Foucault yet. I sort of re-invented him when I opted for a critical analysis, which only aims to show the "temporariness" of systems of domination and does not need an Archimedean point to offer a critical analysis. Michael Burawoy, in his otherwise brilliant criticism of my work published in *AJS* in 2001, misunderstood the nature of my critical methodology believing it criticized state socialism from a genuine socialist perspective. What I tried to develop was a method of "immanent critique," restricting criticism to show temporariness, rather than contrast it with a utopian, ideal state. That is, I tried to develop an "ironic" view, which I will elaborate on in the last section of this paper. All three volumes of my "trilogy" are firmly committed to this method of critical analysis.

As socialism collapsed the cross-systemic comparison I followed in my earlier work lost its power. Therefore in *Making Capitalism without Capitalists*, it became necessary to readjust my method of critical inquiry. To follow Burawoy's advice and to shift to a "utopian standpoint" of a post-socialist theory would have been a major departure. The logical move was retaining the perspective of "immanent critic," keeping "irony" as the critical tool. Instead of using the cross-systemic comparison as a way to show temporariness of the phenomena under investigation, I moved to the neo-classical comparative sociology of capitalism, the project elaborated with Gil Eyal and Eleanor Townsley in our various recent publications (Eyal et al., 1998, 2001) and what I will summarize in the concluding section of this paper.

In the rest of this paper I review the substantive arguments proposed in the "three volumes" and try to explain from the social conditions, the varying constellation of class and elite struggles, why the diagnosis, and in particular the predictions of the volumes, proved to be false.

THE "GOLDEN AGE" OF REFORM COMMUNISM

The Intellectuals and the "New Class"

Milovan Djilas' path-breaking book, *The New Class* was the point of departure for *The Intellectuals on the Road to Class Power*. Djilas' powerful analysis – in arguably the most influential book ever written on state socialism – persuasively argued that socialism did not deliver on its promises. "Actually existing socialism" is neither the "dictatorship of the proletariat" nor a "classless society" – or a society on its way to become classless. Socialism, as Djilas knew it during the late 1940s and early 1950s, produced a new dominant class, which was composed by the bureaucracy and which faced the intelligentsia and the working class as its opponent (the intelligentsia being probably in Djilas view the main opposition to bureaucratic rule).

We also came to the conclusion that socialism – as we knew it during the 1960s – had absolutely nothing to do with the "dictatorship of the proletariat." It was a puzzle to explain what sort of society it was. The bureaucracy was at the center of the power structure all right, but was it really a new "class" and was the intelligentsia indeed the "opposing force"? We began to work with Konrad in 1965 on a series of empirical projects with urban planning agencies and the data we generated and our experience with planners made us rethink the Djilas thesis. I can recall three events which put me on the road to write the book on intellectuals. First, during the early 1960s I worked in the library of the Central Statistical Office, and Istvan Bibo, a cabinet minister from the 1956 Imre Nagy government, an old left-populist theorist and arguably the best Hungarian political philosopher of all time, just came out of jail and became my colleague and friend. In one conversation he told me: "the biggest lie of socialism is that it is the dictatorship of the proletariat. It is rather the dictatorship of the intelligentsia." This shook me and made me think.

Next, I also recall when in 1966 or so Konrad and I looked at the computer output of our survey on housing allocation in Hungary. We expected workers to do better than intellectuals, but the data showed that in the better quality new state housing, workers were badly under-represented, and not only party cadres but all sorts of intellectuals were strongly over-represented. Our initial reaction was that we may have coded the occupations wrong and made our statistical consultant re-run the analysis and eventually found out that wherever we look, bureaucrats and intellectuals are privileged by redistribution and workers have to struggle for shelter and food on the limited markets the bureaucrats tolerated.

The third impetus came from a conversation I had with the father of a high school friend. This person was the son of the inter-war year Mayor of Budapest (hence a rather conservative politician, a close ally of admiral Horthy). Karoly Szendy Jr. – this was his name – was an extraordinary electric engineer, thus, despite his father he was kept in a sensitive job. However, he not only did not join the party, but as a devout Catholic he attended a Mass every morning, even during Stalinist times. Still, given his exceptional expertise he was elected member of the Hungarian Academy of Sciences and in this capacity he was asked to serve on a committee, which reviewed a proposal to liberalize

Hungarian foreign trade. This was during the mid-1960s. Since I had a degree in Economics he asked me to visit his house in order to seek my advice. He was shocked by the proposal, which suggested price deregulation and more room for market forces. "We cannot allow this! This would lead to chaos, anarchy" – he complained. No one could have less sympathy for communism than he – nevertheless as a good engineer he *knew* the anarchy of the market was evil, and society needs a rational order.

And indeed, during the 1960s, that was what I heard from many other anti-communist intellectual friends: socialism is a beautiful idea, the only problem is that the wrong people are in the right place (meaning: if I would be in a decision-making position, I would know what to do). "Counter-selection" – that was the problem. The problem was that bureaucrats, instead of competent intellectuals, were doing the planning. And that was certainly the mind-set of the urban planner Konrad and I worked with closely for several years.

These were the personal motives that led me to revisit Djilas. I concluded that Djilas was probably quite right for the Stalinist epoch. However, the term "class" may not have been appropriate to describe the kind of power the Stalinist bureaucracy had. Trotsky may have been more accurate when he called the bureaucracy a "caste," but I followed Weber and suggested the best way to describe the bureaucracy under Stalinism is to call it a "ruling estate." Caste has rather specific meanings, which do not fit a "modern bureaucracy." "Rank" or "estate," on the other hand, captures well the interesting mixture of "archaic" (paternalistic – to be more precise) and "modern" ("hyper-rational" as Feher called it later in Heller, Feher & Markus, 1983), which characterized socialist bureaucracies (see also Bauman, 1974). The Stalinist bureaucracy, however, with the death of the "charismatic" leader (to the extent Stalin was really "charismatic"), entered a phase of legitimation crisis that culminated in the reforms under Khrushchev. What was the new principle of legitimacy? It turned out to be science and scientific socialism. Socialism is superior in comparison with market capitalism, since the latter one is anarchistic, and the former one, on the other hand, is a rational, scientific order. After the embarrassing meltdown of communism this sounds rather ridiculous, but during the late 1950s, early 1960s it was not. The Soviet Union managed to create a "science scare." The Sputniks, Gagarin in space, scared the hell out of the West. The Soviet Union seemed just about to overtake – if not economically, then in technology, science and education – the advanced West. The expansion of tertiary education in the U.S. and Western Europe to some extent was a response to this scare.

And the appeal of a rational order did appeal broadly to the intelligentsia under communism. If the bureaucracy means business, if it is ready to abandon its practices of counter-selection and to put the professionally competent people in command positions, socialism can be turned into a rational system with a human face (Radovan Richta's book *Civilization at Crossroads* – making exactly this claim – was a sort of manifesto for a broad strata of intellectuals all over in Eastern Europe). Therefore the task was not to "restore market capitalism," but to replace Stalinist voluntarism with a genuinely scientific planning, to create what we called a system of "rational redistribution."

After our studies on housing allocation we now applied the method of "mirrored comparison" to the analysis of social structure. While under capitalism it is private ownership that legitimates the appropriation of surplus by the class of capitalists, under the system of "rational redistribution" (rational planning – if you like it this way better) it is the "teleological knowledge," the scientific knowledge by planners or redistributors, that legitimates why the direct producer should not dispose with the product of his/her labor and why it has to be appropriated by the redistributors and allocated for long term and collective interest. Since intellectuals, by definition, are knowledge monopolists,[5] the prime candidates for the new dominant class position are not just bureaucrats, but an alliance forged by bureaucrats and broad layers of intellectuals (at its core, of course, standing the technocracy).

After 25 years I still believe this was not an unreasonable diagnosis of how socialism appeared to be unfolding during the mid to late 1960s. This was a Golden Age, the epoch of high hopes, the decade when capitalism appeared to be on its way out and socialism with a human face and with democratic institutions, but without too much compromise to markets and mainly regulated by "rational" redistribution, was on the rise, even in the West. Lukacs wrote about the "renaissance" of Marxism. Students (and professors) were reading Marx, Gramsci and Lukacs in Berkeley, Paris and Bielefeld. Gouldner (1979), and others like Bell (1976), Schelsky (1975) – some with enthusiasm, others with horror – were writing about the "rise of the new class" all over the world, about the rise of the knowledge class, about class power as the future of intellectuals.

In retrospect it seems to be obvious that the "new class project" in the West was grossly exaggerated. Sure, the Kennedy administration took in more highbrows occasionally in rather important positions than usual (Eleanor Townsley, 1996, 2000). But that, at best, eased the traditional American anti-intellectuals rather than creating a genuine power-sharing arrangement with old-line bureaucrats, property owners and intellectuals. We certainly can not speak of intellectuals "unseating" the old propertied class as Gouldner (1979) imagined. Therefore my book with Konrad at its core had a more solid empirical reference point. While in retrospect I cannot tell how serious the bureaucratic ruling estate was in what appeared to be an opening to the intelligentsia in general, and its technocratic faction in particular, to share power with them there were enough intellectuals who took the opening seriously. The Prague Spring certainly had nothing to do with yearning to "make capitalism" and it had everything to do with the desire to make a deal between the Enlightened bureaucrats, like Dubcek, and the reform-minded intellectuals such as Richta (1979), Ota Sik and others to create a rational socialism with a human face.

This is what *Intellectuals on the Road to Class Power* tried to capture. It is inexcusable that in 1974 when we were putting the finishing touches on the book we did not see that the love affair between the bureaucratic ruling estate and the intelligentsia was all over (and it was in fact never even consumated). We did not understand properly the irreversible effects of August 1968 in Czechoslovakia and the 1968 events in Poland. We wrote about the "counter-offensive" of the bureaucratic estate, so we knew that the intellectual class project was in some trouble, but as of the early 1970s the regimes in Hungry – and for that matter also in East Germany – were recruiting the technocracy into its ranks.[6] Even in Poland and even during the late 1970s a negotiated settlement between the bureaucratic estate and the technocracy was not completely out of the question. The Polish working class and the Solidarity movement was rather suspicious of the intellectuals (see Szelenyi, 1982, pp. 322–323), whom they distrusted as possible fellow travelers of the bureaucratic estate. This is not a good enough excuse, however. We inexcusably underestimated the disillusionment of the intellectuals with the bureaucratic estate and eventually with the cause of socialism, no matter how much "human face" or "rationality" it might take on.

With this self-critical comment I would maintain that our correction of Djilas as a social analysis of the dynamics of change in socialist societies during the 1960s, during the Golden Age, was accurate. Djilas was right, the bureaucracy held a power monopoly under Stalinism. But he was wrong because it could not establish itself as a new dominant class, it ruled as a dominant estate. During the post Stalinist reform epoch it did experience a crisis of legitimacy. It tried to resolve this crisis by appealing to "science" and "rational order" and at least pretending that it is ready to make an alliance with the technocracy or even generally with the intelligentsia. This action induced a positive response by a substantially large proportion of intellectuals, justifying writing about a new class project, a new class in "statu nascendi."

The Intellectuals on the Road to Class Power had a troubled history, which affected me as well. The book had to be smuggled to the West to be published there for the first time and I myself ended up in exile, not being allowed to return to my native Hungary for seven years.

ON THE "THIRD WAY" TO POST-COMMUNISM

The Fall of the New Class Project and the Rise of "Socialist" Petty Bourgeoisie

I got back my Hungarian passport in 1982. When I returned it was a different country than the one I left seven years earlier. The most striking, and for me, totally unanticipated change, was the explosion of the small private sector and the rapid growth of the informal economy. This did not come as a complete surprise to me. I had been doing research in 1971–1972 in Hungarian villages and already at that time I noticed the vitality of small family businesses. I even wrote an article with Konrad in 1971 about "Social conflicts of under-urbanization," which pointed out that one reason for the relatively slow growth of cities (relative to the urban industrial population) could be attributed to small scale family farming of "family plots" received from collective farms, which generated not only a food supply to the "peasant workers," but also earned them incomes, since they could sell their fresh fruits and vegetables at good prices on urban markets (Konrad & Szelenyi, 1974). Nevertheless, what I saw in 1982 was on a qualitatively different scale – now small private businesses were everywhere – and it was really the way that the system began to operate. People were still required to work in state firms, but by 1982 everyone knew this was much like the mid-19th century labor services on the manorial estate for the serfs. So workers did show up (occasionally) at their place of work, they pretended to work, the government pretended to pay them. But the action began after hours, in the "second economy" (see Stark, 1985).

And I was also astonished how my fellow intellectuals had changed. When I began teaching in 1968 at the University of Economics in Budapest virtually all of my students were Marxists. I had to spend the first year at least to make them read Durkheim and Weber to get them out of Marxism. And even my fellow early "dissidents," like George Konrad, Miklos Haraszti, Janos Kis, Gyorgy Bence, saw themselves as "Left" critics of the communist regime, and some of them were committed Marxists. Let me cite my friend George Konrad – who was never a Marxist, but certainly identified himself with the left, before becoming "liberal." This is what he wrote in 1977 in a Postscript to the Hungarian edition of *The Intellectuals on the Road to Class Power* (published in Bern, Switzerland, an edition at the time in Hungary would have been inconceivable): "For me it was obvious that we have to see society from below, bottom up, and Ivan adapted this way of thinking relatively soon after we met." This is an accurate account of how the two of us grew together in friendship and collegiality during the second half of the 1960s, but is also a testimonial to how traditional left-wing attitudes were rather common at that time even among the non-Marxists.

I came from a traditionally right-wing family and was moving leftward. Now after seven years in the West, confronted with "actually existing capitalism," I became more sympathetic towards Marxism. I was moving further left and I even saw Marxism as more relevant than I did when I lived under socialism. Upon my return to Hungary, much to my surprise, I saw myself as being all the way out on the left. I sensed that not only dissidents, but an increasing number of intellectuals, were turning not only anti-Marxists, but were increasingly having doubts about socialism. While no-one advocated "capitalism" yet, they did advocate a "third way" and were great believers in "civil society" – arguing that the notion of "capitalism" just like the notion of "socialism" is meaningless. Thus, I spotted a dual change: an unexpected rise of the private sector, which mainly offered opportunities to ordinary workers and peasants to make a decent living, and an increasingly disenchanted intelligentsia, which no longer believed that any deal with the bureaucratic ruling estate was possible. Intellectuals certainly were not "on the road to class power." The bureaucratic estate, instead of making a deal with the intelligentsia, was buying political peace by opening up the informal economy to a new petty bourgeoisie (hence Hungarian workers believed Polish workers were dumb for organizing Trade Unions and strikes – they knew the state sector was irrelevant – that life began after one leaves the gates of the state firms).

During my first visit back home after my exile, the department head of scientific affairs at the Central Committee of the Communist Party sent me a message through Alexander Szalai – who was a key figure in Hungarian Sociology at that time – that he wanted to meet with me. The man, Andras Knopp, was largely responsible for my expulsion from Hungary, but I did not take this personally. I was curious and wanted to meet with him. He was generous enough, I did not have to visit him in the offices of the Central Committee, and we met in a coffee shop. We talked for about an hour, or to be more precise he talked for about an hour, as I could hardly insert a question or two from time to time in his long diatribe. Finally I got a chance to ask something, so I asked this silly Western lefty question: "Are you not concerned that you are restoring capitalism here?"

He found the question amusing. "Look, the small private business is good for us. I myself buy my bread from a private bakery, since they sell better bread than the state factory. Good bread is good for us, people are satisfied and that is good for politics." Well, I thought, if you would have had the same idea in 1949 the whole story could have been quite different. . . .

Upon my return to the United States I quickly applied for a major grant from NSF to study the emergent Hungarian private sector. I got my hands on the 1982 income study of the Hungarian Bureau of Census – and extraordinary source of information – and I began to work on what turned out to be *Socialist Entrepreneurs*. By now I knew the time had come for a serious auto-critique (Szelenyi, 1986–1987), and indeed I conceded that the new class project of the intellectuals had failed. The bureaucracy stubbornly resisted sharing its power and instead opted to make concessions to the small private sector, mainly workers and peasants, to buy political peace. Socialism was not making progress towards "rational redistribution" as I anticipated ten years earlier. Instead, it became a mixed economy. The state sector was still dominant and at the top of the social hierarchy the bureaucratic estate was firmly entrenched. However, another, secondary private sector was emerging, and at its top sat a new socialist petty bourgeoisie, the "socialist entrepreneurs." This was the end of socialism "as we knew it." I began to use the term "post-communism" in 1986, but unfortunately did not get it in print before March 1989 (so I cannot claim copyright for the term, which I think was coined by Brzezinski in 1988 – so I lost a lot of good citations). But I made it clear that by the mid-1980s socialism as we knew it did not exist any more, at least not in Hungary. I called the emergent new system a "socialist mixed economy" in which I expected the public sector to remain dominant in the foreseeable future and the private sector to play only a supplementary role.

My research – crunching numbers from the 1982 income survey – tried to understand the origins of this "new class," not composed of intellectuals, but by a new petty bourgeoisie. I estimated the size and dynamics in the growth of the new petty bourgeoisie, and their social origins. I spotted that some of the cadres began to "commodify their bureaucratic privileges" and send their children into the private sector. But I also noticed a return of children of former entrepreneurs into the new stratum.

The book was about the return of the past, how old trajectories resurfaced. I wrote about "interrupted embourgeoisement" – how families, which were on the road to bourgeoisification, were pushed off that road during socialism. As long as they could resist the dual pressures of "cadrefication" and "proletarianization" they were returning to their original trajectory.

My terminology was rather awkward and I was not smart enough to conceptualize the problem I was writing about as path dependence. David

Stark, who has an unusual talent to find the right concept for phenomenon, did so in his 1992 article, "Path Dependence and Privatization Strategies in East Central Europe." In a footnote he acknowledges my work, but for some reason he criticizes my "trajectory" term as "teleological." While I am grateful to him for finding a better term for what I tried to describe, I cannot quite understand what makes "trajectory" more teleological than "path" – don't they both "lead" somewhere?

Socialist Entrepreneurs was a humble book, a serious auto-critique of "Volume One": *The Intellectuals on the Road to Class Power.* In this auto-critique I did not confess that I was a fool – I claimed that working with evidence from the 1960s it was not unreasonable to spot a "class project" by intellectuals. It was a potentiality within the "wombs" of state socialism, just the baby aborted. Instead a dual social structure, the co-existence of a socialist rank order and a subordinated, though emergent, class order, characterizes the socialist mixed economies by the mid-1980s.

Was this the "restoration of capitalism," or "market transition?" I was struggling a lot with this issue. I asked this question of Andras Knopp already in 1982. Then my old friend Pal Juhasz, with whom I collaborated on the *Socialist Entrepreneurs* book, visited me for a semester in 1985 in Madison, Wisconsin with his young colleague, Balint Magyar. I invited them to my house the first evening for a dinner, during which I asked again: "is this capitalism, which is restored?" Juhasz, who after the fall of communism became an MP in the Liberal Party, and Magyar, who for a while was even the president of the Liberal Party, were irritated even by the question. "Why does it have to be either 'capitalism' or 'socialism' – why cannot it be a 'third way', which is neither one nor the other." Their response made a lot of sense to me (though by 1989 for my liberal friends in Hungary the "third way" was an arch-enemy: "on a Third Way to the Third World" was their slogan by then). As of 1985–1986 I indeed could not see that the system was just about to break down. I could not spot signs of the meltdown, which took place in 1989, thus it sounded reasonable that the "socialist mixed economy" could indeed be thought about as a "third way" between a monolithic system of the communist economy and our market capitalism, which might be capable of reproducing itself for a long time.

"The third way" is a loaded term – and became even more loaded and confusing than it was in 1986 when I used it. Tony Blair's application of the term indeed created a great deal of confusion around it. Before "New Labor" the "Third way" referred to something which is neither capitalist nor communist. Now Blair's ideologues, Tony Giddens (1998) in particular, use it to describe a position that is between neo-liberalism and traditional social democracy. The term originated in 19th century German political philosophy, where it designated the German "special road," or "Sonderweg." During the inter-war years it was often used by populists, often on the left, but occasionally on the right as well. For the political left "the third way" implied an agricultural development, which did not accept the Soviet kolkhoz system, but aimed at radical land-reform, breaking up large semi-feudal estates and creating a large land-owning peasantry. During the post second world war years the idea was used by the anti-communist Left, which insisted that the communists are misleading the public when they claim there is just one choice: either communism, or colonial dependence on the West. They claimed there is a third way of independent national development. After 1989 the concept was appropriated by the nationalist right, which pursued an anti-Western ideology and emphasized nation, religion and tradition against the West and globalization. For all those who used the concept, from Left to Right, the Third way implied the "best way," it was an ideological concept. In *Socialist Entrepreneurs* I distanced myself forcefully from the value laden, ideological use of the term. I insisted that I use the term Third Road or Third Way in a value neutral (p. 17) and indeed ironic (p. 212) sense of the term. It does not mean the "right way," it means the most likely outcome under the conditions of late socialist Eastern Europe. Thus, I emphatically plead not guilty to the blame that I advocated the third way. *Social Entrepreneurs* had no anti-Western bias.

Nevertheless, history proved me wrong. My analysis was correct in 1986–1988: communism was coming to an end, we were entering a post-communist era. However, the idea that this will result in a socialist mixed economy, in some "third way" which will be capable of reproduction, proved to be absolutely wrong in Eastern and Central Europe. In 1989–1991 the system simply "melted down." My friends, who, as recently as 1985 persuaded me that capitalism was not being restored, took upon themselves the task to build capitalism from above, and they did so in a relatively short period of time.

Socialist Entrepreneurs could have been an important book, had it been published a few years earlier. But my publisher was slow, it came out in 1988 (though it was finished by the late Spring 1986). By the time it was ready to be reviewed, communism was gone and socialist mixed economy proved to be a brief interlude in the transition from socialism to capitalism. The old East European joke proved to be right and I proved to be wrong. The old joke goes this way: "What is communism?" Answer: "The longest and most painful way from capitalism to capitalism."

VARIETIES OF POST-SOCIALIST CAPITALISMS

The Return of the Intelligentsia and the Ways Intellectuals as a Cultural Bourgeoisie "Build" Capitalism

After 1989 it was time for me to re-group and to face the errors of *Socialist Entrepreneurs*. I was ready for a second round of auto-critique. This is what I was trying to do with my co-authors in *Making Capitalism without Capitalists*. One did not need much brains to realize that what was going on in Eastern Europe right after 1989 was a full-scale move towards capitalism. By the early 1990s it was obvious there is no "third way," no mixed economy, and what we were witnessing was a full-scale transition to capitalism. There has been a little hesitation whether to call this "transition" or "transformation," but when the chips came down this became word twisting – the systems which were emerging were capitalist all right, though not necessary homogeneous and not necessarily on a trajectory of convergence or even rapprochement. In this respect Stark (1992) was indeed right in emphasizing that the change is not "transition," but "transformation," though his later formulation of "comparative capitalism" (Stark & Bruszt, 1998, 2001) captures the unique features of the transition from socialism to capitalism better. The notion of "transformation" provides room to speculate that the new "destination" may not be capitalist – but this is off target. It is capitalism all right, but not necessarily the capitalism as we know it from Western Europe or North America. The challenging intellectual task is to figure out what sort of capitalisms are emerging (since former communist societies were increasing different from each other – they were not even approaching one model of post-communist capitalism). Rather than trying to put some old label (peripheric, or dependent development, political or state capitalism, etc.) on what may very well be a new set of phenomena, one should conceptualize those new forms in novel ways. As I will elaborate later, post-communist socio-economic systems represent various varieties of capitalisms. To what extent and when or whether they will converge into one unified system is the subject matter of speculation, but there can be little doubt that *Socialist Entrepreneurs* was off the mark when it anticipated some lasting, self-reproducing hybrid system between capitalism and socialism.

A qualification is in order at this time. East Asian socialism follows a different trajectory. It is a question of debate whether China or Vietnam can be called "capitalist" at all. In some ways they cannot. They retained the political monopoly of the Communist Party, which still legitimates itself with Marxism-Leninism, and they both still maintain a large public sector, and another sector of the economy is indeed a hybrid that cannot be clearly classified as either private or public. Victor Nee correctly writes about the "hybrid" form in China (Nee, 1992). China may be a "socialist mixed economy" and it certainly comes the closest to what I characterized as the "third way." But by all indications, of course, China is also on its way to capitalism, it just follows a different path than Eastern and Central Europe. In *Making Capitalism without Capitalists* we labeled China as "capitalism from below," a system in which rather than moving first with full scale privatization of the public sector, the making of capitalism follows more the traditional patters. New spaces are created, deregulated, and are filled gradually with private or semi-private firms, while the more traditional, in this case publicly owned sector of the economy, grows slowly and gradually loses ground to the emergent private economy.

So indeed *Making Capitalism without Capitalists* is an auto-critique of *Socialist Entrepreneurs*. The socialist mixed economy in Central and Eastern Europe did not last, the new petty bourgeoisie did not emerge as the winner of the transition, capitalism did not grow from below, it was implemented 'by design" from above. But who are the winners? Who is making capitalism if there are no capitalists (and indeed this is the first instance when capitalism is emerging from a social formation in which there was NO private ownership, and no class of private proprietors)? Here the received wisdom was the nomenclatura. What emerged was political capitalism: the communist nomenclatura turned into a cleptocratura and transformed itself into a new grand bourgeoisie (Hankiss, 1990; Staniszkis, 1991). Is this just "old wine in a new bottle?" Plus ca change, plus c'est la même chose? And what happened to our intellectuals?

This is the point where *Making Capitalism Without Capitalists* returns to the theme of *The Intellectuals on the Road to Class Power*, but in a new – "aufgehebt" – way. Our analysis follows closely the work of Erzsebet Szalai (1989). She in her various publications – few of them available in English – identified the struggle between the technocracy (what she called the "new elite") and the old line political apparatchiks, as the major driving force of social change in Hungary during the 1980s. Her analysis fits the dynamics of change in The Soviet Union and in Poland as well. The technocratic faction of the communist elite, in its struggles against the political apparatchiks, over time forms an alliance with the dissident intellectuals. During the Spring–Summer of 1989 it is this alliance which defeats the communist party rule both in Hungary and Poland and prepares the way for post-communist transition. Since the same process is under way in the Soviet Union Soviet tanks do not crush down the movements. On the contrary the Soviet Union melts down, confronted with the rapid change in its key satellites.

Szalai also shows in her later writings that the following decade during post-communism can be understood as a struggle, changing alliances between the different factions of the elites. The pact between dissident intellectuals and former communist technocrats did not last too long. During the summer of 1989 it was already breaking down and during the 1990 elections both in Hungary and Poland a "new elite," a by now anti-communist intellectual elite – often composed by humanistic intellectual with little or no connection to the former communist party – grabs political power and turns against the technocracy. The technocratic-managerial elite retreats temporarily to the economy. In some countries they "do" political capitalism, thus appropriate as private property public goods. In others they finesse privatization of state firms to Western investors in exchange for maintaining their managerial positions, now with substantially increased incomes and occasionally even with property shares in the newly privatized companies. But in the second round of free elections the technocratic elite (or those of them who remained in politics rather than settling themselves in the new economy), often comes back to power, unseating the "new new elite" (this happened both in Hungary and Poland and also in Lithuania) and they open up a post-communist political electoral cycle. Governments change colors from patriotic-Christian humanistic intellectuals to former communist technocrats and their liberal intellectuals allies (only to change back again). Thus, using the broad definition of "intellectuals" we developed in *The Intellectuals on the Road to Class Power*, the answer to the question who won 1989 is clear. Certainly the winners of the 1989 revolution are not the "socialist petty bourgeoisie" from the "second economy" from the 1980s (they actually lost, usually in a big way, very few of them became major entrepreneurs, many of them were unable to keep competing on the new, "real" market place). The winner is the intelligentsia: some combination of former communist technocrats with liberal or patriotic-Christian humanistic intellectuals. So from socialism, where there are no capitalists, capitalism is made by intellectuals. *Making Capitalism Without Capitalists* does NOT suggest that post-communist capitalism will be without a class of private property owners – hence the emphasis on the term *Making* in the title. Once capitalism was established, it of course will have its propertied bourgeoisie. What is unique – at least in our view – is that in the transition from socialism to capitalism, in contrast to all previous "transitions," occurs in a society which, unlike the ones Marx analyzed, did not have in its "wombs" the institutions of private ownership or an emergent property-owning class. Under these circumstances making capitalism had to be left to an unusual agent: the intellectuals.

Hence intellectuals did come to power, but not in the way we assumed in *The Intellectuals on the Road to Class Power.* They did not establish themselves as "rational redistributors" – on the contrary they abandoned the socialist project altogether and defined as their "mission," the task to create a capitalist social order. During the late 1980s (it happens rather late even in the most "progressive" countries, like Hungary and Poland, probably as late as 1987 or 1988) they began to see their task as "building capitalism" – this becomes an ethical task, just like "building socialism" was. The formerly left intelligentsia turns "from Saulus into Paulus" on the road to Damascus. They not only accept capitalism as "inevitable," a bitter pill one has to swallow in order to achieve civil liberties, they begin to "believe" in capitalism.

At this point the German historiography, in particular the work of Jürgen Kocka (1988), inspired my work. After all there is an historic precedence for intellectuals to take the lead towards modernization in this region. During the late 18th and early 19th centuries, arguably intellectuals in Central Europe constituted themselves as a "Bildungsbürgertum," as a "cultural bourgeoisie", which – given the weakness in the region of the propertied bourgeoisie or "Wirtschaftsbürgertum" – had little choice but to carry out the task what the propertied bourgeoisie carried out further West in the European continent and in North America. While the very term "Bildungsbürgetrum" was coined during the 1920s and became a key category in historiography only after World War II, the notion of "Bildung" (a concept difficult to translate into English, since it has a broader meaning then "culture" or "education" and is deeply rooted in the idea of Enlightenment) goes back to the 18th century, to Kant and Goethe. Intellectuals did play a crucial role in modernization projects during the late 18th and early 19th century. Armed with Kocka's theory, I was now ready to re-interpret *The Intellectuals on the Road to Class Power.* Intellectuals in the European semi-periphery were indeed the "vanguard" of modernization and indeed they were pro-capitalist. Their first project, the project of "Bildung," intimately connected the making of the modern educational system with the modernization of other institutions, including the capitalist modernization of the economy. This was the FIRST project of the central European intelligentsia. But by the mid to late 19th century intellectuals learn that the project is at least very difficult, if doable at all, and they begin to doubt whether the price that one has to pay for capitalism is worth the benefits one would gain from other aspects of modernization. Cannot we think of a less costly and faster way to arrive at modernity? Thus, by the turn of the 19th/20th century the intelligentsia in the region is radicalized, it is increasing attracted to leftwing and rightwing radicalisms and turns anti-capitalist, anti-bourgeois. The very term "Bildungsbürgertum" was coined during the 1920s with such anti-bourgeois sentiments (by right wing theorists, but could have been coined by a lefty just as well). Combining the two terms was supposed to point out how impossible it is to be a 'genuine' intellectual and a "Bürger" or bourgeois. The terms gained a positive, affirmative connotation only after World War II, when liberal intellectuals wanted to demonstrate in Germany that the intelligentsia were not, could not possibly be, Nazi, since it was deeply committed to "Bürgertum," to bourgeois values. The point is, however, that by the end of the 19th century Central European intelligentsia (and the Russian intelligentsia does not simply joins their ranks, but takes a leading role soon in this transformation) adopts a SECOND project. Now it sees itself as the vanguard to by-pass capitalist development and to create a hyper-rational social order. *The Intellectuals on the Road to Class Power* focused on the leftwing version of this project, on communism, and claimed that communism, in particular reform communism, can be seen as a "new class project." There were intellectuals – and not in trivial numbers and some of them quite prominent like Heidegger, or Knut Hamsun, just to name the best of them – who took the rightwing turn. The Bildungsbürgertum had to go into hiding during the first half of the 20th century, being intellectuals and being Bürger or bourgeois was out of fashion for quite some time.

This re-interpretation of the social history of Central European intellectuals therefore accepts the auto-critique of *Socialist Entrepreneurs*, but with a twist. Yes, the intellectual class project failed, but it was a real project (and may not have been necessarily doomed to failure, but failed because of the contingent constellation of world historic events). After all, as a Bildungsbürgertum, the intellectuals were the ones who won the 1989 revolution and not the new socialist petty bourgeoisie.

By the 1970s the Central and East European intellectuals begin to see that the SECOND project will not work either, so they begin to develop their THIRD project. They re-read the liberal thinkers of the 18th and 19th century, and rediscover "Bildung" in its original sense of the term. Much like their predecessors of the late 18th and early 19th century, they first rediscover the notion of civil society: a society, which is civil, without necessarily being at the same time bourgeois, or capitalist, before realizing that private property and market capitalism is the price one has to pay for the liberties only civil society can offer. So now they return to the FIRST project of the Central European intellectuals and constitute themselves as a "second Bildungsbürgertum," as that cultural bourgeoisie, which now will build capitalism on the ruins of socialism.

Making Capitalism Without Capitalists returns in this sense and only in this sense to the theme of *The Intellectuals on the Road to Class Power.*

Intellectuals are not on their road to class power, not even on the road to become a propertied bourgeoisie. They did win the 1989 revolution, but only in alliance with the former communist technocracy. During post-communist transition of the 1990s they belong to the dominant elite, but they are from the beginning and as time goes by increasingly only a "subordinated faction" of the dominant elite – the lead is taken by the technocratic-managerial and the new political elite. And of course, as the capitalist socio-economic order will be consolidated, the dominant elite will give way to a new dominant class. After all, the transition from socialism to capitalism is a transition from a socialist rank order to a capitalist class stratified society, and the power hegemony of the elite lasts only as long as the new class relations do not form properly.

The most general conclusion of the book is that "new class" theories are likely to err, since "cultural capital" can probably never become in a lasting way the dominant form of capital. Cultural capital is like Charisma in weberian sociology. It is a revolutionary force, which helps the movement from one system to the next, but once the change is complete either the rule of bureaucrats, or the domination by a propertied class, will be firmly established, and the possessors of cultural capital will have to take the back seat.

The constellation of social forces, which brought communism down and which are creating the new post-communist socio-economic order, varies a great deal across countries. The unique role of the cultural bourgeoisie we describe in our last book, the alliance between former communist technocracy and dissident humanistic intellectuals, best describes the transformations in Central Europe. Post-communism, however, is not a single destination. As we can see at the present time (King & Szelenyi, forthcoming; Kitschelt et al., 1999), former communist countries are heading towards different destinations. After decades of "convergence" under communism (the differences among nations narrowed at least somewhat under communist rules both in terms of level of economic development and arrangements of socio-economic institutions) is now followed by a strong trend towards "divergence." And which way various societies go depends primarily on the constellation of class forces and intra-elite struggles.

Only in Central Europe did the alliance of the technocracy and the humanistic intellectuals unseat the communist apparatchiks. Where this happened (in Hungary, Poland and Slovenia) capitalism took a neo-liberal turn. The new power elite did carry out quite successfully neo-liberal reforms, and on the whole prevented the communist apparatchiks from walking away with public property and turning it into their private wealth. Privatization, which colored with some corruption, was on the whole carried out under the rule of law, in some cases done by voucher mechanism and in other cases by public auctioning. Neo-liberal regimes, after a sharp drop in their economic output, turned around by the mid-1990s, and they opened up to the world market and foreign investors. Foreign capital plays a crucial role in the corporate sector: it drives economic growth and limits the role of the domestic bourgeoisie to small and middle-sized firms.

In Eastern Europe properly defined and in Russia, with the exception of the Baltic states, the alliance of the technocracy and humanistic intellectuals (which Gorbachev, following the Hungarian and Polish examples, also tried to form) was non-existent or far too weak to defeat the communist apparatus. The old nomenklatura survived the meltdown, and, operating in a weak civil society, managed to privatize as its private property the public sector, and created a neo-patrimonial version of capitalism. Finally, in East Asia the technocracy gained a great deal of influence after the death of Mao, but the old-line bureaucracy until now managed to maintain its monopoly of political power. Under these circumstances the communist bureaucracy is strong enough to prevent the technocracy from going "too far" with neo-liberal reform, but the technocracy has enough clout that it can stop the national level apparatchiks from moving towards political capitalism. As a result, East Asia capitalism evolves more gradually and unlike in Europe it does not happen from "above," but it is growing from "below," giving credence to Nee's assertion that under these circumstances the "direct producers" (especially if they are on their way to become private entrepreneurs) may even benefit from market transition.

My last qualification therefore is that intellectuals did win the 1989 revolution, but that claim has validity only for Central Europe and only with the qualification offered above: namely that even in Central Europe their victory could be achieved only in alliance with the former communist techno-managerial elites. They did not transform themselves into a new class, but rather limited their role as a "revolutionary force" to complete the new historic task of "making capitalism without capitalists." In other post-communist or late socialist contexts the history of capitalism unfolds in different ways.

METHODOLOGICAL CONTINUITY

Irony as the Method of Critical Inquiry in Neo-classical Sociology

While the three books, which I claimed here can be read as three volumes of the same work, negate each other in their content and aim at gradual adjustment of the analysis to the rapidly changing realities of socialism and post-communism, the methodology applied in these works remains pretty much the same.

And here I just would like to respond briefly to an intriguing criticism by Michael Burawoy (2001) of the *Making Capitalism Without Capitalists* (some of the arguments were made by Eyal et al., 2001). In the last book we suggested that with the collapse of communism sociology faces a new task. Until there was a socialist alternative sociology could use socialism (the actually existing one, or the "real" one) as a critical vintage point either to argue for or against the status quo. Even more importantly, since the idea of socialism was at least in the back of the mind of social analysts, sociologists were rarely sensitized to the diversity of actually existing capitalism. Now, with socialism gone from the agenda, we can see with more clarity that capitalism is not a single destination, so "comparative capitalism" can become a central concern for macro-sociological inquiry. With a bit of immodesty we even called this "neo-classical sociology."[7] The point was that the fall of communism forced macro-sociologists to return to some of the originating questions of the discipline: what is modernity, what is capitalism and what are its origins? But this is not simply a return to the classics. Classical sociology, even more so than sociology in the 20th century, was pre-occupied with the promise or threat of socialism, therefore classical sociologists tended to think about capitalism as a homogeneous system.[8] So we claimed neo-classical sociology will re-visit the agenda of the classics, but pose the same questions in a different way. The central project of neo-classical sociology is "the sociology of comparative capitalism" – as David Stark calls it (Stark & Bruszt, 1998).

It should have been clear that the "classical turn" in sociology we believed we spotted is different radically from the classical turn in economics. This classical turn in sociology does enable – so we believed and I still believe – sociology to address the same big issues than neo-classical economics. I do not accept that sociology is just the hand-maiden of economics, and that all sociology can do is bring in some understanding of more micro-mechanisms, such as embeddedness of economic action, into economic analysis. The neo-classical turn in sociology implies that sociology will engage neo-classical economics in the same polemical way as classical sociology engaged classical economics.

Michael Burawoy in his critical review (2001) asserts that this neo-classical turn is nothing less than "market triumphalism" and it is the abandonment of the critical social science project he believes I was committed to in my earlier work, in particular in *The Intellectuals on the Road to Class Power.*

I believe I remained committed to "critical analysis." I think that Burawoy misunderstood the critical method used in my earlier work, which is not different, so I claim, for the method used in the last book. Nevertheless, I want to concede that Burawoy asked an important question to which the answer is not obvious. Is critical analysis possible without a critical vintage point, which is somehow outside the system I try to develop a critical understanding of? Burawoy's answer is a clear "no" – one needs a critical vintage point – and therefore instead of neo-classical sociology he recommends post-socialist theory, which posits a "positive utopia" as such a vintage point. This is a perfectly logical and respectable position and has been consistently the position of many social scientists that practice critical theory.[9] But I would insist this is not the only way to offer critical analysis, and I tried to stay away from such a "utopian" vantage point in my earlier critical analysis as well.

Here, briefly, I would like to return to the method of "mirrored comparison" of inequality under socialism and capitalism. I adopted this method, since I did not want to accept as justification for inequality under socialism that capitalism is also inegalitarian, or that it is even less equal. The point was that one has to understand and offer a critical analysis of socialist inequality on its own terms – you may say it in an "immanent critique" or in an "ironic" way. This analysis, as much as the analysis about the class aspiration of intellectuals, was "ironic" in the sense that it maintained that one does not have to show a better solution in order to understand that the phenomenon under investigation is not inevitable, it is "temporary" (to put it with Foucault), that it could be otherwise.

Similarly in *Socialist Entrepreneurs* I insisted that my diagnosis that late socialism is on a sort of third way is an ironic one. I again used the term not to recommend a third way, to claim it is a change for the better. The only point was to show the phenomena under investigation was not inevitable, that there are other ways to act or live and it is not the task of social science to tell what is the desirable or right way. With Weber I believe it is not the task of social scientists to tell people what they ought to do, the best we can do is to tell them what they can or may do. The rest should be left to social praxis.

Yes, positing a utopia is one way to offer critical analysis. But since the aim of critical analysis is to raise the critical self-consciousness of actors, irony is an equally valid method. "The term irony has its roots in the Greek comic character Eiron, a clever underdog, who by his wit repeatedly triumphs over the boastful character Alazon. The Socratic irony of the Platonic dialogues derives from this comic origin. Feigning ignorance and humility, Socrates goes about asking silly and obvious questions of all sorts of people on all sorts of subjects, only to expose their ignorance as more profound than his own." (Encyclopedia Britannica, 1998, Vol. 6, p. 390)

This paper was supposed to be an exercise in self-irony. It is up to the reader to decide how successful this attempt was. I can only hope that humility was not just "feigned" and ignorance, though real, was not excessively embarrassing for someone who wants to be seen as a social scientist.

NOTES

1. I begin to develop this method on my work on housing in some of my publications, which appeared as early as 1968. In the first English language publication which adopts this method, it appeared in print in 1972 in my article "Housing system and social structure," in *The Sociological Review Monographs*.

2. I used this term for the first time (I believe) in 1972 in my Ph.D. dissertation, which was eventually published in English under the title *Urban Social Inequalities under State Socialism* in 1982 by Oxford University Press. It took a long time before the idea of socialism as a "redistributive economy" sank in. Western readers misunderstood it, since they did not get the difference between welfare redistribution and a "redistributive economic system." Victor Nee's 1989 market transition theory finally introduced the theory of redistributive economy into the literature successfully.

3. For us this was a "counterintuitive" finding in more than one way. The received wisdom – at least since Trotsky and at least among the left of the social sciences – was that inequalities do exist under socialism, but they are the results of "surviving market institutions." Markets create inequalities, no matter what. Now we found instances when inequalities were reduced as a result of workings of markets! Furthermore, socialist societies were supposed to be "workers states" – even if deformed ones – therefore workers were not supposed to be "negatively privileged" and certainly not as a result of government policy, nor as an outcome of redistribution. And now we found that workers compensated for disadvantages they suffered as a result of redistribution by engaging in market type of activities!

4. János Kornai in his masterpiece, *Economics of Shortage*, applied the same method in 1980. In my reading of this book his fundamental point was that socialism creates chronic shortages, while market capitalism tend to produce cycles of "over-production." This book does not suggest that one is better or more desirable than the other, it rather shows that the systems are mirrored images of each other. In neither system can you have your cake and eat it. In his later work, *The Road to a Free Economy* (1990) and *The Socialist System* (1992), Kornai's analysis changes and now he believes capitalism is the desirable system and the only way to go. I never went down this road – again Burawoy misunderstand our *Making Capitalism Without Capitalists* in his 2001 *AJS* piece, by missing the irony of our analysis there.

5. We defined as intellectuals people who can persuade society that they dispose with knowledge that is necessary for society and deserves therefore power and privilege – in hindsight a rather foucauldian, or gouldnerian, definition.

6. Erzsèbet Szalai called them the "new elite" and saw the 1980s as an intense power struggle between the new technocratic line and the old guard (Szalai, 1988).

7. I coined this term in a conversation I had with Victor Nee sometime in the fall of 1997 or spring 1998 at UCLA. I cannot recall any more who used the term first, Victor or me, but nevertheless I am grateful to him for this provocative label, which may not have occurred to me without his inspiration.

8. This is not really true for Weber. In some sense, Weber is the first of "neo-classical" sociologists, since he was well aware that capitalism had various historic

forms, and developed a complex theory of political, or politically oriented, capitalism, and even wrote about state capitalism. Even Weber, however, tended to think about "modern capitalism" as closer to the "pure type," and regarded political capitalism as a temporary, though occasionally fatal, deviation.

9. Critical theory itself – in the sense of the Frankfurt School – offers a more complex point of view. By the late 1930s the theorists of the Frankfurt school abandoned the possibility of offering a critical analysis from the "viewpoint of the proletariat" or "socialism," that they did not believe in any more. They insisted instead to offer an "immanent critique" – an approach that has similarities with what I describe as the "ironic view of history."

REFERENCES

Bauman, Z. (1974). Officialdom and Class – Bases of Inequality in Socialist Society. In: F. Parkin (Ed.), *The Analysis of Class Structure* (pp. 129–148). London: Tavistock.

Bell, D. ([1973] 1976). *The Coming of Postindustrial Society.* New York: Basic Books.

Burawoy, M. (2001). Neoclassical Sociology: From the End of Communism to the End of Classes. *American Journal of Sociology, 106*(4), 1099–1022.

Djilas, M. (1957). *The New Class.* New York: Holton, Rinehart and Winston.

Eyal, G., Szelenyi, I., & Townsley, E. (1998). *Making Capitalism without Capitalists.* London: Verso.

Eyal, G., Szelenyi, I., & Townsley, E. (2001). The Utopia of Postsocialist Theory and the Ironic View of History in Neoclassical Sociology. *American Journal of Sociology, 106*(4), 1121–1128.

Heller, A., Feher, F., & Markus, G. (1983). *Dictatorship over Needs.* London: Blackwell.

Giddens, A. (1998). *The Third Way: The Renewal of Social Democracy.* Cambridge: Polity Press.

Gouldner, A. (1979). *The Future of Intellectuals and the Rise of the New Class.* New York: The Continuum Publishing Corporation.

Hankiss, E. (1990). *East European Alternatives.* Oxford: Clarendon Press.

King, L. P., & Szelenyi, I. (Forthcoming). The New Capitalism of Eastern Europe – Towards a Comparative Political Economy of Post-communist Capitalisms. In: N. Smelser & R. Swedberg (Eds), *Handbook of Economic Sociology* (2nd ed.).

Kitschelt, H., Mansfeldova, Z., Markowski, R., & Toka, G. (1999). *Post-Communist Party System.* Cambridge: Cambridge University Press.

Kocka, J. (1988). *Bürgertum in 19 Jahrhundert: Deutschland in europäischen Vergleich.* Munchen: Tachenbuch Verlag.

Konrad, G., & Szelenyi, I. ([1971] 1974). Social conflicts of under-urbanization. In: A. A. Brown, J. A. Licari & E. Neuberger (Eds), *Urban and Social Economics in Market and Planned Economies* (Vol. 1, pp. 206–226). New York: Praeger.

Konrad, G., & Szelenyi, I. (1979). *The Intellectuals on the Road to Class Power.* New York: Harcourt, Brace and Yovanovich.

Kornai, J. (1980). *The Economics of Shortage.* Amsterdam: North Holland.

Kornai, J. (1990). *The Road to a Free Economy.* New York: Norton.

Kornai J. (1992). *The Socialist System.* Princeton: Princeton University Press.

Kostello, E., & Szelenyi, I. (1996). The Market Transition Debate – Toward a Synthesis? *American Journal of Sociology, 101*(4), 1082–1096.

Lal, D., & Myint, H. (1996). The Political Economy of Poverty, Equity and Growth – A Comparative Study. Oxford: Clarendon Press.

Nee, V. (1989). A Theory of Market Transition. *American Sociological Review*, *54*(5), 663–681.

Nee, V. (1992). Organizational Dynamics of Market Transition: Hybrid Forms, Property Rights, and Mixed Economy in China. *Administrative Science Quarterly*, *37*, 1–27.

Nee, V. (1996). The Emergence of Market Society – Changing Mechanisms of Stratification in China. *American Journal of Sociology*, *101*(4), 908–949.

Nee, V., & Lian, P. (1994). Sleeping with the Enemy. *Theory and Society*, *23*(2), 253–296.

Richta, R. (1969). *The Civilization at the Crossroads*. White Plains, N.Y.: Sharpe.

Schelsky, H. (1975). *Arbeit tun die Anderen*. Opladen: Wesdeutscher Verlag.

Staniszkis, J. (1991). Political Capitalism in Poland. *East European Politics and Societies*, *5*(1), 127–141.

Stark, D. (1985).The micropolitics of the firms and the macropolitics of reform – new forms of workplace bargaining in Hungarian enterprises. In: P. Evans, D. Rueschemeyer, E. Huber (Eds), *States vs. Markets in the World-System* (pp. 257–273). Beverly Hills: Sage.

Stark, D. (1986). Rethinking Internal Labor Markets: New Insights from a Comparative Perspective. *American Sociological Review*, *51*, 492–504.

Stark, D. (1992). Path Dependence and Privatization Strategies in East Central Europe. *East European Politics and Societies*, *6*(1), 17–51.

Stark, D., & Bruszt, L. (1998). *Postsocialist Pathways: Transforming Politics and Property in East Central Europe*. Cambridge: Cambridge University Press.

Stark, D., & Burszt, L. (2001). One Way or Multiple Path: For a Comparative Sociology of East European Capitalism. *American Journal of Sociology*, *106*(4), 1129–1137.

Szalai, E. ([1988] 1989). The New Elite. *Across Frontiers*, *5*(Fall-Winter), 25–31.

Szelenyi, I. (1972). Housing System and Social Structure. *Sociological Review Monographs*, February, 269–297.

Szelenyi, I. (1982). The Intelligentsia in the Class Structure of State Socialist Societies. *American Journal of Sociology*, *88*(Supplement), 287–326.

Szelenyi, I. (1986–1987). Prospects and Limits of the East European New Class Project – an Auto-Critique. *Politics and Society*, *15*(2), 103–144.

Szelenyi, I. (1988). *Socialist Entrepreneurs*. Madison, Wisc.: University of Wisconsin Press.

Szelenyi, I., & Szelenyi, B. (1994). Why socialism failed? *Theory and Society*, *23*(April), 211–231.

Townsley, E. (1996). Academics and the U.S. government in the 1960s. UCLA, unpublished Ph.D. dissertation.

Townsley, E. (2000). A History of Intellectuals and the Demise of the New Class: Academics and the U.S. Government in the 1960s. *Theory and Society*, *29*(6), 739–784.

Trotsky, L. (1972). *The Revolution Betrayed*. New York: Pathfinder.

WHAT HAPPENED TO THE WORKING CLASS? ERRORS OF AN UNREPENTANT MARXIST

Michael Burawoy

In a 1990 article, "Marxism is Dead, Long Live Marxism," I claimed that working class movements against state socialism – from Berlin in 1953 to Hungary in 1956, Czechoslovakia in 1968, Poland in 1980 and finally to the Soviet Union in 1989 – had laid the basis for powerful challenges to the emerging capitalist economies of the region.

> The Soviet democratic revolution has already unchained national struggles on the periphery of the Soviet Empire. But even if these republics were to secede there still remains the heartland of the Soviet Union, the Russian Federation with 50% of the population, 76% of the land area,70% of the national production and the bulk of the natural resources. Here class struggle could still advance toward the renewal of socialism, much as Solidarity was advancing in 1981. Here the collapse of the party state and the construction of political pluralism could engender a democratic socialism.
>
> There was after all a revolution in Russia. Its nationalism may not be closely tied to the fate of the party but it is still tied to the future of socialism. What such a democratic socialism might look like is unclear but it is likely to be more attractive than a peripheral, clientalistic, booty capitalism (Burawoy, 1990, pp. 18–19).

I was more or less on the mark in my diagnosis of the emerging peripheral capitalism but I could not have been further from the mark in expecting a resurgence of working class mobilization. Notwithstanding the restoration of

The Future of Market Transition, Volume 19, pages 69–76.

ISBN: 0-7623-0835-4

factory councils in Hungary, across the swath of disintegrating Central European socialisms the working class slumbered. By 1989 Polish Solidarity had dissolved its militant past and resurfaced to embrace what many of its leaders hoped would be the quickest and most radical transition to capitalism. Workers bore their degradation, marginalization and destitution for the most part in silence.

This was not the first time that workers had failed the predictions of intellectuals, especially those who have endowed workers with some historic mission. There is a long pedigree of working classes giving lie to revolutionary optimism! Indeed, the pedigree goes back to Marx and Engels who complained that the English working class had let them down after being enfranchised in the election of 1867. Engels wrote to Marx: "What do you say to the elections in the factory districts? Once again the proletariat has discredited itself terribly . . . It cannot be denied that the increase of working class has brought the Tories more than their simple percentage increase; it has improved their relative position" (cited in McKenzie & Silver, 1968, p. 14). In my own prognostication of working class mobilization against capitalism and for a democratic socialism was I simply another deluded intellectual, one in a long line, who could not learn from history?

What does history tell us about the working class? To be sure the working class never achieved that messianic character anticipated by the young Lukács – that universal subject-object of history. That is not to say, however, that it has never been a major protagonist in social transformation. Under early European capitalism, the working class demonstrated its radical potential first in England around the middle of the 19th. century, then in France towards the end of the 19th. century, in Germany in the early years of the twentieth century, and in Russia and Italy during and after World War I. In advanced capitalism, similarly, we see how significant working class mobilization was in the United States in the 1930s and subsequently in Europe during the 1960s, especially in France and Italy. Finally, the working class has been a leading force for change in the industrializing semi-periphery, in such countries as South Africa, Brazil and Korea. Thus, it was not so unreasonable to anticipate that the working class would extend its covert struggles into an open movement against the primitive capitalism that followed in the wake of state socialism. Still I was wrong, but why was I wrong?

Social science does not advance by making correct predictions but by making plausible mistakes.[1] So what was the "plausibility" of my argument? The argument began from two premises,[2] that workers revolt if: (a) they see it to be in their interests; and (b) they have the collective capacity to undertake such a project. Let us start with "interests," and the theory expounded by

Konrád and Szelényi in *Intellectuals on the Road to Class Power.* They argue that under state socialism there is a transparent and central appropriation of surplus by, what they call, rational or teleological redistributors. This rational redistribution calls forth the need for legitimation,[3] characteristically performed by intellectuals who represent their own interests as the interests of all. In other words, the inner dynamics of state socialism leads intellectuals to class power. Leaving aside the many debates and issues raises by this classic treatise, for my purposes it posed a clear antagonism between working class who had an interest in controlling the product of their labor and the teleological redistributors – planners, bureaucrats, apparatchiki – who had interests in appropriating that surplus and who did so in the name of collectively defined needs for justice, equality and efficiency.

Based on many stints as a worker in Hungarian enterprises – champagne factory, machine shop, steel mill – I argued that socialist workers turned socialist ideology against the ruling classes, exclaiming the latter's failure to live up to their ideological pretensions, their socialist promises. Compulsory participation in socialist rituals had led them to imminent critique, had led them to embrace socialism – justice, equality and efficiency – but *against* the workers' state. It was here that I made my first mistake. I underestimated the degree to which workers had withdrawn from any serious engagement with socialism.[4] When they showed disgust with existing socialism they were not striving for some better, superior socialism but were cynically dismissing socialism tout court. Perhaps in the 1950s in Hungary, workers may have held out hope for upgrading socialism. Indeed, successive reforms did bring improvements although not necessarily the improvements for which they had hoped and which they had been promised. Socialism manufactured dissent but not in the name of some higher socialism but for some unarticulated alternative to socialism. As market reforms allowed socialism to work better, so workers began to embrace these alternatives that they had constituted from below. Inasmuch as they partook of the second economy – the celebrated inside contracting systems, the cooperatives outside employment – so they were preparing themselves, willy nilly, for an alternative order. Positive experience with markets under socialism made capitalism an attractive prospect.[5]

Interests were not generally aligned with some future socialism but even where they were there was still the question of class capacity. Here I had begun with János Kornai's classic treatise, *The Economics of Shortage* and argued that state socialist economies systematically generated shortages which appeared on the shop floor as unreliable machinery, unpredictable and scarcity of materials, and even inadequate labor supplies. Production, therefore, could work only if workers were given the autonomy to improvise. There was, in other words, a tendency toward a spontaneous self-organization on the shop floor. Of course, I had found such informal organization in capitalist workplaces but it was not as fundament and structurally central to production as it proved to be in state socialism. In capitalism constraints are from the side of demand and these fluctuations can be more easily accommodated within a Taylorized work process. In state socialism, supply side constraints called for flexible specialization, thereby giving workers the resources for collective organization. To be sure, I argued, this could only be realized if, beyond the workplace, there was space to organize. This was the case in both Hungary and Poland but with one major difference: in Hungary the second economy channeled worker dissent in individualist directions, whereas in Poland without such an atomizing second economy, the organization of the Church was an umbrella for expanding labor organizations. Still, persuasive though it might have been, the argument was flawed by its insufficient attention to the absence of well established oppositional organizations such as trade unions or parties. Autonomous work organization and a relatively open (if empty) civil society do not provide the basis for an enduring working class movement.

If the pre-existing conditions for working class mobilization were not as favorable as I anticipated, still there was an eeriness to the silence with which workers embraced their own demise once the market blossomed forth. There is, after all, ample evidence that workers spontaneously contest market society, especially when they are offered no protections against its depredations. Karl Polanyi (1944), for example, argues that once released from the reactionary paternalism of the hated Speenhamland welfare system and the abolition of outdoor poor relief, workers in 19th century England were both free and motivated to spontaneously organize in their self defense against the unrestrained market. They were able to organize a factory movement, co-operatives and even stage demands to extend their political participation. Why not against the capitalism that followed state socialism? Again we must deal with both interests and capacities.

Workers could have drawn on the more favorable conditions of the past – the multiple material and welfare guarantees of socialism. In contesting capitalism they could have appealed to the egalitarian ideology of socialism.[6] But the rhetoric of socialism had been so abused by the communists that it was inaccessible to the working class. Because socialism had discredited any alternative to capitalism, the working class was ideologically disarmed, bereft of any vision of the future. The past was not only ideologically discredited but its material foundations were rapidly eroding. With the market, came the inevitable plant closures and the bases for working class organization collapsed. In terms of both ideology and capacity the working class was ill-equipped to contest the capitalist offensive.

In Russia the destruction of the means of production has been most dramatic and continuous, and there the retreat of the working class most far reaching – a retreat into petty commodity production, self-provisioning, subsistence and the reciprocity of kin networks, you might say a retreat to Polanyi's premarket society based on the household, reciprocity and redistribution. But this retreat to premodernity was also accompanied by a hypermodernity that linked Russia into global circuits of finance, natural resources, information and so forth. A merchant or rentier capitalism emerged on the basis of Russia's enormous natural resources. The realm of exchange profited at the expense of the realm of production upon which it preyed. The new Russian ruling class, the so-called oligarchs who run financial-industrial cartels, had no need for a working class which thereby lost the leverage it used to wield. Class struggle has turned through 180 degrees, from a struggle between the bureaucratic and working classes to one between bureaucratic and rentier classes, between the old and the new Russian dominant classes.

This is so different from Polanyi's 19th. century England where a manufacturing bourgeoisie rose to economic domination in *collaboration* with the ruling landed classes. In the English case the bourgeoisie depended upon the working class for its very existence. The working class could, therefore, more easily organize the defense of vibrant craft and cultural traditions. Equally important the English working class could organize from strength in an economy that was expanding. To be sure there was proletarianization and deskilling, but that was not as demobilizing as deproletarianization and reskilling for Russia's premodern economy. Russian primitive disaccumulation poses almost insuperable obstacles to class organization.

If the circumstances of the Russian working class are so bleak perhaps the diametrically opposed situation in China are more propitious for working class mobilization. This is precisely the argument of Ching Kwan Lee (forthcoming) – that China may yet prove to be the exception to the passivity of "post-socialist" labor. There the market transition has not made a sharp break with the past. There the state continues to regulate and incubate the market economy. There the market has not been the effective instrument for working class advance as it was for Hungarian workers in the 1980s, so much as a vehicle for state imposed degradation. It is still possible, therefore, for Chinese workers to appeal to the state and the continuing socialist ideology in order to make claims against the market. And in China the economy continues to expand so that there is a firmer ground from which at least certain sections of the working class can organize itself. There the working class has retained what it lost in Russia: both the power of leverage and the legitimacy of critique.

Wrong or right, whether the working class mobilizes against capitalism or not should not decide whether it enters sociological analysis. To abandon the working class for a study of elites because they are the ones who appear to be taking initiatives is poor sociology.[7] In forging the transition to a market economy those initiatives of the dominant classes are formulated and adopted in the light of constraints posed by subaltern classes – different constraints in different countries. Constraints from below are as significant in establishing trajectories as the various resources wielded by dominant classes. Moreover, one key to the character of the new postsocialist order lies in the experience of class exploitation and oppression. It is an old Hegelian truism that the greatest insight into social orders are gleaned from below, looking up.

If abandoning the working class for a study of elites is poor sociology, it is equally poor Marxism! Marxists may throw up their hands in despair when workers fail to contest capitalism's assault on the human condition. The working class may betray the intellectuals' hopes and aspirations for emancipation, but this is no reason for intellectuals as a group to then return the favor by betraying the working class, that is by abandoning the working class for some other class upon which it can ride to power. To turn from the working class to the study of elites and policies because they appear to be forging history is to abandon the critical perspective of the subaltern. To continue to study the working class in times of retreat entails recovering past visions to which it was attached but it never had the power to realize, the visions of the Solidarity movement in Poland, the visions of the militant and radical miners of Russia, even the novel institutions created by Hungarian workers within the interstices of socialism. To continue to study the plight of the working class is to offer a continuing critique of a peripheral, derivative, imitative bourgeoisie that falsely dresses itself up in the garb of the general interest.

NOTES

1. Of course, a more practical, social engineering science cannot afford the luxury of being wrong which is often why it is so intellectually boring and conservative.

2. The argument was presented most comprehensively in Burawoy and Lukács (1992).

3. Capitalism by contrast does not need the same legitimation as capitalist relations of production tends to reproduce themselves of themselves and exploitation (the appropriation of surplus) is invisible. In capitalism, I argued, the problem is more consent than legitimacy.

4. Linda Fuller (1999) has a much more adequate explanation of working class passivity in Eastern Europe. Based on her study of GDR she argues that the

inefficiencies and injustices of the workplace, the weakness of trade unions and the hostility to intellectuals led to most (but not all) passivity and cynical withdrawal in the face of the 1989 turbulence of civil society.

5. Zbierski-Salameh (1999) makes a similar point with respect to the appeal of agrarian reforms to the Polish peasantry. The benefits of market concessions under state socialism made a market economy appealing from within state socialism, but it actually turned into a "bitter harvest" when market forces were unleashed by the Solidarity government. Róna-Tas (1997) goes even further in arguing that the expansion of market reforms was not only popular among large sections of the Hungarian population but eroded the very basis of state socialism. In the case of Russia, Crowley (1997) argues that the militant miners were also attracted by market ideology which they grafted onto their critique of communism. They were the dynamite that brought down the Soviet order but also among its first victims. Embracing market ideology ill-equipped them to deal with mine closures, non-payment of wages, and the degradation of working and living conditions.

6. Indeed, Lynne Haney (1999) argues this is precisely what Hungarian women did when the postsocialist government threatened to end their welfare benefits.

7. I'm thinking here, for example, of Eyal et al. (1998) and Stark and Bruszt (1998). See Burawoy (2001) for a critique of these books for their abandonment of class analysis.

REFERENCES

Burawoy, M. (1990). Marxism is Dead, Long Live Marxism. *Socialist Review, 2*, 7–19.

Burawoy, M. (2001). Neoclassical Sociology: From the End of Communism to the End of Classes. *American Journal of Sociology, 106*(4), 1099–1120.

Burawoy, M., & Lukács, J. (1992). *The Radiant Past*. Chicago: University of Chicago Press.

Crowley, S. (1997). *Hot Coal, Cold Steel: Russian and Ukrainian Workers from the End of the Soviet Union to the Post-Communist Transformations*. Ann Arbor: University of Michigan Press.

Eyal, G., Szelényi, I., & Townsley, E. (1998). *Making Capitalism Without Capitalists: The New Ruling Elites in Eastern Europe*. London: Verso Books.

Fuller, L. (1999). *Where was the Working Class?* Urbana and Chicago: University of Illinois Press.

Haney, L. (1999). "But We Are Still Mothers": Gender, the State, and the Construction of Need in Postsocialist Hungary. In: M. Burawoy & K. Verdery (Eds), *Uncertain Transition* (pp. 151–188). Lanham, Maryland: Rowman and Littlefield.

Konrád, G., & Szelényi, I. (1979). *The Intellectuals on the Road to Class Power*. New York and London: Harcourt Brace Jovanovich.

Kornai, J. (1980). *The Economics of Shortage* (Two Volumes). Amsterdam: North-Holland Publishing Company.

Lee, C. K. (Forthcoming). In the Twilight of Socialism: Labor Insurgency and Subjectivity in Reform China. *Theory and Society*.

McKenzie, R., & Silver, A. (1968). *Angels in Marble*. London: Heinemann.

Polanyi, K. (1944). *The Great Transformation*. (Rev. ed. 2001). Boston: Beacon Press.

Róna-Tas, Á. (1997). *The Great Surprise of the Small Transformation*. Ann Arbor: University of Michigan Press.

Stark, D., & Bruszt, L. (1998). *Postsocialist Pathways: Transforming Politics and Property in East Central Europe*. Cambridge: Cambridge University Press.

Zbierski-Salameh, S. (1999). Polish Peasants in the "Valley of Transition": Responses to Postsocialist Reforms. In: M. Burawoy & K. Verdery (Eds), *Uncertain Transition* (pp. 189–222). Lanham, Maryland: Rowman and Littlefield.

PART II:
INSIGHTS INTO THE TRANSFORMATION OF ORGANIZATIONS AND MARKET INSTITUTIONS

BIRTH OF A MARKET ECONOMY: HUNGARIAN AGRICULTURE AFTER SOCIALISM[1]

Anthony Oberschall and Zsuzsa Hanto

ABSTRACT

Based on field work, surveys and statistics from the 1980s to 1995, we compare socialist with postsocialist farming in Hungary on dimensions that differentiate socialism from capitalism: private property; markets; farm entrepreneurship; incentives, bankruptcy and soft budget constraints; market coordination. Some theorists have called for shock treatment and abrupt change as the most effective and in the long run least costly way from socialism to capitalism. Others have favored institution building and a gradual transition to the market economy, and in farming, cooperative enterprises as a halfway house to capitalism. We studied privatization of collective farms into shareholder-owned agribusinesses, and how agromanagers, skilled farm employees, unskilled workers, and the retired fared. Mature capitalism is complemented by social welfare institutions. The dismantling of collective farming in Hungary weakened the enterprise social safety net. Those who had human and social capital have fared relatively well. For the retired and unskilled workers, the job rights, user rights and social entitlements under socialism that they lost were compensated only in part by the private property they gained. Losses in farm output, employment and profitability were due both to the

The Future of Market Transition, Volume 19, pages 79–104.

ISBN: 0-7623-0835-4

economic depression and to privatization. Farm enterprises have become more efficient but the market economy is not yet working satisfactorily.

SOCIALISM AND CAPITALISM

The change from socialism to a market economy in Eastern Europe is an opportunity to compare the performance of socialist and capitalist institutions, and to understand how a market economy is created by human agency (North, 1990). Jeffrey Sachs (1991) advocated shock treatment as the least costly and surest means in the long run of establishing a market economy. Pryor (1990, 1991) argued that in contemporary scientific agriculture it would be inefficient to convert large collective agribusinesses into a multitude of commercial family farms rather than into downsized, privately owned, corporate agribusinesses. Przeworski (1991) believed that market socialism was a viable alternative to both socialism and to capitalism. How well do their views match up against Hungarian privatization in farming? (Sachs, 1996). We have studied Hungarian agriculture in the last years of socialism and the first years of post-socialism when collective farms were privatized.[2] We compare and contrast socialism and capitalism on several dimensions.

Capitalism is an economic system in which the means of production, distribution and exchange are in large measure privately owned and directed (Webster dictionary). For there to be capitalism, owners must have a stake in the profitability of their enterprises and assume personal responsibility for failure. Ultimately, that means bankruptcy results in a real loss (Kornai, 1990). Hard budget constraints and meaningful profit-loss measures are necessary for a successful transition to capitalism (Stiglitz, 1994). We must inquire how enterprise failure was dealt with in socialism and what changed in the 1990s under capitalism.

Competitive markets are central in efficient capitalism: labor markets, capital markets, land markets, commodity markets. Markets allocate scarce economic resources by supply responding to demand (Swedberg, 1994). The integration of all these markets into an economic system is what constitutes a market economy. In socialism Kornai (1990) demonstrated that allocation was determined by bargaining between state officials and state managers. We must inquire how resources were allocated in socialism and how markets functioned in the 1990s.

A third dimension of the difference of socialism and capitalism are work incentives for managers and ordinary employees. A frequent criticism of socialism and of state enterprises is the high job security of workers regardless of performance and of organization need, and the weak linkage of performance to wages and bonuses. Stiglitz (1994) underscores changing the incentive structure for management.

Closely related to work incentives is the organizational structure of an enterprise. Under socialism, planners and politicians created huge, multivillage collective farming enterprises which were difficult to manage centrally and which diluted personal responsibility. Williamson (1975) has shown organizations vary greatly on transaction costs. Under the competitive pressures of capitalism, the size and internal structure of an organization will change in response to transaction costs. We compare the internal organization structure and organizational configuration of agriculture under socialism and in post-socialism.

Private property rights are at the heart of capitalism. A common criticism of socialism is that without well-defined and secure property rights, people have no incentives to invest and that they devote their talents and energies to the small islands of private property that survived within socialism. We examine how managers and workers disposed of common property and user rights and what changed when private property was instituted.

Lastly, we look at the change from "redistributive integration" in the economy under socialism to "market coordination" under capitalism (Szelenyi et al., 1994). What integrated the agricultural economy in the 1980s and how did that change in the 1990s? Did these changes result in a market economy with market coordination? How well are economic actors responding to market signals, incentives, and opportunities?

THE AGRARIAN ECONOMY IN 1980s SOCIALISM

Hungary in the 1980s had 133 large state farms, 1253 large collective farm enterprises, and over a million small plots cultivated by part-time family farmers, and very little in between (Juhász, 1990). The largest enterprises were state farms which were similar to large state industries except for what they produced, with an average of 950 employees on 7600 ha. The other large enterprise was the collective farm, with an average of 400 workers on 4400 ha., combining what used to be the agricultural resources of several villages under one management team. The collective was owned by the members, including numerous retired members. The land itself, by the late 1980s, was owned by the collective farm in common (about 2/3) and by the members separately (1/3). Members could not withdraw their land or a share of other assets, nor could they sell their share, nor did they receive more than a nominal rent for land. Members' ownership of the collective was not the same as private property in capitalism (Bell, 1984; Swain, 1985).

In the 1960s and early 70s Hungarian agriculture had mechanized and collective farms became agribusinesses. Management, professional staff, and some skilled workers were graduates of technical institutes. Collective farms were highly stratified and specialized, which was reflected in the hierarchic structure and the salary and wage scale (Held, 1980). Unskilled labor had only a minimum number of days per year work guarantee. Job security was almost 100%, and children of members were guaranteed employment after a period of apprenticeship. Villagers stayed in the collective farm because it provided them important benefits.

The most important benefit was the right to a plot of land, called a "household" plot, about 0.5 to 1 ha. For unskilled workers, the earnings from small farming might be as much as the earnings from collective farm employment. Small farming was known as the "second economy" and produced an abundant supply of labor intensive farm products, vegetables, fruit, pork, poultry eggs, etc. In 1984, it was estimated that 62% of vegetable production, 59% of fruit, 57% of hogs and 44% of poultry were produced in the small farm sector (Kovách, 1988).

Managers faced a labor surplus after the busy months and solved it by diversifying into non-agricultural activities. The 1980s collective farm usually had several divisions: one or two for the principal crops; one or two for livestock; one for farm machinery and repair; a dairy; a cannery or other food processing; a transportation branch; timber and sawmill; rural industry, i.e. manufacturing shoes and handbags, where unskilled female labor was employed. Some of these non-farm sideline activities were more profitable than farming, especially in marginal farm districts. Diversification was security against farm price fluctuations.

By the 1980s, collective farm managers knew about the problems of large and diversified agribusinesses, and in particular the problem of incentives for managers and workers alike. Some created a decentralized enterprise giving more responsibility to division heads and holding them accountable for division performance, with bonuses matching performance. Within divisions, a contract might be signed by a team of workers with the collective under which a facility, e.g. a dairy, would be rented by the team and earnings beyond the contract amount kept as its profit. Another incentive scheme was "putting out." Families would sign a contract for picking cherry trees or raspberries to be sold to the collective at a stated price. The collective might spray and market, the family would prune, pick and pack. The contracting family could make a profit, but also assumed risk of loss from frost and pests, or neglect. Thus limited features of a market economy were adopted in some collective farms. In the 1980s a third of the collectives were loss making and half had accumulated large debts (Juhász, 1990; Toth & Varga, 1995). Socialist farming was caught up in the general malaise and economic slow down of the entire Hungarian economy in the late 1980s, indeed of the socialist economies as a whole.

At the margins of these large collective agribusinesses, there existed some 20,000 small to medium-sized family farms which had broken with socialism (Szelenyi, 1988). Until the demise of socialism, the expansion of an independent farmer into crop farming was curtailed by lack of access to credit and land. According to Kovách (1988), only about 15% of these farm entrepreneurs had the capacity for substantial commercial farming. In the aggregate, they were a small part of the total agriculture economy.

THE PRIVATIZATION LAWS

The transition to a market economy, from 1989 to 1995, took place under difficult macro-economic conditions, in a hostile political milieu for collective farms, and severe droughts in 1992 and 1993. Farm subsidies declined sharply, exports to East Europe and post-Soviet successor states were down, the domestic food market shrunk as real incomes fell and unemployment rose. Farm prices rose less than energy prices and farm inputs; capital equipment was not renewed; animal stocks were cut; less crop acreage was planted; employment in agriculture nosedived (AKII, 1995). Banks lent at a prohibitively high 30–40% interest rate.

Economists and farm experts expressed doubt about whether technologically sophisticated socialist megafarming could be privatized into entrepreneurial family farm enterprises (Pryor, 1990, 1991). It was not possible to divide common property into private property when much common and state property was immovable and non-divisible, e.g. a huge cold storage facility or a huge dairy, and when much farm equipment was not suited for small-scale farming. The farm infrastructure was made for large agribusinesses. Farm workers had become specialized and many had no knowledge of the spectrum of activities necessary for commercial family farming. How was the debt of collective farms to be allocated among new owners? After a survey of collective farming in several countries, Pryor (1991, p. 3) wrote that "in certain historical situations, collectivization is not reversible so that any large-scale measures taken to return to individual farming are doomed to failure."

The first post-communist government, however, intended to dismantle collective farms altogether and to create in their stead a vigorous commercial family farm economy. To accomplish this purpose, three important pieces of legislation were passed in the early 1990s: a partial compensation law for restoring land to pre-communism owners and their heirs; a common property division law for collective farm members and employees; and an enterprise transformation law (Comisso, 1995). Land compensation (kárpotlás) partially restituted collectivized land to original owners and their heirs under a voucher scheme and local land auctions. By mid-1999, two million ha. were transferred to 708,000 individuals from common to private property in 26,000 auctions. About half this land is now farmed by small family farmers, many part-time; the other half is rented by cooperatives and farm enterprises that succeeded the collective farms (AKII, 1995).

Under common property division (vagyonnevesités), active members, retired members, former members and heirs, and employees all had a legal claim to farm assets. Shares were allocated according to criteria voted by a majority of members, most frequently length of employment and wages. Collective members had choices within broad guidelines for division. In our sample of cooperatives, one third allocated shares on years of employment alone; almost all the others weighted years and wages within the range of 25% to 75%, and 50% mode. Members could take out a physical asset, but less than 10% did because their share of assets was insufficient for starting a family farm. It is estimated that 40% of assets in the form of shares passed to retired members, 20% to former members heirs and employees (so-called "outsiders"), and 40% to current working members (Andorka, 1994; Oberschall, 2000). The new shareholders have seen the value of their shares steadily decrease, most obviously in bankruptcies and liquidations, but more commonly when farm enterprises are downsizing, selling assets, and are unprofitable. Although common property division legally created private property, for many, especially the retired, ownership of shares is of little value.

The reorganization of collective farms (átalakulás) made them into cooperatives, limited liability companies and other farm enterprises. As shown in Table 1, at the end of 1998, the 1300 collectives had become 1715 cooperatives, 4772 limited liability companies (Kft), and 4770 other types of agricultural enterprises. The cooperatives are much smaller than the mega-collectives – instead of 400 employees the average was down to 44, and the other companies tend to average just 11 employees (AK11, 1994). These trends show no sign of halting because downsizings and bankruptcies continue. Agribusiness employment in agriculture in the mid-1990s was down to 180,000 from 600,000 in the late 1980s. At the same time small family farming declined from one and a half million to a little under a million, mainly because the older and retired farm families on dwarf plots no longer get assistance for farming as they used under the collective farm regime. The others who farm are often part-timers who spend an average of about 70 days per year farming. Yet the number of full-time commercial family farmers (those with 10–100 ha.) jumped from

Table 1. Farm Enterprises, 1980s to 1998.

	Enterprise Type	Number	Labor Force	Size in ha*	% all farm land
1980s	State Farm	133	950	7,600	29
	Collective Farm	1253	400	4,400	61
	Family Plots	about 1.5 million	–	0.5 to 1 ha	10
	Agriculture Enterprises				50
1998	Cooperatives	1715	44	689	
	Limited Liability (kft)	4772	11	147	
	Other	4770	11	147	
	Households				50
	Incorporated	27832	?	70%	
	Other	960,000	–	have less than 3 ha	

* 1 ha equals 2.3 acres

Sources: Reports and yearbooks of the Central Statistical Office and The Ministry of Agriculture.

a thousand under socialism to 49,000 in the late 1990s. These data show growing inequality within the small farm sector. Those who are no longer employed by the agribusinesses are part-time farmers on the land they got under compensation, have retired, are unemployed, work part-time in the district, or commute to a city job.

STRATEGIES OF SURVIVAL AND CHANGE

In socialism, the profitability of collective farming depended on the assured sale of Hungarian agricultural and food industry products in the socialist countries. Collective farm success also depended on subsidies, price supports and tax write-offs. The comprehensive social insurance and welfare expenditures of collectives for members and families were not taxed. Capital goods were purchased with low interest loans. The untaxed non-wage benefits were substantial and provided at no or low cost: firewood for heating, fodder for household farm animals, holiday camps for children, cash or corn in lieu of farming the family plot, ambulance service, etc. It was usual for village families to use collective farm machinery, tools and materials for home improvement. Even farm districts with poor soil increased the standard of living. Some family members commuted daily, weekly or monthly to industry jobs. The family plot output, barnyard animals and garden produce were consumed and sold. Though wages and incomes were low by Western European standards, rural households in much of Hungary at the end of socialism had autos and appliances, electricity and hot water, attractive brick and cement houses with tile roofs.

The changes to the market economy during the first non-communist government under prime minister Antall starting in 1990 impacted negatively on all dimensions of production and livelihood of rural people, especially collective farm members and their families. The collapse of the Soviet Union and the socialist economic system disrupted Hungarian agriculture export markets. The Antall government terminated or reduced most tax benefits, subsidies and price supports; interest rates skyrocketed ahead of inflation; bankrupt middlemen, suppliers and wholesalers didn't pay their bills to collectives and farmers; and there was a severe two-year drought. The land restitution law meant that farm enterprises had to rent land they used to farm virtually for free. What that meant for enterprise viability was expressed by the president of Veszpremvarsanyi cooperative: "43% of the land we used to own and farm was auctioned off under compensation, and we are unable to rent from 30–40% of this lost crop land from the new owners, many of whom live in cities. At the moment, only 20–30% of the land we use is owned by our members."

Total agricultural output indexed at 100 for the late 1980s fell to 67 in 1994, then slowly rose to 73 in 1998. To avoid bankruptcy, and many didn't, collectives and their successor enterprises cut back employment, including that of members, closed sideline industries, sold some branches, cut down animal stock for quick cash, tried to refinance loans, cut social insurance benefits and welfare services, used less fertilizer, repaired aging farm equipment, and planted less acreage. Village employment and incomes plunged. Though local government was charged with welfare and development that used to be the collective farms' responsibility, these programs were poorly funded. Rural Hungary was in recession through much of the 1990s.

The organizational transformations of farming enterprises are summarized in Table 1. As Pryor predicted, a multiplicity of smaller enterprises hived off the collective farms, and they themselves by law had to change into cooperatives. Here is the logic and the constraints behind such changes.

Members of collectives could exit by taking their physical share from the division of common property, though less than 10% did since the share was not large enough for starting independent commercial farming. The others, the majority, continued their agribusiness as a cooperative of shareholders. Many of these were retired and not active farm workers. Aside from the exogeneous factors, reviewed above, that threatened all agriculture, the cooperative had to deal with internal threats to viability as a continuing agribusiness. There could be too many individual exits depleting the physical assets and jeopardizing contiguous crop land. With an aging membership many of whose heirs lived in cities, plus the shares owned by non-locals from common property division, a massive bleeding of the enterprise assets was a real threat, especially if outsiders expected bankruptcy and hoped to salvage some benefit before other creditors. As one agromanager put it for his collective farm: "The people leaving the cooperative are absolutely not motivated by the spirit of the law, which is to continue as a cooperative in agricultural activity. Instead they are looking to acquire instantly marketable property and to exit with it."

Another danger was that managers and skilled workers would appropriate the profitable branches of the agribusiness and leave the retired and unskilled members with debt, unprofitable and unusable assets, or, as an interviewee remarked, "with the ashtrays and the broken coffee maker in my office." This might be (and was) done sometimes dishonestly, and sometimes simply as a means of protecting local farm assets from "outside" creditors. An example of honest bankruptcy and its consequences for local agriculture was provided in an interview with the head of a new "service" cooperative that succeeded a collective farm: "When the collective went bankrupt no one got anything from the common property, which remained with creditors (banks). Some of us who became unemployed decided to form a new cooperative. Everyone had to buy at least one share worth 20,000 Ft. (about $200 at that time). With this capital, we rented the farm equipment and facilities from the creditors and bought a few items. Because of land compensation many village people own a small amount of land, but have no equipment for farming it. So we sell farm services to those unable to perform farm operations on their own. Two-thirds of our earnings are from farm services, only one third from own production. At the moment we are just surviving."

There existed an honest strategy for cooperatives not facing immediate bankruptcy that maintained enterprise viability and protected the shares of members, including the retired and the unskilled: create a limited liability company (Kft) for each profitable branch or division, issue shares in these Kfts and require the managers and employees to purchase these shares for cash and some of their cooperative shares, and reorganize the cooperative as a holding company for the Kfts, creating interlocked directors and board members all having a voice on how to invest or distribute profits to cooperative shareholders. After such change, a further investment strategy that made sense was vertical integration into food industries, e.g. when a dairy acquired a cheese and butter-making plant under privatization, which the cooperative could bid for with the vouchers it received in land compensation. Unfortunately the government often blocked vertical integration because it favored foreign investors in the food industry, hoping they would bring new technology and capital into Hungary. The manager of the successful vertically integrated cooperative at Jaszbereny described that strategy: "Fortunately we added meat processing to animal husbandry already in the 1970s. We built a slaughterhouse for hogs, and later for cattle and sheep. Seventy percent of our earnings comes from processed meat that we market ourselves."

Two brief case studies will breathe some life and variety into this simplified account of the strategies of survival and change in the new market economy.

The Magocs collective farm drew members and resources from seven villages. Because of average quality land, crops were grown principally to feed hogs and cattle. Members' families raised poultry on household plots. Though centralized administration and physical facilities created waste, high transportation and fuel costs, subsidies and low cost loans nevertheless enabled profitability under socialism. The collective sponsored small businesses operated by members with leased equipment and floor space, technology and accounting assistance. Nineteen eighty-three was the peak year of prosperity. As subsidies were terminated and interest rates rose after 1990, and the drought deepened, the agribusiness cut back social expenditures, reduced employee size from 641 to 444, yet couldn't extricate from the spiral of debts made worse by the bankruptcy of a turkey processing plant it had invested in heavily and which owed it a huge debt that defaulted. It went bankrupt. Under bankruptcy, nine independent Kfts formed from the branches and divisions, e.g. the mechanics incorporated a machine repair business and rented tools and workplace from the collective, the poultry workers got the poultry farm, etc. In time, the assets of these Kfts were purchased by the Kft managers and employees from the new cooperative and have a combined employment of 20% of the earlier employment peak. Two Kfts are doing relatively well, the other seven just manage. Although the shares of the Kfts were advertised nationally, only local people bought them (who wants to buy into failing agribusiness with meager family savings?), and at a very favorable price. In effect, the creditors (state banks and other state owned institutions) got only a fraction of what they were owed, i.e. the national debt increased; a fraction (maybe 25%) of the original collective farm members acquired common property at a discount price, and saved their jobs, and the others were left with raising a few turkeys on their now privately owned plots. Those who lost employment in these changes work as small farmers, commute to work elsewhere, and are unemployed.

The Pecsvaradi collective in 1992 transformed into a cooperative with no members exiting, thus keeping all its assets. Nevertheless it had many aging retireds who were dying and leaving their shares to urban kin. Together with other "outside" shareholders from the common property division, these urban owners wanted quick cash from their shares rather than promises of dividends a decade hence when farming might once again become profitable. The agribusiness came under pressure to sell productive assets. The cooperative members decided in November 1996 to reorganize as an enterprise owned only by the active members, and the cooperative's shares and assets were acquired by the new enterprise. The actives bought out the retireds and some outsiders at 30% of nominal share value. Since the shares were not going to pay dividends for years, most agreed to the buyout. Ten shareholders ended up with 50% of all shares; this is not surprising or unusual because only agromanagers and highly skilled farm workers had cash to spare for such privatization. Under new enterprise rules only shareholders can purchase shares, and that solves the problem of absentee ownership. This reduced the shareholders from 400 to 280, and subsequently to 130. The enterprise employs however only 72, half in the animal husbandry branch, and the CEO interviewed believes it will eventually drop to 45. Although the agribusiness was saved, there is a huge debt to be serviced, and not enough cash for optimum fertilizer amounts. Capital expenditures barely cover what aging machinery has to be replaced when it is beyond repair.

It is likely that the active members of Pecsvaradi would have been better off by letting the enterprise go bankrupt, and buying the useable agribusiness assets cheaply in auctions as private property for themselves, but local families had a great deal of solidarity binding actives and retireds, and bankruptcy would have meant that retireds would end up with nothing from common property. The membership rejected this choice, and the retired got 30% of share value; anything more would have terminated the agribusiness. Nevertheless that 30% was much less than the continuous stream of monetary and non-monetary benefits from the collective farm social and welfare system under socialism. And whereas the actives, at least some, saved their farm jobs and got agribusiness shares (not worth much until the corporation becomes profitable, lowers its debt and starts paying dividends), most had to make a living from vineyards and winemaking and other private small farm activities, which earned more than the very low wages and land rents from the agribusiness. Still, with an improving economy, these shares will eventually become valuable.

SOFT AND HARD BUDGET CONSTRAINTS: BANKRUPTCY

A crucial flaw in socialism is the avoidance of bankruptcy for state enterprises. Instead, under soft budget constraints, managers bargain with ministry officials and state banks for financial support when enterprises fail. Over time unprofitable and inefficient enterprises accumulate and the economy stagnates. Was this true for Hungarian collective farms? What happened after privatization?

According to Juhász, (1990, p. 11) "one third of Hungary's large scale farming operations became loss making for a lasting period [under socialism] and there were no mechanisms in the system which could make the necessary corrections."

From 1990 to 1995, 30% of collective farms and their successors were in various stages of bankruptcy. In a nationwide survey of the newly organized cooperative farms, another third expected to go bankrupt (Toth & Varga, 1995). Bankruptcy was new in post-socialism, yet there were disguised bankruptcies under socialism, and bankruptcies in capitalism are not as "hard" as they are meant to be.

In 1982, the collective farm at Lövöpetri was forced by state officials to merge with a neighboring collective when it became hopelessly indebted. In the merger, jobs were terminated; offices, repair shops, a warehouse were closed; and all the farm equipment transferred. Lövöpetri was stripped down to a single grocery store, and farm workers commuted daily 15 km. to work. Although the change was termed a "merger", there were very real costs to the collective and the inhabitants of Lövöpetri.

We don't know how common such disguised bankruptcies were under socialism. In the post-socialist 1990s, bankruptcies are common. Failed enterprises and their employees lose most of their farm assets and their jobs, and a nearby enterprise and/or a small team takes over the salvageable part. In a 1995 interview, the president of Veszprémvarsányi cooperative said it "took over" parts of the bankrupt Bakonyszentkirály coop. One third of the debt was written off by the creditor banks, one third was paid by auctioning assets, and the remaining third of the debt was assumed by a new company owned jointly by the two cooperatives. All this occurred, he said, "not without sacrifices", since many lost their jobs and the sale of assets reduced the failed coops' remaining farm and livestock operations. This 1990s takeover, which is reported as a bankruptcy, resembles the 1982 Lövöpetri "merger".

It is worth noting that under both socialism and capitalism a large part of the debt of a bankrupt enterprise ended up and keeps ending up in the national debt. In the 1980s as in the 1990s, when a state bank "writes off" or forgives part of the debt – because it is uncollectable – it passes it on to a state ministry which then merges it into the national debt. This will go on for the foreseeable future since in a bankruptcy the state ends up holding a devalued asset it, and not farmers, created in the first place. This fact puts a constraint on the speed with which "hard" budget constraints can replace "soft" constraints. The mayor of Rozsály underscored this when he said that the collective farm members hadn't lost much when they went bankrupt. Over the years, they converted their earnings into improved houses and their own small farms, and had not invested in the collective because they counted on the state to do it. They still have their houses and small farms, and now they also own some land. What they lost in bankruptcy auctions was a lot of aging farm equipment, some livestock, a few buildings, and farm jobs that paid low wages.

CREATING PRIVATE PROPERTY

There were two obstacles to the privatization of collective farm assets. First, physical division of assets was either impossible without destroying a facility (a cold storage house) or much reduced the value of an integrated facility (when chicken are taken from a huge chicken coop). Second, much farm equipment was worth more than a member's share and there weren't enough movable assets to distribute among members. The average share value of active workers was 578,000 ft (about $5000), and considerably less for retireds and "outsiders (Toth & Varga, 1995). When only a few members wanted to exit, it was possible to provide physical assets without impairing viability of the enterprise. In fact, less than 10% of collective members exited singly or in a group. Pryor had been right: privatization by physical division of common property does not work in an agribusiness. There remained asset division by shares.

Share privatization may look good on paper and legally does create private property. Yet share values are worth only what an enterprise's earnings prospects are. With many farm enterprises going bankrupt and even the survivors struggling and not planning to pay dividends for some years, shares' market value is far below their nominal value. In our survey, shares were traded at 10 to 30% of nominal value. Under socialism, a farm worker could not convert his share of common property to cash or some other movable private asset; in capitalism, the same farm worker could sell her private share, but only for a pittance. The value of private property is contingent on other market institutions functioning well: it is not just a legal fact.

LAND

The other main farm asset is land. What did land privatization accomplish? Under socialism there was no private property in land except on a very small scale. The collective farms had obtained land through political coercion in the 1950s for free. Villagers had their house gardens at their village homes, and many had user rights with membership in the collective to a "household" plot. It was impossible to put together a holding of 50–100 ha. for crop farming. Socialism had no market in farmland.

Land compensation favored former owners over the producers. The compensation law had several important features. (1) A large number of people, former owners, their heirs, former farm employees, in addition to current and retired farm workers, got land in some fashion, either through compensation vouchers and auctions or through common property division; (2) Compensation was partial, according to a declining schedule, with 300 ha. maximum; (3) One could not physically repossess earlier owned land; instead vouchers were issued against claims at the value of 1000 Ft. per acre per Ak ("golden crown" quality rating). Vouchers valid only in a particular locality would then be used to bid at local land auctions with a fixed minimum bid of 500 Ft. per ha. per Ak; (4) Vouchers could be bought, sold, and used for acquiring other property, e.g. an apartment owned by a local government; (5) The cooperative farms received these vouchers for the land they lost; and (6) The land market was frozen for five years: new land owners had to rent or farm the land, but couldn't sell it. Important consequences followed.

Since the auctions were restricted to a limited number of mostly local buyers, the locals agreed on 500 Ft. minimum bids rather than compete against one another. Exceptions were for land near cities and along highways that people expected to convert to valuable urban and commercial real estate. Thus privatized land was almost twice what legislators had expected. It was massive: seven hundred thousand people got two million ha. Though much went to members and retireds, a lot ended up the property of non-resident, non-farming "outsiders." Renting farm land from outside the community drains cash from agribusinesses at a time when they are hard put to survive and need to invest more. At the same time, since grain farming for a full-time family farm requires a minimum of fifty ha. plus farm machinery, given the small size (less than 5 ha.) of most new land acquisitions, commercial family farmers have to rent most of their farm land, and often farm machinery. The new land ownership system thus weakened agribusiness without strengthening middle and small independent farming.

Two other laws contributed to an emerging land market, in addition to a temporary, flourishing "black" market in covert land sales to get around the five year freeze. In 1989 it became possible for former collective farm members (and heirs) to claim ownership of land their families had entered the collective with so long as the land continued to be farmed, and in 1990 it became legal for a member to do the same. Unlike compensation land these properties could be bought and sold. All these measures broke the state monopoly on land. How much land consolidation is going on is difficult to tell until the black market sales have been legalized and recorded, but observers think land ownership is going to become quite unequally distributed.

LABOR AND CAPITAL MARKETS

Two complaints were common in socialism: farm managers were burdened with redundant labor due to obligation to employ collective members, and were unable to dismiss unreliable, thieving, drinking, shirking workers. A farmer who quit his collective in 1992 said "the collective did not punish for bad work . . . I don't want to work with unproductive people . . . there is overstaffing." During privatization, all this changed dramatically as farm enterprises downsized employment to cope with the economic depression and to become efficient and increase labor productivity. In addition to the unmotivated and unreliable workers, many others lost their jobs, especially older workers and women.

Under socialism there was no capital market. The small and part-time family farmers, many of whom were members of the collective farm, received interest free credit, below cost farm services and free farming advice from the collective. Agribusinesses financed some capital from earnings, and for large projects and amounts bargained with ministries and state banks. In the transition, socialist redistribution ceased yet no capital market took its place. Agricultural credit collapsed completely. The most usual problem for farm enterprises was that wholesalers and food corporations were not paying their debts, yet farmers had to buy fuel, fertilizer and other necessities for cash, not to mention their payroll. At 35–40% short term interest rates, it was ruinous to borrow.

In 1996 there was still no capital market, at least not for farming. The economist Csaba Csáki underscored in an interview (March, 1996) that a market economy in agriculture cannot function without a rural banking system for continuous financing of farming activities. Banking and capital markets have to be created, but no one had created them.

ADAPTING TO A MARKET ECONOMY: DOWNSIZING, DECENTRALIZATION, INCENTIVES

In the 1990s transition, farm enterprises took many measures to cut costs and increase efficiency. Cutting the labor force was universal. Very common as well was the splitting of huge, multi-village collective farms into smaller enterprises. In the process, one or more parts of the megabusiness would go bankrupt. In a downsized agribusiness, the new president there told us he made efficiency gains from shortened travel time, reducing idle farm equipment, and fewer administrative and supervisory costs.

Downsizing is ubiquitous. In a national sample of cooperatives, Toth and Varga found that the average workforce declined from 377 to 142 in four years, and keeps shrinking (1995, p. 50). Labor is used more efficiently, as shown in Table 2, from several surveys.

Also, Toth and Varga (1996) found that despite downsizing, the total stock of farm machinery had increased somewhat. These figures show the effort made to cut costs, increase efficiency, and substitute machinery for labor.

Cutting the workforce was done in many cases with early retirement. As for those who were still employed in farming, their real wages fell. One agro-manager expressed it thus, "great sacrifices had to be made . . . I lift my hat to the vast majority of the workers."

In the post-socialist transformation, decentralization became corporate restructuring with the formation of limited liability companies attached to a central cooperative. Just how a large privatized agribusiness operates in the 1990s market economy is best explained with a case study from 1991 and 1995 at Veszprémvarsányi. In 1991 it was a huge eight village, 7000 ha., 1500 cows and 1200 hogs, collective farm.

Realizing that such a "mammoth" and diverse farm enterprise could not be managed efficiently from one center and that it destroyed cost consciousness

Table 2. Trends in Cropland Per Worker for Agribusinesses.

		(Toth & Varga)		(Oberschall & Hanto)
	1989	1992	1995	1995
Cropland/ worker	8.5 ha	16 ha	17.4 ha	23 ha
Number of enterprises	104	84	84	90

and incentives for workers, the cooperative decided on major restructuring. Six production entities were made into limited liability companies: two crop and livestock companies, a hog farm, horticulture, two repair and service companies. Each was made the responsibility of an independent management team who hire and fire workers, set wages, make production decisions, and increase their earnings with profitability. The sawmill, an apparel plant and another workshop were leased to their former managers. Forestry and construction could not be sold or leased and remain for the time being under cooperative management. The cooperative became a holding corporation that owns most of the six companies' shares, and provides financial and other business services to them for a fee. Company managers had to buy company shares and workers are advised to do the same. Company employees are also shareholders in the cooperative; thus cooperative managers sit on the company boards and company managers are represented on the cooperative board.

In this successful transition, Veszprémvarsányi cooperative created a central cooperative linked to satellite operating companies that was a continuation of the autonomous accounting units under socialism. For the longer run, as Pryor (1990, p. 12) foresaw in his privatization plan for socialist agribusiness, the satellite companies can buy a majority of their shares from the coop and form a separate, independent, privately owned farm enterprise. Such a gradual "buyout" is in fact what the director of the cooperative anticipates some years hence.

COMMERCIAL FAMILY FARM ENTREPRENEURS

According to farm statistics, the total number of crop farmers on the 100–200 ha scale hadn't changed since the late 1980s despite privatization (Harcsa, Kovach & Szelenyi, 1995). Both the Central Statistical Office and AKII surveyed commercial farmers and found them in difficulties (KSH, 1996; Szijjarto, 1996). Half were part-time farmers, i.e. depended on another job for income. Only 13% managed to get a farm loan. Some 80% needed to rent some farm equipment. Family farm entrepreneurs are nearly as marginal after privatization as they had been in socialism.

As for the over one million small family farms which formed the second economy under socialism, most have become owners of cropland as a result of land compensation, but lack the tools, equipment, farm buildings, and access to credit to break out of part-time into commercial farming. Many rent some land to the cooperatives and other large farm enterprises and purchase farm services, e.g. ploughing. According to a nationwide survey of small farmers in 1993, 60% farm out of necessity and for lack of other opportunity for making a living: they lost their jobs when cooperatives downsized or went bankrupt, though 20% are part-time employed in coops (Varga & Szijjarto, 1994). They do sell some crops and livestock in the marketplace. A majority is over 40 years old and uncertain whether another family member will continue farming. Most have family members with non-farm jobs. Some may one day grow into medium-sized farm enterprises when economic conditions improve. Yet the survey demonstrates that the small farm sector after privatization is mostly a continuation of the socialist second economy.

MARKET COORDINATION

The change from socialist redistributive integration to capitalist market coordination has been chaotic. In socialism, two forms of integration had developed over the years, neither organized by state planners. The highly competitive small farm sector, referred to as the "second economy", was embedded in the "household" plots and putting-out system of the collective farms. The collective farms supplied farm equipment and farm services, fertilizer, seed, and animal fodder at below cost to thousands of small farmers who were members of the collectives for the most part, and provided transportation and marketing for produce. Thus production and marketing decisions in the second economy were made in bargaining between hundreds of agromanagers and thousands of small farmers. A second integration stemmed from state agribusiness introducing, selling and managing high yield crop technologies and livestock systems to collective farms.

The integration of small farming, state and collective farming, state farms and the food industry in socialism created contract certainty: all could calculate what and how much to produce at stable prices, and what costs would be. Exports to communist countries were secure.

In the early 1990s everything in agriculture became uncertain and problematic: landownership, jobs, credit, export markets, prices, costs, privatization politics and legislation, not to speak of the drought. In the second economy, the new cooperatives performed services for small farmers but no longer for free. In our survey and in that of Toth and Varga (1995, 1996) as well, between half to 80% of coops sold seed and fertilizer, provided farm services (e.g. ploughing), gave advice, and bought crops from small farmers. On their part, between 50 and 95% of the commercial small farmers reported buying farm services and supplies (seed, fertilizer, fodder, ploughing, breeding, drying), mostly from the cooperatives in their locality (Szijjárto, 1996). Weak integration between agribusiness and small farming was a problem for market coordination because small farmers produce a large share of fruit, vegetables, grapes, pork, eggs and poultry. In 1996, according to the Central Statistical Office, small farmers owned 25% of cattle, 50% of hogs, 70% of sheep, and 50% of poultry in Hungary. The nationwide small farm study found that 76% had no contract for their produce, 47% decided what to grow before they had any idea about prices and who to sell to, and 50% of those who had contracts reported problems with contract enforcement (Varga & Szijjárto, 1994). Just as telling, nine of ten said their situation had not improved or worsened in the past two years, and eight of ten did not expect improvement.

THE MORAL ECONOMY OF CHANGE: WINNERS AND LOSERS

The economist Kenneth Arrow (1974) has written that "the principles of ethics and morality . . . are agreements, conscious or, in many cases, unconscious to supply mutual benefits . . . which are essential to the survival of the society, or at least contribute greatly to the efficiency of its working." With 15% of Hungary's assets earmarked for privatization in agriculture – the nation's farm land, livestock, farm machinery and buildings – and hundreds of thousand farm jobs at stake, how was the problematic and contentious change from socialism to a market economy accomplished? Did people weigh justice, not just interest, equity, not just efficiency, in decisions? Who are the winners, and who the losers, and was the change game played fairly?

Rural folk in Hungary differed on human capital, on social capital, and on access to resources, i.e. user and job rights under socialism, and private property in land and farm assets under capitalism. In agriculture, human capital entails far more than schooling in agrotechnical institutes and universities. Competence in managing a complex, technologically sophisticated agribusiness could be gotten only from years of experience. Social capital comes from investing in personal relationships, social networks and group memberships that provide advice, assistance, information, access and reciprocity in one's business dealings. It too is a function of years' experience in a managerial post. In the 1980s communist party membership was no longer a necessary source of social capital in agriculture. Be that as it may, human and social capital were very unequally distributed. Agromanagers had lots of both, unskilled farm workers and many retireds had little of either, and office administrators and technical workers were somewhere in between.

In the change to a market economy, human capital endowment did not change. Those who possessed it in the late 1980s still possessed it in the mid-1990s. Social capital did not change either. The transition was peaceful. Incumbents remained in their positions in all institutions except for national politics at the top. Most agromanagers were re-elected to executive positions in the cooperatives. The greatest change occurred with the termination of collective farm user rights and job rights, and the introduction of private property for land and farm assets. On privatization, agromanagers, accountants, agronomists, veterinarians, and technicians had no advantage. The division of common property would have to be approved by a majority vote in the collectives' general assembly. At best the division was a zero-sum game: a fixed pie was divided, and if anyone got more others would get less. At worst, the division could become a negative sum game in which all or most would be losers. Which game was going to be played, and what share of the pie each got depended on negotiations and compromises, and not least on the solidarity of members.

Collective farms were huge, hierarchic, stratified agribusinesses. Though democratic in their constitution, the collectives were controlled by agromanagers. There was no workplace democracy (Swain, 1985). The farm workers had an "employee mentality" and thought that administrators had soft jobs for high pay (Bell, 1984). They put their energies into small family farming in the "second economy." Solidarity was strong among kin and friends, with limited commitment and loyalty to the collective farm, as was true also for industrial workers in state enterprises (Andorka, 1993).

One should not exaggerate the divisions between agromanagers and other farmers. In our field work we discovered no large gap in the standard of life of agromanagers and employees. Managers lived in houses and drove autos somewhat larger than many villagers' but not more luxurious. They wore work clothes and boots suitable for getting about the farm and not business suits. They worked long hours. The manager of a very large agribusiness, with 9600 ha. and 630 employees, put it this way: "I earn more from my six hectares of peppers than from my salary."

Within the village the division of common property was surprisingly consensual (Andorka, 1994; Oberschall, 2000). Collective members well knew the losses from physical division of an agribusiness into small farm units. They agreed on privatization by shares, and voted to allocate shares proportional to years worked, and with lesser weight to wages. The division favored the retired members and unskilled workers who were a majority. As one agromanager put it, "the night watchman got a larger share than I did." It was a concession to the elderly who, had they insisted on physical division, would have gained some quick cash at the cost of destroying the agribusiness. What farmers considered inequitable is that heirs of former members and former employees – most long gone from the district – were also entitled to shares (though not voting rights in the new cooperative). The transformation law put village solidarity and morality to a great test. Whose jobs would be kept, and whose would be terminated? Under the law, a new cooperative no longer had an employment obligation, and could terminate the household plot and social benefits. Most of the unemployed were unskilled workers, older workers, and women. As for the retired, though some gained land and rental income from land compensation, they lost household plots, user rights, free farming services and other benefits. In employment and in member benefit and welfare decisions, survival and efficiency overruled all other criteria. Even so, many agribusinesses went bankrupt.

In dressing a balance between relative winners and losers from privatization, those who got more property in the legal sense did not end up as the winners. The elderly and the retired received a large share of land and much in cooperative shares. Nevertheless, without well functioning land and shares markets their property cannot be transformed into resources for living. User rights to land, farm services and social benefits under socialism were more useful to the retired than private property in land and shares in capitalism. The well-being of the older generation depends on family, neighborly relations, local government and village solidarity as much as, if not more than, before privatization.

Unskilled workers and many women had low human capital and social capital limited to the village economy. They received little land and few shares, and lost their jobs. They are the greatest losers in privatization. Agromanagers did not get more than the average villager in land and enterprise shares. They were knowledgeable about running an agribusiness and possessed translocal business networks. Privatized agribusiness needs them. They have cash savings for buying land and acquiring enterprise shares at a fraction of nominal value and for starting a private business. Should they quit, they become wholesalers, specialized service providers, consultants, and heads of small companies that hived off the large enterprise. Skilled farm workers, drivers, repairers, and technicians possessed human capital in short supply and useful to start a private business or farm. They got land and shares. Many continue working in agribusiness. They too are gainers. The trend is clear. Despite land compensation and common property division, those with human and social capital will end up with the largest share of private property and with the good jobs. The fate of the others will depend on how much industry is successfully restarted in rural districts.

Has privatization caused "pauperization" of rural Hungary and the accumulation of land and assets by an agromanagerial elite? (Harcsa, Kovach & Szelényi, 1995). No one doubts that in an economic depression and with high unemployment the population is worse off than earlier, in cities as well as villages, in fact throughout Eastern Europe. But is pauperization inevitable? Unemployment support, part-time work, private farming, farm services to the retired, two-earner families, some public works projects, have all cushioned the impact of the depression. Villagers own land: even when not enough to farm commercially, they grow food and get a small rental income. There were signs in 1995 that the depression has bottomed out in some counties. It is premature to describe these folk as a new agrarian proletariat.

As for a new agromangerial elite accumulating private property at a rapid rate, what they got was aging farm equipment and buildings, some livestock, some land, a struggling farm business they have to share with some others, which will need a lot of hard work and investment before it makes anyone rich.

CONCLUSION

Now that we have described how agriculture was organized under socialism and what changes occurred with privatization in the early 1990s, we return to questions on socialism and capitalism. Were the seeds of a market economy present in the 1980s in socialism? Did shock treatment work, and what were its consequences? Can an employee-owned producer-cooperative with a social safety net survive in the market? Has a market economy become institutionalized? How do agents create new institutions?

The seeds of a market economy existed before the downfall of socialism, but the seeds had produced some trees and not a forest. Some prices were set by market forces. Enterprise decentralization, internal contracting and putting out resembled outsourcing, subcontracting and enterprise division autonomy in capitalism. State policy and enterprise practice supported a thriving second economy based on the private property and family labor of hundreds of thousand villagers. With extreme failure bankruptcy did occur. All of these were requirements of a market economy. At the same time, redundant and incompetent labor could not be fired, and most loss making enterprises continued to be subsidized. There was no land market. Private commercial farming was limited, and private investment in agriculture discouraged. The state was the main source of capital. State officials and policies interfered in enterprises, as on favoring large agribusiness over small. As long as capital formation and allocation was by the state, there were limits to marketization. That is not to take away from the successes of Hungarian agriculture under socialism. It provided the country with abundant food and lots to spare for export, and it had raised rural living standards to urban levels.

What of shock treatment? Within five years, all collective farms were privatized, and 70% of all arable land, some 3.3 million hectares, became the private property of 535,000 individuals, the largest land reform in Hungarian history. In this process, 30% of all collective farms went bankrupt or where under court supervised reorganization. From 1989 to 1993, agricultural output declined from an index of 100 to 65, and animal stock from 100 to 60. Total employment in farm enterprises decreased from six hundred thousand to two hundred thousand, some of it reflecting the cessation of rural industry attached to collective farms. In 1995, average farm wages were 25% below the national average, and on some farms below the minimum wage. In 1992 farm enterprise income before taxes on total sales was –8.3% (i.e. loss making); however by 1995 it was 3.8% (i.e. a modest profit), largely due to downsizing and selling or closing loss-making divisions. In 1995 for the first time in five years, there was some improvement in agriculture and better prospects for the privatized agribusinesses: 62 of 84 privatized agribusinesses in one study and 64 of 109 in another expected some pretax profits, though only a modest amount (Toth & Varga, 1996). Hungarian agriculture underwent the shock treatment. Much of it survived. The economic and human consequences were deeper, the pain was a lot worse and is lasting longer than Sachs had expected.

Has a capitalist market economy been institutionalized in agriculture? There is no longer any common property and very limited state property in land and other farm assets; private property has replaced them. Bankruptcies are frequent and not disguised. Enterprise management has taken many steps to cut costs and to become profitable by reducing the work force by two-thirds. Private entrepreneurs are free to enter farming, and do. State officials have stopped intervening in enterprises. State subsidies have diminished. Unlike industry and banking, there is no blurring of private and state property and no interlocking directorships and shareownership between agribusinesses and state banks (Stark, 1996). In agriculture there exists a fully capitalist market economy. But why isn't it working well?

Institutions, as North reminded us, are not created overnight by enacting laws. People have to learn new knowledge, new ways of thinking, new habits of conduct and norms of transacting, new forms of social control. All of these are costly and take time. Contract certainty is most likely when businesses are in the market for the long haul, benefit from a lasting reputation and are profitable. In Hungary, many enterprises in the market are new, transient and failing. Contract certainty will improve with settled business conditions, but these have not come yet. Capitalism needs capital. When the state withdrew from agriculture, it created a capital vacuum. It will take time for a capital market to emerge.

It is instructive to examine private property in the new market economy (Pryor, 1990, 1991). Farmers became shareowners, but shareownership does not yet confer the same benefits in Hungary as it does in Western countries. In the absence of a market in shares, one cannot exercise the "exit" option (Hirschman, 1970). All analysts of socialist collective farming concurred that despite the democratic charter of collectives, they were run by an oligarchic agromanagement (Swain, 1985; Bell, 1984). The new right of hiring and firing has increased management's power in the cooperatives. Members may well own most of the shares, but without exit they have no influence over management. It will take time before a market in agribusiness shares gets going, i.e. when agriculture becomes profitable. Until then, shares will remain a weak form of private property. In socialism, managers had user rights in common property; in the new market economy, for some time to come, they continue to control farm assets, though it belongs to others.

Last, how do people create the institutions they live with? Considering the high stakes of privatization, with most everybody's jobs, earnings, and life chances on the line as resources diminished, the rural people of Hungary acted in a remarkably cooperative fashion. Thousands of hours were spent in meetings, listing and valuing assets and calculating each member's share, reading, debating and explaining the complex details of the privatization legislation and rules; debating and voting in general assemblies of cooperatives; electing and working on land commissions that designated compensation land and rated soil quality; conducting the land auctions themselves, and engaging in land exchanges and consolidation. Bankruptcies and reorganizations too were implemented. All this was an enormous outpouring of human effort. Had the older generation and agromanagers pursued a narrow, short term interest, they could have destroyed the economic foundations of agribusiness in Hungary. They did not. Despite differences, a majority of rural people cooperated to keep agriculture viable during a very trying time.

NOTES

1. We thank the National Council on Soviet and East European Research for supporting this research with a grant, and Zoltán Szánto, Sándor Elek, Lászlo Letenyei, and Robert Kovách of the Budapest University of Economic Sciences for assisting with the research. We also thank Elisa Bienestock, Steve Rosefield and Nicholas Harsanyi for comments and assistance. The research started in 1989 and continued in 1991–1991 with in-depth case studies of collective farms. Then in 1995 we surveyed 107 farm enterprises in four counties randomly picked from county enterprise registers. Our data come from this survey and similar farm enterprise surveys conducted by the research

institute of the Ministry of Agriculture (AKII). In most enterprises we interviewed one of the chief managers and often were taken on a tour of the farm as we conducted the interview. Some of these interviews were video recorded, and we have produced a documentary video titled "Privatization of Hungarian Agriculture" (1996) from this research commissioned by USAID, a 45 minute version in Hungarian and a 28 minute version in English. Other aspects of the research have been published in Anthony Oberschall, "Privatizing Socialist Farming in Hungary. Interest, Efficiency, and Equity" in *Rationality and Society*, *12*(1), 2000, 5–24. Publications and findings from research done after 1996 can be obtained by corresponding with Zsuzsa Hanto at <SZOCINFO@mail.datanet.hu>.

2. cf. footnote 1 for description of the study design and sources of our information.
3. One hectare (ha) is 2.3 acres.

REFERENCES

AKII (1995). Agriculture and Food Industry 1994. Budapest: AKII.

AKII (1995). A mezögazdaság helyzete 1994, Budapest: AKII.

Andorka, R. (1994). *Társadalmi Report 1994*. Budapest: TARKI.

Andorka, R. (1993). The socialist system and its collapse in Hungary: an interpretation in terms of modernization theory? *International Sociology*, *8*(3), 317–337.

Arrow, K. (1974). *The Limits of Organization*. New York: Norton.

Bell, P. (1984). *Peasants in Socialist Transition*. Berkeley: University of California Press.

Comisso, E. (1995). Legacies of the Past or New Institutions: The Struggle over Restritution in Hungary. *Comparative Political Studies*, *18*(2), 200–238.

Harcsa, I., Kovách, I., & Szelényi, I. (1995). The price of privatization. *Review of Sociology*, special issue. Budapest: Hungarian Sociological Association.

Held, J. (1980). *The Modernization of Agriculture: Rural Transformation in Hungary 1848–1975*. Boulder: East European Monographs.

Hirschman, A. (1970). *Exit, Voice and Loyalty*. Cambridge: Harvard University Press.

Juhász, J. (1990). Large scale and small scale farming in Hungarian agriculture. Budapest: Cooperative Research Institute.

Kornai, J. (1990). *The Road to Freedom*. New York: Norton.

Kovách, I. (1988). *Termelök és Válalkozok*. Budapest: TDJ.

Kozponti Statisztikai Hivatal (KSH) (1996). Paraszti gazdaságok, mezögazdasági válalkozok. Budapest: KSH.

North, D. (1990). *Institutions, Institutional Change and Economic Performance*. Cambridge: Cambridge University Press.

Oberschall, A. (2000). Privatizing Socialist Farming. *Rationality and Society*, *12*(1), 5–24.

Pryor, F. (1990). *East European economic reforms: rebirth of the market*. Stanford University, Hoover Institute.

Pryor, F. (1991). When is collectivization reversible? *Studies in Comparative Communism*, *24*(1), 3–24.

Przeworski, A. (1991). *Democracy and the Market*. Cambridge: Cambridge University Press.

Sachs, J. (1991). Crossing the Valley of Tears in East European Reform. *Challenge*, *34*(Sept/Oct), 26–34.

Sachs, J. (1996). The Transition at Mid Decade. *American Economic Review*, *86*(2), 128–133.

Stiglitz, J. (1994). *Wither Socialism*. Cambridge: MIT Press.

Swain, N. (1985). *Collective Farms Which Work?* Cambridge: Cambridge University Press.

Swedberg, R. (1994). Markets in social structures. In: N. Smelser & R. Swedberg (Eds), *Handbook of Economic Sociology* (p. 271). Princeton: Princeton University Press.

Szelényi, I. (1988). *Socialist Entrepreneurs: Embourgeoisement in Rural Hungary.* Madison: University of Wisconsin Press.

Szelényi, I., et al. (1994). The socialist economic system. In: N. Smelser & R. Swedberg (Eds), *Handbook of Economic Sociology.* Princeton: Princeton University Press.

Szijjárto, A. (1996). *A mezögazdasági termelök helyzetérol és szándékairol.* Budapest: AKII.

Toth, E., & Varga, G. (1995). *A mezögazdasági termelöszövetkezetek helyzete és sorsa az átalakulás idöszakában.* Budapest: AKII.

Toth, E., & Varga, G. (1996). *A mezögazdasági szövetkezetek.* Budapest: AKII.

Varga, I., & Szijjárto, A. (1994). *Közelkep a Mezögazdasági Termelök Egyes Rétegeiröl és Csoportjairol.* Budapest: AKII.

Williamson, O. (1975). *Markets and Hierarchies.* New York: Free Press.

PARTY POWER, MARKET AND PRIVATE POWER: CHINESE COMMUNIST PARTY PERSISTENCE IN CHINA'S LISTED COMPANIES

Sonja Opper, Sonia M. L. Wong and Ruyin Hu

ABSTRACT

Structural changes of the elite have been a particular focus of sociological and economic research and debate since the outset of reforms in the post-communist transition countries. While most studies on elite changes focus on the relative income position as the indicator for the changing position of the old elite, we concentrate on the strength and pattern of decision-making power of China's old elite in newly emerging economic entities, such as listed companies. In line with the power persistence thesis, our analysis shows that the local party committees still succeed at keeping their fingers in the decision-making process even after two decades of economic transition, due to diverse lock-in effects between the party and various areas of the institutional environment. We hypothesize that the decision-making power of the local party committees is weakened by the emergence of market and private power during the economic reform and test our hypothesis by employing a survey conducted by the Shanghai Stock Exchange. This study supplements and broadens empirical evidence on the market-transition model and emphasizes the particular importance

The Future of Market Transition, Volume 19, pages 105–138.

ISBN: 0-7623-0835-4

of a major private shareholder as the central constraint on the persistence of old elite in enterprise decision making.

INTRODUCTION

The investigation into the survival of the Chinese Communist Party (CCP) grassroots organizations at enterprise level during the two decades of economic reform has been a focus of research for several years (You, 1998; Steinfeld, 1999; Shanghai Stock Exchange, 2000; McGregor, 2001).[1] Most of the studies so far are descriptive in nature, however. Policy implications are usually based on generalizations of anecdotal evidence and selective case studies. You (1998) classified the current party-management relationship into four types and substantiates his analysis with several case studies. In his extensive study on the internal decision and operating processes of China's listed companies, Tam (1999) states that party influence prevails at the enterprise level, but the study fails to present empirical evidence. Others provide some evidence that the local party committees continue to hold their influence in decision making (McGregor, 2001; Zhongguo Qiyejia Diaocha Xitong, 1997a, b). On the whole, these studies do not offer systematic evidence on the prevailing pattern and trend of local Party power persistence. To a certain extent the prevailing ideas on current local Party power in China's enterprises resemble a sort of myth; belief in it is widespread, but empirical evidence is scarce.

In this respect, our paper presents some recent empirical findings on the interplay between economic transition and survival of the political elite. Specifically, we examine the market and private power as the determinants of decision-making power of the local party committees in companies listed at Shanghai Stock Exchange (hereafter referred to as "listed companies"). We also reflect on the important question as to whether remaining political interference follows commands from the central party authority or represents the spontaneous and uncoordinated activities of local branches at the grass-root level. The answer to this question has important implications for the relationship between central policy making and local enforcement.

The focus on the ownership form of listed companies is intriguing for two reasons. First, listed companies are generally regarded as the incarnation of capitalist ownership and were propagated by the government as the role-model of China's evolving modern enterprise system. From this viewpoint listed companies ought to be subject to the least amount of party involvement. We should stress however, that most listed companies are former SOEs that have been reorganized and privatized to varying degrees. They are typically large companies, which have to be able to show three years of profit-making directly preceding their listing at the Exchanges. Since the listing procedure in China was tightly administered by a quota system until 2000 and competition for listing was keen, successful listing-application usually reflects a certain level of political favoritism. As a result, caution must be used when generalizing the findings of this study to China's enterprise sector as a whole. Second, the legal extent of Party power in listed companies is defined by the Company Law, which was promulgated in 1993. The Law includes a relatively clear specification on the rights and authorities of various power holders in China's shareholding companies and thus provides us with a benchmark for the evaluation and analysis of the degree and the pattern of party involvement.

VIEWS ON ELITE CHANGES

Structural changes of the elite have been a particular focus of sociological and economic research and debate since the outset of reforms in the post-communist transition countries. Comparable to a large-scale field experiment, the investigation of changes in the elite promises to provide some hints on the way societies tend to stratify. In the narrower context of economic reform, an investigation of changes in the elite also helps to identify the potential supporters and opponents, thus revealing the forces and obstacles of reform. Three major conflicting views are debated in current literature (Bian & Logan, 1996): First there is the "power-conversion thesis", which predicts that the old elite will be the primary beneficiary of marketization (Oi, 1989; Shirk, 1989; Rona-Tas, 1994). Second, the "power-persistence thesis" proposes a temporary persistence and a phasing out of the old elite, depending on the speed and dynamism of institutional market reforms. The thesis is based on Nee's market-transition model (1989, 1991), which predicts that cadres lose from reform due to an increasing importance of market institutions. Originally Nee (1989) assumed a fast decline of cadre privileges, but later (1991) stated that due to a gradual reform approach, the privileged elite will only slowly recede (see Fligstein, 1996). And finally, the thesis of a complete change in the elite has been discussed, which suggests that the main beneficiaries are those, who were less privileged in the previous system (Szèlenyi, 1988).

Most studies on elite changes focus on the relative income position as the indicator for the changing position of the old elite (Nee, 1991; Zhou, 2000; Bian & Logan, 1996). Though we do not share Oberschall's doubts as to whether income and income inequality can "give us any clue about the shape of emerging institutions" (Oberschall, 1996) or Guthrie's criticism that income related studies on elite change "show no direct or concrete evidence about the fate of the hierarchy of former command economies" (Guthrie, 1997), we share Guthrie's idea that the focus on economic decisions might offer a useful extension of the existing literature. While Guthrie (1999) focuses on types of decisions and practices of firms however, we decided to concentrate directly on the changing decision-making power of the Chinese Communist Party's (CCP) grass-root organizations at enterprise level (hereafter referred as the local party committees). Although decision-making power and the income position of the old elite are related to each other, the direct analysis of decision-making power allows a clearer comprehension of the changing driving forces and control mechanisms at operational level. In this respect, our study seeks to supplement and broaden available income-related empirical evidence related to elite survival; particularly the still unsettled "market transition debate".

In line with the power persistence thesis, our analysis shows that the local party committees still succeed at keeping their fingers in the decision-making process even after two decades of economic transition, due to diverse lock-in effects between party and various areas of the institutional environment. We hypothesize that the decision-making power of the local party committees is weakened by emergence of market and private power during economic reform process and support our hypothesis by employing a survey conducted by the Shanghai Stock Exchange.

INDIVIDUAL INCENTIVES AND INSTITUTIONAL LOCK-IN EFFECTS

The de-facto Party power at the enterprise level is determined by a wide range of formal and informal institutions (North, 1990) that govern economic transactions. There is a high probability of path-dependent change, similar to the evolution of other institutions. Although we do not yet know enough about path dependence to fully understand the ways societies change over time, we have sufficient evidence that changes in enterprises' governance mechanisms are constrained by their institutional environment (North, 2000; Greif, 1997). Our survey of the current local Party power in China's listed companies starts with an examination of the factors most likely to influence the relationship since the outset of reforms. Among the decisive factors is the interest and incentive of members of the local party committees. We apply a two-step analysis of the legal-political and economic institutional environment including the observable party-law, party-government and party-economy linkages.

Individual Incentives

The redefinition of formal Party power at the enterprise level, similar to other institutional changes, provokes a concurrent re-allocation of rights and respective wealth-maximizing opportunities (Eggertson, 1996; North, 1990). The transfer of formal decision-making rights from the local party committees to the management, board of directors (BoD) and shareholders severely damaged the interests of the local party unit members. Goodman (2000) remarked elsewhere "that (local) cadres are likely to be resistant to any change regardless of its intent, especially when that change seems to threaten their position, or socio-economic well-being". Shirk (1992) also finds that party's resistance in general to any reduction of power were strongest at local and provincial levels. In view of these observations, it is doubtful that members of the local party committees, which were highly involved in decision-making processes for decades, will immediately accept a deprivation of power and voluntarily retreat from decision-making processes within the enterprises. First and foremost, the local party committees need to have a minimum of control rights in order to demonstrate their continuing importance in a rapidly changing economic system and to safeguard their future position as members of a local elite. Members of the local committees have a strong interest in developing power-preserving strategies to secure both their former political and social status as well as their economic rent-seeking possibilities which allow them to pursue individual utility maximization and opportunistic activities (Fewsmith, 2001). As a result, the immediate acceptance of the new power balance after the promulgation of the Company Law was not be taken for granted. Instead, it had to be expected that the local party committees would attempt to protect their vested interests and shape the new formal constraints to their advantage. Empirical evidence in Russia has clearly shown that the probability of blocking privatization is especially high at the local level (Boycko, Shleifer & Vishny, 1995). As Nee and Ingram (1998) have elsewhere stressed, "when . . . formal norms are perceived to be at odds with the interests and preferences of actors in subgroups, informal norms opposing formal rules will emerge to 'bend the bars of the iron cage' of the formal organizational rules." With respect to Olson's findings on the logic of collective action (1965), such an inclination is all the more likely to be successfully realized since the local party committees are small and well-organized subgroups following common interests.[2] In addition, the Chinese authoritarian system did not allow the emergence of competing independent interest groups (Chhibber & Eldersveld, 2000), which could act as a potent counterbalance and constraint to party activities.

Political and Legal Framework

The existence of lock-in effects in the political and legal environments is closely connected with the fact that China is still a Marxist state where most governmental and legal organs are mirrored by political organs of the Communist Party (Shirk, 1992). In such a hybrid party-state with a high degree of organizational penetration and the political hegemony of the CCP (Shambaugh, 2000), chances for enterprise depoliticization at the grass-roots level are particularly determined by the legal and political framework.

The most important legal constraint affecting enterprise depoliticization in China is the Company Law. The original intent of the Law was to institutionalize a corporate governance structure modelled on modern business corporation.[3] By providing a clear specification and distribution of decision making rights among shareholders, board of directors and managers, it was expected that the Law could help to depoliticize enterprise decision making.[4] Even foreign observers have high hopes for the Law's contribution to enterprise depoliticization; among others the World Bank (1997) judged "the Chinese corporate form has become the vehicle for separating governmental and business functions." With regard to the position of the local party committees, the Company Law significantly reduced its formal authority and challenged their encompassing power in China's enterprises for the first time ever. The power to appoint or remove, reward and punish managers is explicitly transferred to the Board of Directors. With regard to the party's formal rights however, the Law remains quite vague and provides local party committees with a certain leeway to continue their involvement and interventionist activities. Concerning party activities, Art. 17 of the Company Law states that "the activities of the local party committees of the CCP in a company shall be carried out in accordance with the Constitution of the CCP."[5] It can be taken for granted that the ambiguity of the legal framework did not occur by happenstance, but instead reflects the Party's strong sense of stability and power reasoning. On the one hand politicians accepted the need to increase managerial autonomy and market orientation to revitalize the severely troubled state enterprise sector. On the other hand, a complete loss of direct political control at enterprise level seemed to be unbearable and destabilizing. The last minute addition of Art. 17 was therefore necessary to appease possible opposition from members of the local party committees (Wang & Tomasic, 1994). The lack of a more precise clarification on the role of the local party committees within the companies might have been the most feasible way to handle this sensible subject politically without risking critical opposition.

In addition to law-making, the tendency of the local party committees to keep their fingers in enterprise decision making is reinforced by the low degree of legal independence, which inevitably leads to weak and arbitrary law enforcement. In spite of the fact that there have been far-reaching legal reforms and re-definitions of the party-legal relations since 1982, which explicitly forbid local party committees to replace the formal law with directives of local party secretaries, the legal system is still anything but independent from the Party. Local courts are actually still subordinate to the local party committees (Zheng, 1997; Findlay, 1999), which allows local party committees to provide political guidance that the local courts can hardly oppose. A major organizational device of the Party Committees is the Party's Political and Legal Affairs Committee, which directly controls the legal system by reviewing the local legal matters (Jayasuriya, 1999). Actually, it has even been observed that judges directly report to district party committees and discuss major cases before they come to court (Liou, 1998). In general, political interests prevail over legal justice if their views call for different actions.[6]

The lock-in effects of the legal environment are reinforced by the official position of China's leadership towards the role played by the local party committees. In spite of the fact that the government regularly emphasizes its will to increase enterprise autonomy, current efforts obviously do not go so far as to ban the party from the economic sphere. This was made perfectly clear by the 15th CCP National Congress, which stressed the party's unquestioned core leadership and made clear that there is no intent to reduce the party's overall presence. Official statements from various members of China's political top-leadership reinforce that a continuation of party involvement at the enterprise level is highly appreciated. Wu Bangguo (1997) for instance, claims that the "party must absolutely not lose its political leadership powers with regard to the enterprises" and even adds that the "party should take part in the decision making in the enterprise with regard to major issues."[7]

Economic Framework

The lock-in effects of the economic institutional environment are closely related to the legacies of the central planning system. It is widely accepted that the survival of re-distributional activities and bureaucratic procedures are what gives the old elite the necessary bargaining power to persist in a reforming economic environment. After two decades of economic reform the administrative controls in China's economy shrank dramatically. The economy is still characterized by the coexistence of market institutions and legacies of the central planning system however, which can be partly attributed to China's dual track reform approach (Naughton, 1992). Gradual reforms caused the rapid development of markets such as the markets for consumer goods. At the same time, scarce key resources and basic factors of production – capital, land and labor – have not been completely liberalized and exposed to free market competition. The cadre elite still controls access to selected sensible resources. This is especially true for the local party and government officials who control resources at the local level (Putterman, 1997). In particular, the liberalization of the financial markets lags far behind the reforms in other sectors, with capital access (both in banking sector and securities market) still being tightly controlled by the government. A recent survey revealed that about 50% of the interviewed managers regard access to financial capital as a major problem of enterprise management (Keister & Lu, 2001). In addition, administrative procedures in a wide range of business-related matters (for instance application procedures for enterprise listings, decisions on enterprise de-listings, decisions on bankruptcy filings and social plans for laid-off surplus workers) are in general not formalized by transparent rules and consistently enforced. Instead, the outcome of these administrative procedures is still determined by the relative bargaining power of the involved interest groups.

Such a quasi market economic system provides the management and the local party committees with a different edge in the contest for power and control in enterprises. On the one hand, the increasing liberalization and marketization of the economy requires an increasing degree of professional skills and expertise in enterprise management. The relative importance of managerial functions like purchasing, marketing, distribution, financial and personnel management increases in response to the phasing out of production plans and price controls. The replacement of plan-fulfillment with productivity and profit maximization as enterprise objectives calls for entrepreneurial rather than political qualities. This increasing demand for professional business skills will raise the bargaining power of the managers and provide them with leverage to resist interference from the local party committees. As shown by Yep (2000), the growing functional indispensability of the managers in rural China has contributed to their emerging influence and created a new power balance in favor of enterprise managers.

On the other hand, the legacies of the socialist planned economy have generated a hybrid business environment in which political capital still plays an active role (Rona-Tas, 1994). Based on panel survey data from Hungary, Rona-Tas finds that former communist cadres succeed in maintaining their former advantageous position. Particularly in the newly generated dynamic segment of Hungary's transitory economy, being a cadre contributes to the financial success of start-up enterprises. Connection with government officials is also considered to be the key to business success in China (Oi, 1985; Pearson, 1997). Generally, government-enterprise ties serve two major objectives: first they facilitate access to scarce resources (Oi, 1985), and second, close ties with representatives of government reduce uncertainty caused by institutional weaknesses and serve as a shield against arbitrary interference (Pearson, 1997). Having cultivated close informal vertical ties between enterprise and administration helps to evade or re-interpret existing rules, accelerates administrative procedures and guarantees a relatively stable business environment. Thus, the evolution of informal business networks in which government and party agencies both play an active role is an interest-maximizing strategy for both members of the economic and administrative/political elites. Pearson (1997) argues that even managers of foreign funded enterprises in China consider good relations with official representatives as crucial for business success. In support of these observations Peng and Luo (2000) conducted a survey that systematically investigates the link between managerial ties and firm performance. Their results suggest that managerial interpersonal ties with government officials do indeed have a positive effect on enterprise performance. The government-enterprise ties are necessary but not sufficient for improved performance. In other words, ties with government officials are important complements but not substitutes for business capabilities.

The CCP and the Chinese government can best be described as a 'delegation relationship' with the party being the principal and the government agencies representing diverse agents (Shirk, 1992, 1993). The local party committees can therefore offer access to most administrative bureaus at the local level. For instance, the party can provide an indispensable network outside of which bank credit is much more difficult to access or permissions to list a company are unattainable. This explains why even private companies in China must also cultivate party ties when they reach a certain size and want to continue growing (McGregor, 2001). Hence, from an individual manager's perspective, it is still sound to collaborate with local party committees; in some cases the continuing interference/involvement at the decision-making process may even be welcomed (Guthrie, 1999; Goodman, 2000).

Summarizing our discussion on the lock-in effects in China's economic institutional environment, we conclude that the quasi-market institutions endow government officials with opportunities to offer particularly favorable treatments to enterprises. By providing access to administrative bureaus at the local level, there is a demand for involvement of the local party committee in enterprises. Available evidence suggests that the importance of personal networks to business success is probably negatively correlated with the degree of economic liberalization and marketization (Nee, 1989, 1991; Bian & Logan, 1996). This implies that the demand for the party network may also decline.

Hypotheses

Our analysis so far has shed some light on diverse links connecting party power and the relevant institutional environment of China's enterprises. Against this background, we argue that the formal constraints of the Company Law are not likely to induce a complete withdrawal of the local party committees from enterprise decision-making processes. Instead, members of the local party committees will keep their fingers in enterprise decision-making processes.

The market-transition model suggests a temporary persistence and a relative decline in power (in the original model measured by earnings advantage) of the old elite, depending on the speed and dynamism of institutional market reforms. An important issue involved in testing the model is the appropriate measurement of economic reform progress. For the role of market power, Nee (1989) predicts that entrepreneurs, professionals and managers gain in power relative to the old political elite (redistributors) due to an increase of market power, material incentives and wealth-maximizing opportunities outside of the redistributive sector. Briefly, a higher degree of market liberalization and hence a relative decrease of bureaucratic mechanisms constrains the power of the old redistributive elite. Thus we formulate

> *Hypothesis 1*: The decision-making power of the local party committees is negatively related to the degree of market liberalization.

Though not explicitly specified in Nee's original market-transition model, there are various hints that market liberalization (market power) needs to be complemented by privatization (private power). As to the importance of private power, Nee (1989) clearly stresses that "transitions to markets in the urban sector would bring the issue of ownership to center stage". Elsewhere Cao and Nee (2000) stress the importance of the formation of a market sector either by the emergence of a secondary economy or through ownership diversification. Exclusive, undiluted private property rights guarantee the complete internalization of costs and benefits and serve as a strong individual incentive to make the best use of property (Alchian & Demsetz, 1972). Socialist ownership in comparison is characterized by diluted property rights that weaken individual incentives for property owners, since full internalization of costs and benefits is not possible. Against this background it is quite clear that privatization should be a centerpiece of market transition. Only privatization generates *real*, highly-motivated property owners, who have sufficient economic incentives to defend their individual interests against state or party interference, which typically causes a deviation from profit-maximizing objectives. Thus, we predict

> *Hypothesis 2*: The decision-making power of the local party committees in enterprises is negatively related to the emergence of private power.

Private power and market power are not independent constraining forces of the old elite's power, but the development of market institutions is a prerequisite for a viable private property regime (Rapaczynski, 1996). Without functioning product and factor markets, even exclusive property rights fail to generate *real*, highly-motivated property owners, since profit-realization is impeded by the weak market infrastructure. The guarantee of private property rights may therefore not provide sufficient incentives to tie the old elite's hands. As we have argued before, shareholders and managers in China may have an incentive to seek cooperation with the old elite because of the quasi-market institutional environment. On the other hand, the existence of private property rights for means of production is also a central determinant of the constraining effects of market power. Without exclusive property rights, state-owned enterprises lack real owners who have a strong incentive to maximize profits and avoid bankruptcy. As a result, market competition fails to generate disciplinary pressure on the state as the ultimate owner and may not provide the necessary incentives to restrain the old elites. As the constraining effects of market power also depend on the prevailing property regime, we formulate

> *Hypothesis 3*: The constraining effects of market power and private power on the decision-making power of the local party committees are mutually reinforcing.

DATA SOURCES AND METHODS

We test the above hypotheses using data obtained from a survey conducted by the Shanghai Stock Exchange (SSE) and Integrity Management Consulting Firm (the survey is referred to as SSES hereafter). SSES is part of a three-year project devoted to the investigation of the corporate governance structure of China's listed companies.[8] The Shanghai Stock Exchange has surveyed all the companies listed in the Exchange early in 2000, 257 companies returned the questionnaires, making the response rate 53.54%. Compared with all companies listed at the Shanghai Stock Exchange, the respondents had no obvious bias in terms of industrial structure, shareholding structure or corporate performance (Shanghai Stock Exchange, 2000).

The questionnaires were supposed to be filled in by the secretary to the chairmen of the board of directors. The survey includes a question that asks the listed companies to rate the level of involvement of shareholders, board of directors, managers and party committees in 63 decisions on a 5-point scale, ranging from no involvement at all (score = 1) to complete control (score = 5). It also provides information on board composition and market conditions of the listed companies. This study utilizes this valuable data set to investigate the power persistence of the local party committees in China's listed companies.

Dependent Variable

We utilize the firm-level data on the involvement of the local party committees in 63 decisions to construct an index for measuring the power of local party committee (PI) for each company. Among the respondents, only 110 companies provide a complete set of ratings on the decision-making power of the local party committees in 63 decisions ($SAMPLE_{63}$). If we expand our sample to include those companies that have provided ratings for 50 decisions or more, we yield a sample consisting of 143 listed companies ($SAMPLE_{50}$). The comparative summary statistics of the decision-making power variables are presented in Appendix B. As the two samples share very similar characteristics, we decided to include the companies that had provided ratings for 50 decisions or more into this study. For each company we construct an index of party power by averaging the decision-making power of the local party committees in all decisions where data is available.

$$PI_i = \frac{\sum_{j=1}^{n} S_{ij}}{n}$$

Where S_{ij} is the level of involvement of the local party unit of company i in decision j

$$j = 1 \ldots n$$

Covering at least 50 decision-types in enterprise decision making, the index provides a particularly complete measurement of party interference in major areas of enterprise decision-making. The averaged scores of the major decision-makers of $SAMPLE_{50}$ (143 companies), ranked by the level of involvement of the local party committees, are provided by Appendix C. It shows clearly that the local party committees have stayed involved in all enterprise decisions (with score > 1), even though their overall level of decision-making power (mean = 1.69) is lower than those of managers (mean = 3.07), shareholders meeting (mean = 2.63) and board of directors (mean = 3.6).

Further analysis of the relative level of party interference by decision-type reveals that party interference concentrates on personnel policy issues like recruitment decisions, performance appraisal and dismissals of leading personnel. Thus, local party branches cling to the tradition of the socialist nomenclature system to control and interfere in enterprise decision-making by establishing personnel dependencies.

Independent Variables

Private Power

All listed companies are partially privatized in China. From the perspective of resisting political interference, it is not meaningful to use the proportion of shares held by all non-state-owned entities and individual shareholders as an index for the degree of private power, because small individual shareholders are usually not involved in enterprise decision making. Even in mature market economies individual minority shareholders are rarely active shareholders seeking to monitor the efficiency of enterprise policy. Since the potential benefits of monitoring activities accrue equally to all shareholders, while monitoring costs are covered individually, minority shareholders frequently take a free-rider position. Due to this common "public good problem," only large shareholders may expect net-benefits from exercising monitoring activities (Shleifer & Vishny, 1986; Hart, 1995). Large shareholders (typically institutional investors) also have the necessary knowledge and capacity to perform professional monitoring activities. Empirical surveys have shown that the monitoring activities of shareholders actually increase with the ownership share (Grossman & Hart, 1980; Shleifer & Vishny, 1986). These findings are consistent with recent empirical evidence on the positive effects of ownership concentration on the corporate performance in China's listed companies (Xu & Wang, 1997; Qi, Wu & Zhang, 1999). Based on the existing corporate governance theories and empirical evidence, we use the ownership identities of the largest shareholders to proxy for the emergence of private power in listed companies. The annual reports of China's listed companies only provide information on the types of shares held by the top ten shareholders but not the ownership identity of the largest shareholders. The listed companies in China typically have three distinctive types of shares – state shares, legal persons shares and individual shares. The types of shares held by the largest shareholders consist of state shares and legal persons shares only because individual investors are not allowed to hold more than 0.5% of individual shares.[9] We refrain from using the proportion of legal persons shares as an index of private power because some of the legal persons shares are held by wholly state-owned enterprises, which represent state power rather than private power. Fortunately, SSES provides information on the ownership identity of the largest shareholders so that we can classify the largest shareholders into two types. The first type of shareholders consists of non-state shareholders (NSS); the second type of shareholders are state shareholders (SS). Thus, SS include both governmental institutions and state-owned enterprises and NSS are non-state-owned entities including private and foreign funded enterprises. The SSES reveals that 83% of the largest shareholders are state-owned entities. Only 17% of the largest shareholders are non-state owned entities.

Market Power

We purposely refrain from using industrial classification as a proxy for the degree of competition for our sample companies for two reasons. First, industrial classifications are usually highly aggregated and they typically fail to reveal the specific competition conditions of individual firms. Second, China has adopted a regional approach to economic reform under which companies in the same industry may face very different degrees of competition if they are located in different regions. As a result, industrial classification is not an appropriate indicator to proxy the degree of competition faced by enterprises. The popular measurement of market concentration ratios is not adopted due to the lack of data.

We obtain three variables from the database to proxy the degree of market competition to which the listed companies are exposed. The selected variables benefit from the fact that they refer to the specific market conditions of the companies and thus better reflect de facto market competition than broad industry classifications. The first dummy variable indicates whether there are close substitutes for products produced by a listed company (CS). The existence of close product substitutes indicates a higher level of competitive pressure in product markets as consumers can easily substitute products of firm A by products of firm B if the latter offers higher product quality or sells at lower prices. Thus, the existence of close substitutes ties enterprise policy closely to the activities of its competitors and leaves less room for political interference. The second dummy variable indicates whether the products produced by a listed company require production licensing arrangements (NPLA). Product licensing arrangements serve as market entry barriers that impede free competition (Baumol, 1982). As a result, companies can enjoy a certain degree of monopolistic power which provides a more tolerant environment for political interference. The third variable is also a dummy variable. It denotes whether the prices of products are controlled by the government (NPC). It is expected that the ruling out of price competition will reduce the level of market competition and is therefore associated with a higher degree of party power.

Control Variables

The major focus of this study is to examine the relationship between private and market power on the one hand and decision-making power of local party committees on the other. There are some factors that can jointly affect party interference and the two types of power and thus may induce a spurious correlation between them. We introduce two control variables in this study. The first control variable is the age of listing. Before 2000, listing at the two exchanges in China had been strictly controlled by the government through a quota system. It was the local government and line ministries who decided which enterprises would be listed. As there is an intense competition among enterprises, the order of listing reflects the degree of government favoritism and the closeness of the government-enterprise connection to a certain extent (Cao, 2000). As a result, companies listed earlier tend to have a higher degree of political involvement in enterprises. They are also more likely to receive/maintain market protection and less likely to be privatized. As the degree of government favoritism jointly affects private and market power on the one hand and the degree of political involvement on the other, we introduce the listing age as a control variable to capture the initial government-enterprise relationship.

In addition to age of listing, we introduce the percentage of seats in the BOD taken up by the largest shareholder (% SEATS) as a second control variable when we examine the relationship between private power and the decision-making power of the local party committees. The variable is used to capture the largest shareholder's direct involvement in enterprise governance, which may be correlated with both private power and decision-making power of the old elite. On the one hand, state and private shareholders may have different motives and incentives to monitor managers. On the other hand, direct shareholder involvement in corporate governance may have some impact on the room for political interference from the local party committees. We preferred the variable of % SEAT to the average decision-making power of the shareholder-meeting, since it is widely known that shareholder-meetings in China generally do not exert any *independent* power. By and large, shareholder meetings just approve the drafts prepared by the BOD.[10] Hence shareholder power is much better reflected by directly focusing on the power of the largest shareholder within the BOD.

Models

We construct the following four models to investigate how the persistence of party involvement is affected by market power and private power. In particular we test stepwise for the isolated market- and ownership-effect and then test the combined effect of market and private power with and without interaction effect. Our regression equations are

Market Model:

$$PI = \alpha + \beta_1 CS + \beta_2 NPLA + \beta_3 NPC + \beta_4 YEAR + \beta_5 \%SEATS + e \qquad (1)$$

Ownership Model:

$$PI = \alpha + \beta_1 NSS + \beta_2 YEAR + \beta_3 \%SEATS + e \qquad (2)$$

Combined Model:

$$PI = \alpha + \beta_1 NSS + \beta_2 CS + \beta_3 NPLA + \beta_4 NPC + \beta_5 YEAR + \beta_6 \%SEATS + e \qquad (3)$$

Interaction Model:

$$PI = \alpha + \beta_1 CS + \beta_2 NPLA + \beta_3 NPC + \beta_4 NSS{*}CS + \beta_5 NSS{*}NPLA + \beta_6 NSS{*}NPC + \beta_7 YEAR + \beta_8 \%SEATS + e \qquad (4)$$

Where

PI is the overall decision-making power of the local party committee.

YEAR is the number of years since IPO.

% SEATS is the percentage of seats in the board of directors taken up by the largest shareholder.

CS is a dummy variable for the existence of close substitutes. It is 1 if there are close substitutes. Otherwise, it is 0.

NPLA is a dummy variable for the existence of production licensing arrangement. It is 1 if licensing is not required. Otherwise, it is 0.

NPC is a dummy variable for the existence of price control. It is 1 if there is no price control. Otherwise, it is 0.

NSS is a dummy variable for the existence of non-state-owned largest shareholder. It is 1 if a largest shareholder is non-state-owned enterprises. Otherwise, it is 0.

e is an error term with a mean of zero.

RESULTS

Descriptive Statistics

Among the 143 companies that provided ratings for the decision-making power of the local party committee, some of them have missing data in our measures of private power, market power and control variables. When we confine our sample to those companies having data in all variables, our final sample includes 88 companies ($SAMPLE_{final}$).

The summary statistics of $SAMPLE_{final}$ are provided in Appendices D and E. On average, the companies have been listed at Shanghai Stock Exchange for 4.09 years with a minimum of 1 and a maximum of 8 years. The age distribution is reasonable because the Shanghai Stock Exchange had been running for a period of 8 years at the time the survey was conducted. The BODs of our sample companies seem to be dominated by the largest shareholder with the averaged ratio of board representation of the largest shareholder reaching 51% and a median of 54%. The mean party involvement of our sample companies is 1.69 with a median of 1.49 and minimum and maximum value of 1.00 respective 4.19 (Appendix D). This is consistent with distributions of $SAMPLE_{63}$ and $SAMPLE_{50}$. With regard to the ownership identity of the largest shareholders, Appendix E reveals that 73 (83%) of our sample companies have a state largest shareholder and only 15 (17%) have a non-state large shareholder. The distribution is consistent with the corresponding distribution of all companies covered by SSES. Statistics on relevant market conditions show that production in China is still subjected to a great deal of administrative control, with 53 (60%) of our sample companies indicating that their production requires product licensing agreements. Direct controls in the economy, however, have considerably decreased as only nine of the companies are still under price control. Twenty-six (29.5%) of our sample companies experience intense competition due to the presence of close product substitutes.

Regression Results and Interpretation

The estimates of Model (1) to (4) are presented in Table 1. As we can see from Model (1) the support for Hypothesis 1 is at best weak. Though all coefficients

Table 1. Determinants of Party Power Persistence in China's Listed Companies.

Dependent Variable: Party Power	Model 1 (*Market*)	Model 2 (*Ownership*)	Model 3 (*Combined*)	Model 4 (*Interaction*)
Independent Variables				
CS	–0.062 (0.156)		–0.033 (0.152)	0.088 (0.167)
NPLA	–0.238 (0.146)		–0.249* (0.139)	–0.158 (0.149)
NPC	–0.077 (0.234)		0.151 (0.234)	0.148 (0.236)
NSS		–0.469** (0.181)	–0.500*** (0.184)	
NSS*CS				–0.430 (0.330)
NSS*NPLA				–0.622** (0.300)
NSS*NPC[a]				–
Control Variables				
YEAR	0.116* (0.033)	0.105*** (0.032)	0.105*** (0.032)	0.103*** (0.033)
%SEAT	–0.506** (0.254)	–0.618** (0.272)	–0.639** (0.275)	
Constant	1.008*** (0.18)	1.603*** (0.219)	1.519*** (0.247)	1.569*** (0.281)
R^2	0.151	0.213	0.250	0.251
Adj. R^2	0.11	0.185	0.195	0.186
Observations	88	88	88	88

Note: Numbers in brackets represent std. error.

[a] No enterprise fulfills both criteria.

*** $p < 0.01$; ** $p < 0.05$; * $p < 0.10$ (two-tail tests).

of the market model (1) generate the expected signs, none of the coefficients are statistically significant. The coefficient for variable of year of listing is corrected and statistically significant. The explanatory power of the model is acceptable with $R^2 = 11.0\%$.

In the ownership model (2), the coefficient for NSS is –0.469 and statistically significant at 5% level, which indicates that the rise of a non-state largest shareholder reduces the level of local party interference. This is consistent with our prediction that private power serves as the basic force to fight off party power and gives strong support to Hypothesis 2. The coefficients for the two control variables (year of listing and percentage of seats taken up by the largest shareholders) have the expected signs and are statistically significant. The explanatory power of the ownership model is 18.5%.

The combined model (3) reconfirms the major findings of models (1) and (2). Under a simultaneous consideration of privatization and marketization, the year of listing as the indicator of initial enterprise-government relations again yields a positive and significant (1% level) impact while the board representation of the largest shareholder yields a negative and significant (5% level) effect on the continuation of local party involvement. The coefficient for NSS rises slightly to (0.5) and is now significant at a 1% level. While the market model did not generate statistically significant coefficients, the coefficient for production licensing arrangement is now significant at 10%. In this context, it should also be noted that the coefficient of price controls loses the expected positive sign, though its effect is statistically insignificant in both model (1) and (3). The explanatory power of the combined model increases slightly to 19.5%. The changes in the coefficients of both privatization and marketization variables suggests that the constraining effects of market and private power are not totally independent of each other and some form of interaction effect may exist between them.

In order to seek more insights into the underlying interaction effects between private and market power we finally included three additional interaction terms in model 4 to reveal possible interaction between private power and the three specific market characteristics represented by the dummy variables. All market variables remain statistically insignificant. Coefficients of the interaction term NSS*NPLA give strong support to the mutual interdependence between market and private power formulated in Hypothesis 3. First, the coefficient of NSS*NPLA (0.622) is higher than the coefficient of NPLA (0.249) in model (3). This indicates that the constraining effect of production market liberalization increases when there is a NSS. Second, the coefficient of NSS*NPLA (0.622) is also higher than the coefficient of NSS (0.5) in model (3). This shows that the constraining effect of NSS also increases when there is no production licensing arrangement. The direction of the interaction term NSS*CS is also in line with the prediction of H3. The effect however, remains statistically insignificant which is probably attributable to the small panel size.

On the whole, we find clear evidence for the validity of Hypotheses 2 and 3 while Hypothesis 1 is not verified. This implies that the power constraining effects of market liberalization cannot evolve unless markets are complemented by private power as represented here by the rise of a dominant private shareholder. Briefly, dismantling the planning system and the transfer to liberalized market allocation does not significantly threaten the established power structure at enterprise level. Liberalization of markets can therefore be accompanied by a relatively stable power structure and survival of the political elite. A significant threat of the power structure is only brought about if private property rights are introduced.

Private power on the other hand, is able to constrain the power of the old political elite in the absence of market liberalization. Even in a strictly regulated economic environment, exclusive property rights give property owners sufficient incentives to protect their property and oppose against interference from third parties. Nevertheless, the constraining effect of private power increases with market liberalization, since expected economic benefits of exclusive property rights are higher in a liberalized than in a strongly regulated market environment.

Our results prove that it is in fact the existence of private property rights that determines the fate of the old political elite at enterprise level. The degree of power persistence and – from a dynamic perspective – the speed of relative power decline during market transition both crucially depend on the emergence and the magnitude of private power. As Shleifer and Vishny (1994) have argued in their seminal paper on politicians and firms, the existence of private owners and their individual interests in profit maximization reduces the bargaining power of politicians and thereby increases costs of political interference in enterprise decision-making. This change of relative interference costs eventually threatens the existing power structure and helps to depoliticize the economy.

CONCLUSION AND DISCUSSION

Summarizing our major findings, the paper gives empirical evidence of the widespread, though also empirically poorly proven, idea of continuing party involvement in China's modern enterprise system, specifically in China's listed companies. We confirmed that the economic institutional environment actually does have a decisive impact on the degree of elite survival and continuing involvement of local Party power as representative of the former redistributive elite. We particularly emphasize the role of private power. On the whole, our findings support the validity of the power-persistence thesis and supplement available income-related empirical evidence to the market-transition model. The importance of private power as revealed by this study suggests that the application of the market-transition model (which was originally designed to explain power transfers in China's rural areas) to urban areas and large corporations demands a stronger focus on the specification and distribution of property rights. Though market liberalization was proven to be instrumental in reducing party power, it is not effective as an independent constraint but has to be accompanied by the emergence of private property rights. Private property rights constrain the old elite even in the absence of a liberal market environment. Politicians obviously have a very clear intuitive understanding of these interdependencies and the underlying causal mechanism of power transfer. In almost all transition economies, particularly in China, political resistance against full-scale privatization programs was high while market liberalization itself was in general quickly accomplished.

The question of whether the detected phenomenon of political involvement is coordinated and guided by the Party center or it is a completely spontaneous and individual reaction cannot be resolved by directly referring to our data set and will need much closer investigation in future research. For a first tentative reflection we instead draw on the available theoretical and empirical literature to differentiate between two distinct scenarios. In the first scenario we see the intentional and centrally guided integration and survival of the old elite under changing formal rules of governance. In the second scenario, members of the old elite (not the elite as a defined homogenous social group) survive in a newly evolving system by taking advantage of their still existing but significantly weakening old status and relying on lock-in effects of the gradually changing institutional environment.

Actually, little seems to speak for the first scenario while much seems to be in favor of the second. The increasing disintegration of the center and local units is reported by many observers and it must be doubted whether the central party office still enjoys the necessary strength to monitor coordinated political action throughout the country's grassroots. White observed as early as 1983 that "the leaky quality of power in a complex hierarchy, has also led to informal decentralization within the party, notably the phenomenon of 'independent kingdoms' under local party 'bosses' " and remarked, that these 'kingdoms' cause a "constant headache for the strategic chess players of the Politburo" (White, 1983). Even though the Party control on personnel and organization can still be a sharp sword to discipline and supervise activities of the political cadres, it has been reported that the Party's organizational control has been greatly eroded when compared to the pre-reform era (Zheng, 1997). Corruption and other illegal activities of local officials are a clear signal of the center's weakness to tightly monitor and sanction the behavior of the local cadres. A similar influence is to be expected from the decreasing importance of socialist ideology (the widely discussed ideological vacuum, see Fewsmith 2001), which no longer serves as a binding commitment to bring activities of the local political agents in line with the central Party leadership's interest. Thus, we tend to the assumption that our survey is basically a case study of the spontaneous struggle for survival of individual members of the old political elite in a gradually changing institutional environment. Here, we are in full accordance with Cao and Nee's (2000) assumption that marketization and liberalization of economic systems probably does not allow the survival of the former elite as a social group, but will only allow the survival of the individual elite members who successfully adapt to the new situation. There is no question however, that a seizure of the established personnel party-enterprise dependencies (i.e. for the enforcement of central party guidelines and directives at the enterprise level) is generally possible, regardless of whether continuing involvement of party members followed a central directive or developed spontaneously.

NOTES

1. The local Party power has been a regular focus of policy debate and concern since the founding of the PRC because it determines the relative influence of political control and economic forces at work at the enterprise level. The relative importance of political forces as represented by formal party rights at the enterprise level has undergone frequent changes since 1949. In retrospect, during the last five decades the ratio between party-strength and management-strength forms a reversed u-form with a peak in the Cultural Revolution and a following downturn of relative party strength since the shifting of national development objectives from class struggle to economic growth and development in the post-Mao period (You, 1998).

2. The unwillingness of the local party committees to withdraw from the decision-making process is reinforced by arguments borrowed from the theory of bureaucracy, which has broken with the assumption that the individual utility functions of 'political bureaucrats' are identical with the general interests of society. Thus, the existence of an army of benevolent civil servants whose highest interest lies in the utility maximization of a Benthamite social welfare function has long been banned to the land of fairy tales. Instead, it is assumed that bureaucrats as individuals desire to maximize their own individual utility function and behave opportunistically. Typical objectives of bureaucrats are status, income, power, authority and the size of the administrative budget. In order to realize their objectives they seek decision-making rights, since control broadens their bargaining opportunities (Niskanen, 1971). Theda Skocpol (1985, p. 15) hypothesizes that one feature of all autonomous state actions will be the reinforcement of the prerogatives of collectivities of state officials.

3. An English translation is to be found in Howard Gensler and Yang Jiliang, A Guide to China's Tax and Business Laws (Hong Kong: Sweet & Maxwell Asia, 1995).

4. The distribution of decision-making rights among various power holders as specified in the Company Law is provided in appendix A.

5. But, the Constitution of the CCP does not contribute much to the clarification of the party activities within the enterprise, since Art. 31 only vaguely delegates the implementation of higher party decisions to the local party committees at the enterprise level. Any advice on the concrete implementation of tasks and techniques is completely absent.

6. In fact, in Chinese history, the legal system has never been independent from the state or political leadership and was uninterruptedly regarded as part of the executive branch (Jayasuriya, 1999). Thus, law was traditionally regarded as an instrument to control society; it was not concerned with the regulation of public-civil relations (Fewsmith, 2001).

7. The general secretary Jiang Zemin, only recently gave a detailed picture of the party's activities in enterprises. According to Jiang, the party's influence at the enterprise level should include at least the four following tasks (FBIS-CHI-1999-0817): (1) Implementation of the basic party line; (2) Fulfillment of its duties under special consideration of production and management; (3) Participation in important operational decisions; (4) Assistance to the Board of Directors, Board of Supervisors and management. It should be noted that these tasks have been assigned to wholly state owned enterprises according to Art. 32 of the Chinese Constitution.

8. The major findings of the research project were presented in an international conference held on 2–3 November 2000 and is also published under the title of "Corporate Governance Structure of China's Listed Companies".

9. "Gupiao faxing yu jaioyi guanli zanxing tiaolie" (Preliminary regulations on the stock distribution and stock trading), 22.04.1993, Art. 46, in *Zhongguo Zhengquan Fagui Zonghui* (*Compendium of Chinas Securities Laws and Regulations*) edited by Chen Gong, Zhou Shengye and Wu Xiaoqiu, 2000.

10. However, we have to stress that the weak position of the shareholder meeting is not a phenomenon specific to China's listed enterprises, though the problem is certainly very severe in China. Epstein for instance criticized – not with respect to China, but addressing listed companies of mature market economies – that "shareholder elections are much more akin to the elections held by the CP of North Korea than those held in Western democracies" (Monks, 1995).

ACKNOWLEDGMENTS

We are grateful to Kevin T. Leicht and Victor G. Nee who provided helpful criticism and valuable comments on an earlier version of this paper. We also thank David Kalok Yuen for excellent research assistance.

REFERENCES

Alchian, A., & Demsetz, H. (1972). Production, Information Costs, and Economic Organization. *American Economic Review*, *72*, 777–795.

Baumol, W. J. (1982). Contestable Markets: An Uprising in the Theory of Industrial Structure. *American Economic Review*, *60*, 1–15.

Bian, Y., & Logan, J. R. (1996). Market Transition and the Persistence of Power: The Changing Stratification System in Urban China. *American Sociological Review*, *61*, 739–758.

Boycko, M., Shleifer, A., & Vishny, R. V. (1995). *Privatizing Russia*. Cambridge, MA.: MIT Press.

Cao, L. (2000). Chinese Privatization: Between Plan and Market. *Law and Contemporary Problems*, *63*, 13–62.

Cao, Y., & Nee, V. G. (2000). Comment: Controversies and Evidence in the Market Transition Debate. *American Journal of Sociology*, *105*, 1175–1189.

Chen G., Shengye, Z., & Xiaoqiu, W. (Eds) (2000). *Zhongguo Zhengquan Fagui Zonghui* (*Compendium of Chinas Securities Laws and Regulations*). Beijing: Zhongguo Caizheng Jingji Chubanshe.

Chhibber, P., & Eldersveld, S. (2000). Local Elites and Popular Support for Economic Reform in China and India. *Comparative Political Studies*, *33*, 350–373.

Eggertson, T. (1996). A Note on the Economics of Institutions. In: L. Alston, T. Eggertson & D. C. North (Eds), *Empirical Studies in Institutional Change* (pp. 6–24). Cambridge, MA.: Cambridge University Press.

Fewsmith, J. (2001). *Elite Politics in Contemporary China*. Armonk, NY: M. E. Sharpe.

Findlay, M. (1999). Independence and the Judiciary in the PRC: Expectations for Constitutional Legality in China. In: K. Jayasuriya (Ed.), *Law, Capitalism and Power in Asia* (pp. 281–299). London: Routledge.

Fligstein, N. (1996). The Economic Sociology of the Transitions from Socialism. *American Journal of Sociology*, *101*, 1074–1081.

Foreign Broadcast Information Service (FBIS), various volumes.

Gensler, H., & Yang, J. (1995). *A Guide to China's Tax and Business Laws*. Hong Kong: Sweet & Maxwell Asia.

Goodman, D. S. G. (2000). The Localism of Local Leadership Cadres in Reform Shanxi. *Journal of Contemporary China*, *24*, 159–184.

Greif, A. (1997). On the Interrelations and Economic Implications of Economic, Social, Political, and Normative Factors: Reflections from Two Late Medieval Societies. In: J. N. Drobak & J. V. C. Nye (Eds), *The Frontiers of the New Institutional Economics* (pp. 57–94). San Diego: Academic Press.

Grossman, S., & Hart, O. (1980). The Costs and Benefits of Ownership: A Theory of Vertical and Lateral Integration. *Bell Journal of Economics*, *11*, 42–64.

Guthrie, D. (1997). Between Markets and Politics: Organizational Responses to Reform in China. *American Journal of Sociology*, *102*, 1258–1304.

Guthrie, D. (1999). *Dragon in a Three-Piece Suit*. Princeton, NJ: Princeton University Press.

Hart, O. D. (1995). Corporate Governance: Some Theory and Implications. *The Economic Journal*, *105*, 678–689.

Jayasuriya, K. (1999). Corporatism and Judicial Independence within Statist Legal Institutions in Asia. In: K. Jayasuriya (Ed.), *Law, Capitalism and Power in Asia* (pp. 173–204). London: Routledge.

Keister, L. A., & Lu, J. (2001). The Transformation Continues: The Status of Chinese State-Owned Enterprises at the Start of the Millenium. *NBER Analysis*, *12*(3), June.

Liou, K. T. (1998). *Managing Economic Reforms in Post-Mao China*. London: Praeger.

McGregor, R. (2001). The Little Red Book of Business in China. *Financial Times*, July 2.

Monks, R. A. G. (1995). Corporate Governance in the Twenty-First Century. A Preliminary Outline. *Corporate Governance Quarterly*, *2*, 11–28.

Naughton, B. (1992). Hierarchy and the Bargaining Economy: Government and Enterprise in the Reform Process. In: K. Lieberthal & D. Lampton (Eds), *Bureaucracy, Politics, and Decision Making in Post-Mao China* (pp. 245–279). Berkeley: University of California Press.

Nee, V. (1989). A Theory of Market Transition: From Redistribution to Markets in State Socialism. *American Sociological Review, 54*, 663–681.

Nee, V. (1991). Social Inequalities in Reforming State Socialism: Between Redistribution to Markets in State Socialism. *American Sociological Review, 56*, 267–282.

Nee, V., & Ingram, P. (1998). Embeddedness and Beyond: Institutions, Exchange, and Social Structure. In: M. Brinton & V. Nee (Eds), *The New Institutionalism in Sociology* (pp. 19–45). New York: Russell Sage Foundation.

Niskanen, W. (1971). *Bureaucracy and Representative Government*. Chicago: Atherton.

North, Douglass C. 1990. *Institutions, Institutional Change and Economic Performance*. Cambridge: Cambridge University Press.

North, D. C. (2000). Understanding Institutions. In: C. Menard (Ed.), *Institutions, Contracts and Organizations. Perspectives from New Institutional Economics* (pp. 7–10). Cheltenham: Edward Elgar.

Oberschall, A. (1996). The Great Transition: China, Hungary, and Sociology Exit Socialism into the Market. *American Journal of Sociology, 101*, 1028–1041.

Oi, J. (1985). Communism and Clientelism: Rural Politics in China. *World Politics, 37*, 238–266.

Oi, J. (1989). *State and Peasant in Contemporary China*. Berkeley: University of California Press.

Olson, M. (1965). *The Logic of Collective Action, Public Action and the Theory of Groups*. Cambridge, MA.: Harvard University Press.

Pearson, M. M. (1997). *China's New Business Elite. The Political Consequences of Economic Reform*. Berkeley: University of California Press.

Peng, M. W., & Luo, Y. (2000). Managerial Ties and Firm Performance in a Transition Economy: The Nature of a Micro-Macro Link. *Academy of Management Journal, 43*, 486–501.

Putterman, L. (1997). On the Past and Future of China's Township and Village-owned Enterprises. *World Development, 25*, 1639–1655.

Qi, D., Wu, W., & Zhang, H. (1999). Shareholding Structure and Corporate Performance of Partially Privatized Firms: Evidence from Listed Chinese Companies. *Pacific-Basin Finance Journal, 8*, 587–610.

Rapaczynski, A. (1996). The Roles of the State and the Market in Establishing Property Rights. *Journal of Economic Perspectives, 10*, 87–103.

Rona-Tas, A. (1994). The First Shall be the Last: Entrepreneurship and Communist Cadres in the Transition from Socialism. *American Journal of Sociology, 100*, 40–69.

Shambaugh, D. (2000). The Chinese State in the Post-Mao Era. In: D. Shambaugh (Ed.), *The Modern Chinese State* (pp. 161–187). Cambridge: Cambridge University Press.

Shanghai Stock Exchange (2000). *Corporate Governance in China*. Shanghai.

Shirk, S. L. (1989). The Political Economy of Chinese Industrial Reform. In: V. Nee & D. Stark (Eds), *Remaking the Economic Institutions of Socialism: China and Eastern Europe* (pp. 328–364). Stanford: Stanford University Press.

Shirk, S. L. (1992). The Chinese Political System and the Political Strategy of Economic Reform. In: K. Lieberthal & D. Lampton (Eds), *Bureaucracy, Politics, and Decision Making in Post-Mao China* (pp. 59–91). Berkeley: University of California Press.

Shirk, S. L. (1993). *The Political Logic of Economic Reform in China*. Berkeley: University of California Press.

Shleifer, A., & Vishny, R. W. (1986). Large Shareholders and Corporate Control. *Journal of Political Economy, 94*, 461–488.

Shleifer, A., & Vishny, R. W. (1994). Politicians and Firms. *The Quarterly Journal of Economics, CIX*, 995–1025.

Skocpol, T. (1985). Bringing the State Back in: Strategies of Analysis in Current Research. In: P. B. Evans, D. Rueschemeyer & T. Skocpol (Eds), *Bringing the State Back In* (pp. 3–37). Cambridge, MA.: Cambridge University Press.

Steinfeld, E. S. (1999). *Forging Reform in China: The Fate of State-Owned Industry* (2nd ed.). Cambridge: Cambridge University Press.

Szèlenyi, I. (1988). *Socialist Entrepreneurs: Embourgeoisement in Rural Hungary*. Madison: University of Wisconsin Press.

Tam, O. K. (1999). *The Development of Corporate Governance in China*. Cheltenham: Edward Elgar.

Wang G., & Tomasic, R. (1994). *China's Company Law: An Annotation*. Singapore: Butterworths.

White, G. (1983). The Postrevolutionary Chinese State. In: V. Nee & D. Mozingo (Eds), *State and Society in Contemporary China* (pp. 27–52). Ithaca and London: Cornell University Press.

World Bank (1997). *Chinas̀ Management of Enterprise Assets. The State as Shareholder*. Washington, D.C.: World Bank.

Wu, B. (1997). Several Questions Concerning the Reform and Development of State-Owned Enterprises. *The Chinese Economy, 2*, 6–47.

Xu, X., & Wang, Y. (1999). Ownership Structure and Corporate Governance in Chinese Stock Companies. *China Economic Review, 10*, 75–98.

Yep, R. (2000). Bringing the Managers in: A Case of Rising Influence of Enterprise Managers in Rural China. *Issues and Studies, 4*, 132–166.

You, J. (1998). *China's Enterprise Reform. Changing State/Society Relations After Mao*. London and New York: Routledge.

Zheng, S. (1997). *Party vs. State in Post-1949 China*. Cambridge: Cambridge University Press.

Zhongguo Qiyejia Diaocha Xitong (1997a). Dangqian Wo Guo Qiye Jingyingzhe Dui Jili yu Yueshu Wenti Kanfa de Diaocha. (Research on Enterprise Managers' Opinion on Problems with Incentives and Constraints in Today's China.) *Guanli Shijie* (*Management World*), *4*, 119–132.

Zhongguo Qiyejia Diaocha Xitong (1997b). Qiye Jingyingzhe dui Dangqian Jingji Gaige yu Fazhan de Panduan he Jianyi. (Enterprise Managers' Evaluation of Recent Economic Reform and Development and Suggestions.) *Jingji Gongzuozhe Xuexi Ziliao* (*Study Material of the Economic Worker*), *22*, 17–47.

Zhou, X. (2000). Economic Transformation and Income Inequality in Urban China: Evidence from Panel Data. *American Journal of Sociology, 105*, 1135–1174.

APPENDIX A

Distribution of Formal Rights Granted by the Company Law

	Shareholder Meeting	Board of directors	Manager	Board of Supervisors
Investment and operating plan	Decides on the plan	Determines plan	Implements the plan	
Personnel decisions	Elects member of BoD/ remuneration decisions. Elects board of supervisors/ decides on remuneration	Appoints and removes managers, vice-managers, persons in charge of finance and accounting. Determines remuneration	Suggests appointment/ removal of vice-manager. Appoints/ removes managerial personnel.	Supervises BoD and manager's activities
Reports/meeting	Examines and approves report of BoD	Reports to shareholder meeting		Attends the BoD meetings as non voting delegate
Financial budget/ accounting	Examines and approves	Drafts the plan		Examines
Distribution of profits	Examines and approves	Drafts the plan		
Increase/ Decrease of capital	Adopts resolution	Drafts the plan		
Company bonds	Adopts resolution	Drafts the plan		
Mergers/ separation/ clearance	Adopts resolution	Drafts the plan		
Company constitution	Amends			
General meeting		Convenes general meeting/work report		Proposes convention of a provisional stockholder's general meeting

APPENDIX A *Continued.*

	Shareholder Meeting	Board of Directors	Manager	Board of Supervisors
Management system		Establishes internal management organization	Drafts the establishment of the internal management organization; drafts basic management system	

APPENDIX B

Descriptive Statistics Decision-making Power

	SAMPLE$_{63}$			*SAMPLE*$_{50}$		
	Party Committees	Board of Directors	Managers	Party Committees	Board of Directors	Managers
Mean	1.601	3.575	3.051	1.681	3.628	3.094
Median	0.059	0.042	0.051	0.053	0.039	0.046
Mode	1.413	3.635	3.032	1.508	3.698	3.063
Minimum	1	3.333	2.873	1	3.333	2.873
Maximum	1	2.397	2.016	1	2.397	1.700
Standard Error	3.508	4.444	4.683	4.194	4.698	4.683

APPENDIX C

Decision-making Power of Various Power Holders of $SAMPLE_{50}$*

	Local Party Committees	Managers	Shareholders' Meeting	Board of Directors
1. Agenda Setting in Shareholder Meeting	1.40 (0.61)	2.16 (0.86)	3.45 (1.37)	4.25 (0.76)
2. Call of Shareholder Meeting	1.42 (0.60)	2.13 (0.82)	3.24 (1.49)	4.25 (0.81)
3. Call of Board Meeting	1.44 (0.69)	2.37 (0.94)	2.07 (1.06)	4.57 (0.71)
4. Agenda Setting in Board Meeting	1.47 (0.68)	2.44 (0.95)	2.00 (1.03)	4.61 (0.72)
5. Call of Supervisory Committee Meeting	1.52 (0.69)	1.76 (0.94)	1.91 (0.97)	1.96 (1.06)
6. Agenda Setting in Supervisory Committee Meeting	1.50 (0.70)	1.74 (0.94)	1.89 (0.97)	1.87 (0.97)
7. Call of Manager's Office Meeting	1.90 (0.95)	4.64 (0.62)	1.44 (0.70)	2.44 (1.00)
8. Agenda Setting in Manager's Office Meeting	1.87 (0.91)	4.66 (0.59)	1.44 (0.66)	2.38 (0.96)
9. Selection of Representatives Attending Manager's Office Meeting	1.75 (0.95)	4.65 (0.68)	1.34 (0.63)	2.08 (1.00)
10. Making Amendments to Company's Charter	1.51 (0.67)	2.19 (0.83)	4.39 (1.06)	3.71 (0.75)
11. Organizational Change	2.04 (1.07)	3.60 (1.02)	2.15 (1.27)	3.99 (1.01)
12. Creation and Abolition of Functional Departments	2.03 (1.07)	4.07 (0.86)	1.60 (0.93)	3.51 (1.24)
13. Selection of Functional Department Manager	2.27 (1.23)	4.40 (0.76)	1.35 (0.67)	2.90 (1.29)
14. Performance Appraisal of Functional Departments	2.21 (1.16)	4.46 (0.72)	1.38 (0.71)	2.51 (1.23)
15. Creation and Abolition of Business Departments	1.97 (1.09)	4.36 (0.76)	1.38 (0.70)	2.88 (1.35)

APPENDIX C *Continued.*

	Local Party Committees	Managers	Shareholders' Meeting	Board of Directors
16. Selection of Business Department Managers	2.27 (1.21)	4.46 (0.71)	1.32 (0.64)	2.45 (1.25)
17. Performance Appraisal of Business Department	2.16 (1.16)	4.42 (0.81)	1.31 (0.61)	2.35 (1.21)
18. Creation and Abolition of Branch	1.86 (1.08)	3.78 (0.97)	2.04 (1.27)	3.65 (1.14)
19. Selection of Branch Manager	2.24 (1.24)	4.25 (0.87)	1.43 (0.73)	3.03 (1.34)
20. Performance Appraisal of Branch	2.01 (1.11)	4.33 (0.84)	1.40 (0.71)	2.76 (1.33)
21. Creation and Abolition of Subsidiaries	1.87 (1.09)	3.61 (1.00)	2.25 (1.37)	3.80 (1.08)
22. Selection of Subsidiary Manager	2.20 (1.22)	4.04 (1.03)	1.48 (0.82)	3.27 (1.28)
23. Performance Appraisal of Subsidiaries	2.02 (1.12)	4.18 (0.95)	1.42 (0.72)	2.88 (1.35)
24. Election and Dismissal of Chairman of Board of Director	1.68 (0.94)	1.46 (0.76)	3.18 (1.44)	4.18 (1.01)
25. Performance Appraisal of and Remuneration Enjoyed by Board Chairman	1.68 (0.91)	1.49 (0.72)	3.22 (1.46)	3.73 (1.17)
26. Election and Dismissal of Board Members	1.63 (0.88)	1.51 (0.77)	4.43 (0.96)	3.32 (1.03)
27. Performance Appraisal of and Remuneration Enjoyed by Board Members	1.60 (0.80)	1.54 (0.76)	3.64 (1.41)	3.64 (1.12)
28. Election and Dismissal of Board Secretary	1.67 (0.88)	1.85 (1.00)	2.35 (1.36)	4.52 (0.78)
29. Performance Appraisal of and Remuneration Enjoyed by Board Secretary	1.64 (0.90)	2.07 (1.14)	2.02 (1.21)	4.39 (0.94)
30. Selection of Supervisory Committee Members	1.78 (0.93)	1.61 (0.86)	4.31 (1.01)	2.10 (1.08)

APPENDIX C *Continued.*

	Local Party Committees	Managers	Shareholders' Meeting	Board of Directors
31. Performance Appraisal of and Remuneration Enjoyed by Supervisory Committee Members	1.73	1.70	3.66	2.20
	(0.94)	(0.94)	(1.47)	(1.18)
32. Selection and Dismissal of Manager	1.99	1.96	2.15	4.63
	(1.09)	(1.06)	(1.20)	(0.68)
33. Performance Appraisal of and Remuneration Enjoyed by Manager	1.90	2.13	2.01	4.51
	(1.02)	(1.17)	(1.11)	(0.78)
34. Selection and Dismissal of Vice-manager	2.13	3.26	1.83	4.15
	(1.11)	(1.31)	(1.09)	(1.03)
35. Performance Appraisal of and Remuneration Enjoyed by Vice-manager	2.01	3.21	1.73	4.07
	(1.09)	(1.31)	(1.00)	(1.10)
36. Change in Shareholding Structure	1.41	2.26	4.24	3.76
	(0.70)	(1.05)	(1.01)	(0.80)
37. Change in Debt/Equity Ratio	1.36	2.63	3.67	3.93
	(0.65)	(1.12)	(1.39)	(0.76)
38. Dividend Plan	1.31	2.43	4.40	3.90
	(0.63)	(1.05)	(0.99)	(0.63)
39. Share Placement and New Issue	1.33	2.48	4.42	3.87
	(0.66)	(1.03)	(0.95)	(0.68)
40. New Investment in Technology	1.46	3.29	3.38	4.11
	(0.77)	(1.02)	(1.39)	(0.66)
41. New Investment in Infrastructure	1.46	3.23	3.38	4.10
	(0.78)	(1.02)	(1.38)	(0.68)
42. Financial Investment	1.43	3.12	3.18	4.12
	(0.74)	(1.03)	(1.44)	(0.66)
43. Investment in Other Stock Companies	1.42	3.01	3.50	4.12
	(0.73)	(1.07)	(1.35)	(0.69)
44. Sell of Assets	1.48	2.99	3.53	4.04
	(0.90)	(1.10)	(1.36)	(0.72)
45. Loans for Fixed Asset Investment	1.40	3.41	2.54	3.97
	(0.74)	(1.05)	(1.39)	(0.90)
46. Loans for Liquidity Fund	1.37	3.74	2.13	3.58
	(0.72)	(1.13)	(1.25)	(1.11)

APPENDIX C *Continued.*

	Local Party Committees	Managers	Shareholders' Meeting	Board of Directors
47. Loans Through Mortgaging of Asset	1.43 (0.81)	3.09 (1.04)	3.30 (1.48)	4.03 (0.80)
48. Guarantee for Other Enterprises' Large Scale Loans	1.41 (0.77)	2.95 (1.09)	3.32 (1.43)	4.05 (0.79)
49. Amount of External Donation	1.63 (0.92)	3.02 (1.25)	2.59 (1.47)	4.00 (0.92)
50. External Donation Plan	1.66 (0.94)	3.15 (1.26)	2.33 (1.36)	3.61 (1.13)
51. Contracting of Large Scale Construction Project	1.53 (0.83)	3.58 (1.13)	2.14 (1.32)	3.63 (1.15)
52. Merger with Other Enterprises	1.55 (0.84)	3.00 (1.04)	4.07 (1.10)	3.95 (0.58)
53. Being Merged By Other Enterprises	1.65 (1.00)	2.75 (1.05)	4.16 (1.09)	3.83 (0.76)
54. Formulation of Long-term Development Plan	1.76 (0.98)	3.25 (0.98)	3.57 (1.28)	4.18 (0.67)
55. Formulation of Strategic Plan	1.74 (0.96)	3.32 (0.96)	3.18 (1.42)	4.22 (0.74)
56. Establishment of Long-term Relationship with Other Enterprises	1.61 (0.93)	3.69 (1.01)	2.33 (1.31)	3.69 (1.07)
57. Change of Direction, Entry into New Industry and Market	1.68 (0.99)	3.32 (0.97)	3.71 (1.30)	3.98 (0.79)
58. Selection of Accounting (Auditing) Firm	1.36 (0.72)	2.62 (1.20)	3.97 (1.38)	3.88 (0.86)
59. Selection of Law Firm	1.39 (0.76)	2.87 (1.25)	2.90 (1.56)	3.99 (1.09)
60. Selection of Financial Consultant	1.39 (0.78)	3.14 (1.27)	2.40 (1.46)	3.89 (1.08)
61. Selection of Management Consultant	1.45 (0.84)	3.38 (1.28)	2.14 (1.32)	3.84 (1.13)
62. Training and Education for Board Members and Higher Management	1.71 (1.06)	2.99 (1.25)	1.66 (0.92)	4.21 (0.97)

APPENDIX C *Continued.*

	Local Party Committees	Managers	Shareholders' Meeting	Board of Directors
63. Training and Education for Middle Management	1.95 (1.16)	4.30 (0.91)	1.44 (0.76)	2.65 (1.36)
Overall Average Decision-making Power	1.69 (0.28)	3.07 (0.94)	2.63 (1.01)	3.60 (0.74)

- Our sample companies include 143 companies which provide rating on the involvement of various power holders in 50 decisions or above.
- Average score on a five-point scale ranging from no involvement at all (score = 1) to full decision-making power (score = 5)
- Figures in parentheses are standard deviations.

APPENDIX D

Descriptive Statistics of Sample Companies (I)

$SAMPLE_{final}$	Year of IPO	Ratio of Largest Shareholder on Board	Party Involvement
Mean	4.091	0.509	1.693
Standard Error	0.232	0.030	0.075
Median	4.000	0.542	1.492
Mode	3.000	0.571	1.000
Minimum	1.000	0.000	1.000
Maximum	8.000	1.000	4.194

APPENDIX E

Descriptive Statistics of Sample Companies (II)

	$SAMPLE_{final}$
A. Nature of Largest Shareholders	
Number (Percentage) of Non-State Shareholders (SS = 1)	15 (17%)
Number (Percentage) of State Shareholders (NSS = 1)	73 (83%)
B. Market Condition	
Number (Percentage) of Companies Whose Product Prices are Controlled by the Government (PC = 1)	9 (10.2%)
Number (Percentage) of Companies Whose Products Have Close Substitutes (CS = 1)	26 (29.5%)
Number of (Percentage) of Companies with Production Licensing Agreements (PLS = 1)	53 (60%)

THE TRANSFORMATION OF LABOR RELATIONS IN CHINA'S EMERGING MARKET ECONOMY

Doug Guthrie

ABSTRACT

The economic reforms in China have set in motion a process of change that is transforming Chinese society and politics in fundamental ways. Gradual reforms in China often lead critics to argue that little substantive change has actually occurred with respect to labor relations in China. However, the transformation of labor relations in reform-era China has been fundamental and deep, and this transformation plays a crucial role in the "quiet revolution" currently underway in the Chinese economy and in society at large. From the changes in the workplace to the new institutional contexts in which firms are situated, the current position of labor in China marks a radical break from the past. An explanation of these changes must strive to integrate three levels of analysis. First, state level institutional changes, led by reform-minded leaders, have driven this process forward. Second, a rights-based labor regime is emerging in factories through on-the-ground pressure from foreign investors. Third, at the individual level, workers are no longer tied to their workplaces; fluid labor markets, and opportunities elsewhere, afford workers a bargaining power that was previously impossible in China. The emergence of a rule of law society in general provides a context within which changing labor relations in China are situated.

The Future of Market Transition, Volume 19, pages 139–170.

ISBN: 0-7623-0835-4

"Doesn't a work unit have to heed national law? We want an explanation. We are just protecting our rights."

Plaintiff in labor dispute, April 1998[1]

INTRODUCTION

For more than a decade, a quiet revolution has been taking place in the Chinese economy. It is a revolution that is not hidden from China scholars and business leaders, but it is one to which policy makers in the U.S. have been largely oblivious. In China today, workers experience much greater freedom, much more protection from capricious authoritarian rule, and many more avenues for recourse against unfair labor practices. Since the economic reforms began, the Chinese government has been gradually building the scaffolding upon which rational and fair labor practices rest. By the end of the 1980s, Chinese workplaces had begun adopting the types of systems and structures that are most often found in workplaces of advanced capitalist economies. Chinese workers and citizens today experience the greatest sense of freedom since the founding of the PRC. These changes in labor relations have important implications for the emergence of a democratic society in China.

In my past work, I have focused on two forces that have driven these changes forward. The first feature of the Chinese economy upon which I focused is the institutional hierarchy of the former command economy. I have argued that this system has had profound implications for the ways that firms experience the reform era, and I have shown this to be the case empirically across a number of different economic and social indicators. Second, I argued that the role of foreign investment has played a crucial role in the changes sweeping across Chinese firms. Foreign investment and, in particular, joint ventures with large multinational firms have played a fundamental rule in the type of capitalism that is currently emerging in China. While these institutional forces have been crucial for the process of economic reform in China, the problem with this approach is that I have told only a partial story. I have omitted several of the crucial factors that allow us a fuller understanding of these processes of change. Where I have focused on firm level forces of change, a broader understanding of the economic reforms in transforming socialist economies must, at the very least, also account for the activities of elites and the changes in labor markets. In other words, understanding the forces shaping Chinese capitalism must begin with an understanding of the processes that drive market formation and individual level economic behavior.

Concretely, three critical factors are shaping the structure of labor relations in China today. First, state level institutional changes have laid the backdrop against which changing labor relations have emerged in China. From governmental policies propelling the reform of state enterprises to a host of new laws and institutions, reform-minded leaders have set in place the institutional underpinnings of a rational economy, and these changes stand at the center of China's transition from an authoritarian system to one based on rational law. Second, exposure to the international community has helped push forward the emergence of a rights-based labor regime in China. Third, an increasingly fluid and open labor market has meant that workers now hold the most basic form of bargaining power – they have the ability to leave the workplace and find employment elsewhere. While such a right might seem simply inalienable from a Western perspective, this change has been a crucial step in the transformation of labor relations in China. Finally, the emergence of a rule of law society more generally has provided an ethos of legalism, a context in which workers can now place their understanding of the changing labor relations they experience.

THEORY AND PRACTICE

Many economists tell a story of the spontaneous rise of markets and the natural gravitation toward rational, economic efficiency within these newly established markets. Markets in this conception are believed to arise spontaneously as bureaucrats step back from central planning (see, e.g. Sachs, 1993). Taking a page from the modernization theorists of the 1950s, economic advisors from the West have viewed rational, "modern" economies as something that will simply emerge as long as the market's invisible hand is given free reign. "Shock therapy" economists – advocates of rapid reform – have further argued that it is only through an immediate unleashing of market forces that transforming economies can avoid the pitfalls of cronyism and corruption. The logic here is that rational, economic efficiency cannot be engineered by meddlesome authoritarian governments; modern, rational institutions are best left to the sculpting power of the market, which will inevitably push for the most efficient outcome. Advocates of shock therapy have described the goals of institutional change in transforming communist economies in the following way: "The long-run goals of institutional change are clear, and are found in the economic models of existing market-based economies" (Sachs & Woo, 1997, p. 5). Translation: the West has already figured out what institutions work, so enough with the hand-wringing and experimentation among governments that have not followed the shock therapy prescription; these governments need to step back and let the market work its magic.

China presents a conundrum for scholars and practitioners who ascribe to some version of the ideas espoused above. First of all, where economists advocated radical reform, China's strategy has been based on gradual transition from plan to market economy, an approach that has been extremely successful from an economic standpoint.[2] This reality has left some advocates of shock therapy in the odd position of arguing that, despite China's success, the country would have been even more successful if it had followed the shock therapists' prescriptions (Sachs & Woo, 1997), a position that has become even more odd in the face of Russia's economic turmoil. Instead of the path of rapid privatization that has been enacted in such places as Russia and various places in the Eastern Block, China has slowly pushed economic responsibilities onto firms directly, while at the same time it has built the institutional foundations of the market economy. The 1980s were marked with a slow transition away from direct enterprise control and a great deal of experimentation with new laws and institutions that would eventually define China's market economy.

Second, because of the absence of a clear, radical break with the authoritarian past, China is often portrayed as a place in which institutional change has not yet occurred in any substantive way. It is much more common to speak of corruption and the authoritarian nature of the system than about the fact that these gradual reforms have, in many ways, begun the process of constructing a rational economy (see, e.g. Lu, 2000; Shao, 1998; Sik, 1994, 2000; Boist & Child, 1996).[3] Yet, despite the fact that such changes are dismissed if not ignored, China has created the foundations for an economy based on rational-legal principles and individual civil liberties. As the state gradually receded from direct control over enterprises, it left in place a rational economy that will eventually govern the decisions of the economic actors that survive the transition. New laws and new institutions have created the basis for a new conception of labor rights that few scholars of China acknowledge much less explore.

So we are left with two critical issues in the exploration of labor in China's emerging market economy. First there is empirical reality: an analysis of economic reform in China must begin with an acknowledgment of the changes and progress that have actually occurred there. Of course it is still the case that abuses of labor, a curtailing of individual freedoms, and many other violations of human rights still occur in China. However, this is only part of the story; the other part is one in which the government has sought to create a society in which individual civil liberties and a protection of labor sit at its core. Second, there is explanation: understanding the forces driving these changes forward must avoid the simplistic assumptions of efficiency, the invisible hand, and the progress toward modern capitalist markets and instead strive to isolate the institutional forces and actors that are guiding this process of change. More than a simple logic of the freedom to pursue profits, the decisions and practices of managers and entrepreneurs in China are shaped by willful political decisions by the government and the economic models to which Chinese managers and entrepreneurs are exposed. Economic pressures are important in economic decision making, but markets are more than purely economic systems; they are also political and social settings in which economic actors make decisions based upon the social, normative, and political pressures they experience. As state officials and economic actors are exposed to different models of economic structure in the global marketplace – and as they receive different kinds of pressure to adopt new models of economic structure – they implement economic strategies that reflect these pressures. The forces behind the changes occurring in the Chinese economy must be analyzed through this prism. As we observe the emergence of a rational economy in China, we must begin with a social, political, and normative understanding of the origins of these models of economic behavior.

The emergence of a rational economy in China is not based upon an inevitable march toward rational economic action or the result of some inexorable drive of modernization. Instead, economic actors in China are adopting Western models of economic behavior because of normative pressure to take seriously the new laws and institutions emerging from the government; as a way of attracting foreign investment; as a result of the pressure from international organizations, such as the World Trade Organization; and as a result of the changing demographics and the changing structure of labor markets in China. The Chinese government, for its part, is willfully creating a rational economy as an institutional and political project that is shaped by the dominance of neoliberal ideology and the success of market systems in the West. In this framework, modern rational capitalism is not an inevitable outcome of laissez-faire economic systems as neoclassical transition economists have argued. It is the outcome of a power struggle between nations (and between ideological camps within nations) in which capitalist nations and powerful economic actors force these models onto the economic agenda. Modern rational capitalism arrives as the result of particular social and political forces in a particular historical moment. The ideas of this economy are, in cases such as China's, exported overseas to governments and economic actors within developing nations.

One might raise the question here of why it would be that capitalist nations and capitalists themselves would care about exporting rational-legal capitalism to China. Indeed, there are many examples of development around the world in which Western nations and Western capitalists have happily undercut the institutional framework as a way of supporting despotic regimes or of extracting profits through the exploitation of labor. And the Chinese government has hardly been a champion of rational law, at least in the first thirty years of the People's Republic. But the case of China, in this particular phase of development and in this particular moment in the global economy, brings together a different set of dynamics and a different set of principles about development and the transition from socialism to capitalism. The point here is that, while it is empirically true that Chinese firms and the labor relations within them are becoming more rationalized, this is not the inevitable outcome of a march toward modernization or the inevitable outcome of market reforms.

Rather, changing labor relations in China are the unintended consequence of a particular set of power relations that involve large-scale Western capitalists, the Chinese government, and the international agencies organizing the global economy. Because Western capitalists are intent upon conquering the Chinese market – it is simply too large and lucrative to cut off the way we have Cuba – and they are unwilling to wait until China's authoritarian government collapses, pressuring the government to create a rational economy, one in which rational law and contracts are respected, is the next best thing. The Chinese government and Chinese factories, for their part, know that their own survival lies in continued economic development, which in turn, relies heavily on the attraction of powerful investors that will bring with them new technologies. Changing labor relations and more generally the creation of a rational environment within the firm become important markers and signals that Chinese firms can set in place to attract powerful foreign investors and thereby secure their own future.[4] In the sections that follow, I will first lay out some of the fundamental changes occurring in the Chinese economy. There are many other critical changes occurring, but due to space constraints, I limit my discussion to only a few of the critical changes that are transforming labor relations in China. Following that discussion, I will explain the reasons behind these changes.

THE TRANSFORMATION OF LABOR IN CHINA

Under Mao, labor was organized according to authoritarian principles. Workers were subject to the caprice of organizational and Party authorities, and they had little recourse against this system. To the extent that labor relations in market economies are based on "independence, contract, and universalism," labor relations in pre-reform China were based primarily on "dependence, deference, and particularism" (Walder, 1986, p. 10). Walder's study of factories and labor relations in pre-reform China revealed a system organized around political and social relations in the firm, and central to these relations was the notion that workers were dependent upon management and supervisors. If formal rational (or legal rational) systems imply a structure in which the benefits and rights of the worker are defined independent of personal ties, factories in the pre-reform Chinese system were decidedly *in*formal. The relationships between workers and supervisors were personalized, and supervisors had considerable discretion over processes in the workplace.[5] In other words, supervisors within factories made decisions about worker advantages and advancement based on personal relations and personal decisions, unrestrained by formal rules or routinized decision-making systems. This system has changed radically in the reform era. While the transformation is far from complete, the fundamental building blocks for a new set of labor relations have been set in place in China.

Labor Contracts

The transformation of labor relations in China begins with the institutions that are rationalizing these relationships. Labor contracts are the first among several important institutional changes that have transformed labor relations. In Mao's China, under the command economy, employment was guaranteed by the state.[6] Workers were assigned to work units by the Labor Bureau, and from that point on, the work unit was responsible for dispensing income, benefits, and retirement pay for the rest of the worker's life. In different periods, especially in the late 1970s, a small fraction of the population was classified as "waiting for employment" [*diaye*], but for the most part, the state still fulfilled its promise of finding employment for everyone.[7] Although by 1980 state sector jobs had become more competitive than ever before (only 37% of workers were assigned jobs in state enterprises [*guoyou qiye*]), still 80% of workers were assigned jobs in either state enterprises or collectively-owned enterprises [*jiti qiye*] in that year (Walder, 1986, pp. 57, 68–74). Once jobs were assigned, except for in rare cases of disciplinary firing and even rarer cases of layoffs (which were often followed by reassignment to another enterprise), the job assignment was for life. This is not to say that workers never changed jobs or resigned from a given enterprise, but once workers were assigned to a work unit, except in exceptional circumstances, they had the option of staying at that organization for life.

The emergence of labor contracts in China marks an important turning point for the socialist system created under Mao. Labor contracts began a new system in which enterprises are only responsible to workers for as long as the contract specifies. If the enterprise and individual sign a one-, three-, or five-year contract, the enterprise is only responsible for the worker for one, three, or five years and is under no obligation to renew the contract at the end of this period. At the end of a contract period, the enterprise has no obligation to continue to pay income or benefits to the worker. One manager in the chemicals sector explained the gravity of this change saying,

> The labor situation has changed tremendously over the last few years. . . . I think that probably the most significant change is that we have everyone on labor contracts now. Now if workers violate the terms of their contracts, they can be fired. . . . We've never had this type of labor relationship before (Personal interview, Shanghai, 1995; originally reported in Guthrie [1999]).[8]

The labor contract was officially introduced in 1986 with Document No. 77 and Decree No. 99, both promulgated by the State Council.[9] These documents explicitly define three types of contracts: the fixed limited term contract [*guding qixian laodong hetong*], the non-fixed limited term contract [*wuguding qixian laodong hetong*], and the per-project work limited term contract [*yixiang gongzuo wei qixian laodong hetong*]. Although these institutional arrangements officially emerged in 1986, experimentation with labor contracts dates back as early as 1983, as defined by the 1983 State Council Notice for Trial Implementation (PRC, 1983). Following the 1986 documents, the legitimacy of the labor contract was further enhanced by the Enterprise Law (PRC, 1988, Ch. 3, Art. 31), which states that, "The enterprise shall have the right to employ or dismiss its staff members and workers in accordance with the provisions of the State Council." Though such a statement does not sound radical as far as enterprise rights go in market economies, in fact, turning the rights of hiring and dismissing of workers over to the enterprise was extremely radical in the context of China's recent institutional history. Other institutional changes, such as the establishment of the unemployment and social security funds, set up to protect workers in the event that their organization would let them go, have also given legitimacy to the use of labor contracts (Naughton, 1995, pp. 210–212).

In 1984, 1.8% of the labor force or 2,090,000 individuals were on labor contracts.[10] By 1994, about 26% of the labor force or 38,390,000 individuals were on labor contracts. By sector, the labor contract has been most readily adopted in manufacturing, where 41% of workers were on labor contracts in 1994.[11] While I have argued elsewhere (see Guthrie, 1998, 1999) that labor contracts are adopted by managers and factories as a way of protecting themselves from the economic duress of supporting a labor force with lifetime employment – in other words, they are adopted to end lifetime employment and therefore not in the interests of workers – there are positive unintended consequences of this transformation for the rights of workers. This is a common theme that will come through in many of the transformations occurring with regard to labor in China: while a series of changes have been adopted for a variety of reasons, there are positive unintended consequences for the emergence of a rational economy in general and the rights of the worker specifically. Despite the fact that factories have adopted labor contracts as a cost-cutting measure, they have rationalized the labor relationship in fundamental ways. These contracts provide workers with an institutional basis upon which employment relations are defined. They lay out the terms of the labor relationship, forcing workers and managers to acknowledge that labor relations have taken on a formal, rationalized, contractual quality. If workers want to file grievances for their treatment in the firm, they can rely on a formal document to present their case. In the past, the rules of the workplace were defined solely on the caprice of authoritarian rule; today, they are increasingly based upon previously agreed upon terms that are depicted in a formal document.

Transformation of the Firm

Another way that labor relations have been transformed in fundamental ways lies in the transformation of the workplace itself. Since the late 1980s, Chinese factories have been experimenting with a number of formal institutions in the workplace that rationalize the labor relationship in crucial ways. Little systematic work has been done on this phenomenon to capture the true breadth of these changes. However, in my own research on the topic, I found that these changes were indeed widespread.

As Table 1 shows, more than 60% of workplaces in industrial Shanghai have adopted formal organizational rules, formal grievance filing procedures, and formal pay scales. More than 8% have institutionalized Worker Representative Committee Meetings, which many workers and managers informally refer to as

Table 1. Percentage of Workplaces in Shanghai's Industrial Economy that have Adopted Various Institutional Changes.

Formal organizational rules	64%
Formal job descriptions	57%
Formal grievance filing procedures	64%
Mediation institution in firm	56%
Institutionalized WRC meetings	85%
Promotion test	28%
Pay scale	64%
Formal hiring procedures	27%

Source: Guthrie (1999, Ch. 3).

"our own [factory's] democratic institutions" [*women zijide minzhu zhidu*] (personal interviews, Shanghai, 1995, 1996). More than 50% of workplaces in Shanghai's industrial economy have institutionalized formal job descriptions and mediation institutions within the firm. The emergence of some of these changes is remarkable, given that many of these formalized institutions only emerged in American firms in the 1970s (Dobbin et al., 1993; Sutton et al., 1994).

Other Institutional Changes: The Labor Law and Labor Arbitration

Beyond the emergence of a rationalized and formalized labor relationship within the firm, other formal institutions have emerged to create an environment outside the firm that further rationalizes the labor relationship. The Labor Law (PRC, 1994) and the Labor Arbitration Commissions are two governance structures that have had the largest influence on firms' institutional environments and, by extension, the internal practices firms adopt in the period of economic reform. For example, Chapter Ten of the Labor Law, entitled "Labor Disputes," is specifically devoted to describing the process laborers are legally entitled to follow should a dispute arise in the workplace. The law explains in an explicit fashion the rights of the worker to take disputes to outside arbitration (the district's Labor Arbitration Commission) should she or he be unsatisfied with the manner in which grievances are being handled within the organization. These institutional shifts have exerted pressure on organizations to alter their internal structures, much as changing institutional environments in the 1960s in the United States forced U.S. organizations to alter their internal structures by experimenting with job ladders, employment tests, job descriptions, and the like (Dobbin et al., 1993).

The Labor Arbitration Commission (LAC) is an institution under the jurisdiction of the Labor Bureau. There is a LAC in each urban district and county. The emergence of the institution of labor arbitration in China is directly related to the issues of the economic transition and the emergence of a market economy. An official in the Labor Bureau, who now oversees the Labor Dispute Office in Shanghai's Labor Bureau, explained this relationship in the following way:

> The need for arbitration in China grew as we moved away from the planned economy. In the planned economy, everything was fixed and decided by the government. No one could be fired from his/her job, and everyone was secure. In the early 1980s we started to move into a market economy. With this came the labor system reform [*laodong zhidu gaige*] . . . At the same time as we were introducing contracts that allowed factories to only hire workers for a fixed amount of time, we realized that the labor relationship would become much more complicated with this change. We realized we would need a way to settle labor

disputes. So also in 1987 we formed the first Labor Arbitration Commission (Personal interview, Shanghai, 1995; originally reported in Guthrie [1999]).

The emergence of the LAC is grounded in a number of legal and institutional changes of the period of reform. The document that first defined these changes was the State-Owned Enterprises Labor Dispute Resolution Temporary Rules [*guoying qiye laodong zhengyi chuli zhanxing guiding*], which was adopted by the State Council in 1987. While this document dealt only with dispute resolution in state-owned organizations, the 1993 People's Republic of China Labor Dispute Resolution Regulations [*zhonghua renmin gongheguo qiye laodong zhengyi chuyi tiaoli*] expanded the rules to include all types of labor relationships. Later, the Labor Law solidified the role of the local Labor Arbitration Commissions as an institution for labor dispute resolution, as Chapter Ten of the Labor Law is devoted exclusively to labor disputes and the use of these local institutions. Finally, the Arbitration Law (PRC, 1995) established the practice of arbitration as a formally supported legal structure in the governance of labor relations in China's economic transition.[12]

Within the Arbitration Commission, there are two sections: there is the arbitration court [*zhongcaiyuan*], and there is the labor section [*zhuanzi laodong bumen*], which primarily takes care of labor disputes. One group within the labor section is made up of volunteer workers, while the other group is ruled by the presiding official. The volunteer system is dependent upon participation of workers (i.e. they are not paid). Basically the labor union at each organization submits names of individuals to occupy this position, and the LAC chooses from this list of names.[13] Three groups are represented in the labor arbitration process: the government is represented by the Labor Bureau [*laodongju*], the organization is represented by the Economic Commission [*jingji weiyuanhui*] in the Central Economic Administrative Unit [*zhonghe jingji guanli bumen*], and the worker is represented by the organization's Labor Union [*gonghui*].[14] This governmental unit actually only represents state-owned organizations; if the dispute is with a private company, a separate governmental department represents the organization.

There are basically three types of problems that go through the LAC. The first relates to disagreements over contractual issues surrounding firing [*kaichu*] or quitting [*cizi*]. The second type of dispute relates to salaries, insurance, and benefits. The third type of problem relates to vacation days and work leave. These three kinds of problems are each handled by three different sections in the Commission. The greatest problem area for applications to the LAC is contractual disputes [*hetong zhengyi*], which comprised over 50% of the applications to Shanghai's LACs as of 1995. Most often, the problem is that people have signed contracts and the work unit is not adhering to the terms of the contract; these cases are usually decided in favor of the workers.[15] The state has created this system, in conjunction with the Labor Law, as an institutional structure to help facilitate due process in the workplace. One official in the Labor Bureau explained the goal of this system, saying: "Our main focus in creating this system is to build a system of legal structures [*jiancheng falu zhidu*] that will make all labor relationships the same. If there is a problem we want all resolutions to be simple and straightforward" (Personal interview, Shanghai, 1995).

Thus, between the Labor Law, the Labor Arbitration Commissions, and the institutional changes within the workplace, an infrastructure is now in place to institutionally protect workers from the whim of authoritarian rule. Do these institutional changes matter? That is a more difficult question to answer. However, over the course of the 1990s, cases brought before courts and arbitration boards have been steadily on the rise. In 1999, more than 115,000 cases were brought before Labor Arbitration Commissions throughout the country. Of these, workers won more than half outright, while only about 10% were decided fully in favor of the firm (about one-third of the cases were partially decided in favor of both parties). Table 2 shows the breakdown of these cases for 1999 by organizational type and by outcome. Firms owned and run by overseas Chinese have the highest number of disputes and the greatest number of cases won by laborers. Following in descending order are: state-owned enterprises, urban collectives, private firms, rural collectives, joint ventures, and government organizations.

Despite the gradual nature of their emergence in Chinese society, these changes mark a radical break from the past. From the national level institutional changes that have redefined workers' rights to the institutional changes that have rationalized labor relations within the firm, Chinese workers have more access to rational institutions and rational law than ever before. As important as the empirical reality of these changes, however, is an understanding of the forces driving this process of change. As mentioned above, if it is true that Chinese workers are experiencing a rationalized economic system, it is an anomaly for developing economies in general and for authoritarian societies in particular. What particular circumstances in the Chinese case have led to the emergence of a rational economy there?

EXPLAINING THESE CHANGES

Market transition in China has been informed by a particular dynamic that amounts to a struggle between a government that wants to stay in power and an

Table 2. Labor Disputes by Outcome and Organizational Type.

	Totals	SOE	Urban coll.	Rural	Overseas Chinese*	Private	JV	Govt	Other
Won by Firm	15,674	4,836	3,028	1,972	2,013	876	1,046	335	1,379
Won by Laborer	63,030	12,742	9,613	5,156	16,317	8,411	3,411	1,014	5,018
Partial victory	37,549	7,560	4,867	2,685	9,313	4,235	1,904	777	5,469
Totals	116,253	25,138	17,508	9,813	27,643	13,522	6,361	2,126	11,866
Percent won by workers	54%	48%	53%	52%	59%	62%	53%	47%	42%

Source: *Zhongguo Tongji Nianjian* [*Statistical Yearbook of China*], 2000, pp. 750–751.

* Taiwan and Hong Kong-owned firms depicted in this category.

international community that wants access to that mythical market of a billion consumers. The Chinese government has resisted rapid economic and political change. The Communist Party made it resoundingly and brutally clear in 1989 that it would not undertake the path of rapid political and economic reform. Instead the government has maintained political control – at least to the extent that China is still a one-party system – while gradually reforming the economy. Why, then, do the proponents of the international economy not simply write China off the way it has Cuba and North Korea? The answer here is that there is simply too much to gain in China; the prospect of gaining access to the internal market there is too enticing to ignore. So the U.S. government and Western capitalists find themselves in a position of wanting to invest in this gradually transforming economy but at the same time forced to deal with an authoritarian government that, at least when the economic reforms began, was unpredictable at best. The Chinese government, for its part, recognizes the importance of Western capitalists and international markets on at least two levels. First, since the economic reforms began, the architects recognized the need for a "modern" rational economy. From Zhao Ziyang to Zhu Rongji, the leaders of this reform have clearly focused on the creation of rational accountability and the embracing of international standards. Indeed the "modern enterprise system" and all of the accounting practices that stand behind it are based upon international models and standards of firm management. Second, the government and enterprises themselves recognize the need for foreign capital and technology. The desire to attract foreign investment and technology leads to institutional accommodations that support the role of contracts, legal-rational accountability, and the rule of law within the firm. The rationalization of labor relations is an unintended consequences of this larger dynamic.

As we examine the changes behind the transformation of labor in China, our focus will be on three critical factors. First, contrary to representations of the Chinese government as an unchanging, unresponsive, authoritarian government, China's leaders have aggressively enacted state-level institutional changes that have formed the basis of the rationalized economy emerging in China. Second, pressure from international organizations and Western investors have led to a rationalized economy both at the state level but also within firms. Third, changing labor markets and changing opportunities have transformed the bargaining power of workers in the economy. All these factors have come together to facilitate the emergence of a rule-of-law ethos in China, which has changed the extent to which workers approach the issue of rights. We will explore each of these changes in greater depth below.

Transformation from Above: The Heavy Hand of the State

Economic reform in China has been a state-driven process, as the architects of the reform have aggressively led this transition. Despite the fact that markets have steadily emerged in China, the gradual creation of the new institutions of the market, the experimentation with these institutions and their measured, steady implementation in the reform-era economy, has been a process that has emerged from elite ideologies and reform-minded leaders. At the center of their strategies has been the gradual freeing of firms from reliance on the planned economy system and the implementation of a rational economy. Zhu Rongji and Zhao Ziyang before him have been fundamentally focused on the creation of a rational economy in China, one that operates by independent, transparent accounting systems, one that respects formal rational laws and contracts. However, where Zhao's goal was to help newly autonomous enterprises survive in the face of economic uncertainty, Zhu's goal has been to create a stable investment environment that will help further integrate China into the global economy. Zhu knows all too well that China's only hope for integrating into the global economy lies in the creation of an institutional framework that will put corporate investors from advanced capitalist nations at ease. For with these corporate investors comes much needed technology, and critical technology transfer is now, more than ever, a central part of China's transition plan.

In the early years, the institutional changes were about experimentation with new forms of enterprise management, the creation of a rational economy at the firm level, and the weaning of firms from the purse strings of the state. However, if the 1980s was defined by the creation of a rational economy, the 1990s has been defined by the creation of the laws that will govern this society for years to come. Since the economic reforms began, the National People's Congress has passed over 700 new laws, and local people's congresses have passed an additional 2–3,000. An estimated half of these laws are directly tied to the creation of a rational economy. The Company Law, the Bankruptcy Law, and the Joint Venture Law are the most famous among these, but there are many more laws and resolutions that have reshaped the economy in fundamental ways. Several of these laws have had fundamental consequences for labor relations in the economy. The important point here is that, despite the depictions of a stolid, unresponsive and unreformed government in China, the last two decades of reform have, on the contrary, been marked by an activist approach to economic and social reform, one which brought about many new economic practices inside the firm and many new laws to govern the economy in which these firms were embedded.

Western Systems in Chinese Companies

While an activist state has been crucial in setting the institutional framework of changing labor relations in place, equally important are the face-to-face negotiations in the marketplace with the very economic actors the government seeks to attract, as Western investors pressure Chinese firms to take seriously the institutional changes the government has set in place. These negotiations play out differently in the "old" and "new" economies, but they play a central role in the ways these economies are taking shape. The transformation of Chinese factories has been dramatic, and policy makers in debates over trade with China often ignore the radical changes occurring in this sector of the economy. Policy makers focus almost exclusively on issues such as regime type and treatment of political dissidents, but meanwhile a "quiet revolution from within"[16] has been occurring in the Chinese workplace. As I described above, a process of rationalization is occurring in the Chinese workplace, where Chinese companies are adopting a number of the rational bureaucratic systems that are most often found in Western organizations, such as grievance filing procedures, mediation committees, formal organizational rules and guidelines, and many others. It is striking to see these kinds of changes in Chinese factories, given that this type of legalization within the workplace only occurred in American firms as recently as the 1970s.[17]

Foreign investment, and more importantly, joint venture relationships play a crucial role in this process of change. In my own study of Shanghai's industrial economy, I showed that joint venture relationships have a statistically significant and consistent effect on the organizational decisions and practices Chinese factories (Guthrie, 1999). This relationship amounts to a significant positive effect of foreign joint ventures pushing their partner organizations to adopt stable rational-legal structures and systems in their organizations. In other words, it is not only joint venture firms that are different than classical, old-style Chinese factories, but the Chinese parent companies in these joint venture relationships are also changing as a result of the joint venture negotiations. While these stable, rational-legal systems are adopted more often to attract foreign investors than they are for the good of workers, they nevertheless have radical implications for the structure of authority relations and therefore for the lives of individual Chinese citizens.

Chinese factories that have formal relationships with foreign firms are significantly more likely to have formal organizational rules, they are almost 20 times more likely to have formal grievance filing procedures, they are more likely to have worker representative committee meetings and formal hiring procedures. They pay significantly higher wages (about 50% higher), and they are more likely to adopt China's new Company Law, which binds them to the norms of the international community. Those with Western partners are significantly more likely to have arbitration clauses in their joint venture contracts, which subject them to the authority of international legal institutions such as the Chinese International Economic Arbitration and Trade Commission. I have had many conversations with managers in which they openly acknowledge that the changes they have set in place have little to do with their own ideas of efficient business practices and much more to do with pressure brought on them by their foreign partners.

Human rights advocates, as well as others who are knowledgeable about the alliance between capitalists and repressive regimes in developing countries often remain skeptical of these developments within China. However, the Chinese case is different than most circumstances of labor exploitation in the developing world – at least with regard to Western investors, which tend to bring large-scale, high profile investment projects to China. It is rarely the case that corporations are the leading advocates of civil liberties and labor reform, but they push for these reforms in China for a couple of reasons. Because many foreign investors in China are often more interested in long-term investments to capture market share than they are in cheap labor, they generally seek Chinese partners that are predictable, stable, and knowledgeable about Western-style business practices and negotiations. They want partners who will understand the issues at stake in contractual law and arbitration clauses. In short, they seek partners that have familiarity with Western laws, institutions, and negotiations.

Chinese factories, for their part, want desperately to land these partnerships, and they position themselves as suitable investment partners by adopting a number of the practices that Western partners will recognize as stable, reform-minded business practices. Among the basic reforms they adopt to show their fitness for partnerships the international corporations are labor reforms, as they are often the most visible internal structural changes Chinese factories can make. Thus, Chinese companies signal a commitment to stable Western-style business practices through making a visible commitment to labor reform. Foreign investors and Chinese firms are not interested in human rights per se, but the negotiations in the marketplace lead to transformed workplaces, which affect millions of Chinese citizens on a daily basis. As one general manager of a large industrial factory in Shanghai put it,

> [These practices are] very important part of the economic reforms happening in China. . . . It's a way of linking up with the international world [*yizhong guoji jiegui*]. If a foreign company comes to China and wants to invest, who are they going to look for? They are going to look for the organizations with the most progressive and most Western ways of management and organization. . . . It's a way of acting the way the foreign companies act,

so they will see what kind of organization we are (Personal interview, Shanghai, 1995; originally reported in Guthrie [1999]).

The implication here is that Chinese factories are not simply adopting the practices that are most efficient in the market; rather, they are imitating the models of economic practice that are most respected and admired in the marketplace as a way of attracting foreign investment.

With joint ventures, the stakes are often very high, so the pressure from foreign investors for a rationalization of economic processes is not surprising. However, the new legal institutions are also touching the piece-rate economy, as Western businesses seek to avoid public relations debacles, such as Nike, Adidas, and The Gap have experienced. One senior manager of an American garments company, who spends much of his time inspecting the labor and human rights situations in the factories he uses, explained to me:

> We're not trying to make [managers of Chinese companies] do anything that they don't already have on the books over here. We just want them to follow the laws that the Chinese government has already set up. The fact is, the Chinese government has set in place a good number of laws and institutions that protect the interests of workers . . . We think we can play a positive role by emphasizing the importance of these laws. If we don't like the way they're running things, we can take our business elsewhere. They need the business, so they're generally pretty cooperative. . . . Believe me, we have our own interest in this. The last thing we want is the public relations disaster of allegations that our products are manufactured by a factory that violates human rights. It's just best for everyone that we do these visits (Personal interview, Shanghai, 1995; originally reported in Guthrie [1999]).

Even within China's emerging New Economy, which is much younger and much more fluid than the industrial economy, while the players are different than in the industrial economy, the basic issues are the same. For example, in the industrial economy, where we see powerful industrial giants from the West working to shape Chinese markets in their images, in the New Economy, companies like Chinadotcom, Eachnet, and Sina.com have a great deal invested in creating a market that is viable for the virtual economy – one that makes foreign investors feel secure. And where investment banks have played critical roles in helping to finance major projects in the industrial sector – like the IPO of Petro-China – in the New Economy, the important players are as likely to be the venture capitalists who are setting up incubators to help in the development of a high tech economy in China. Nevertheless, despite the differences in who the players are, the themes to bring capitalism to China from the players who are most powerful in the international economy are ever present in the emergence of these new Chinese markets.

New Labor Markets and New Freedom

Workers in China today are also exposed to changing labor markets and a greater autonomy within these markets than ever before. In the planned economy, workers were placed in jobs by the Labor Bureau. This fact, combined with the reality of lifetime employment, meant that there was very little movement in the labor market. Workers had few options for new employment and therefore no bargaining power in the labor market. Further, with the state controlling the allocation of jobs, there were significant incentives against the dissention and for the cultivation of relationships with Party officials and managers of state enterprises.[18] But over the course of the economic reforms, these incentives keeping workers beholden to the state have withered away. Andrew Walder's (1994) essay articulating an institutional theory of regime change in transforming communist societies is relevant for the discussion here. Attempting to explain the groundswell of movement activity that emerged, seemingly suddenly, in 1989, Walder points out that, while the emergence of civil societies, public spheres, economic grievances, and political instability may have contributed to movement activity in communist societies in the late-1980s, these phenomena were nothing new to these societies. And while these elements were important for the groundswell of support for movement activities in these societies, deeper, more fundamental changes were occurring that made these movement activities possible in the first place. As Walder (1994, p. 298) puts it,

> [A] theory of political order is a necessary starting point for any theory of change. There must have been institutional mechanisms that served to maintain order in the old regime in spite of longstanding and obvious economic problems and political liabilities; and these institutions must have been eroded in ways we do not yet understand. The current emphasis upon the triumph of 'society' over 'the state' tends to obscure the logically prior question of how such a triumph, if it is that, could occur . . . [W]hat changed in these regimes in the last decade was not their economic difficulties, widespread cynicism, or corruption, but that the institutional mechanisms that served to promote order in the past – despite these longstanding problems – lost their capacity to do so.

Economic grievances and political struggles have played longstanding roles in communist societies, and they therefore cannot be viewed as causal agents in unprecedented movement activity or social change. The point here is that an analysis of regime change must begin with the underlying mechanisms that kept these regimes stable and, as they changed, that eventually allowed for large-scale social upheavals.

Walder goes on to specify the mechanisms that were crucial for maintaining order in communist societies as: (1) hierarchically organized and grass-roots mobility of the Communist Party; and (2) the organized dependence of individuals within social institutions, particularly workplaces. With the beginning of the economic reforms in China, both of these institutional bases of power began to erode. In the first case – the decline of Party power – there are two ways this change had fundamental implications for the organization of Chinese society. First, the Party no longer had strict control over its own agents. Party cadres operated with an autonomy that increasingly grew in scope throughout the 1980s. This was, in large part, a direct consequence of the movement away from central planning of the command economy. As the reforms progressed, the new economic policies of the 1980s essentially mandated that local-level bureaucrats assume administrative and economic responsibilities for the firms under their jurisdictions (Walder, 1995; Guthrie, 1997, 1999). As administrative and economic responsibilities were pushed down the hierarchy of the former command economy, local-level bureaucrats exercised more and more power in the struggle to control resources and survive in the markets of China's transforming economy. In many cases, local-level bureaucrats abused this new autonomy, leading to the corruption that was one of the central problems in what has been called the crisis of succession in the late 1980s (Calhoun, 1995). Thus, the institutional changes of the reform economy led to the decline of central Party control over its own members.

Second, and perhaps more importantly, the Party no longer exercises grassroots control over individual citizens. In pre-reform China, the Party meticulously exercised grassroots control through local Party meetings, usually conducted through an individual's work unit or neighborhood association (Walder, 1986; Whyte & Parish, 1984). In the reform era, this centrally mandated practice eroded quickly. Managers and administrators no longer required their workers to attend meetings for the dissemination of Party ideology. This change is closely related to the institutional changes of the economic transition described above: as economic imperatives replaced strict compliance with detailed directives of the Party and the command economy, managers and administrators began to run their organizations less around the dissemination of Party ideology and more around the ideals of performance. Dingxin Zhao (1997) makes a similar point in his study of the 1989 Chinese movement. Arguing that it is problematic to place causal primacy on China's nascent civil society, Zhao, like Walder, pushes the analysis to the underlying mechanisms that allowed a civil society to emerge in the first place: the declining control of the Party on university campuses, as well as in the workplace.[19] Zhao (1997, p. 161) argues that "the political control system in Chinese universities was greatly weakened between the mid- and late eighties. This weakening had changed patterns of student interaction and the nature of the control system itself; in turn, it facilitated the rise of the the 1989 [movement]."[20]

In addition to the declining role of the Party on university campuses, one of the major mechanisms weakening the sanctioning power of the Party was the rise of alternative paths to status attainment, which came with an expanding economic sphere (Zhao, 1997; Walder, 1994). Under the command economy, when students entering the labor market and were assigned jobs by their municipality's Labor Bureau, the system was highly political, and the most prestigious jobs were jobs in the Party-State bureaucracy or in state-owned enterprises. Thus, the Party not only had a highly functioning monitoring system on university campuses, but the incentives against rebellion were very strong: consequences were nothing less than a blocked career path for life, regardless of a student's academic performance. With the economic reforms came alternative paths to status attainment. The growth of the private, foreign, and joint-venture economies, as well as the growth of the service sector economy, have afforded workers many options for employment. The implications of this shift are that workers have greater bargaining power within their own workplaces. Ultimately, the increasingly autonomous labor markets mean that workers can vote with their feet, as it were, if they do not approve of the way they are being treated in their workplace. Table 3 shows the changes in the labor market for the availability in different sectors of the economy. While the relative size of these labor markets are not large (except for the growth of the service sector economy, which is quite significant), they do provide significant outlets for workers to seek employment elsewhere. But more important than whether there are jobs in these emerging sectors is the fact that they exist and that workers are no longer tied to their workplaces with no options elsewhere.

The Rule of Law

The specific changes in labor relations should be viewed in the context of a wider movement toward the rule of law in Chinese society. The last decade has seen amazing changes in this area. In the Spring of 1999, several relatives of students who were killed in the early hours of June 4, 1989, decided to sue the government for the slaughter of their children. They invoked two relatively new laws, the Administrative Litigation Act, passed in 1990, and the National Compensation Law, passed in 1995, which effectively allows Chinese citizens to sue the government for compensation for restitution for past wrongs. Passage of this law seemed to occur as a matter of course, as the National People's Congress passed many rights-based legal institutions in the mid-1990s in

Table 3. Changes in Labor Markets: Percent Employed in Each Category.

	Primary	Secondary	Tertiary	SOE	Collectives	Private	Overseas Chinese*	Other Foreign	Self-employed
1978	70.7	17.6	11.7	17.5	5	–	–	–	
1980	68.9	18.5	12.6	19	5.7	–	–	–	0.1
1985	62.5	21.1	16.4	18	6.6	–	–	–	0.5
1990	60	21.4	18.6	16.1	5.5	0.1	0.1	0.1	1
1995	52.2	23	24.8	16.6	4.6	0.7	0.4	0.4	2.3
1997	49.9	23.7	26.4	15.8	4	1.1	0.4	0.4	2.7
1998	49.8	23.5	26.7	12.9	2.7	1.4	0.4	0.4	3.3
1999	50.1	23	26.9	12.3	2.4	1.5	0.4	0.4	3.4

Source: *Zhongguo Tongji Nianjian* [*Statistical Yearbook of China*], 2000, pp. 118–119.

* Taiwan and Hong Kong-owned firms depicted in this category.

China, including a Labor Law, a Prison Reform Law, and many others. Yet, while the government may not have anticipated such an employment of these laws, the event marked a dramatic step forward in the evolution toward a rational legal system in which the government is held accountable for its actions just the same as individual citizens are. In 1989, the participants in the Tiananmen movement were operating completely outside of the institutional system they were criticizing; they were branded "counter-revolutionaries," "hooligans" and enemies of the state. A decade later, their relatives are employing the legal system to criticize the state for its actions.

These events are important for two reasons. First, it is important to understand the extent to which this society is indeed evolving in a dramatic fashion, despite the fact that the evolution instead of revolution make changes seem all too slow to come about. That individuals can now sue the government for past wrongs stands in stark contrast to the society that existed even a decade ago. Second, the creation of a predictable, rational legal system has been a central part of the Chinese government's path toward the creation of a market economy; it has been a necessary part of China's transition to a global market economy. A number of scholars have argued that the construction of a rational legal system to ensure market transactions that match the standards of the international community is a necessary precondition to participation in the global economy. It is possible to have an economic system that is not based on rational-legal principles – for example, an economy could be based on social ties and particularistic relations – but this type of economy is unlikely to attract significant amounts of foreign capital, as investors from overseas will be at a disadvantage in this type of market. Yet, a market still requires enforcement mechanisms for meting out justice, and if cultural norms and social ties cannot serve this function, other institutional standards must form the basis for the governance of the market. In the mid 1990s, the National People's Congress adopted a certain urgency with respect to legal reforms, affirming that legal reform would be the backbone for a stable and regulated marketplace. As Pei (1995, p. 68) puts it, the rule of law is "the institutional foundation of a market economy and a constitutional government," and China is hurtling headlong toward this type of institutional system.

In the two decades since the economic reforms began, the National People's Congress has written and passed literally hundreds of new laws, resolutions, and policies that gradually move the country away from the governance of capricious leaders and toward a rational-legal system in which newly defined laws and market institutions govern society. New laws such as the National Compensation Law and the Labor Law (1994), which rationalizes the labor relationship in significant ways, fundamentally change the structure of Chinese society, at least on an official level. These laws and many others have dramatically transformed the institutions and rules that define labor relations and economic transactions in China's reforming economy. With regard to the Administrative Litigation Act, the case of the Tiananmen suit is only the highest profile example of a trend that is actually quite common in China today: with the passage of the Administrative Litigation Act in 1990 came a rush of suits against the government – about 25,000 per year. Perhaps more amazing is that the courts ruled with the plaintiffs in about 28% of the cases (Pei, 1995). Also in line with the high profile Tiananmen case, there have been many cases in which political dissidents have filed suit against the government for violation of their constitutional rights.

We might ask, at this point, whether the creation of all these new laws and institutional frameworks is having any impact on the way society is actually governed. Indeed, it could very well be the case that while these new laws and institutions exist on paper, they have little impact in practice. Table 4 shows evidence of the Rule of Law in everyday governance in a number of different spheres. At this point, China only has one-tenth the number of lawyers that we have in the United States, however, for the number of professionals in this field to have tripled over the course of a decade suggests dramatic growth in the litigiousness of this changing society. The number of cases brought before the Chinese legal system has increased by about seven-fold over two decades of economic reform. Most remarkable, is the emergence and dramatic rise of economic and administrative cases: in the pre-reform era, these two spheres were simply not subject to law in any way, yet they have emerged as central features of the Chinese legal system in the reform era.

The rule of law, which many of scholars of the transition to capitalism have argued is a centerpiece of the transition to a market economy, is also the foundation of a rights-based society and the gradual transformation of an authoritarian political system. The Chinese government has institutionalized so many new laws – laws that govern the economy and extend to the level of individual civil rights – that it is obviously far down the road toward the creation of a rule of law society. Skeptics might still argue that, in China, change has not come quickly enough, that the laws are a formal shell, more symbolic than substantive, or that the only true marker of political reform is a dismantling of the authoritarian one-party system itself. To some extent, this view is right: there have been many accounts of the ways that new laws have been ignored or openly defied in practice, and, although the Rule of Law is often bandied about as evidence of true change, constitutional rights can still be overthrown at the Party's whim. However, deeming this infant system a failure also places unrealistic expectations about the process of institutional change in

Table 4. Evidence of the Rule of Law in China.

No. of Lawyers	No. of First Trial Cases	Criminal	Civil	Economic	Administrative	
1980	NA	763,535	197,865	565,679	NA	NA
1985	34,379	1,319,741	246,655	846,391	225,541	916
1990	90,602	2,916,774	459,656	1,851,897	591,462	13,006
1995	NA	4,545,676	495,741	2,718,533	1,275,959	52,596
1996	100,198	5,312,580	618,826	3,093,995	1,515,848	79,966
1997	98,902	5,288,379	436,894	3,277,572	1,478,822	90,557
1998	101,220	5,410,798	482,164	3,375,069	1,450,049	98,350
1999	111,433	5,692,434	540,008	3,519,244	1,529,877	97,569

Source: *Zhongguo Tongji Nianjian* [*Statistical Yearbook of China*], 1999, 2000.

China – which is necessarily a gradual process – especially given that this country was devoid of such formal institutions when the economic reforms began. In addition to the construction of new legal institutions it is also necessary for norms, legal cultures, and general public awareness to follow these changes. These norms and cultures are being built in China gradually and over time, and they have significant implications for the rights of the population in general and for workers specifically.

CONCLUSIONS

The changes in China, over the course of the last two decades have been dramatic and deep, and these are changes that extend beyond the economy into the realm of labor relations and society in general. There are three central implications to the changes discussed above. First, while economists want to imagine that economic actors simply gravitate toward the type of economic practices that are the most efficient in the face of market constraints, the reality is that the shape of a market is the result of a variety of pressures, and efficiency is only one of them. Also important are the types of economic leverage that are brought to bear in the negotiations of the marketplace and the political actors shaping these institutions. Powerful actors in the marketplace often push Chinese companies to take seriously the very institutions that the Chinese government has set in place to govern the market. Second, because of the uncertainties in the Chinese legal system itself – and the uncertainties of investing in a country that is ruled by an authoritarian government – economic negotiations in China have a more positive outcome for workers than is often the case in overseas investment. Corporations push for stability and commitments to Western institutions – including labor laws – as a way of ensuring that their partners understand the workings of the global economy. In 1998, the United States surpassed Japan as the largest foreign investor in China both in terms of capital and number of ventures. It is crucial that we understand the implications of the U.S. presence there. Corporations must always be monitored, just as repressive governments must, but in the Chinese case, the pressure to adopt Western-style economic systems is overwhelmingly positive for the legalization and rationalization of Chinese labor practices. Labor relations are being transformed in fundamental ways in China, and an activist government, self-interested foreign investors, an open labor market, and the emergence of a rule-of-law society in general are all behind these changes.

Third, an institutional framework has emerged that allows workers to seek rational-legal protection from capricious authority. The fact that workers can file grievances against employers in an institutional context separate from the firm is a radical departure from the employment relations of the past. Some concerns still exist in this realm. Namely, Labor Arbitration Commissions are institutions of a still-authoritarian government, a fact that may reduce our confidence in the extent to which these institutions are actually set up to protect workers. And not surprisingly, workers have the least chance of winning cases that are filed against State-Owned Enterprises and governmental organizations (see Table 2). Yet, across all other organizational types, the majority of cases filed against workplaces are won by laborers. In addition, individuals in China have greater freedom to move throughout the economy than they have for 50 years. This is perhaps the greatest leverage that workers have over their workplaces: with the end of the job assignment system and the new freedom that workers have to participate in open labor markets, they can now vote with their feet.

The concerns over abuses of human rights and the abuses of labor that are inextricably tied to China's reputation in the global economy are significant and it is not my purpose here to dismiss the importance of the horrors the Chinese government has enacted on its people. However, it is also the case that gradually implemented reforms have transformed labor relations in China in fundamental ways, and it is important to depict an accurate and empirically-grounded picture of those changes. By looking beyond the workplace, we can begin to understand the forces pushing these reforms forward. The programs of reform-minded elites, who are creating the "quiet revolution" occurring within China, are reshaping the institutional terrain within which labor relations occur in China. Pressure from foreign investors to show commitments to the rational principles of the international economy are reshaping the normative environments in which managers make decisions about labor. Changing labor market dynamics afford the most talented workers to test the boundaries of the rational-legal reforms that are transforming labor. As China continues to evolve under the normative pressures of the international economy, these changes are likely to become deeper still.

NOTES

1. See *New York Times*, April 27, 1998, pp. A1, 6.
2. Reform in China has been wildly successful from an economic standpoint: Throughout the 1980s, China's real Gross Domestic Product grew at an average annual rate of 10.2%, a level that was only equaled by the growth rate in Botswana. From 1990–1996, the average annual rate of growth for real GDP was 12.3%, the highest rate of any country in the world for that period. It has also had the highest industrial growth rate (an amazing 17.3% average annual growth from 1990–1996) and the second highest growth in services (9.6% per annum, 1990–1996) in the world (World in

Figures, 1999). These are amazing figures given China's size, as growth figures are usually dominated by small countries.

3. This is not to say there are not proponents of the rational capitalism view. For example Pei (1994), Naughton (1995) and I (Guthrie, 1999) have all taken the view that the emergence of a rational-legal based economy in China is significant and real. However, the overwhelming tenor of scholarship on China's transition is that, despite the success of the reforms, corporatism, corruption, crony-capitalism, and a still-authoritarian government are all impeding the development of a rational, legal-based economy in China.

4. See Guthrie (1999, esp. Chs 3, 7, 9) for discussion.

5. As Walder (1986, p. 11) puts it, "The discretion of supervisors, relatively unrestrained by enforceable regulations and contracts, [was] quite broad . . . [supervisors had] considerable ability to influence the promotions, raises, and, more importantly, the degree to which a worker and his or her family may enjoy the many non-wage benefits and advantages potentially supplied by the enterprise."

6. As a document from the State Council put it in 1983, "The current system of employment in China, under which the majority are permanent workers, in practice operates as a kind of unconditional system of life tenure" (PRC, 1983); See also Guthrie (1998) and Josephs (1989) for discussion.

7. The Great Leap Forward (1958–1960) provided a caveat to this system, as approximately sixteen million workers were laid-off and sent down to the countryside during that campaign. This is the only period, however, where layoffs were not accompanied by reassignment (Walder, 1986). For further discussion of "waiting for employment", see also Gold (1989).

8. Despite the force of this manager's (and many other managers') statements regarding the importance of the labor contract, there is still significant variation surrounding the meaning of this institution in China today, and there are still places where the labor contract is viewed to have little meaning (see below). However, my argument here is that the labor contract lays the foundation for fundamental changes in the labor relationship; and these changes are already meaningful in many industrial organizations and will become increasingly meaningful in years to come.

9. See PRC (1986a, b). See also *Zhongguo tongji nianjian* (1994, p. 131) and Guthrie (1998).

10. While the official Provisional Regulations document (see PRC, 1986a, b) was promulgated in 1986, local governments began experimenting with contracts as early as 1983, by order of the Trial Implementation Notice of the State Council promulgated in 1983 (see PRC, 1983). Typically, this is the way broad institutional changes are set in motion in China: an institutional change begins with a policy idea that emerges as a "Notice" from the State Council is then experimented with in different localities and different sectors of the economy. When the kinks have been worked out to some degree, the institutional change is legitimized through an official law, rule, regulation, or decree from the State Council.

11. There is significant variation across provinces and municipalities in China: Shanghai has a considerably higher proportion of its laborers on labor contracts with 49.9% of its labor force on labor contracts or 2,378,000 individuals. The less developed areas of Tibet and Anhui Province are among the lowest with 10.5% (18,000 laborers) and 12.5% (621,000 laborers) of the labor force on labor contracts respectively. However, it is also clear that the implementation of the labor contract is not only

a function of industrial development, as Tianjin – one of the major industrial municipalities in China – is also among the lowest with 13.8% (404,000 laborers) of the labor force on labor contracts.

12. Some officials and managers hold the view that these legal frameworks have a direct impact on use of outside arbitration. As one government official explained: "We believe that the Labor Law will have a huge impact on the labor arbitration situation. We think this is already beginning to happen. Over the last few years there has been a steady increase of applications to the Labor Arbitration Commission. But this year we expect a huge increase because of the Labor Law. Because of the Labor Law, everyone will start to know what kind of personal power they have. The Labor Law is changing peoples' understanding of their rights. . . . We are hoping that the combination of the Labor Law and the Labor Arbitration Commission will force all types of organizations to focus on the laws more and more. Now that we are developing a market economy, changes are happening so quickly, and it's very important that everyone is protected by the laws" (Personal interview, Shanghai, 1995, originally reported in Guthrie [1999]).

13. Individuals can also apply to serve in this group, but few do, because it is not a paying position. Of the people that do apply to volunteer, most are lawyers working at universities who want to get some experience with the legal changes that are happening in China. According to officials, there are really not enough individuals working in this capacity, and as a result, many cases are simply heard by the presiding governmental official.

14. The representation of workers in dispute resolution and more generally overseeing the implementation of the Labor Law have become the primary functions of labor unions in China. As of 1999, labor unions had set up more than 140,000 agencies to oversee the implementation of the Labor Law in local workplaces.

15. Although there is a separate section for disputes relating to benefits and pay in the LAC, individuals generally rely on labor unions to solve such problems.

16. For discussions of the "quiet revolution" within China, see: The Quiet Revolution from Within: Economic Reform as a Source of Political Decline. In: A. Walder (Ed.), *The Waning of the Communist State* (pp. 1–24), (Berkeley: University of California Press, 1995); and D. Goodman and B. Hooper (Eds), *China's Quiet Revolution* (Melbourne: Longman Cheshire, 1994).

17. For discussion of the adoption of these systems in U.S. workplaces, see J. Sutton et al., The Legalization of the Workplace. *American Journal of Sociology*, 1994, 944–971.

18. It was this system that led to what Walder (1986) called "principled particularism," where workers were beholden to officials and managers for the distribution of goods (including jobs) and benefits in the planned economy. There was little autonomy and little room for dissention within this system.

19. Though not central to my discussion here, workers were actually an important part of this movement, and declining Party power operated in workplaces and universities in similar ways. Walder and Gong (1991) and Calhoun (1995) examine the importance of workers in the movement.

20. Craig Calhoun, a first hand observer of the movement notes that the university campuses themselves had become an important part of the "free space" that facilitated the students' organizational activities, a situation that was very different from the era before the economic reforms began (Calhoun, 1995).

ACKNOWLEDGMENTS

This paper was prepared for presentation at the American Sociological Association's Annual Meetings, August 16–20, Anaheim, CA. Thanks to Marc Blecher, Michael Burawoy, Ching Kwan Lee, and Kevin Leicht for helpful comments on earlier drafts. Address correspondence to doug.guthrie-@nyu.edu.

REFERENCES

Boisot, M., & Child, J. (1996). From Fiefs to Clans and Network Capitalism: Explaining China's Emerging Economic Order. *Administrative Science Quarterly*, *41*, 600–628.

Calhoun, C. (1995). *Neither Gods nor Emperors: Students and the Struggle for Democracy in China*. Berkeley, CA: University of California Press.

Dobbin, F., Sutton, J. R., Meyer, J. W., & Scott, W. R. (1993). Equal Opportunity Law and the Construction of Internal Labor Markets. *American Journal of Sociology*, *99*, 396–427.

Gold, T. B. (1989). Guerilla Interviews Among the *Getihu*. In: P. Link, R. Madsen & P. Pickowicz (Eds), *Popular Culture and Thought in the People's Republic* (pp. 175–192). San Francisco: Westview Press.

Goodman, D., & Hooper, B. (Eds) (1994). *China's Quiet Revolution*. Melbourne: Longman Cheshire.

Guthrie, D. (1997). Between Markets and Politics: Organizational Responses to Reform in China. *American Journal of Sociology*, *102*, 1258–1303.

Guthrie, D. (1998). Organizational Uncertainty and Labor Contracts in China's Economic Transition. *Sociological Forum*, *13*(3), 457–494.

Guthrie, D. (1999). *Dragon in a Three-Piece Suit: The Emergence of Capitalism in China*. Princeton, NJ: Princeton University Press.

Lu, Xiaobo. *Cadres and Corruption: The Organizational Involution of the Chinese Communist Party*. Stanford, CA: Stanford University Press.

Naughton, B. (1995). *Growing Out of the Plan: Chinese Economic Reform 1978–1993*. New York, NY: Cambridge University Press.

Pei, M. (1994). *From Reform to Revolution: The Demise of Communism in China and the Soviet Union*. Cambridge, MA: Harvard University Press.

Pei, M. (1995). Creeping Democratization in China. *Journal of Democracy*, *6*(4), 65–79.

People's Republic of China [*Zhonghua renmin gongheguo*] (1981a). Economic Contract Law of the People's Republic of China. Adopted on December 13, 1981 at the Fourth Session of the Fifth National People's Congress.

People's Republic of China [*Zhonghua renmin gongheguo*] (1983a). Notice of the Ministry of Labor and Personnel on Active Trial Implementation of the Contract Employment System [*laodong renshi bu guanyu jiji shixing laodong hetong zhide tongzhi*]. 6 State Council Gazette 213.

People's Republic of China [*Zhonghua renmin gongheguo*] (1986a). Provisional Regulations on the Implementation of the Contract Employment System in State Enterprises [*guoying qiye shixing laodong hetong zhanxing guiding*]. Promulgated by the State Council on July 12, 1986, effective October 1, 1986.

People's Republic of China [*Zhonghua renmin gongheguo*] (1986b). Provisional Regulations on the Dismissal of Workers and Staff for Work Violations in State Enterprises [*guoying qiye citui weiji zhigong zanxing guiding*]. Promulgated by the State Council on July 12, 1986, effective October 1, 1986.

People's Republic of China [*Zhonghua renmin gongheguo*] (1986c). Provisional Regulations on the Hiring of Workers in State Enterprises [*guoying qiye zhaoyong gongren zhanxing guiding*]. Promulgated by the State Council on July 12, 1986, effective October 1, 1986.

People's Republic of China [*Zhonghua renmin gongheguo*] (1988b). Law of the People's Republic of China on Chinese-Foreign Contractual Joint Ventures. Adopted at the First Session of the Seventh National People's Congress and promulgated by Order No. 4 of the President of the People's Republic of China on April 13, 1988.

People's Republic of China [*Zhonghua renmin gongheguo*] (1993). The Company Law of the People's Republic of China. Adopted at the Fifth Meeting of the Standing Committee of the Eighth National People's Congress on December 12, 1993, and effective as of July 1, 1994.

People's Republic of China [*Zhonghua renmin gongheguo*] (1994). The Labor Law of the People's Republic of China. Adopted at the Eighth Meeting of the Standing Committee of the National People's Congress on July 5, 1994, and effective January 1, 1995.

People's Republic of China [*Zhonghua renmin gongheguo*] (1995a). The National Compensation Law of the People's Republic of China. Adopted at the Seventh Meeting of the Standing Committee of the Eighth National People's Congress on May 5, 1994, and effective as of January 1, 1995.

Sachs, J. (1993). *Poland's Jump to the Market Economy.* Cambridge: MIT Press.

Sachs, J. D., & Woo, W. T. (1994). Experiences in the Transition to a Market Economy. *Journal of Comparative Economics, 18*(3), 271–275.

Sachs, J. D., & Woo, W. T. (1997). Understanding China's Economic Performance. Working Paper No. 5935, National Bureau of Economic Research, Inc. Working Paper Series.

Shao, C. (Ed.) (1998). *Zhong gong fan tan da an zhong an* (*Big cases and serious cases on the Chinese communists fight against corruption*). Hong Kong: Xiafeier publishers.

Sik, E. (1994). Network Capital in Capitalist, Communist, and Post-Communist Societies. *International Contributions to Labor Studies 4*, 73–70.

Sik, E. (2000). The Bad, the Worse and the Worst: Guesstimating the Level of Corruption. Presented to the Princeton University-CEU Joint Conference on Corruption. TARKI, Budapest, April.

Sutton, J. R., Dobbin, F., Meyer, J. W., & Scott, W. R. (1994). The Legalization of the Workplace. *American Journal of Sociology, 99*, 944–971.

Walder, A. (1986). *Communist Neo-Traditionalism: Work and Authority in Chinese Industry.* Berkeley, CA: University of California Press.

Walder, A. (1989). The Political Sociology of the Beijing Upheaval of 1989. *Problems of Communism, 38*, 30–40.

Walder, A. (1991). Workers, Managers, and the State: The Reform Era and the Political Crisis of 1989. *China Quarterly, 127*, 467–492.

Walder, A. (1994). The Decline of Communist Power: Elements of a Theory of Institutional Change. *Theory and Society, 23*, 297–323.

Walder, A. (1995). The Quiet Revolution from Within: Economic Reform as a Source of Political Decline. In A. Walder (Ed.), *The Waning of the Communist State* (pp. 1–24). Berkeley: University of California Press.

Walder, A., & Gong, X. (1993). Workers in the Tiananmen Protests: The Politics of the Beijing Workers' Autonomous Federation. *The Australian Journal of Chinese Affairs*, *29*, 1–29.

Whyte, M. K., & Parish, W. L. (1984). *Urban Life in Contemporary China*. Chicago, IL: University of Chicago Press.

World in Figures 1999. John Wiley & Sons.

Zhao, D. (1997). Decline of Political Control in Chinese Universities and the Rise of the 1989 Chinese Student Movement. *Sociological Perspectives*, *40*, 159–182.

CORPORATE LABOR POLICIES AND PRACTICES DURING CHINA'S TRANSITION: AN EXPLORATION OF IMPLICATIONS FOR SOCIAL STRATIFICATION

Lisa A. Keister

ABSTRACT

Labor reform in post-socialist economies has the potential to shape the nature of emerging stratification systems in these countries in important ways. Yet researchers have not explored how labor policies and practices are changing. This paper describes changes in firm labor practices and policies in China and discusses how these are likely to affect the nature of stratification. I highlight differences between state-owned enterprises (SOEs) and non-SOEs to explore the role that firm ownership structure is likely to play in defining the future of inequality in these countries. I provide estimates from longitudinal (1994–1999) quantitative survey data on 800 Chinese SOEs and non-SOEs to examine current labor conditions in Chinese firms, characteristics of workers, and the nature of current hiring and termination practices.

The Future of Market Transition, Volume 19, pages 171–187.

ISBN: 0-7623-0835-4

INTRODUCTION

Labor reform, among the most far-reaching changes taking place in transition economies, has the potential to shape the nature of emerging stratification systems in important ways. China's socialist labor system was begun in the 1950s and provided regular workers in well-endowed enterprises secure incomes and a wide range of benefits for almost four decades. Although socialist planners prided themselves in this system, the country's labor practices have had to be transformed because they precluded a number of other reforms that are vital to transition. The previous labor system was also problematic because it favored urban workers in state-owned enterprises (SOEs) at the expense of rural residents and those in the increasingly common non-SOEs. In socialist economies, the firm's ability to provide wages and benefits determined a great deal about the nature of stratification (Szelenyi, 1983; Walder, 1992). During transition, corporate labor practices have continued to differentiate workers and to shape well-being. Questions about worker retention, the fate of terminated workers, and the use of temporary and contract workers have increasingly found their way into both mainstream academic journals and the popular press. Yet we have little concrete evidence to support conjectures about how critical labor policies and practices are changing in China and other transition economies. Moreover most data on China's reform still come from official sources, and researchers seldom have access to current data from the companies themselves.

In this paper, I describe changes in firm labor practices and policies and discuss how these are likely to impact the nature of stratification in China. I emphasize differences between state-owned enterprises and non-SOEs in order to highlight the role that firm ownership structure is likely to play in defining future stratification systems. I draw on recently-collected longitudinal (1994–1999) quantitative survey data on 800 Chinese SOEs and non-SOEs, including 433 SOEs and 367 firms with other ownership structures (e.g. collectives, stock-owned, joint ventures, and privately-owned companies). In the next section, I provide a brief synopsis of the nature of enterprises prior to reform and describe the way labor reform affected firms. I then present an overview of the survey and discuss how information from this survey informs understanding of the relationship between changing labor practices and stratification. I explore current labor conditions in Chinese firms, characteristics of workers, and the nature of current hiring and termination practices. My objective is to provide a snapshot of the nature of labor conditions in China at the turn of the millenium and to discuss the potential for these conditions to shape the future of social stratification in that country.

THE TRANSFORMATION OF LABOR PRACTICES

Prior to reform, organizations in China were all state-owned and were part of an immense system of redistribution and central planning. In many ways, individual firms were branch plants of a single, albeit very large, firm (Groves, Hong, McMillan & Naughton, 1994). The hierarchical planning system included multiple layers from central ministries, to provinces, municipalities, counties, and townships, with each level redistributing resources within its jurisdiction (Guthrie, 1997; Nee, 1992). While central planning was less comprehensive in China than in the former Soviet Union, all industrial profits in China were remitted to the state after fixed deductions were taken by the factory. Central planners then redistributed remitted profits according to long-term state plans (Jefferson & Rawski, 1994; Walder, 1992). Production targets and mandates regarding production methods forced firms to conform to state-specified standards. Similarly, the government controlled labor resources. State agencies permanently assigned workers to factories based on firm needs, worker qualifications, and unofficial factors such as personal contacts. Factories could not fire workers and quitting was unheard of. Wages were set and tightly controlled by central authorities, workers did not receive material rewards for superior performance, and promotions were dictated from above (Naughton, 1995).

Beginning in 1978, industrial reform began to change the way state-owned enterprises operated in China. The state gradually began to allow firms to retain profits, transferred some responsibility for firm inputs and outputs to managers, and otherwise reduced the degree to which enterprise activities were centrally coordinated. Although reformers initially intended to experiment with profit retention in a small group of firms, the practice was widely adopted almost immediately. In fact, 6,600 large enterprises, accounting for 60% of the output and 70% of the profits of state-owned factories, had begun to retain profits by 1979 (Naughton, 1995). Reformers also sought to increase productivity by improving incentives for workers and by transferring responsibility for factory operations to managers. The "factory manager responsibility system" gave managers clear authority over the organization, and most enterprises adopted long-term managerial contracts (often tied to performance) that prompted the development of a labor market for managerial personnel (Groves, Hong, McMillan & Naughton, 1995). Central and local government control was not eliminated, nor did the reduction in control happen instantaneously. Rather, the state loosened its control gradually and, by many accounts, unevenly. Yet the loosening was clear, and this change prompted firms to respond or face being disbanded.

Firms and their managers have faced a number of challenges during reform that have affected the nature of labor practices during transition. Budget constraints have gradually hardened. That is, firms have become increasingly responsible for meeting expenses with revenues and have been less able to rely on state subsidies to cover overspending. As a result, managers have gained control of many business decisions, but, at the same time, the nature of management has changed because bargaining and political maneuvering have become less effective. Markets have begun to develop, but development has been uneven. Labor markets developed slowly, beginning on the coasts and near major cities, and remained local at least initially. Similarly, the development of financial markets and product markets was slow and varied regionally. State reformers encouraged labor and product market development in coastal cities, usually identified as special economic zones, and restricted reform in other areas. The intention of this strategy was to introduce reform slowly rather than shocking the entire economy with reforms whose outcome was unknown but likely to be extreme. The state allowed financial markets to develop as well, but it constrained development even more in this sector. Reformers limited the operations of private and foreign banks, regulated stock trading until the 1990s, and continues to closely monitor and restrict the actions of foreign banks. As a result, financial market development has happened but it has been even more delayed than the development of other markets. Financial market development indirectly affected labor practices by constraining fiscal resources in SOEs (who were often adjusting to reduced government subsidies) and in non-SOEs (who were struggling to be competitive with state-backed companies).

In addition, competition has gradually increased, both because the state has relaxed its control over firms and because firms have become more competitive in an effort to survive. Perhaps the greatest force motivating competition has been the threat of closure that remained only a threat in the early stages of reform but that has become increasingly real in recent years. At the end of the twentieth century, even the largest firms found themselves competing for resources with innovative state firms, non-state firms, and foreign companies.

As a result of these changes, firms began to adjust their labor practices and to experiment with various new policies. For example, many firms began to hire temporary and contract workers, and while labor migration remained relatively rare, it increased enormously by Chinese standards (Howard, 1991; Korzec, 1988). As profit retention spread, worker bonuses and welfare funds (used to finance investment in benefits such as housing and health clinics for workers) grew rapidly. Bonuses accounted for most of the 14% increase in real wages in urban areas between 1978 and 1980, and housing construction resulting primarily from increases in worker welfare funds increased more than 300% between 1978 and 1982 (Naughton, 1995, p. 103). Evidence that managers made decisions to hire, promote, demote, and alter the compensation of workers suggests that reform did, indeed, increase firm autonomy (Groves, Hong, McMillan & Naughton, 1994, 1995).

There is some evidence that firms also began to use completely new strategies that were more capitalist than socialist in nature. Paying workers piece wages, for example, is a quintessential capitalist practice that some firms began to experiment with during transition (Keister, Forthcoming). Linking pay to output had been somewhat common in earlier historical periods, but the use of incentive-based compensation schemes was prohibited following China's 1949 communist takeover (Naughton, 1995). Beginning in 1978, firms were again allowed to use piece wages, and by the late 1980s, their use had become taken for granted. The use of piece wages was less common in China than in European transition economies where they played a major role in worker compensation (Naughton, 1995, p. 343). Yet both in terms of the percentage of firms using new practices such as piece rates and the percentage of the total wage bill accounted for by these strategies, capitalist-oriented labor strategies became increasingly significant throughout the 1980s in China. The use of piece wages was unheard of in 1978, for instance, but in some regions and economic sectors, nearly 70% of firms used them as early as 1981. Similarly, by that same year, up to 20% of some firms' total wage bill was accounted for by piece wages (CASS/UCSD, 1990).

At the same time, because firms continued to use socialist labor practices, the adoption of new policies and practices created a dual system of socialist and capitalist labor practices within firms (Keister, 2000). Reformers pushed for the development of a socialist market economy, and organizations correspondingly began to adopt capitalist practices such as the use of piece rates while retaining socialist methods of hiring, firing, and compensating workers (often because the state required it). The state continued to regulate labor practices, but as managerial authority over the operation of firms expanded, reformers transferred responsibility for many of these practices to the firm (Naughton, 1995). Most firms continued to employ permanent workers through the end of the 1980s, but in 1984, all new employees were considered contract workers (those who had been hired previously as permanent employees were still guaranteed life-time employment). Likewise, most organizations continued to accept workers allocated by state agencies even while beginning to acquire workers from newly developing markets (Dong & Hu, 1995). The continued use of socialist-oriented labor practices reflected coercion to some degree, but it was also a voluntary, risk-reduction strategy on the part of organizational decision makers (Keister, 1998).

SURVEYING FIRMS AND THEIR LABOR PRACTICES

In previous decades, stratification in China and other socialist economies rested largely on worker affiliation with enterprises. Well-endowed enterprises – often those with significant bargaining power – were better able to provide housing and other benefits that allowed their workers to gravitate to the top of the socialist stratification system. The changes that China's economic reform initiated have altered the relationship between the state and firms, thus the conditions in firms that determined worker well-being in the past are currently less salient. Yet we know very little about the nature of labor conditions in China's companies in recent years. To explore these issues, I draw on new data on 800 enterprises in four provinces. The sample includes 433 state-owned enterprises and 367 firms that were collective enterprises, joint ventures, private firms, and other types of companies. I collected these data together with Mark Frazier, University of Louisville; David Li, Hong Kong University of Science and Technology; Barry Naughton, University of California-San Diego; and Wang Hongling, Chinese Academy of Social Sciences (CASS). The National Bureau of Asian Research, the National Science Foundation, and the Luce Foundation funded the data collection.

CASS administered the survey during the summer and fall of 2000 in face-to-face interviews with firm managers and financial officers. The questionnaire had two parts. The first was a set of 92 questions regarding the structure of the enterprise, manager appointment, participation in reform, organizational and management structure, manager incentives, firm strategy, relations with government offices, investment strategies, and related information. This section also included information about contract disputes, the presence of mediation committees in the companies, worker participation in firm management and governance, and the nature of firm pension plans and retirement options. The second part included 141 quantitative questions, designed to be answered by the enterprise's accountant, covering enterprise operations from 1994–1999. The second portion of the survey gathered information about output, production expenses, investments, assets and liabilities, costs, profits, and related firm traits. The second portion of the survey also included information about workforce size, worker characteristics, hiring, firing, and the current status of terminated workers.

Table 1 provides an overview of the firms in the sample and their managers. As the table indicates, 26.75% of the firms (or 214 firms) were located in

Table 1. The Nature of Firms in the Survey.

Firm characteristics (%)			
Location		*Level of subordination*	
Jiangsu	26.75	Central ministry	6.25
Sichuan	24.50	Province	6.88
Jilin	25.38	Municipality	49.75
Shanxi	23.38	County	7.38
		Other	29.75
Size			
Large	24.25		
Medium	52.75	*Ownership*	
Small	23.00	State-owned	54.13
		Collective	29.00
Age		Stock	11.51
Less than 20 years	46.88	Joint venture	2.63
21–40 years	21.51	Private	1.50
Greater than 40 years	31.63	Other	1.25
Manager characteristics (%)			
Age		*Tenure*	
40–49 years	36.40	Fewer than 3 years	49.88
50–59 years	57.53	4–6 years	35.50
Greater than 60 years	6.15	More than 6 years	14.63
Education level		*Party status*	
College degree or more	38.75	Secretary or vice-secretary	74.01
Post-2nd tech school	54.00	Committee/branch member	19.75
Upper middle or 2nd tech school	7.25	Ordinary party member	0.50
Elementary school or less	0.00	Not a party member	5.75

Jiangsu, 24.5% were located in Sichuan, 25.38% were in Jilin, and 23.38% were in Shanxi. The survey included a number of estimates of firm size, including a subjective self report. On this measure (included in Table 1), approximately one-half of the firms reported that they were medium-sized enterprises, with 25% each reporting that they were large or small companies. Nearly half of the firms were under the jurisdiction of a municipal government at the time of the survey, and nearly half (46.88%) had been formed within the last 20 years. A large number of the firms, more than 30% and primarily including the SOEs, were formed more than 40 years before the survey was conducted. The majority of managers of firms in this sample were between 50 and 59 years old and had a post-secondary technical education. Very few of the managers were older than 60, and very few had not completed some post-secondary education. The vast majority of the managers were either the secretary or vice-secretary of the local Communist Party branch, although nearly 6% were not Party members.

LABOR CONDITIONS IN SOEs AND NON-SOEs

An important element of the firm's role in shaping emerging stratification systems are policies regarding laid-off workers. Prior to reform, corporate bankruptcy was unknown, and workers were guaranteed lifetime employment. State-owned factories might have been reorganized or merged, with all workers being assured positions in the new factory or given a comparable position in another factory, but the closure of a plant was extremely rare. Reform gradually introduced provisions to allow firms to close entirely and leave all employees unemployed. Early labor reform efforts met with varying degrees of success. One relatively successful effort was the "three linkages employment policy" that encouraged workers and firms to begin using various methods (including individual effort, employment agencies, and the traditional state placement procedures) to match workers and jobs. In 1986, the employment system underwent a major restructuring, and all state sector employees became part of the contract employment system under which employees began signing contracts of limited length with their employers (Naughton, 1995). While it was still unusual in the mid-1980s for a contract not to be renewed, the days of permanent, guaranteed employment (the iron rice bowl) were clearly over.

Employment policies had changed even more dramatically by the late-1980s, and firms were actually encouraged to "reoptimize" their labor forces, cutting down on redundant employees. Local governments established programs to re-train and place workers who found themselves unemployed, but the number of jobless, particular in large urban areas, increased steadily through the late 1990s. In 1997, the State Council (similar to a cabinet) developed a task force to oversee and enforce bankruptcies and other closures. The task force was responsible for identifying unprofitable state-owned firms, determining the long-term prospects of the enterprise, and, where there was a negative prognosis, auctioning off their assets. As a result, bankruptcy (and thus unemployment) increased dramatically, demonstrating to managers that poor financial performance may result in failure for the firm and unemployment for the firm's managers and workers alike. Of course, the closures primarily affected small and medium enterprises, as the state continues to protect larger firms in hopes of stabilizing the economy. Yet while it seemed unlikely that the state would allow millions of urban workers to be unemployed, state-owned firms laid off more than 10 million workers in 1996, and layoffs continued through the end of the decade (*Economist*, 1997).

What effect did these changes have on labor practices? Table 2 provides some insight into conditions in SOEs and non-SOEs in the late 1990s. As the data indicate, more than 40% of workers in SOEs who were terminated took an early retirement, while only 12% of those in non-SOEs retired early. This indicates that a sizable number of those leaving did so under the guise of a retirement, but this was true primarily in SOEs. Before reform or in the early days of reform, this practice was much less common. Early retirement has, however, allowed managers to deal somewhat effectively with increasing demands to streamline labor forces. The difference between SOEs and non-SOEs suggests that an important determinant of well-being in the future will be the ownership structure of the firm at which workers are employed. Those working in formerly state-owned enterprises will be more likely to face long-term unemployment when forced to leave their jobs, while those in firms that are owned in other ways will likely re-enter the labor pool and find jobs in other settings.

Table 2. Labor Conditions in SOEs and non-SOEs.

	SOE (%)	Non-SOE (%)
Laid-off workers who . . .		
Took early retirement	40.50	12.07
Found a new job	12.81	42.44
Remained at firm to do service work	15.02	11.79
Went to a re-employment center	17.23	3.50
Are awaiting placement	4.16	11.68
Other	10.12	17.99
Firms that had . . .		
A dispute mediation committee	32.33	12.81
A contract dispute in 1999	25.17	6.81
Firms that contribute to . . .		
Firm-funded retirement accounts for individuals	100	88.56
A supplementary pension fund	0	14.64

* Authority refers to entities to which the enterprises are subordinated, including central ministry, province, municipality or county (see Table 1).

The relatively high percentage of laid-off workers who found new jobs when terminated from non-SOEs (42%) suggests that these workers are, indeed, finding jobs in new firms rather than remaining unemployed. In contrast, fewer than 13% of workers terminated from SOEs found new jobs. This estimate also suggests that labor markets, at least local labor markets, are indeed developing. However, this suggests strongly that labor markets are functioning outside the state-owned system. Because workers in the non-SOEs sought non-state employment in previous years, it is not entirely surprising that these workers had a higher propensity to seek employment on the market again. Yet the differences between state and non-state workers' behavior following termination does indicate that there may be a first-mover's advantage. That is, those who move to non-state firms early may benefit long-term, including in their well-being following termination.

The degree to which workers' rights are protected in the firm will also shape well-being in the future, and an important indicator of worker rights is the presence of a committee devoted to dispute mediation. On this front, SOEs appear to offer workers better conditions. As the estimates in Table 2 suggest, 32% of SOEs in the sample had dispute mediation committees, while only 12% of firms out of the state-owned sector had committees designated to address disputes. More than a quarter of firms in the SOE group reported that workers actually used the committee in 1999, while 12% of the non-SOEs reported a contract dispute in that year. To some degree, these differences reflect greater state control of worker well-being prior to reform, and the dispute resolution committee in many of the SOEs are likely still in place from prior to reform. Yet these differences between the two types of firms do suggest that an important advantage of employment in an SOE is the protection of worker rights. This does not imply that firms in the non state sector are more abusive, rather it implies that the infrastructure in non-SOEs may be less well-developed than in SOEs.

Given that SOEs were previously required to care for workers during retirement, it would be reasonable to expect these firms to provide better retirement plans currently. The results in Table 2 suggest, however, that at least among the firms in the sample, conditions in non-SOEs for retirees are actually quite promising. All of the SOEs in the sample provide firm-funded retirement accounts for individuals, while nearly 90% of the non-SOEs had these accounts in the late 1990s. Moreover, while none of the SOEs provided supplementary pension funds in 1999, 14.64% of the non-SOEs offered these funds, which resemble pension funds in the U.S. more than Chinese pension systems. It is likely that many of the SOEs in the sample will begin providing supplementary pensions as well in the future as independent insurance companies become more common and as the burden of caring for pensioners competes with other SOE needs. When these data were collected, however, these changes had not yet begun to occur. What these differences imply for stratification, however, is unclear. There are clearly advantages in terms of retirement benefits to remaining in the state-owned sector. Yet evidence that SOEs are going to have to reduce pension support and begin adapting to the radical changes they are experiencing suggests that these advantages are not going to be permanent (Keister, Forthcoming).

WORKER TRAITS AND EMPLOYMENT STATUS

During transition, labor market development is necessary, and the way markets for workers emerge varies both across and within countries. In China, the development of labor markets varied regionally, and the rate of development of local markets usually outpaced the rate at which the national market for labor emerged. Yet labor markets clearly began to shape the way people found jobs and the way business was done in China. Managers began to hire workers independent of state assignment, and workers started to realize that they could change jobs if the opportunities were right. Of course, labor migration remained relatively rare, but it increased enormously by Chinese standards (Howard, 1991; Korzec, 1988). Moreover, as profit retention spread, worker bonuses and welfare funds (used to finance investment in benefits such as housing and health clinics for workers) grew rapidly. Bonuses accounted for most of the 14% increase in real wages in urban areas between 1978 and 1980, and housing construction resulting primarily from increases in worker welfare funds increased more than 300% between 1978 and 1982 (Naughton, 1995).

An important indicator that markets were developing was the increased use of temporary workers. As we would expect, there were very clear differences between firms in the state sector and the non-SOEs in terms of their use of permanent and temporary employees. The estimates in Table 3 summarize these differences. Between 1995 and 1997, the total number of employees in both SOEs and other firms declined gradually. However, six million SOE workers are being laid off each year. The implications of this finding are not evident in the data, but one possible explanation is that the lay-offs are largely coming from bankrupt firms. Another potential explanation is that the surviving SOEs have merged with other firms or acquired subsidiaries. Consistent with this second explanation, output for these SOEs increased markedly during this same period, perhaps indicating that workers were added during a merger (Keister & Lu, 2001).

Table 3. Worker Traits and Employment Status.

	1995		1997		1999	
	SOE	Non-SOE	SOE	Non-SOE	SOE	Non-SOE
Workers who were (%) . . .						
Permanent employees	84.39	14.55	85.22	14.68	85.42	14.96
Temporary employees	15.61	85.22	14.78	85.13	14.51	84.85
Managers	9.43	9.99	9.68	9.83	9.76	9.89
Female managers	36.64	37.14	36.08	37.06	36.51	37.66
Engineers/technicians	6.32	5.88	6.58	6.11	6.80	6.47
Female engineers/technicians	35.46	33.40	34.84	33.61	34.93	33.96
Front-line workers	57.99	60.20	56.87	58.73	57.29	58.08
Purchase & sales personnel	4.06	4.46	4.25	4.50	4.44	5.02
Auxiliary workers	7.15	8.94	7.46	8.70	7.77	8.72
College graduates	8.22	3.12	8.86	3.45	9.47	4.24
Vocational & 2nd school grads	32.19	28.97	34.37	30.30	36.99	33.34
Middle school grads (or less)	59.60	67.91	56.83	65.86	53.65	62.10
Total employees (thousands)	2.53	1.20	2.44	1.18	2.36	1.13

It is also notable that the proportion of the work force accounted for by permanent versus temporary workers remained relatively constant in both types of firms. The estimates in the table do indicate, however, the stark difference in the types of employees working in SOEs and non-SOEs. In 1999, for example, permanent (state-assigned) employees accounted for 85% of the workforce of SOEs in the sample. In that same year, fewer than 15% of the employees in the non-SOEs were permanent employees. When we look at the composition of the work forces of these companies by job, there is little difference between the SOEs and non-SOEs. In other words, both employed approximately 60% front-line workers, 4 to 5% purchase and sales personnel, and 7 to 9% auxiliary workers. Similarly, the distribution of managers (including female managers) and engineers (including female engineers) was comparable across firm types. These similarities indicate that the firms are comparable on many dimensions, with the notable exception of the temporary versus permanent status of the employees. There is also only minimal difference between the two types of firms in the percentage of college graduates in the work force. A higher percentage of SOE employees are college graduates, but the difference between SOEs and non-SOEs is minimal on this dimension. It appears from these estimates, then, that there are few differences in the nature of employees working in SOEs and their non-state counterparts.

THE END OF THE IRON RICE BOWL

Details about hiring and terminating workers highlight the differences between firms that remained in the state sector and those that were not SOEs. State owned enterprises and other firms clearly differed in the manner in which employees were hired and terminated. The SOEs hired more than 26% of their workers through the state in 1995, and while this number declined by 1999 the decline was slight. Non-SOEs did hire some workers through state channels, but the firms in the sample never added more than 3% of their new workers through state allocation in the years depicted in Table 4. What is perhaps most striking is that the state-owned enterprises in the sample hired about three-quarters of their workers independently in the years included in the Table. It is less surprising to learn that non-SOEs found their workers this way – indeed the non-SOEs hired the vast majority of their new workers independently – but both trends indicate strongly that labor markets were rather well-developed by the late 1990s.

Similarly, SOEs and non-SOEs differed on the way they terminate workers. SOEs eliminated more employees on average in the early years of the survey,

Table 4. Hiring and Eliminating Workers.

	1995		1997		1999	
	SOE	Non SOE	SOE	Non SOE	SOE	Non SOE
Workers added (mean No.)	28.11	49.08	31.81	54.56	33.42	41.42
New workers who were (%) . . .						
Allocated by the state	26.14	2.03	24.75	2.91	24.81	2.50
Hired independently	73.81	96.60	74.59	96.90	75.13	96.77
Workers eliminated (mean No.)	61.00	48.56	64.02	53.71	65.57	65.46
Eliminated workers who (%) . . .						
Quit	4.09	17.13	4.33	19.41	4.62	20.86
Retired	90.98	25.27	89.54	25.41	89.11	25.63
Were transferred	3.45	6.55	3.72	5.75	3.67	4.15
Were fired	1.53	50.34	2.29	48.81	2.41	48.88
Welfare payments (1,000 yuan)	734.00	792.47	808.39	879.35	907.68	947.85
Pensions (1,000 yuan)	1,702.05	424.87	2,233.63	523.32	2,836.61	658.13
Pensioners (number)	504.66	90.61	606.40	106.97	712.03	123.17

although elimination of employees by non-SOEs increased during the period the firms were surveyed. By 1999, both SOEs and non-SOEs eliminated 65 workers per year on average. In the SOEs, 90% of those eliminated were listed as retired. This is consistent with arguments that managers forced early retirements in order to reduce work force size. In the non-SOEs, because workers were not considered permanent employees, early retirement was naturally less common. In contrast to the SOEs, when other firms terminated workers, they were more likely to fire the workers or have them quit. These differences in commitment to workers both while they are employed and after retirement are reflected in the pension burden borne by the firms. The final rows of Table 4 indicate the average total welfare payments and the average total pension payments made by the firm as well as the average number of pensioners dependent on the firm. While SOEs make much higher payments in pensions and had many more pensioners on average than the non-SOEs, the firms were relatively comparable in their payment of welfare benefits (i.e. the difference in welfare payments between SOEs and non-SOEs is not statistically significant, but the difference in pensions and pensioners is).

CONCLUSIONS

Research on market transition has been accumulating in recent years, but most evidence about how transition occurs is derived from research on individuals or economic aggregates (Bian, 1997; Nee, 1996; Xie & Hannum, 1996; Zhou, Tuma & Moen, 1997). Important exceptions exist (Guthrie, 1997; Nee, 1992), but direct observations of the economic choices made by actors during transition are rare (Oberschall, 1996). My results concern one of the most fundamental changes that occur during transition – transformation of labor practices and policies in firms – and my estimates suggest that there are important ways in which labor changes are likely to shape the nature of stratification in coming years. The estimates suggest strongly that employment in SOEs and non-SOEs may well be a dimension along which Chinese workers are stratified in coming years. My estimates indicated that SOEs still have substantially more permanent workers than non-SOEs, although both types of firms are hiring and terminating workers in ways that would have been unheard of until quite recently. Workers who are terminated from SOEs, however, are more likely to remain long-term unemployed while those from non-SOEs appear to be returning to the labor market and returning to new jobs.

The results also suggest that there may be some first-movers' advantage in going to work for a firm out of the state sector in terms of acquaintance with the labor market and ability to regain employment in the event of termination.

Does this imply that there are clear advantages currently to employment in either the state sector or the non-state sector? Not at all. In fact, my estimates indicated that there is not a definite advantage to employment in either sector. Worker rights are perhaps better protected in SOEs and that retirement benefits are still at least adequate in state-owned firms, yet such factors as more progressive forms of retirement benefits make employment in the non-state sector appealing. Taken together, these findings suggest that reform has certainly changed the nature of Chinese firms and the way business is conducted in China. They also suggest that worker well-being in the future will be determined in ways that are very different from past patterns.

It is important to note the limitations of my estimates. An important limitation is the setting. While China's transition offers important advantages for a study of the changes occurring in labor practices in transition economies, China is by no means a representative context and Chinese firms are by no means representative of firms in all transition economies. The degree to which the state continued to monitor and influence firm practices and the economy, more general, is likely to have shaped the nature of managerial behavior in ways that are not evident here and that are not generalizeable to other times or settings. Likewise, while the data I employ were gathered systematically and included a large number of typical Chinese firms, data on Chinese firms are almost always limited to some degree. For example, my intention to discuss the placement of terminated workers was necessarily limited by the nature of the data. Firm-level data have important advantages, but it is likely that these estimates would differ from estimates obtained by workers. Missing values were not particularly problematic in these data relative to other data on Chinese firms, but again, the difficulty in accessing Chinese managers inevitably produces more missing data than is desirable. Once again, my estimates may have differed somewhat had the data been more complete.

These results provide insight into the behavior of organizations in China during a unique time period. Generalizing from the findings to other firms in transition economies seems plausible, but in fact, the findings can be generalized to organizations in other contexts as well. The study began with the observation that the complexity of changes the firms face has increased in recent decades and has increased interest among researchers in the process by which organizations adapt to this change. While there are certainly characteristics of the Chinese case that make it unique, many of the findings are useful as research attempts to understand these more general processes. In particular, the notion that uncertainty and social diffusion processes matter, but that they matter differently at different points in the diffusion process is relevant in nearly all contexts. Likewise, the finding that pluralism in the organization has important effects on the adoption process is relevant across time and context, as all organizations are pluralistic to some degree. Finally, my findings highlighted the importance of including notions of process in understanding firm behavior.

Taken together, these findings suggest that reform has certainly changed the nature of Chinese firms and the way business is conducted in China. More importantly, the results are suggestive of the ways in which firms will affect stratification in the future. It is clear that Chinese firms have changed dramatically in recent years, but the coming decade likely holds more change for the firms, their managers, and their workers. It is also clear that there are important differences between the state owned enterprises that have survived and non-SOEs, and These differences are likely to provide important insight into the process of reform in general and the particular character of China's transformation. What is not clear at this point is exactly how stratification will change as a result of these changes in firms. Future research will be able to specify the exact nature of changes in the stratification system, but these estimates will provide a useful starting point for that research.

ACKNOWLEDGMENTS

I appreciate funding from the National Science Foundation (SES-9875147), the Luce Foundation, and the National Bureau of Asian Research. I am grateful to my co-investigators: Mark Frazier, David Li, and Barry Naughton. Donald Clarke, Rich Ellings, Meira Meek, Jin Lu, and Hongling Wang also made very significant contributions to data collection and analysis.

REFERENCES

Bian, Y. (1997). Bringing Strong Ties Back In: Indirect Ties, Network Bridges, and Job Searches in China. *American Sociological Review*, *62*, 366–385.

CASS/UCSD (1990). Survey of 769 State-Owned Industrial Firms. University of California, San Diego: Graduate School of International Relations and Pacific Studies and Chinese Academy of Social Science: Beijing, China.

Dong, J. L., & Hu, J. (1995). Mergers and Acquisitions in China. *Federal Reserve Bank of Atlanta Economic Review*, *80*, 15–29.

Economist (1997). Beijing Rules. *The Economist*, May 3, 54–55.

Groves, T., Hong, Y., McMillan, J., & Naughton, B. (1994). Autonomy and Incentives in Chinese State Enterprises. *Quarterly Journal of Economics*, *109*, 183–209.

Groves, T., Hong, Y., McMillan, J., & Naughton, B. (1995). China's Evolving Managerial Labor Market. *Journal of Political Economy*, *103*, 873–891.

Guthrie, D. (1997). Between Markets and Politics: Organizational Responses to Reform in China. *American Journal of Sociology*, *102*, 1258–1304.

Howard, P. (1991). Rice Bowls and Job Security: The Urban Contract Labour System. *Australian Journal of Chinese Affairs*, *25*, 93–114.

Jefferson, G. H., & Rawski, T. G. (1994). Enterprise Reform in Chinese Industry. *Journal of Economic Perspectives*, *8*, 47–70.

Keister, L. A. (1998). Engineering Growth: Business Group Structure and Firm Performance in China's Transition Economy. *American Journal of Sociology*, *104*, 404–440.

Keister, L. A. (2000). *Chinese Business Groups: The Structure and Impact of Interfirm Relations During Economic Development*. New York: Oxford University Press.

Keister, L. A., & Lu, J. (2001). The Transformation Continues: The Status of Chinese State Owned Enterprises At the Start of the Millennium. *National Bureau of Economic Research Analysis Report*, *12*, 5–31.

Keister, L. A. (Forthcoming). Adapting to Radical Change: Strategy and Environment in the Adoption of Piece Rates During China's Transition. *Organization Science*.

Korzec, M. (1988). New Labour Laws in the People's Republic of China. *Comparative Economic Studies*, *XXX2*, 117–149.

Naughton, B. (1995). *Growing Out of The Plan: Chinese Economic Reform, 1978–1993*. New York: Cambridge University Press.

Nee, V. (1992). Organizational Dynamics of Market Transition: Hybrid Forms, Property Rights, and Mixed Economy in China. *Administrative Science Quarterly*, *37*, 1–27.

Nee, V. (1996). The Emergence of a Market Society: Changing Mechanisms of Stratification in China. *American Journal of Sociology*, *101*, 908–949.

Oberschall, A. (1996). The Great Transition: China, Hungary, and Sociology Exit Socialism into the Market. *American Journal of Sociology*, *101*, 1028–1041.

Szelenyi, I. (1983). *Urban Inequalities Under State Socialism*. Oxford: Oxford University Press.

Walder, A. G. (1992). Property Rights and Stratification in Socialist Redistributive Economies. *American Sociological Review*, *57*, 524–539.

Xie, Y., & Hannum, E. (1996). Regional Variation in Earnings Inequality in Reform-Era Urban China. *American Journal of Sociology*, *101*, 950–992.

Zhou, X., Tuma, N. B., & Moen, P. (1997). Institutional Change and Job-shift Patterns in Urban China, 1949–1994. *American Journal of Sociology*, *62*, 339–365.

PART III: ANALYSES OF OCCUPATIONAL ATTAINMENT AND GENDER INEQUALITY

OCCUPATIONAL ATTAINMENT IN EASTERN EUROPE UNDER SOCIALISM

Raymond Sin-Kwok Wong

ABSTRACT

This study explores the characteristics of the socialist stratification system through a comparative analysis of the determinants of occupational attainment in five Eastern European countries (Russia, Bulgaria, Czechoslovakia, Hungary, and Poland) at three time points during socialist rule (1970, 1980, and 1988). Besides the conventional measures of family environment, parental cultural capital and parental social capital are included as independent factors. The study finds that although individual educational attainment, particularly tertiary education, was the most important determinant of occupational attainment, parental cultural capital had significant direct influence in all five countries throughout the period studied. Together with the continued significance of family background (parental education, father's occupation, and parental cultural capital) ***indirectly*** *via individual attainment, this makes clear the tenacity and resilience of the family in intergenerational transmission of inequality even under socialism. The significance of individual social capital (Communist party membership) in occupational attainment, especially in Russia, indicates that social network through political affiliations was a major stratification agent developed specifically under socialism. There are, however, significant cross-national differences. The*

The Future of Market Transition, Volume 19, pages 191–230.

ISBN: 0-7623-0835-4

appeal and advantage of party membership have largely disappeared in Hungary and Poland by 1988 but remained relatively strong in the other three countries. Finally, the findings confirm that a distinctive achievement of the socialist stratification system was the closing of the gender gap. Women, particularly those who received secondary education with diploma or better, had advanced so much that some even surpassed men in their occupational attainment.

INTRODUCTION

More than a decade has passed since the fall of socialism in Eastern Europe and much of the socialist legacy has disappeared there. Yet we are still on our way to a thorough understanding and learned assessment of this ambitious and massive social experiment to fundamentally transform pre-existing (pre-capitalist or early capitalist) inequality systems. Eschewing the kind of sweeping conclusions about socialism's inevitable demise and utter failure favored by Western media and politicians, researchers have probed the more illuminating questions of how successful the socialist efforts were in altering and transforming the stratification order, the nature and characteristics of the socialist stratification system, and what determined who got what and why under socialism (see Kolosi, 1988; Kolosi & Wnuk-Lipinski, 1983; Krejcí, 1972; Lane, 1971, 1982; Parkin, 1971; Simkus & Andorka, 1982; Słomczynski & Krauze, 1986; Szelényi, 1998 for some discussion). These studies have generated a wealth of theoretical knowledge and empirical evidence about the socialist experiences in various East European countries. However, based largely on data from single countries or, at most, a comparison of two or three countries, the empirical findings have limited generalizability about systematic differences (or similarities) in socialist stratification systems. Furthermore, as most of the studies examine only one time point, the findings shed little light on possible changes in the stratification order over time. Most importantly, previous studies rely solely on conventional factors listed in traditional status attainment literature (such as parental education and occupation) to represent the influence of family environment on individual status attainment, thus neglecting the possible effects of additional agents particular to the socialist inequality system.

Drawing on cumulative findings from previous research, the present study seeks a more encompassing cross-national and temporal examination of occupational attainment under socialism. To provide a general profile of systematic differences and/or similarities in socialist stratification systems across countries and over time, occupational attainment in five countries (Bulgaria, Czechoslovakia, Hungary, Poland, and Russia) at three time points (1970, 1980, and 1988) are analyzed and compared. The period covers approximately the last two decades of socialism, a period that some critics speculate to have seen re-stratification in the "classless" system. To better capture the effects of stratification agents that were particular to the socialist system, the study incorporates two previously neglected dimensions – parental social capital and parental cultural capital – into its measures of family environment. Though the *direct* effects of parental human capital are expected to be negligible in socioeconomic attainment, with *indirect* influences mediated through individual human and social capital (see Featherman & Hauser, 1978 for the United States), it is possible that the direct influences of parental cultural and social capital have been significant under the socialist stratification regime. Their effects may then shed new light on social inequality under socialism.

In general, social capital stands for the "ability of actors to secure benefits by virtue of membership in social networks or other social structures" (Portes, 1998, p. 6). Relative to other forms of capital, social capital is intangible, as it exists only in relations among persons and is defined by its function (Coleman, 1988, 1990). In socialist countries, an indisputably characteristic and prominent social network was the Communist party. Given the Communists' monopolistic hold on power, party membership constituted a significant form of social capital. It not only conferred power and privileges on the holders themselves, but could also secure benefits for the holders' offsprings. Its importance in educational attainment under socialism has been established in a recent work (Wong, 1998), though its influence on other attainment outcomes has yet to be empirically confirmed. To determine whether and how much it affected occupational attainment, Communist party membership is taken as the primary measure of parental social capital (and individual social capital) in this study.[1]

Cultural capital, on the other hand, is a set of institutionalized high status cultural signals (attitudes, preferences, formal knowledge, behavior, and credentials) used for social and cultural exclusion (Lamont & Lareau, 1988).[2] Its importance in intergenerational inequality is widely established in cultural reproduction literature (Bernstein, 1975; Bourdieu, 1977; Bourdieu & Passeron, 1977; Collins, 1979; DiMaggio, 1982). In this study, parental cultural capital refers to the *quality* of home environment and time that parents spent with their children. Through activities such as regular visits to theaters, concerts, galleries, and libraries, or through books, classical music, and other resources at home, parental cultural capital establishes the intellectual climate for children's academic development, educational aspirations, motivation to achieve, and performance in schools.[3] It also socializes children to understand what is desirable, acceptable, and valued in society, teaches them how to relate to others, and inculcates adaptability in changing conditions. All these qualities are influential in work and career advancement. Family lifestyle and consumption pattern thus shape children's cultural formation, which in turn provides valuable educational resources that aid children's motivation and performance at school, work, and beyond. Given its intangible nature, parental cultural capital will be much more difficult to equalize, and its influence on status attainment could conceivably persist throughout the period of socialist rule, significantly undermining the deliberate efforts to alter the inequality structure. Thus, its inclusion in the conceptualization of family environment may shed particular light on the pattern of inequality under socialism.

In short, with an expanded measurement of the multidimensional family environment (human, social, and cultural capital) and individual social and human capital, the current study proffers a systematic and nuanced analysis of the relative significance of each of these factors in accounting for individual occupational achievement under socialism. The cross-national and temporal design further affords the possibility of uncovering some distinctive characteristics of the socialist stratification system.

SOCIALIST STRATIFICATION SYSTEM

Based on the cumulative empirical analyses of the East European experiences, the following observations about socialist stratification can be made. First, there is evidence that the early policies of destratification and reverse discrimination against formerly privileged classes in favor of the working class had some success in creating openness in the class mobility regimes and reducing the influence of family background, and that socialist mobility patterns were quite distinct from their Western counterparts (Simkus & Andorka, 1982; Wong, 1995; but note Szelényi, 1998). In particular, the extent of long-distance upward and downward mobility was notably larger in socialist countries than in capitalist countries. Some of this openness in relative mobility chances can be attributed to the abolition of private property, active demotion of the propertied class into other destinations, and selective promotion of workers and farmers into professional and managerial positions, though the contribution of industrialization, especially during the immediate postwar period, should not be understated. However, there are also signs that these equalization policies were not effective for long. Many of the class-based discrimination policies in education and employment were abolished in the 1960s or 1970s, and replaced by more merit-based and credential-oriented selections. At the same time, the dominance of the Communist party bureaucracy, with its significant influence on the inequality structure, has led to the postulation of the rise of a new class in the "classless" society (Djilas, 1957; Konrád & Szelényi, 1979). And there is indeed some empirical evidence that the socialist stratification systems in several Eastern European countries have become more unequal over time, with possible restratification in later years (Wong & Hauser, 1992).

It is therefore reasonable to postulate some significant temporal changes in the socialist inequality system. Specifically, the demand for particular individuals to fill vacant positions may differ under such differing historical conditions as the active construction of a new order in the early years of socialist rule, the consolidation of the new power structure, or the institution of new policies to stimulate a sagging economy in later years. During the early period of socialist construction, the active demotion of previously privileged classes and the rapid expansion of state bureaucracies created rooms for long-distance upward mobility that would not have been possible otherwise (see Simkus & Andorka, 1982; Szelényi, 1998 for a detailed discussion of education and labor policies instituted in Hungary). This openness is most likely to have benefitted loyal party members, particularly those with limited educational training. That is, besides advantages conferred on Communist party membership, some of the less educated but loyal party members might have been selectively promoted to positions of power and prestige when ideological purity was the dominant factor in social selection. On the other hand, if the destratification programs indeed had some early success, the level of status attainment would be lower for individuals of self-employed origins. In both cases, however, the effects are unlikely to have persisted over time.

The demand for qualified personnel to fill important positions after the Communist party has consolidated power suggests a possible resurgence of the importance of individual achievement in status attainment over time. Besides the return of the old stratification agents, new agents may have also developed in the course of socialist stratification. The factors that may have affected the pattern of restratification include parental cultural capital, parental social capital, and individual social capital. Since parental cultural capital is difficult to equalize through political and administrative means, its influence on status attainment is likely to have persisted and remained relatively stable throughout socialist rule. For parental social capital, the net effect, after one controls for individual social capital, would probably decrease to non-significance, since individual's immediate social network should provide greater and more visible benefits in individual status attainment than indirect networks through parents. However, the total and indirect effect may nonetheless remain strong and significant throughout the entire period.

Whether the significance of individual social capital (party membership status and seniority within the party, measured by the total number of years in the party) would change over time is less clear. Everything else being equal, the advantages of party membership and seniority within the party would be particularly strong during the early years, and then decline over time, but they should remain significant throughout socialist rule. The reason is twofold. First, as a vehicle of career advancement, party membership would have continued to attract the ambitious, whatever their political convictions. Second, as a highly selective organization with repeated purging of undesirable elements, the ruling Communist party tended to entrust positions of power and prestige more to its members than non-members. After all, party membership was a not-so-secret prerequisite for many high-ranking positions with decision-making power. Hungary may be the only exception here because political credentials were abandoned as a criterion for appointments to leadership position under the Kádár regime (Szelényi, Szelényi & Kovách, 1995). However, whether party membership interacts with other factors in affecting the pattern of socialist (re)-stratification remains to be empirically explored.

Regardless of possible restratification in later years, a particularly notable achievement of socialism is the narrowing gender gap in educational and occupational attainment (Parkin, 1969, 1971; Lane, 1982; Yanowitch, 1977; Simkus & Andorka, 1982). The constitution of many socialist countries granted every citizen the same opportunity of education, and the abolition of private schooling and rapid expansion of seats at various levels of the school system created ample opportunities for the new generations, benefitting especially women who had been disadvantaged in the past. Indeed, the relative success of women in obtaining secondary grammar education (or *gymnasium*) rather than vocational training after primary education in some countries has led to the postulation of the "feminization of the gymnasia" (von Kopp, 1988). This is a significant development because about two-thirds of university students were directly recruited from gymnasia graduates, who also enjoyed greater chances to attain non-manual rather than manual occupations.

Besides the universalization of education, the socialist regimes' undertaking the "forced emancipation" of women as part of their agenda also promoted gender equality in status attainment.[4] Women were officially liberated from the limited role of housewife and bearer and caretaker of labor to become fellow members of the proletariat. Their employment was typically full-time and continuous, with relatively short breaks around child birth. As a result, women's rates of participation in the labor market in socialist countries were not only significantly higher than those in Western countries, but almost equal to men's (Yanowtich, 1977; Bakker, 1988). Furthermore, compared to women in the West, socialist women enjoyed better access to prestigious male-dominated occupations. Although a substantial proportion still found themselves channeled into clerical, sales, and personal service jobs just like women in the West, some managed to break into professional and skilled manual jobs, especially in the medical profession such as physicians, pharmacists, and nurses (Garnsey, 1982; Heitlinger, 1979, 1985).

Many socialist governments also instituted pro-family and pro-natalist policies to accommodate women's reproductive and family needs, granting maternity and family leave and guaranteeing women the right to return to the *same* or similar job after their temporary leave of absence (see also Szelényi, 1998, pp. 14–15). This resulted in levels of occupational attainment for women that were equal to or even higher than men as early as 1970 (detailed below). Such a phenomenon was unmatched in the West, where interrupted job histories and dual responsibilities, among other factors, led to women's relatively low level of occupational attainment (Reskin & Padavic, 1994). Socialism, then, has arguably generated two, not one, revolutions: the oft-cited eradication of the ownership class and the incorporation of women into the formal economy (Szelényi, 1998). Of course, this does not mean that women achieved parity with men under socialism. The right to return to the same or similar jobs after temporary absence, in actuality, often means that women could retain their social status but still incurred lower rates of career mobility, lower chances to hold positions of power and authority, and lower chances of high earnings (Heitlinger, 1979; Lane, 1976; Matejko, 1974; Jaronsinko, 1983).[5] Be that as it may, the narrowing of gender inequality in status attainment could still be a distinctive feature of the socialist stratification system.

HYPOTHESES

Based on the above discussion, the following hypotheses are formulated for empirical examination. Six of them (H1–H6) pertain to the effects of various factors of family background or environment and individual characteristics on occupational attainment and their changes over time, and the last (H7) is about gender differences.

H1: The direct effects of parental human capital (parental education and father's occupation) on individual attainment were not significant in the early period but gradually regained significance over time. Their influences were largely indirect, via individual education, first occupation, and social capital. The total effects remained significant throughout the period and increased over time.

H2: The direct and total effect of parental cultural capital on status attainment remained strong and stable over time.

H3: The direct effects of parental social capital (Communist party membership) were weak throughout the period studied, but the total effects remained strong and significant.

H4: The effects of individual educational attainment were strong and increasing over time, particularly for those with tertiary education.

H5: The advantage of individual social capital remained strong and significant throughout the entire period, but its effect was most prominent in the early years and then declined over time. In the early period, the effect of party membership interacted with individual education, largely benefitting those who were less educated.

H6: The higher a person's seniority within the Communist party, the higher his/her level of status attainment. The effect remained relatively stable over time.

H7: Gender gaps in status attainment declined significantly over time and possibly reversed in the 1980s, particularly for better educated women.

Given the countries' various level of adherence to Marxist-Leninist ideology, proclamation of the attainment of "communism," and differences due to economic, cultural, and historical particularities, there may be cross-national variations in some of the effects of the variables. The direction and extent of such variations are difficult to predict and no specific hypothesis is postulated.

DATA AND METHODS

The data for this study are derived from the 1993 *Social Stratification in Eastern Europe After 1989: General Population Survey*, coordinated by Ivan Szelényi and Donald Treiman. The comparative project contains national representative probability samples of men and women in six countries: Bulgaria, the Czech Republic, Hungary, Poland, Russia, and Slovakia (see Szelényi & Treiman, 1994 for details). Since the Czech Republic and Slovakia together constituted Czechoslovakia before the split, the two samples are combined to form the present five-country study. Individual education, work, and political activity histories are used to create time-specific attainment in 1970, 1980, and 1988. The analyses are restricted to those aged between 20 and

64 and gainfully employed in the three specified years.[6] To reduce data loss due to missing values, the mean substitution method is applied to those independent variables with missing values. Additional dummy variables representing their missing conditions are also constructed and added as statistical controls in data analysis. They include number of siblings, parental education, father's occupation, father's self-employment status, individual education, first occupation, number of years in the labor force, and Communist party membership.[7]

To facilitate comparison across countries, the international socioeconomic status scale (ISE) is used to measure the socioeconomic standing of father's occupation, respondent's first occupation, and current occupation in 1970, 1980, and 1988 (Ganzeboom, De Graaf & Treiman, 1992). Parental education and individual education are measured by three dummy variables that provide information on the type and level of education attained. The dummy variables are secondary education without diploma, secondary education with diploma, and tertiary or higher education, with primary or less education as the reference category.[8] The dummy variables are derived from the expanded CASMIN educational classification (Müller, Lüttinger, König & Karle, 1990).

Parental cultural capital is a composite factor of eight indicators which measure how often the respondent's parents participated in certain activities when the respondent was growing up. They include: (a) visiting art museums or art exhibits (PMUSEUM); (b) attending ballet, opera, theater, or concert (PPERF); (c) listening to classical music at home (PMUSIC); (d) reading serious books such as history, biography, science, or literature (PREAD); (e) going to the library (PLIB); (f) having dictionary or encyclopedia at home (PDICT); (g) having atlas at home (PATLAS); and (h) number of books at home (PBOOKS). The first five indicators (PMUSEUM-PLIB) are ordinal variables with 7 categories ranging from never to more often than once a week. PDICT and PATLAS are dichotomies, and PBOOKS is an ordinal variable with 9 categories (0, 1 or 2, around 10, 20, 50, 100, 200, 500, and 1000 or more). Results from principal component factor analysis indicate that only one factor can be extracted from the indicators (using eigenvalue greater than 1 as the cutoff). The factor loadings are 0.716, 0.719, 0.606, 0.733, 0.549, 0.599, 0.537, and 0.767, respectively, and are used to construct factors scores of parental cultural capital. To maximize the utility of the constructed variable, imputation method is used to assign values to those cases with missing values, using parental education, father's occupation, and their missing dummies as predictors. About 18.4% of the sample has imputed values of cultural capital. The final sample sizes and a summary of the descriptive statistics of the variables involved are presented in Appendix A.

To examine the relative importance of each independent variable (and their possible interactions) to occupational attainment, ordinary regression models are used. If Y_{it} denotes current occupation in 1970, 1980, or 1988, and $X_{1t}, \ldots, X_{kt}$ represent the list of independent variables, then

$$Y_{it} = \mathbf{b}_{0t} + \mathbf{b}_{1t} X_{1it} + \mathbf{b}_{2t} X_{2it} + \ldots + \mathbf{b}_{kt} X_{kit} + '_{\mathrm{it}} \qquad (1)$$

Additional interaction terms are added to detect non-linear relationships between variables, for example, gender variations and differences involving party membership. The total effects of parental background variables are estimated by omitting all individual attainment variables and their corresponding missing dummies.The regression models are estimated separately for each country and at each time point. The following strategy is applied consistently to derive the final models for each country: first, estimate the main effects models for each period, then add possible interaction effects one at a time, and, finally, test whether the significant interaction effects can be added simultaneously with significant improvement using backward selection method.

GENDER DIFFERENCES IN OCCUPATIONAL ATTAINMENT

Before presenting results from regression analyses, Table 1 summarizes the observed gender differences in socioeconomic attainment across countries and over time. Several observations are noteworthy. First, with the exception of Polish men, the mean status scores for men and women both improved over time. Second, the improvement was substantially greater for women than men. In fact, except in Czechoslovakia, women's occupational status started to surpass men in 1980, and the gain was either maintained or widened in 1988. Russian women's socioeconomic status in 1988 was about 4.5 ISE points greater than their male counterparts. Similarly, noticeable advantage was observed for women in Hungary (3.4 points) and Bulgaria (2.5 points). All of these differences are statistically significant at the 0.001 level. The advantage was substantially smaller in Poland (1.4 points), though still significant at the 0.05 level. Only in Czechoslovakia do we observe equal status attainment between men and women in 1988 (and 1980 as well), but note also the slightly inferior position of women in 1970. Thus, an improvement in the occupational status of women over time is observed in all five countries, with particularly noticeable gains in Russia and Hungary.

To see how substantial these gains by women under socialism were, we can refer to corresponding figures in the United States. Based on a rough benchmark compiled from the *Cumulative General Social Surveys, 1972–1998*

Table 1. Observed Gender Differences in Occupational Attainment Under Socialism.

EGP Classes	1970 Men (%)	1970 Women (%)	1980 Men (%)	1980 Women (%)	1988 Men (%)	1988 Women (%)	1970 Men (%)	1970 Women (%)	1980 Men (%)	1980 Women (%)	1988 Men (%)	1988 Women (%)
	Russia						Bulgaria					
Higher-Grade Professional & Manager	17.04	14.46	17.48	18.21	18.16	20.31	6.67	5.09	7.35	6.80	7.60	8.07
Lower-Grade Professional & Manager	12.16	24.42	13.09	24.25	13.48	26.88	10.63	16.47	11.36	19.05	11.23	19.69
Routine Non-Manual	2.76	17.42	2.98	18.70	3.37	18.76	3.57	14.62	3.40	17.39	3.86	20.55
Skilled Manual/Supervisor	35.71	14.70	34.88	16.70	34.53	14.29	29.37	9.71	29.93	10.13	30.30	11.38
Semi- & Unskilled Manual	20.43	19.67	22.20	16.11	21.39	14.14	32.46	27.66	34.01	28.58	34.22	27.46
Farmer & Farm Worker	11.90	9.33	9.36	6.03	9.08	5.62	17.29	26.46	13.95	18.05	12.79	12.84
Mean ISE Score	42.47	43.82	42.77	46.04	43.16	47.69	35.27	35.40	35.97	37.39	36.39	39.17
Index of Dissimilarity	26.92		27.60		30.94		26.04		25.79		25.68	
	Czechoslovakia						Hungary					
Higher-Grade Professional & Manager	8.87	3.45	9.62	4.48	10.18	5.36	8.43	3.45	7.50	4.41	8.03	6.22
Lower-Grade Professional & Manager	14.19	15.62	13.79	17.00	14.53	18.54	9.25	12.32	11.66	16.22	11.55	18.89
Routine Non-Manual	7.03	31.59	7.43	32.16	6.19	33.89	4.62	21.85	3.55	26.01	4.52	28.71
Skilled Manual/Supervisor	34.72	12.20	36.22	12.72	36.62	12.77	36.26	16.15	38.61	16.82	37.85	15.37
Semi- & Unskilled Manual	28.98	26.01	27.21	25.18	26.79	22.46	27.47	29.79	27.90	28.48	29.42	26.46
Farm & Farm Worker	6.22	11.12	5.73	8.46	5.68	6.97	13.96	16.43	10.78	8.07	8.63	4.35
Mean ISE Score	40.25	39.07	40.57	40.06	40.74	41.29	36.59	35.72	37.21	39.06	37.81	41.19
Index of Dissimilarity	30.90		30.67		33.00		25.09		27.59		31.53	

Table 1. Continued.

EGP Classes	1970 Men (%)	1970 Women (%)	1980 Men (%)	1980 Women (%)	1988 Men (%)	1988 Women (%)	1970 Men (%)	1970 Women (%)	1980 Men (%)	1980 Women (%)	1988 Men (%)	1988 Women (%)
			Poland									
Higher-Grade Professional & Manager	14.52	8.17	14.67	8.99	13.39	8.49						
Lower-Grade Professional & Manager	15.26	14.33	13.43	17.85	16.39	20.55						
Routine Non-Manual	6.06	32.80	6.68	32.94	6.47	33.85						
Skilled Manual/Supervisor	31.87	10.19	32.71	10.37	32.16	9.20						
Semi- & Unskilled Manual	20.48	16.25	22.13	17.85	20.93	16.57						
Farm & Farm Worker	11.81	18.26	10.38	12.01	10.66	11.34						
Mean ISE Score	41.01	40.48	41.00	41.61	40.92	42.29						
Index of Dissimilarity	33.19		32.29		32.21							

Note: Sums may not be equal to 100 because of rounding errors.

(Davis & Smith, 1998), the mean occupational prestige of men and women aged between 20 and 64 in the United States was, respectively, 40.5 and 40.0 in 1980 and 40.8 and 40.5 in 1988. It was only in 1998 that women's occupational prestige began to surpass men and the difference was really small (44.6 vs. 44.2), much less than the advantage Eastern European women gained almost two decades earlier. In general, then, the gains in occupational status women achieved under socialism were quite phenomenal.

Third, the relatively higher socioeconomic standing of women in socialist countries can be explained by their over-representation in lower-grade professional and managerial jobs and clerical positions, under-representation in skilled manual positions, and more or less equal representation in the lower end of the class spectrum (semi-skilled and unskilled manual and farm worker).[9] Also, while the presence of women in higher-grade professional and managerial jobs was generally low in all five countries, significant inroads have been made in Russia and Hungary, where increasing rates of women's representation in these highly desirable occupations are observed. In fact, since 1980, the proportion of Russian women attaining these occupations has been higher than that of Russian men.

Finally, the degree of occupational sex segregation was moderate (ranging from 25 to 33). It remained relatively stable in Bulgaria and Poland between 1970 and 1988, but some slight increase was observed in Czechoslovakia, Hungary, and Russia. According to a five country comparison of occupational sex segregation in the 1970s, the degree of occupational segregation in the two socialist countries (Hungary and Poland) and France was generally lower than that of the Federal Republic of Germany and Sweden (Erikson & Goldthorpe, 1993, p. 243). Unfortunately, the results are not strictly comparable because of the reorganization of the CASMIN classes in that study. But it may be safe to conclude that even if the degree of sex segregation in these socialist countries was similar to that in the West, socialist women had a higher degree of integration into the labor force and had made significant inroads into professional and managerial occupations. Whether the observed gender advantages are robust in multivariate analysis and explainable by women's rising educational attainment will be examined below.

SOCIOECONOMIC ATTAINMENT IN RUSSIA

The regression models that provide the best understanding of the determinants of occupational attainment in Russia in 1970, 1980, and 1988 respectively are reported in Table 2. In each case, the preferred model accounts for more than half of the variance in socioeconomic attainment. At the same time, there is a

Table 2. Occupational Attainment in Russia (Ordinary Regression Models).

Variables	Regression Coefficients 1970	1980	1988
Intercept	17.341***	14.596***	16.908***
Age	0.062	0.047	–0.034
Female	–0.380	0.709	1.438
Number of Siblings	–0.039	0.080	0.031
Parent Educ (Secondary without Diploma)	0.079	0.612	0.133
Parent Educ (Secondary with Diploma)	–0.417	–0.869	–1.053#
Parent Educ (Tertiary or Higher)	–1.447	–2.767**	–0.122
Father Occupation	0.060*	0.043*	0.034#
Father Self-Employed	0.202	0.330	–1.468
Parental Cultural Capital	1.351***	1.029**	0.865*
Parent Communist Party Member	1.148#	0.876	1.300*
Secondary without Diploma	0.296	0.948	0.660
Secondary with Diploma	3.117**	4.191***	4.370***
Tertiary or Higher	19.165***	19.416***	18.825***
First Occupation	0.484***	0.442***	0.410***
Years in Labor Force	–0.008	0.298**	0.353***
Years in Labor Force Squared	–0.181	–0.764***	–0.668***
Communist Party Member	5.437**	7.200***	3.519***
Cumulative Years in Communist Party	–0.033	–0.095	0.121*
Interactions:			
CP Member*Secondary without Diploma	–1.492	0.059	
CP Member*Secondary with Diploma	0.279	0.897	
CP Member*Tertiary or Higher	–6.516**	–4.938*	
Female*Secondary without Diploma	2.786	1.461	1.411
Female*Secondary with Diploma	3.116*	3.194**	2.766*
Female*Tertiary or Higher	–2.214	0.850	0.364
R^2	0.589	0.574	0.544
Adjusted R^2	0.583	0.569	0.540
RMSE	11.539	11.703	12.109
Sample Size	2084	3063	3448

# $p < 0.10$, * $p < 0.05$, ** $p < 0.01$, *** $p < 0.001$.

Note: The coefficients of years in the labor force squared have been multiplied by 100.

steady decline in the respective model's explanatory power, from 59% in 1970 to 54% in 1988, suggesting that factors other than those considered in the current framework increasingly contributed to occupational attainment.

Several important observations emerge from the results. First, similar to status attainment reported in the West (Featherman & Hauser, 1978), the *direct* influences of the conventional measures of socioeconomic background were mostly insignificant in the period covered, even though their total effects were important (see the top panel of Table 3 for details). The only exception is father's occupation where its influence was significant in 1970 and 1980, and marginal in 1988. Furthermore, the level of individual occupational attainment in 1980 was considerably lower if either parent had tertiary or higher education. Contrary to the postulation of possible re-stratification, there is no notable increasing trend for either the direct or total effects of these background variables. Father's occupation is again the only exception, with its total effect increased somewhat over time.[10] As expected, the direct and indirect influence of parental cultural capital was significant in Russia. Its direct impact, however, has declined over time. Most of its influence on socioeconomic status was largely indirect, and the total effects ranged from 4.3 to 5.4 ISE points, higher in the first two years (1970 and 1980) and lower in 1988. Consistent with our hypothesis again, the direct effect of parental social capital was marginal in 1970 and 1980, but gained statistical significance in 1988. Since the total effects were practically the same (slightly less than 4 ISE points) in all three years, the result suggests that the effect of parental Communist party membership had changed from indirect influences to both direct and indirect

Table 3. Selected Effects of Variables in Occupational Attainment in Russia.

Variables	1970	1980	1988
(A) Total Effects of Parental Background Variables			
Parent Educ (Secondary without Diploma)	2.074	2.211#	1.541
Parent Educ (Secondary with Diploma)	3.620**	1.592#	0.998
Parent Educ (Tertiary or Higher)	3.709*	1.328	3.808**
Father Occupation	0.100**	0.122***	0.123***
Father Self-Employed	–2.233	–0.727	–2.766#
Parental Cultural Capital	5.367***	5.312***	4.337***
Parent Communist Party Member	3.557***	3.837***	3.942***
R^2	0.181	0.167	0.165
(B) Net Gender Differences by Education[a]			
Primary or Less	–0.380	0.709	1.438
Secondary without Diploma	2.406	2.170#	2.849*
Secondary with Diploma	2.736**	3.903***	4.204***
Tertiary or Higher	–2.594#	1.559	1.802*

# $p < 0.10$, * $p < 0.05$, ** $p < 0.01$, *** $p < 0.001$.

[a] Positive values indicate women's occupational statuses are higher than men and vice versa.

influences in 1988. Together with the rising influence of individual Communist party membership (to be discussed shortly), this increase in direct effect of parental social capital signifies that in the waning days of Soviet socialism, its stratification system was turning into an exclusive network where power and privileges were largely reserved for Communist party members and their children, at least in the case of socioeconomic status.

None of the coefficients for female are significant at all three time points. But since there are significant interactions between female and education, a more complex interpretation of how Russian women fared in the socialist stratification system is warranted. For Russian men, there was virtually no difference in status attainment between those with primary or less education and those with secondary education but without diploma. A diploma secondary education, on the other hand, would increase ISE status by 3–4 points over primary or less education. The advantage for university graduates was even higher, as much as 19 ISE points. Furthermore, these differentials by the types and levels of education were relatively stable over time. Similar effects are observed for Russian women, except that women holding secondary diploma education attained higher status occupations than their male counterparts. Such advantage for the better educated women was maintained in all three of the years studied. To highlight the gains made by Russian women, the *net* gender differences by types and levels of education are reported in the bottom panel of Table 3. The results confirm that women, especially those with diploma secondary education, made significant inroads into not only male occupations, but also occupations with high socioeconomic status, probably at the expense of men's attainment.

Results from Table 2 also indicate that individual attainments (education, first occupation, years in the labor force, and Communist party membership) were more important than parental background in accounting for socioeconomic attainment.[11] Irrespective of individual education, Communist party membership accounts for about 3 to 7 points gains in socioeconomic status. Although it may appear that the effect of party membership has declined in 1988, there are reasons to caution against such an interpretation. First, the effect of seniority within the party was positive and significant in 1988. In fact, veteran members of 20 years tended to have 6 points higher in occupational status than non-members. Second, as noted earlier, the effect of parental Communist party membership was also significant in 1988, with about two-thirds of its influence transmitted indirectly through individual attainment such as education and party membership. Thus, the cumulative advantages for those party members with "privileged" background can be tremendous. Once again, the evidence suggests that before its collapse in 1991, the Russian stratification system was dominated by networks and social relationships, which played a significant role in socioeconomic advancement.

Consistent with the postulation in H5, there were significant interactions between Communist party membership and individual education in 1970. Surprisingly, the effect persisted in 1980. For both years, party members with primary or less education tended to attain 5 to 7 points higher in socioeconomic status than non-members with similar education. But the socioeconomic attainment by party members with tertiary or higher education were lower than non-members by 6.5 points in 1970 and 4.7 points in 1980, largely diminishing or even erasing the gains afforded by their party membership status. In other words, the Communist party in Russia continued to favor some of its less educated members long after the Stalinist era, and actively promoted them in their occupational (and possibly political) careers. In 1988, as we discussed earlier, Communist party membership per se conferred significant advantages, irrespective of educational level. Such advantages gave people tremendous incentives to join the Russian Communist Worker's Party (CPSU) during the period studied. This may explain why the size of CPSU continued to increase until the late 1980s when hundreds of thousands of members started to leave (Holms, Read & Voskresenkaya, 1995), whereas in the case of Hungary and Poland, the decline in party membership occurred in the early 1980s (Miller, 1982; Staar, 1988; Weydenthal, 1986).

SOCIOECONOMIC ATTAINMENT IN BULGARIA

In Bulgaria, as in Russia, none of the parental background variables had any direct and consistent influences on status attainment (see Table 4), except for parental cultural capital. Their influences were still disproportionately indirect (see top panel of Table 5). It is interesting to observe that an intelligentsia background tended to lower children's occupational attainment. In other words, the actual attainment of children from an intelligentsia family would have been lower had they not also had very high parental cultural capital. Together with the findings on their total effects, this indicates that for the intelligentsia class, the vehicle for intergenerational transmission of inequality is parental cultural capital, not education *per se*. The total effects of the other "additional" agents of stratification, parental social capital, were also significant (slightly more than 2 ISE points). Since these effects were statistically significant in all three years, there is strong evidence against the long-term effectiveness of the socialist regime's deliberate efforts to reduce intergenerational transmission of inequality. It seems that Bulgarian families were able to counteract and circumvent the

Table 4. Occupational Attainment in Bulgaria (Ordinary Regression Models).

Variables	Regression Coefficients 1970	1980	1988
Intercept	10.732***	9.296***	11.539***
Age	0.018	0.010	0.054
Female	–0.961#	–1.101*	–1.046#
Number of Siblings	–0.333**	–0.277**	–0.311**
Parent Educ (Secondary without Diploma)	1.919	1.265	0.968
Parent Educ (Secondary with Diploma)	–1.401	–0.601	–0.074
Parent Educ (Tertiary or Higher)	–3.045#	–2.491*	–3.073**
Father Occupation	0.008	0.037*	0.016
Father Self-Employed	0.723	1.056*	0.748
Parental Cultural Capital	1.425***	1.236***	1.507***
Parent Communist Party Member	0.179	0.128	0.035
Secondary without Diploma	2.477**	1.974*	2.442**
Secondary with Diploma	5.813***	5.023***	4.149***
Tertiary or Higher	11.281***	12.246***	11.791***
First Occupation	0.616***	0.588***	0.537***
Years in Labor Force	0.410***	0.396***	0.169*
Years in Labor Force Squared	–1.245***	–0.833***	–0.345**
Communist Party Member	1.998#	2.251*	2.063*
Cumulative Years in Communist Party	0.150	0.044	0.040
Interactions:			
Female*Secondary without Diploma	0.025	1.350	1.189
Female*Secondary with Diploma	1.165	1.737*	2.789***
Female*Tertiary or Higher	5.746***	5.112***	5.747***
Female*Cum Years in Communist Party	–0.301*		
R^2	0.665	0.660	0.611
Adjusted R^2	0.660	0.656	0.608
RMSE	8.869	9.117	9.801
Sample Size	2116	2971	3292

# $p < 0.10$, * $p < 0.05$, ** $p < 0.01$, *** $p < 0.001$.

Note: The coefficients of years in the labor force squared have been multiplied by 100.

imposed conditions and continue to transmit inequality from one generation to another.

Again, just like in Russia, educational attainment was the most important determinant of individual status attainment.[12] Given the interactions between gender and education, separate interpretations for men and women are in order. For men, the effects of education increased according to the levels and types of

Table 5. Selected Effects of Variables in Occupational Attainment in Bulgaria.

Variables	1970	1980	1988
(A) Total Effects of Parental Background Variables			
Parent Educ (Secondary without Diploma)	4.787**	3.280*	3.182*
Parent Educ (Secondary with Diploma)	2.824*	3.215***	3.071***
Parent Educ (Tertiary or Higher)	0.615	2.389	0.153
Father Occupation	0.026	0.078**	0.063*
Father Self-Employed	0.163	–0.179	–1.069
Parental Cultural Capital	7.564***	6.931***	6.751***
Parent Communist Party Member	2.847***	2.600***	2.223***
R^2	0.228	0.249	0.251
(B) Net Gender Differences by Education[a]			
Primary or Less	–0.961#	–1.101*	–1.046#
Secondary without Diploma	–0.936	0.249	0.143
Secondary with Diploma	0.204	0.637	1.743***
Tertiary or Higher	4.785**	4.011**	4.701***

# $p < 0.10$, * $p < 0.05$, ** $p < 0.01$, *** $p < 0.001$.

[a]Positive values indicate women's occupational statuses are higher than men and vice versa.

education received and were relatively stable over time, though the returns of education for those with secondary diploma education declined somewhat over time (from 5.8 to 5.0 to 4.1 ISE points in 1970, 1980, and 1988, respectively). A secondary education without diploma raised socioeconomic attainment 2 points above a primary or less education. For tertiary or higher education, the returns were 11 points higher. A similar pattern is observed for women, but women with tertiary education had even higher levels of status attainment, as much as 5.7 ISE points higher than their male counterparts. Although the interaction effects between women and secondary education with diploma are statistically significant in both 1980 and 1988, it is only in 1988 that the net effects indicate a clear advantage of women over men with the same credentials (see bottom panel of Table 5). In other words, it is tertiary education, not diploma secondary education as in Russia, that gave Bulgarian women advantages over their male counterparts.

On average, being a member of the Bulgarian Communist Party increased one's socioeconomic status by about 2 ISE points at all three time points, but the effects are significant in 1980 and 1988 only. Seniority within the party, on the other hand, provided little or no significant advantages. For female comrades, it was even a liability in 1970 as they had significantly lower attainment than their male counterparts with similar characteristics and non-members. Thus, even though party membership conferred some advantages in Bulgaria, its influence is definitely not as prominent as in Russia. Finally, similar to the case of Russia, the explanatory power of the models declines somewhat over time, from about 67% of the total variance explained to about 61%.

SOCIOECONOMIC ATTAINMENT IN CZECHOSLOVAKIA

Table 6 presents the final models chosen for Czechoslovakia. A dummy variable for Slovakia is added in each model, since it has been argued that the Czechoslovak Communist government provided preferential treatment to residents of Slovakia (Matějů, 1993). The results here indeed confirm that residents in Slovakia had had a slight advantage of about one ISE point over their counterparts in the Czech lands, but the advantage virtually disappeared in 1988.

As expected, the direct influences of the conventional measures of parental background were marginal in all three years. None of the effects are statistically significant. The total effects (top panel of Table 7), on the other hand, reveal stable indirect influences for parental background with secondary education, regardless of their credential status. But for those with tertiary or higher educational background, its indirect effect has increased over time. Interestingly, no effect whatsoever is observed for parental Communist party membership, whereas parental cultural capital shows both direct and indirect influences in all three years. Thus, though the Czechoslovak Communist government was quite adamant about adhering to the Marxist-Leninist ideology, it was still unable to stem the reproduction of inequality through the transmission of cultural capital. The finding provides clear evidence that individuals from more culturally endowed families had distinct advantages and that a significant proportion of the influence of parental cultural capital was indirect, mediated through individual attainment,including individual cultural capital. In 1980, the effect was stronger for women than for men, but no similar advantage for women applied earlier in 1970 or later in 1988. It is noteworthy that the effect of parental cultural capital appears to be strengthening towards the end of socialism. If the trend is real and barring dramatic changes thereafter, the influence of parental cultural capital is likely to be quite significant in today's Slovakia and the Czech Republic.

Table 6. Occupational Attainment in Czechoslovakia (Ordinary Regression Models).

Variables	Regression Coefficients 1970	1980	1988
Intercept	14.794***	14.186***	13.084***
Slovakia	1.081***	0.985***	0.047
Age	–0.021	–0.009	0.001
Female	–2.270***	–1.023*	–1.211*
Number of Siblings	–0.021	–0.133*	–0.079
Parent Educ (Secondary without Diploma)	–0.263	–0.312	0.173
Parent Educ (Secondary with Diploma)	0.151	0.312	0.173
Parent Educ (Tertiary or Higher)	–0.980	0.296	–0.101
Father Occupation	0.010	0.013	0.014
Father Self-Employed	0.189	0.500	0.080
Parental Cultural Capital	0.787***	0.545*	0.934***
Parent Communist Party Member	–0.140	–0.122	–0.186
Secondary without Diploma	1.029#	1.110*	0.686
Secondary with Diploma	9.325***	9.664***	8.115***
Tertiary or Higher	15.116***	16.002***	15.783***
First Occupation	0.518***	0.508***	0.506***
Years in Labor Force	0.199**	0.137**	0.202***
Years in Labor Force Squared	–0.183	–0.089	–0.231**
Communist Party Member	1.702	0.620	0.712
Cumulative Years in Communist Party	0.173***	0.143***	0.078**
Interactions:			
CP Member*Secondary without Diploma	–0.120		
CP Member*Secondary with Diploma	–2.091		
CP Member*Tertiary or Higher	–3.209*		
Female*Secondary without Diploma	3.143***	2.092***	1.711**
Female*Secondary with Diploma	0.864	–0.513	0.759
Female*Tertiary or Higher	5.180***	1.958*	3.012***
Female*Parental Cultural Capital		0.578*	
R^2	0.625	0.633	0.624
Adjusted R^2	0.622	0.631	0.623
RMSE	9.080	9.045	9.236
Sample Size	4824	6996	7564

# $p < 0.10$, * $p < 0.05$, ** $p < 0.01$, *** $p < 0.001$.

Note: The coefficients of years in the labor force squared have been multiplied by 100.

Compared to Russia and Bulgaria, the advantage of secondary education with diploma was more pronounced in Czechoslovakia, especially for men. For Czechoslovak men, there was virtually no difference in attainment between

Table 7. Selected Effects of Variables in Occupational Attainment in Czechoslovakia.

Variables	1970	1980	1988
(A) Total Effects of Parental Background Variables			
Parent Educ (Secondary without Diploma)	1.255**	0.832*	0.925*
Parent Educ (Secondary with Diploma)	3.973***	3.685***	3.727***
Parent Educ (Tertiary or Higher)	3.362**	4.983***	5.122***
Father Occupation	0.150***	0.145***	0.144***
Father Self-Employed	–0.397	–0.309	–0.800
Parental Cultural Capital	4.799***	3.842***	4.612***
Parent Communist Party Member	0.650	0.560	0.511
Female*Parental Cultural Capital		1.899***	
R^2	0.185	0.206	0.197
(B) Net Gender Differences by Education[a]			
Primary or Less	–2.270***	–1.023*	–1.211*
Secondary without Diploma	0.873*	1.069**	0.500
Secondary with Diploma	–1.406**	–1.536***	–0.452
Tertiary or Higher	2.910**	0.936	1.801**

# $p < 0.10$, * $p < 0.05$, ** $p < 0.01$, *** $p < 0.001$.

[a] Positive values indicate women's occupational statuses are higher than men and vice versa.

those who received primary or less education and secondary non-diploma education. But the advantage of diploma secondary education was quite substantial, about 8 to 9 ISE points. Likewise, the advantage of tertiary education was prominent, boosting socioeconomic attainment by as much as 16 points. For women, the situation falls into two opposite scenarios. On the one hand, women with primary or less and diploma secondary education were worse off than their male counterparts. On the other hand, those with tertiary or higher education and, to a lesser extent, non-diploma secondary education generally attained higher socioeconomic status than men (see the bottom panel of Table 7).

Unlike the case in Bulgaria and Russia, it is not party membership *per se* but seniority within the Czechoslovak Communist Party that boosted individual status attainment. None of the regression coefficients for party membership is significant in any of the three years. Yet, the cumulative number of years spent within the party is highly significant in all three years. In 1970, each additional year of party membership increased one's socioeconomic status by about 0.17 points. In other words, a person who had 20 years of seniority within the party was likely to attain an additional 3.4 points in socioeconomic status over a first-year member. This advantage, however, declined by 17% in 1980, and another 45% in 1988. Clearly, then, while the Czechoslovak stratification system favored long-time party members in promotion and career advancement, the influence of party seniority declined dramatically over time. Finally, consistent with the prediction from H5, party members with tertiary or higher education tended to have significantly lower level of occupational attainment than their less-educated counterparts in 1970.

SOCIOECONOMIC ATTAINMENT IN HUNGARY

Consistent with our findings on the other countries, few of the conventional measures of parental background had any direct influence on status attainment in Hungary (see Table 8). Thus, empirical support for the re-stratification thesis' postulation of a returning importance of parental background in socioeconomic attainment under socialism is quite weak. The stability of the measures' overall influence (see total effects presented in Table 9) further questions the thesis's validity. In fact, of all background variables, only parental cultural capital exerted both significant *direct* and *indirect* influences on socioeconomic attainment in all three years. Since these effects were relatively stable over time, it appears that the efforts to reduce intergenerational transmission of inequality were quite ineffective. Interestingly, the effects did not increase under the more permissive economic reform environment. Furthermore, both the direct and indirect influences of parental social capital were negligible, unlike the case in Bulgaria and Russia.

The returns of education to socioeconomic status were considerably stronger in Hungary than the other countries studied. Since its influences also differed for men and women, we need to discuss them separately. Hungarian men with non-diploma secondary education generally had higher attainment than those with primary or less education, but such advantage decreased consistently over time (from 3 points in 1970 to 2.2 in 1980 and 1.5 in 1988). A similar decline is also observed for those with diploma secondary education, except that the advantage was at a considerably higher level (from 10.6 points in 1970 to 7.8 points in 1988). University graduates, in contrast, have been successful in maintaining their advantages. The attainment gaps between university and secondary graduates have remained remarkably stable over time. This is not the case for Hungarian women. While female university graduates did not fare as well as their male counterparts in 1970, averaging a status about 6.6 points lower, the gender penalty virtually disappeared in 1980 and 1988. The

Table 8. Occupational Attainment in Hungary (Ordinary Regression Models).

Variables	Regression Coefficients 1970	1980	1988
Intercept	15.991***	16.211***	16.610***
Age	–0.034	–0.049	–0.004
Female	0.136	1.682**	0.615
Number of Siblings	–0.021	–0.228**	–0.228*
Parent Educ (Secondary without Diploma)	0.337	–0.303	–0.250
Parent Educ (Secondary with Diploma)	0.069	0.063	–0.656
Parent Educ (Tertiary or Higher)	–0.683	–0.394	–0.668
Father Occupation	0.035	0.004	0.039*
Father Self-Employed	–0.250	–0.165	–0.317
Parental Cultural Capital	1.175***	1.251***	1.151***
Parent Communist Party Member	–0.330	0.528	–0.089
Secondary without Diploma	3.008***	2.193***	1.547*
Secondary with Diploma	10.596***	9.534***	7.781***
Tertiary or Higher	22.021***	20.814***	20.255***
First Occupation	0.409***	0.386***	0.385***
Years in Labor Force	0.382***	0.473***	0.135#
Years in Labor Force Squared	–0.689***	–0.686***	0.000
Communist Party Member	2.917**	3.435*	0.457
Cumulative Years in Communist Party	0.119	0.161**	0.068
Interactions:			
CP Member*Secondary without Diploma		–3.067#	
CP Member*Secondary with Diploma		–2.009	
CP Member*Tertiary or Higher		–5.403**	
Female*Secondary without Diploma	1.691	2.685**	3.629***
Female*Secondary with Diploma	1.002	0.933	3.585***
Female*Tertiary or Higher	–6.353***	–0.867	–0.508
Female*Cum Years in Communist Party		–0.185*	
R^2	0.590	0.576	0.597
Adjusted R^2	0.585	0.571	0.593
RMSE	9.569	9.556	9.478
Sample Size	2174	2804	2840

# $p < 0.10$, * $p < 0.05$, ** $p < 0.01$, *** $p < 0.001$.

Note: The coefficients of years in the labor force squared have been multiplied by 100.

advantage of secondary education for women is also obvious, particularly for those without diploma. In 1988, the advantages for diploma and non-diploma holders converged, and women's socioeconomic attainment was more than 4 points higher than men with similar education.

Table 9. Selected Effects of Variables in Occupational Attainment in Hungary.

Variables	1970	1980	1988
(A) Total Effects of Parental Background Variables			
Parent Educ (Secondary without Diploma)	1.494#	0.437	0.190
Parent Educ (Secondary with Diploma)	4.694***	4.085***	2.185*
Parent Educ (Tertiary or Higher)	1.041	1.927	2.384#
Father Occupation	0.125***	0.086***	0.130***
Father Self-Employed	–1.196#	–0.900	–1.132#
Parental Cultural Capital	6.319***	5.949***	5.496***
Parent Communist Party Member	–0.289	0.232	0.221
R^2	0.257	0.248	0.255
(B) Net Gender Differences by Educationa			
Primary or Less	0.136	1.682**	0.615
Secondary without Diploma	1.827*	4.368***	4.243***
Secondary with Diploma	1.138	2.615***	4.200***
Tertiary or Higher	–6.217***	0.815	0.107

# $p < 0.10$, * $p < 0.05$, ** $p < 0.01$, *** $p < 0.001$.

[a] Positive values indicate women's occupational statuses are higher than men and vice versa.

Being a member of the Hungarian Socialist Workers' Party increased one's socioeconomic attainment by approximately 3 points in 1970 and 1980, but individual social capital *per se* was no longer significant in 1988. However, the declining importance of individual social capital does not apply to men and women equally. In 1980, senior male party members continued to enjoy higher socioeconomic standing than non-members, over 7 points higher if they had 20 years of membership. Generally speaking, together with the larger attainment gaps between university and secondary graduates, the finding here is consistent with the observation by Szelényi, Szelényi, and Kovách (1995) that political credentials were not important in leadership position under Kádár's regime and that non-member appointees did not even have to express absolute loyalty to all principles of Marxism-Leninism. It also confirms that intellectuals gained considerable status in Hungary as the socialist regime evolved (Konrád & Szelényi, 1979). However, this does not necessarily support the prediction of a universal rise of credentialism and decline of social capital under Kádár's pragmatic reform. For instance, the finding also indicates that university trained party members still had significantly lower occupational attainment (by about 5.4 points) than members with primary or less education in 1980. Furthermore, the analysis here pertains only to socioeconomic status and not positions of power and authority. Nonetheless, it is clear that unlike Russia and Bulgaria, Communist party membership in Hungary lost its clout as an additional route in status attainment in the 1980s. Finally, the models consistently account for slightly less than 60% of the variance of occupational status in all three years.

SOCIOECONOMIC ATTAINMENT IN POLAND

Table 10 presents the results of the regression analyses of socioeconomic status in Poland. Consistent with the results from the other four countries, most of the measures of parental background did not have any direct influences on status attainment. Parental cultural capital is the only exception. It benefitted women but not men in 1980, and both sexes equally in 1970 and 1988. However, much of its influence was indirect, just like the other background variables (see the top panel of Table 11). Interestingly, the total effects of parental cultural capital remained remarkably stable for the three years studied. With the exception of a significant effect of parental education at the tertiary level in 1970, none of the other measures of parental background (father's occupation and parental party membership) had any notable direct influence on occupational attainment.

As expected, both the types and levels of education attained were highly influential in status attainment. Other than the fact that women generally attained occupations with lower status, the returns of education were the same for men and women in 1970 and 1980. In 1988, however, some of the returns differed remarkably by gender. Relative to those with primary education or less, university credentials increased the socioeconomic status of both men and women by over 19.5 points in 1970 and 1980, and slightly lower in 1988. The returns for diploma secondary education were considerably lower but still high, about 9–10 points for men in all three years. For women, there were similar returns in 1970 and 1980, but a remarkable 12 points in 1988. Much lower returns are observed for non-diploma secondary education, and the returns steadily declined over time.

Individual social capital was significant only in 1970, when members of the Polish United Workers' Party generally attained 4 points higher in socioeconomic status than non-members. However, since party membership also interacted with individual education, this advantage in fact applied only to members with primary or less education. For those with secondary education (with or without diploma), no *net* advantage is observed, as the main and interaction effects practically cancelled each other out. For well-educated members with university degrees, there was even a net disadvantage of over 4

Table 10. Occupational Attainment in Poland (Ordinary Regression Models).

Variables	Regression Coefficients 1970	1980	1988
Intercept	10.788***	15.088***	15.814***
Age	0.127*	–0.019	–0.016
Female	–1.641***	–0.709#	–2.094**
Number of Siblings	0.028	–0.095	–0.106
Parent Educ (Secondary without Diploma)	–0.091	–0.709	–0.482
Parent Educ (Secondary with Diploma)	0.568	–0.005	0.991
Parent Educ (Tertiary or Higher)	3.044*	0.112	0.036
Father Occupation	0.014	–0.008	0.013
Father Self-Employed	0.737	–0.315	–0.370
Parental Cultural Capital	0.817*	0.357	1.162***
Parent Communist Party Member	0.659	0.480	–0.283
Secondary without Diploma	3.193***	2.606***	1.892**
Secondary with Diploma	9.821***	10.278***	8.732***
Tertiary or Higher	19.789***	19.541***	18.845***
First Occupation	0.495***	0.462***	0.421***
Years in Labor Force	0.233*	0.323***	0.268***
Years in Labor Force Squared	–0.767*	–0.510**	–0.351**
Communist Party Member	4.396**	1.530#	1.422
Cumulative Years in Communist Party	0.111	0.024	0.060
Interactions:			
CP Member*Secondary without Diploma	–4.256*		
CP Member*Secondary with Diploma	–3.293*		
CP Member*Tertiary or Higher	–8.472***		
Female*Parental Cultural Capital		0.886*	
Female*Secondary without Diploma			1.823#
Female*Secondary with Diploma			3.393***
Female*Tertiary or Higher			1.003
R^2	0.689	0.651	0.624
Adjusted R^2	0.684	0.648	0.621
RMSE	9.208	9.665	10.015
Sample Size	1948	3132	3447

# $p < 0.10$, * $p < 0.05$, ** $p < 0.01$, *** $p < 0.001$.

Note: The coefficients of years in the labor force squared have been multiplied by 100.

points. This clearly indicates that the more ideological and repressive Polish Communist Party continued to practice negative social selection in 1970, promoting the uneducated while penalizing the well-educated within its own party rank. But the allure of party membership as an additional route for social advancement disappeared completely in the 1980s, when there was a mass exodus of party members (Staar, 1988; Weydenthal, 1986). Finally, the proportion of variance explained by the models declined modestly over time from 0.69 in 1970 to 0.62 in 1988.

SUMMARY OF FINDINGS

Contrary to the restratification thesis (and the prediction from H1), the study does not find a trend of increasing *direct* and/or *indirect* influences of parental background in socioeconomic attainment.[13] Most of the influences were indirect, mediated through individual attainment such as education, first occupation, and social capital (party membership), and remained relatively stable between 1970 and 1988 in all five countries. This stability highlights the inability of the socialist system to neutralize the intergenerational transmission mechanisms of families.

The persistent significance of the direct influence of parental cultural capital in all five countries throughout the period studied further illustrates the

Table 11. Selected Effects of Variables in Occupational Attainment in Poland.

Variables	1970	1980	1988
(A) Total Effects of Parental Background Variables			
Parent Educ (Secondary without Diploma)	1.832#	1.375#	1.100
Parent Educ (Secondary with Diploma)	4.394***	2.925***	4.081***
Parent Educ (Tertiary or Higher)	8.692***	5.075***	4.837***
Father Occupation	0.096**	0.082***	0.099***
Father Self-Employed	–0.155	–0.772	–0.686
Parental Cultural Capital	6.343***	4.994***	5.967***
Parent Communist Party Member	0.407	0.953	0.283
Female*Parental Cultural Capital		1.802***	
R^2	0.290	0.253	0.264
(B) Net Gender Differences by Education[a]			
Primary or Less	–1.641***	–0.709#	–2.094**
Secondary without Diploma	–1.641***	–0.709#	–0.272
Secondary with Diploma	–1.641***	–0.709#	1.299*
Tertiary or Higher	–1.641***	–0.709#	–1.092

# $p < 0.10$, * $p < 0.05$, ** $p < 0.01$, *** $p < 0.001$.

[a] Positive values indicate women's occupational statuses are higher than men and vice versa.

inadequacies of the socialist system in reducing the intergenerational transmission of inequality. Together with the strong and stable total effects of parental cultural capital, this result lends strong support to H2.[14] In contrast, the support for H3 is inconclusive. Unlike parental cultural capital, the direct effect of parental social capital was weak. In terms of total effects, the remarkable cross-national differences (strong and stable in Russia and Bulgaria, but weak and insignificant in Czechoslovakia, Hungary, and Poland) illustrate that the institutionalization of socialism varied across countries and the power and privileges conferred to Communist party members differed accordingly. Politically derived status differentials were particularly acute in Russia: not only was the influence of individual social capital strong and significant throughout the period studied, but both seniority in the party and parental social capital also became significant in 1988. This suggests that favoritism and nepotism was rampant in the Russian society right before its collapse in 1991. Russia's socialist experience, then, directly challenges the prediction of H3 about the declining influence of parental social capital.

Consistent with H4, both the levels and types of education were important in determining individual socioeconomic attainment. The biggest advantage can be found among university graduates, who achieved about 11 points over those with primary or less education in Bulgaria and 15 to 19 points in the other four countries. Having credentials in secondary education also boosted status attainment, but to a lesser extent. Perhaps the most interesting finding is that not only did women generally attain higher occupational status than their male counterparts, but those with diploma secondary education or tertiary education had greater returns than their male counterparts as early as 1970 in some countries (consistent with H7). Thus, the fact that many socialist women attended *gymnasium* (diploma education) rather than basic vocational training may well reflect a rational response to their better expected returns in occupational status.

Such improvement in women's position in the labor market was particularly impressive because policies for social promotion to equalize opportunities were virtually eliminated in all Eastern European countries by the end of the 1970s. How can we explain the remarkable gains in socioeconomic attainment by women? First, women's high level of occupational attainment can possibly be attributed to institutional and infrastructural support in the labor market, such as the right to return to the same jobs, child care, and paid maternity leave. Although some critics may see the motives behind these policies as purely pronatal or pragmatic resolution for severe labor shortages, it is undeniable that the derived benefits to women's position in the labor market have been spectacular and persistent. Second, and more importantly, the types and specialties of secondary education that women received were instrumental in boosting their levels of occupational attainment and the returns of education. Women in socialist countries were more likely to attend secondary grammar schools, which significantly improved their chances to obtain higher education and non-manual occupations. For those who received technical vocational training, women were more likely to concentrate in professions such as teaching and nursing, while men gravitated towards "male-dominating" jobs such as craftsmen and technicians. In other words, though the levels of education were the same, the types and contents of training at the secondary level differed by gender. As a result, women with secondary education tended to enter occupations that have higher status than those taken by men with similar education. In sum, given the close relationship between education, training, and occupational attainment, it is not surprising to find the returns of education different for men and women. Paradoxically, women achieved higher occupational attainment when socialism was coming to an end in Eastern Europe amidst rising discontent and dissent from their citizens. It would be interesting to see whether the gains women made in the labor market remained, improved, or deteriorated under a different system after 1989.

Like parental social capital, significant cross-national differences are observed in individual social capital. In Hungary and Poland, party membership lost its clout in the 1980s and no longer provided any advantage in socioeconomic attainment. While individual social capital continued to play a particularly significant role in Bulgaria, Czechoslovakia, and Russia, the mechanisms involved were quite different. In Bulgaria and Russia, party membership had direct effects on status attainment, whereas in Czechoslovakia, the influence came through seniority within the party. Given the lack of a visible trend in most countries, the support for H5 is mixed, and for H6 weak. However, it is important to recognize that the findings do not negate the significance of individual social capital in status attainment, especially in the heyday of socialism. To what extent social capital played in advancing individual careers and other status attainment outcomes should be further examined in future research.

DISCUSSION

The findings here show that while the conventional measures of family background had little direct influence on occupational attainment under socialism, parental cultural capital and, to a limited extent, parental social capital, were significant. This underscores the need to broaden our conception of various stratification agents under socialism.[15] Although the influence of parental cultural capital may weaken somewhat if we control for individual cultural capital, its importance nonetheless highlights the significance of cultural capital as a stratifying agent under a socialist regime. Countering the universal access to education and other interventionist policies that aimed at equalizing opportunity structures, the continued significance of parental cultural capital throughout the period studied confirms that such form of family capital is difficult to equalize despite political and administrative measures.

The study also shows that the concentration of power in the hands of state and party bureaucrats resulted in exclusive social networks which provided a different opportunity structure for those who belonged. The significance of individual party membership (in the case of Russia in 1988, parental party membership as well) in occupational attainment clearly indicates the effectiveness of social capital as a vehicle of career advancement. But when the Communist party lost its legitimacy and its constituent base began to dissolve, as was the case in Hungary and Poland toward the end of socialist rule, its utility as a route for socioeconomic success quickly dissipated.

Socialist rhetoric's emphasis on achieving class equality notwithstanding, our findings suggest that the biggest success of the socialist experiment lies perhaps in its promotion of gender equality. If the success of socialism in changing the structures of class inequality was limited to the early years, its achievement in reducing gender inequality was more long-lasting. The study yields unambiguous evidence of considerable improvement in women's position in the labor market over time. Much of the advantages is attributable to the substantial strides women made in educational attainment, particularly secondary grammar education and technical vocational training with diploma. In sum, although we may fault the socialist regimes for failing to realize their stated goals of class equality, their experiences in promoting gender equality contrast quite favorably with the experiences of Western countries such as the United States.

However, with the shift toward market economy, it is unclear whether and to what extent various stratification agents active under socialism may operate in the post-socialist era. Particularly interesting is the question whether and how the role of membership, former or current, in the Communist party changed. The drastically changed political setting and climate would lead one to expect current and former party membership to become less important in status attainment outcomes. Yet, the well-established social networks of the Communist party may continue to be useful under the new system, benefitting "former" and current party members and functionaries, either directly when their enterprises were privatized or as insiders taking advantage of other privatization programs. An examination of how Communist party members holding important and strategic positions before and after the 1989 transition fared under the new system in comparison to the general public would shed light on this question of the staying power of distinctive socialist stratifying agents (for some discussion, see Szelényi, Wnud-Lipinski & Treiman, 1995; Szelényi, 1998).

Given the success of socialism in reducing gender inequality, the question whether the gains women achieved under socialism were reduced or reversed under the new system would also illuminate the extent to which the socialist stratification system survived the changeover. With the abandonment of socialism, several factors may contribute to the erosion of gender equality. As the size of the state sector dwindles and the private sector rapidly expands, families may strategize to boost total income by having women stay in the public and state sectors for continued benefits such as healthcare, housing and food subsidies, while men venture out into the private sector or entrepreneurial activities. At the same time, the decline in state support and other benefits may force some women to quit paid work to take care of the family. Furthermore, the temporary and permanent layoffs brought about by economic downturns and market privatization tend to disproportionately affect women. All these may lead to a significant weakening of women's position in the labor market and perhaps even in the family, thus reversing the gains women made under socialism. A more detailed discussion of post-socialist changes to the stratification system is clearly beyond the scope of this study, but the findings here provide a profile of the socialist stratification systems of five countries that can serve as a benchmark for assessing the post-socialist stratification system.

NOTES

1. Relative positions within the Communist party, such as party functionaries vs. rank-and-file members, would predictably affect the effectiveness of network mobilization. Unfortunately, data limitation prevents the present study from making such distinction in the empirical analysis.

2. Researchers sometimes use parental education as proxies for parental cultural capital. Although the two concepts are related and their measures are highly correlated (0.62 in Czechoslovakia and 0.68 or better in Russia, Bulgaria, Hungary, and Poland), they are not synonymous and each has a separate, independent influence on socioeconomic attainment. A distinction between the two is particularly important in the socialist context. While the socialist governments may have been successful in limiting parental effects by making parental education a criterion in school selection and labor market participation, they would probably be far less successful in reducing the influence of parental cultural capital, which functions in inculcating qualities such as individual motivation, demeanor, and academic orientation, qualities that are generally believed to positively affect socioeconomic outcomes. Indeed, later analyses show that once parental education is properly controlled, the effects of parental cultural capital

either increase in significance or change from insignificance to significance in all five countries.

3. Cultural reproduction theory postulates that schools are not socially neutral institutions and the apparently neutral academic standards are in fact laden with specific cultural resources, typically from the dominant classes, acquired at home (Bernstein, 1975).

4. Some skeptics may interpret the incorporation of socialist women into the labor market as driven by little more than the need to fill vacant positions generated by the rapid pace of industrialization and the severe shortage of manpower due to heavy war casualties. But the implementation of labor policies that aided women workers, and women's exceptionally high rate of labor force particpation, representation in the occupational structure, and improvement in educational attainment all suggest intentional intervention beyond purely pragmatic accommodations.

5. In the case of Hungary, the lower rate of women's participation in the second economy in the 1980s further undermined their position in the stratification order.

6. The age range of respondents in the survey varies by country: 20 to 89 in Russia, 20 to 74 in Bulgaria, 20 to 70 in Czechoslovakia, 20 to 93 in Hungary, and 20 to 78 in Poland. Thus, except for Bulgaria, Czechoslovakia, and Poland in 1970, the distributions of occupations should be quite representative of those aged 20 to 64 at the three time points. The statistical models do not control for urban/rural differentials because information from the residential histories collected in the survey was incomplete. It is also important to recognize that the samples of individuals in 1970 and 1980 might not be representative of the labor force population at the time because of differential mortality and selective out-migration. This is a common problem of retrospective data, aside from data reliability.

7. The mean substitution method may artificially deflate the variance of the estimates, but the introduction of missing dummies in the regression models should minimize its influence. Other statistical procedures such as the multiple imputation method generally provide superior results (Little & Rubin, 1987; Schafer, 1997) but they tend to be computationally intensive, especially for large samples like the current study.

8. To minimize the number of missing cases, parental education, that is, the maximum of either father's or mother's education, is used. There is virtually no difference in the substantive interpretation of results when father's and mother's education are used instead. It should also be noted that when years of parental education are used, the effects of parental cultural capital are not statistically significant in a number of countries and time points and a few of the coefficients of parental education are significant. When educational dummies are used, however, the effects of parental cultural capital either become significant or increase its significance in all cases and only a few of the coefficients of parental education are significant. This clearly indicates that the distinctive influence of parental cultural capital from parental education. These results are available from the author.

9. See Erikson and Goldthorpe (1993) for the specific explanation of the CASMIN class categories.

10. The differences of the effects over time are not statistically significant if we assume that the estimates are drawn from independent samples. This assumption is, however, untenable since some individuals may be observed at more than one time point.

11. Since the regression coefficients for first occupation and years in the labor force (and its corresponding squared term) are not the central focus of this study, they will not be further discussed. Suffice it to say that they both contribute significantly to our understanding of socioeconomic attainment in all five countries.

12. The effects of first occupation were strong in all three years. In fact, they are the strongest among the five countries studied here. This suggests either lower rates of career mobility or a higher extent of path dependencies in career mobility in Bulgaria than in other countries. Both explanations can be plausible, and there is no real means of assessing their relative merit in the present study. Further research into this topic may be warranted.

13. The restratification thesis may still be valid for other stratification outcomes such as educational attainment, but its examination is beyond the scope of the current study.

14. It should be noted that the direct effects of parental background are considerably stronger when the analyses are based on first occupation. For instance, additional analyses (not shown) found direct influences by parental education in Czechoslovakia, Hungary, and Poland; father's occupation in Bulgaria, Czechoslovakia, and Hungary; father self-employment status in Bulgaria and Poland (the effects are negative); and parental cultural capital in all five countries. Remarkably, even with the significance of these conventional measures of parental background, the effects of parental cultural capital on first occupation are stronger than on current occupation. This further affirms our central argument about the importance of attending to different stratification agents in the socialist stratification systems. The results also suggest that some of the direct effects of parental cultural capital in current occupation are mediated through first occupation. None of the coefficients for parental communist party membership are significant. These results are available on request.

15. The logic of incorporating various stratification agents applies to other settings such as capitalist and/or developing countries as well. The forms and strengths of these agents, however, may vary in different contexts.

ACKNOWLEDGMENTS

An earlier version of the work was presented at the 1999 Annual Meeting of the American Sociological Association in Chicago, Illinois. I thank David Grusky and Ming-Yan Lai for helpful comments and Peter Chua for assistance.

REFERENCES

Bakker, I. (1988). Women's Employment in Comparative Perspective. In: J. Jenson, E. Hagen & C. Reddy (Eds), *Feminization of the Labor Force: Paradoxes and Promises* (pp. 17–44). New York: Oxford University Press.

Bernstein, B. (1975). *Class, Codes, and Control*. London: Routledge & Kegan Paul.

Bourdieu, P. (1977). Cultural Reproduction and Social Reproduction. In: J. Karabel & A. H. Halsey (Eds), *Power and Ideology in Education* (pp. 487–511). New York: Oxford University Press.

Bourdieu, P., & Passerson, J-C. (1977). *Reproduction in Education, Society, and Culture*. Beverly Hills, CA: Sage.

Coleman, J. S. (1988). Social Capital in the Creation of Human Capital. *American Journal of Sociology, 94*, S95–S120.

Coleman, J. S. (1990). *Foundations of Social Theory*. Cambridge, MA: Bellknap Press.

Collins, R. (1979). *The Credential Society*. New York: Academic Press.

Davis, J. A., & Smith, T. W. (1998). *General Social Surveys, 1972–1998* (machine-readable data file). Chicago, IL: National Opinion Research Center.

DiMaggio, P. (1982). Cultural Capital and School Success: The Impact of Status Culture Participation on the Grades of U.S. High-School Students. *American Sociological Review, 47*, 189–201.

Djilas, M. (1957). *The New Class: An Analysis of the Communist System*. New York: Praeger.

Erikson, R., & Goldthorpe, J. H. (1993). *The Constant Flux: A Study of Class Mobility in Industrial Societies*. London: Clarendon.

Featherman, D. L., & Hauser, R. M. (1978). *Opportunity and Change*. New York: Academic Press.

Ganzeboom, H. B. G., De. Graaf, P., & Treiman, D. J. (1992). A Standard International Socio-Economic Index of Occupational Status. *Social Science Research, 21*, 1–56.

Garnsey, E. (1982). Growth Strategy, Competing Interests, and the Soviet Occupational System. In: A. Giddens & D. Held (Eds), *Classes, Power, and Conflict: Classical and Contemporary Debates* (pp. 629–642). Berkeley, CA: University of California Press.

Heitlinger, A. (1979). *Women and State Socialism: Sex Inequality in the Soviet Union and Czechoslovakia*. Montreal: McGill-Queen's University Press.

Heitlinger, A. (1985). Women in Eastern Europe: Survey of Literature. *Women's Studies International Forum, 8*, 147–152.

Holms, B., Read, G. R., & Voskresenkaya, N. (1995). *Russian Education: Tradition and Transition*. New York: Garland Publishing.

Jaronsinko, M. (1983). Work Conditions and Activities. In: T. Kolosi & E. Wnuk-Lipinski (Eds), *Equality and Inequality Under Socialism* (pp. 79–105). London: Sage.

Kolosi, T. (1988). Stratification and Social Structure in Hungary. *Annual Review of Sociology, 14*, 405–419.

Kolosi, T., & Wnuk-Lipinski, E. (1983). *Equality and Inequality Under Socialism*. London: Sage.

Konrád, G., & Szelényi, I. (1979). *The Intellectuals on the Road to Class Power: A Sociological Study of the Role of the Intelligentsia in Socialism*. New York: Harcourt Brace Jovanovich.

Krejcí, J. (1972). *Social Change and Stratification in Postwar Czechoslovakia*. New York: Columbia University Press.

Lamont, M., & Lareau, A. (1988). Cultural Capital: Allusions, Gaps, and Glissandos in Recent Theoretical Developments. *Sociological Theory, 6*, 153–168.

Lane, D. (1971). *The End of Inequality? Stratification Under State Socialism*. Harmondsworth: Penguin.

Lane, D. (1976). *The Socialist Industrial State: Towards a Political Sociology of State Socialism*. London: Allen & Unwin.

Lane, D. (1982). *The End of Social Inequality? Class, Status, and Power Under State Socialism*. London: Allen & Unwin.

Little, R. J. A., & Rubin, D. B. (1987). *Statistical Analysis with Incomplete Data*. New York: Wiley.

Matejko, A. (1974). *Social Change and Stratification in Eastern Europe: An Alternative Analysis of Poland and Her Neighbors*. New York: Praeger.

Matějů, P. (1993). Who Won and Who Lost in a Socialist Redistribution in Czechoslovakia. In: Y. Shavit & H-P. Blossfeld (Eds), *Persistent Inequality: Changing Educational Attainment in Thirteen Countries* (pp. 257–271). Boulder, CO: Westview.

Miller, J. H. (1982). The Communist Party: Trends and Problems. In: A. Brown & M. Kaser (Eds), *Soviet Policy for the 1980s* (pp. 1–34). Bloomington, IN: Indiana University Press.

Müller, W., Lüttinger, P., König, W., & Karle, W. (1990). Class and Education in Industrial Nations. In: M. Haller (Ed.), *Class Structure in Europe* (pp. 61–91). Armonk, NY: Sharpe.

Parkin, F. (1969). Class Stratification in Socialist Societies. *British Journal of Sociology, 20*, 355–374.

Parkin, F. (1971). *Class Inequality and Political Order*. London: McGibbon and Kee.

Portes, A. (1998). Social Capital: Its Origins and Applications in Modern Sociology. *Annual Review of Sociology, 24*, 1–24.

Reskin, B., & Padavic, I. (1994). *Women and Men at Work*. Thousand Oaks, CA: Pine Forge Press.

Schafer, J. L. (1997). *Analysis of Incomplete Multivariate Data*. London: Chapman & Hall.

Simkus, A., & Andorka, R. (1982). Educational Attainment in Hungary. *American Sociological Review, 47*, 740–751.

Słomczynski, K., & Krauze, T. (1986). *Social Stratification in Poland: Eight Empirical Studies*. Armonk, NY: M. E. Sharpe.

Staar, R. F. (1988). *Communist Regimes in Eastern Europe* (5th ed.). Stanford, CA: Hoover Institution Press.

Szelényi, I., & Treiman, D. (1994). *Social Stratification in Eastern Europe After 1989: General Population Survey: Codebook*. Department of Sociology, University of California, Los Angeles.

Szelényi, I., Wnuk-Lipinski, E., & Treiman, D. J. (Eds) (1995). Circulation of Elites: Old and New Elites in Post-Communist Societies. Special Issues of *Theory and Society, 24*, 615–800.

Szelényi, S. (1998). *Equality by Design: The Grand Experiment in Destratification in Socialist Hungary*. Stanford, CA: Stanford University Press.

Szelényi, S., Szelényi, I., & Kovách, I. (1995). The Making of the Hungarian Post-Communist Elite: Circulation of Politics, Reproduction in the Economy. *Theory and Society, 13*, 697–722.

von Kopp, B. (1988). Czechoslovakia. In: G. T. Kurian (Ed.), *World Education Encyclopedia* (Vol. 1, pp. 291–309). New York: Facts on File Publications.

Weydenthal, J. B. de. (1986). *The Communists of Poland: An Historical Outline*. (Revised ed.). Stanford, CA: Hoover Institution Press.

Wong, R. S-K. (1995). Socialist Stratification and Mobility: Cross-National and Gender Differences in Czechoslovakia, Hungary, and Poland. *Social Science Research, 24*, 302–328.

Wong, R. S-K. (1996). The Social Composition of Communist Parties of Czechoslovakia and Hungary in the 1980s. *Social Forces, 75*, 61–90.

Wong, R. S-K. (1998). Multidimensional Influences of Family Environment in Education: The Case of Socialist Czechoslovakia. *Sociology of Education, 71*, 1–22.

Wong, R. S-K., & Hauser, R. M. (1992). Trends in Occupational Mobility in Hungary Under Socialism. *Social Science Research, 21*, 419–444.

Yanowitch, M. (1977). *Social and Economic Inequality in the Soviet Union*. White Plains, NY: Sharpe.

APPENDIX A. DESCRIPTIVE STATISTICS OF VARIABLES USED IN THE ANALYSIS

Variables	1970 Mean	1970 S.D.	1980 Mean	1980 S.D.	1988 Mean	1988 S.D.
A. Russia	$N=2084$		$N=3063$		$N=3448$	
Occupational Status	43.301	17.871	44.753	17.832	45.777	17.858
Age	34.125	9.066	36.506	10.810	39.191	11.243
Female	0.617	0.486	0.606	0.489	0.578	0.494
Number of Siblings	2.720	2.207	2.465	2.026	2.280	1.939
Parent Education						
Primary or Less	0.721		0.644		0.558	
Secondary without Diploma	0.046		0.063		0.074	
Secondary with Diploma	0.153		0.198		0.246	
Tertiary or Higher	0.080		0.095		0.122	
Father Occupation at Age 14	35.201	12.538	35.760	12.834	36.463	13.332
Father Self-Employed	0.043	0.203	0.035	0.184	0.034	0.181
Parental Cultural Capital	–0.348	0.865	–0.198	0.867	–0.055	0.889
Parent Communist Party Member	0.214	0.411	0.236	0.425	0.254	0.436
Education						
Primary or Less	0.371		0.256		0.203	
Secondary without Diploma	0.122		0.109		0.097	
Secondary with Diploma	0.366		0.450		0.483	
Tertiary or Higher	0.140		0.185		0.217	
First Occupation	38.445	17.650	40.054	17.264	41.147	17.068
Years in Labor Force	15.018	9.599	17.026	11.302	19.410	11.747
Communist Party Member	0.124	0.330	0.123	0.329	0.119	0.324
Cumulative Years in CP	1.210	4.429	1.543	5.282	1.903	6.102
B. Bulgaria	$N=2116$		$N=2971$		$N=3292$	
Occupational Status	35.335	15.209	36.687	15.554	37.770	15.656
Age	32.601	7.670	37.567	10.124	40.713	11.287
Female	0.511	0.500	0.505	0.500	0.497	0.500
Number of Siblings	2.186	1.685	2.055	1.718	1.946	1.678
Parent Education						
Primary or Less	0.880		0.826		0.774	
Secondary without Diploma	0.030		0.035		0.037	
Secondary with Diploma	0.070		0.110		0.151	
Tertiary or Higher	0.020		0.029		0.038	
Father Occupation at Age 14	29.198	10.784	30.506	11.979	31.606	12.510
Father Self-Employed	0.310	0.463	0.241	0.428	0.187	0.390
Parental Cultural Capital	–0.572	0.753	–0.448	0.826	–0.308	0.886
Parent Communist Party Member	0.155	0.362	0.174	0.379	0.197	0.397

APPENDIX A. *Continued.*

Variables	1970 Mean	1970 S.D.	1980 Mean	1980 S.D.	1988 Mean	1988 S.D.
B. Bulgaria continued.	*N*=2116		*N*=2971		*N*=3292	
Education						
Primary or Less	0.491		0.414		0.341	
Secondary without Diploma	0.127		0.116		0.106	
Secondary with Diploma	0.326		0.391		0.460	
Tertiary or Higher	0.056		0.079		0.093	
First Occupation	32.701	14.434	34.262	14.794	35.543	14.966
Years in Labor Force	12.607	8.284	17.052	10.640	19.988	11.720
Communist Party Member	0.108	0.310	0.130	0.336	0.145	0.352
Cumulative Years in CP	0.716	3.086	1.263	4.643	1.676	5.718
C. Czechoslovakia	*N*=4824		*N*=6996		*N*=7564	
Occupational Status	39.642	14.777	40.316	14.896	41.006	15.036
Slovakia	0.404	0.491	0.445	0.497	0.471	0.499
Age	32.856	8.092	37.174	10.374	39.625	10.626
Female	0.516	0.500	0.504	0.500	0.483	0.500
Number of Siblings	2.592	2.155	2.521	2.102	2.385	2.001
Parent Education						
Primary or Less	0.527		0.470		0.406	
Secondary without Diploma	0.326		0.343		0.356	
Secondary with Diploma	0.113		0.142		0.176	
Tertiary or Higher	0.034		0.046		0.062	
Father Occupation at Age 14	32.895	12.200	34.162	12.771	35.289	13.103
Father Self-Employed	0.154	0.361	0.114	0.318	0.077	0.267
Parental Cultural Capital	0.043	0.835	0.129	0.837	0.235	0.839
Parent Communist Party Member	0.187	0.390	0.211	0.408	0.232	0.422
Education						
Primary or Less	0.288		0.238		0.180	0.384
Secondary without Diploma	0.393		0.406		0.398	0.490
Secondary with Diploma	0.250		0.269		0.311	0.463
Tertiary or Higher	0.068		0.088		0.111	0.314
First Occupation	37.303	14.592	38.170	14.376	39.394	14.280
Years in Labor Force	12.953	8.050	16.792	10.528	19.041	11.077
Communist Party Member	0.109	0.312	0.122	0.328	0.138	0.345
Cumulative Years in CP	1.489	4.548	1.882	5.796	2.290	6.666

APPENDIX A. *Continued.*

Variables	1970 Mean	1970 S.D.	1980 Mean	1980 S.D.	1988 Mean	1988 S.D.
D. Hungary	$N=2174$		$N=2804$		$N=2840$	
Occupational Status	36.160	14.844	38.089	14.594	39.401	14.853
Age	35.778	10.531	37.489	11.072	38.957	10.537
Female	0.493	0.500	0.477	0.500	0.470	0.499
Number of Siblings	3.154	2.522	2.746	2.336	2.449	2.171
Parent Education						
Primary or Less	0.741		0.681		0.610	
Secondary without Diploma	0.156		0.182		0.218	
Secondary with Diploma	0.051		0.067		0.094	
Tertiary or Higher	0.052		0.069		0.078	
Father Occupation at Age 14	30.835	11.965	32.161	12.690	33.193	12.847
Father Self-Employed	0.287	0.452	0.214	0.410	0.169	0.375
Parental Cultural Capital	–0.364	0.870	–0.198	0.903	–0.042	0.905
Parent Communist Party Member	0.120	0.325	0.146	0.353	0.169	0.375
Education						
Primary or Less	0.509		0.394		0.299	0.458
Secondary without Diploma	0.236		0.266		0.300	0.458
Secondary with Diploma	0.184		0.244		0.275	0.447
Tertiary or Higher	0.072		0.096		0.126	0.332
First Occupation	30.949	13.760	33.138	13.595	34.918	13.540
Years in Labor Force	16.525	10.966	17.969	11.370	19.513	10.954
Communist Party Member	0.103	0.303	0.106	0.308	0.094	0.292
Cumulative Years in CP	1.210	4.184	1.514	5.220	1.723	5.706
E. Poland	$N=1948$		$N=3132$		$N=3447$	
Occupational Status	40.743	16.387	41.309	16.299	41.590	16.274
Age	32.180	7.458	35.722	10.159	39.658	11.018
Female	0.509	0.500	0.508	0.500	0.489	0.500
Number of Siblings	2.876	2.064	2.702	1.973	2.593	1.948
Parent Education						
Primary or Less	0.699		0.641		0.591	
Secondary without Diploma	0.120		0.138		0.164	
Secondary with Diploma	0.122		0.145		0.158	
Tertiary or Higher	0.059		0.077		0.087	
Father Occupation at Age 14	32.472	12.377	33.804	13.114	34.339	13.369
Father Self-Employed	0.477	0.500	0.423	0.494	0.391	0.488

APPENDIX A. *Continued.*

Variables	1970 Mean	1970 S.D.	1980 Mean	1980 S.D.	1988 Mean	1988 S.D.
E. Poland continued.	*N* = 1948		*N* = 3132		*N* = 3447	
Parental Cultural Capital	–0.242	0.894	–0.110	0.908	–0.038	0.897
Parent Communist Party Member	0.110	0.313	0.155	0.362	0.186	0.389
Education						
Primary or Less	0.398		0.300		0.247	0.432
Secondary without Diploma	0.177		0.223		0.246	0.431
Secondary with Diploma	0.317		0.341		0.359	0.480
Tertiary or Higher	0.108		0.135		0.147	0.355
First Occupation	37.512	15.560	38.400	15.399	38.814	15.257
Years in Labor Force	12.728	7.714	15.615	10.400	19.163	11.457
Communist Party Member	0.135	0.342	0.133	0.340	0.077	0.266
Cumulative Years in CP	1.080	3.629	1.713	5.200	1.971	6.123

OCCUPATIONAL SEX SEGREGATION IN STATE SOCIALIST AND MARKET ECONOMIES: LEVELS, PATTERNS, AND CHANGE IN EAST AND WEST GERMANY, 1980s AND 1998

Rachel A. Rosenfeld and Heike Trappe

ABSTRACT

From 1949 to 1989, East Germany was a state socialist society, while West Germany remained capitalist. In 1990, the East again became one country with the West. What were the level and nature of occupational sex segregation in the former East and West Germany in the decade before reunification? How had East/West differences in occupational sex segregation changed by the end of the first decade after unification? Much of the discussion about changes with unification is based on the assumption that in the GDR compared with the West, there was less overall segregation and more integration especially of predominately-male occupations because of the East's stronger ideology of gender equality and higher need for labor. Such arguments fail to take into consideration East Germany's higher rate of women's labor force participation, more extensive support for working mothers, and slower development of the service sector. In this paper we use detailed occupational information from 1980s East and West German population

The Future of Market Transition, Volume 19, pages 231–267.

ISBN: 0-7623-0835-4

censuses and from the 1998 German micro-census. We recode occupations to be comparable across surveys using the 1988 International Standard Classification of Occupations. We find that before 1989, the East had a ***higher*** *level of occupational gender segregation and* ***more*** *concentration in predominantly female occupations. It also had somewhat more integration of "male" jobs and a greater overall range of occupations for women than in West Germany. By 1998, these patterns had largely converged to those of the West.*

INTRODUCTION

In the labor markets of modern societies, jobs and occupations are more or less identified and enacted as "male" or "female," with consequences for pay, prestige, benefits, employment stability, autonomy, promotion, and authority. Which jobs are "male" and "female," though, differs across countries, as does the overall extent of gender segregation (Charles & Grusky, forthcoming; Jacobs & Lim, 1995). What is behind such variation? This paper focuses on occupational sex segregation in East Germany (German Democratic Republic, GDR) and West Germany (the old Federal Republic of Germany, FRG) in the 1980s and in the two parts of the united Germany in 1998. Comparing a market and a state socialist society that had a common past and continued to have similar educational systems and then looking at the changes that occurred with the demise of the socialist system may give us some perspective on why countries differ in their levels and patterns of gender segregation.

By most measures, West Germany has a moderately high level of occupational gender segregation, not as high as Sweden or Switzerland, but higher than the U.S. (Charles & Grusky, forthcoming). Even a decade after the former GDR ceased to exist, however, it is unclear how separate women's and men's occupations really were in that country. Public debate and government policy are proceeding on assumptions and speculation about the nature of occupational sex segregation in the East and changes after unification. Some research (e.g. Trappe & Rosenfeld, 1998) suggests that, overall, occupational gender segregation was higher in the East than the West. On the other hand, commentators point to how women in state socialist societies held positions in the professions (e.g. physician) and manufacturing that are considered men's in the West. The same *level* of gender segregation, though, may exist along with different *patterns*. For example, what are considered "male" occupations elsewhere may be filled predominantly by women in a particular country or set of countries. Or there may be more integration of higher-pay and higher-status occupations in one country and of lower ones in another (Chang, 2000).

Comparably-coded, yet detailed data have not been available to satisfactorily answer questions about the nature of occupational sex segregation in the former East and West Germanies. In this paper, we use data from the GDR and FRG population censuses for the 1980s and from the 1998 German micro-census. We recode occupations comparably into the 3-digit 1988 International Standard Classification of Occupations (ISCO) categories. Such data give what is probably the best available overview of the distribution of women and men across occupations in the 1980s and 1998, representative of the entire employed populations. We address two questions. First, what were the level and nature of occupational sex segregation in the former East and West Germany in the decade before reunification? Second, how had East/West differences in segregation changed by the end of the first decade after unification? These comparisons provide opportunities to better understand how societal-level processes are related to the gendered division of labor among advanced industrialized countries, with a natural control for common history and institutions and the abrupt shift in political and economic system for the East.

EXPLANATIONS FOR OCCUPATIONAL SEX SEGREGATION

Explanations for patterns of segregation across countries and time consider the supply of and demand for different kinds of labor. Reskin and Roos' (1990) gender queuing model provides a framework for understanding the intersection of these factors. The basic idea of this model is that workers rank jobs (job queues) and employers rank workers (labor queues). Employers want to get the "best" workers, those at the head of the labor queue for a particular type of job, and workers want to get the jobs they consider most desirable. Employers' rankings are affected by estimates of workers' productivity and costs. These estimates may be indirectly related to gender, but may also be influenced directly by gender and similar characteristics, for example having a strong preference for African American women for certain jobs, and for white men for others. Workers' preferences reflect jobs' rewards and conditions of work, but may also be shaped by lack of access to training and positions, perceived discrimination, and other constraints, such as family responsibilities. How far down in the labor queue an employer must go depends on how many workers there are of different kinds (e.g. how many men and how many women workers), while the shape of the job distribution affects the types of jobs workers get. As the rankings and shapes of the queues vary over time and place, the degree and nature of occupational sex segregation varies. (See Reskin, 1991.)

Growth, decline, and reorganization of occupations and industries, changes in technology and skill demands, shifts in the relative sizes and power of various groups of workers, increases in education or training for one group relative to another, change in ideological and legal support for equal opportunity and affirmative action may all change the level and patterns of sex segregation. Rubery and Fagan (1995) point out that for cross-national studies of labor market divisions by gender, one needs to keep in mind variations in social, political, and economic institutions that affect the supply of and demand for workers. They list women's employment patterns, women's relative access to education and training, and social attitudes as societal-level factors affecting the shape of labor queues, while systems of pay determination, industrial organization, consumption patterns, and the nature of career paths affect the rankings in job queues.

Chang (2000) focuses on two dimensions of state action that help create the context within which job queues and labor queues are gendered across countries: extent of legislation facilitating women's access to all occupations and level of supports for working parents, especially mothers. Broadly, in "traditional family-centered systems," such as the FRG, there is little legal or other support for employed women. What entitlements there are tend to reinforce women's roles in the home. In West Germany, the main equal employment policies are directed towards women's access to employment, such as re-integrating housewives, and do not address women's position in the labor market per se. Legislation against persistent discrimination facing employed women has been of secondary importance (von Wahl, 1999). In "economy-centered systems," such as the GDR, despite egalitarian ideologies, the economy shapes sex segregation. Support for women workers is more a response to the need for their labor than commitment to gender-based equality.

Chang predicts that the level of occupational sex segregation will be higher in "traditional family-centered" countries, with women who enter the labor force especially likely to choose "women's" jobs. These may be the "traditional" care-giving jobs, but may also be jobs structured as part-time or temporary, to correspond to the family life cycle. Women would be especially unlikely to have higher-level, full-commitment managerial and administrative positions. In the "economy-centered" societies, she expects concentrations of women in the professions and in production, because of women's relatively high levels of training and employment continuity in combination with labor shortages.

EXPECTATIONS ABOUT OCCUPATIONAL SEX SEGREGATION IN GERMANY

Pre-Unification

Among the factors discussed above that influence job queues and labor queues, some of those most salient to the comparison between the GDR and FRG are the differences in official gender ideology, overall labor needs, and family policies. Differences in these factors between the countries combined to produce striking contrasts in women's employment histories and, directly and possibly indirectly, to differences in the sorts of jobs women held. Differences in industrial structure, interacting with the educational and vocational training systems, were important sources of cross-national variation in job opportunities by gender as well.

Gender Ideology, Labor Needs, and Family Policies

Both countries had a rather traditional, Catholic-influenced gender ideology before World War II. And both countries included gender equality as a goal in their 1949 constitutions. The GDR, however, followed Marxist ideology in conceptualizing gender equality as largely coming about from equal participation in paid labor. As well, after World War II, the East had a high demand for labor to rebuild the country and compensate for extensive migration to the West before 1961. Overstaffing, to deal with changes in government plans and regulations, may also have contributed to a later labor shortage (Uunk, Mach & Mayer, 1998). A range of state policies facilitated the incorporation of women into the skilled labor force, including free or inexpensive child care covering the large majority of children by 1989 (Statistisches Amt der DDR, 1990, pp. 57, 62; Trappe, 1996) and paid maternity leave with a job return guarantee (a "baby year" by 1986) (Sørensen & Trappe, 1995). The strategies and pressures to include women in the work force seemed to be effective in producing a very high rate of female employment. By the end of the 1980s, 78% of East German women ages 15 to 60 were employed and comprised almost half the work force (Statistisches Amt der DDR, 1990). Most of these employed women were also mothers, and employment rates varied little by marital or maternal status (Ostner, 1993). Women's employment was mainly full-time and continuous, with relatively short breaks around childbirth.

After World War II, refugees flooded into the FRG from former German territories and the East, and later guest workers met a large part of demand in lower-level jobs (Münz, Seifert & Ulrich, 1997). There was less need than in the East for women's labor. Much of legislation and social policy treated women solely as wives and mothers and men as "breadwinners," reinforcing traditional gender roles. There was little full time child care, and care for infants and toddlers was scarce (Berghahn & Fritzsche, 1991). The length of paid maternity leave increased, but leaves did not guarantee a return to a job at the same level. School schedules and store hours made it difficult for women to hold full-time jobs and care for the home (Buchmann & Charles, 1995; Gornick, Meyers & Ross, 1997). With men's wages relatively high, many middle-class families could afford to have the mother stay home with young children or work only part time. Increases in women's employment did come about mainly through growth in part-time work. By 1989, roughly 30% of working-age women in the FRG were employed full time (37 hours a week), and 30% part time (Blossfeld & Rohwer, 1997). Wives' employment was very sensitive to the presence and ages of children, more so than in many other Western countries (Gornick, 1999; Ostner, 1993).

On the one hand, the GDR's ideology of gender equality through employment and high post-World War II labor needs would put women higher in the labor queues and force managers to go farther down in the queues. This suggests there was less segregation overall than in the FRG, especially in crucial, predominantly-male occupations. And indeed this was the state intention, at least in the 1950s and 1960s,[1] and public perception.

On the other hand, contrary to Chang's prediction and the common assumption, the increasing support for employed mothers in the GDR, especially from the 1970s on, may have led to more statistical discrimination against women in important technical crafts and positions of authority. They may have been channeled out of some "critical" occupations on the basis of the expectation that almost all women would take child leave and other benefits, putting women lower in labor queues because of higher costs and lower perceived productivity. Such arguments are often used to explain the high level of gender segregation in Sweden, despite its egalitarian ideals (Rosenfeld, Van Buren & Kalleberg, 1998). In addition, and again contrary to Chang's logic, high women's employment in East Germany, compared with the relatively low level in West Germany, may have resulted in less selection of women into the labor force in the East, with more concentration in predominantly women's jobs as a consequence: While women with more traditional interests and values may have stayed out of the labor market in the West, in the East, these may have been women who took on "typical" women's jobs (Beckmann, 1996; Quack, Maier & Schuldt, 1992). Especially in the state socialist context of a more compressed earnings distribution, East German women may have ranked predominantly women's occupations higher in their job queues than women in the West (Schober, 1994).

Another aspect of gender ideology associated with occupational segregation is protective legislation. If some occupations are considered too dangerous or unhealthy for women (especially potential mothers), then this limits their options, while reducing competition with men in queues for these occupations. In the GDR, women were excluded from underground mining, jobs at higher atmospheric pressures, and occupations that involved working around toxic gases, dust, and steam. They were present in other, physically hard occupations. Protective legislation was more extensive in the FRG. For example, women were excluded from the main occupations in construction and prohibited from working nights if they were blue collar workers (Berghahn & Fritzsche, 1991). From this description, one would expect to see East German women's having a wider range of jobs and being more integrated into "male" occupations than women in the West.

Industrial Structure and Shape of Job Queues

Large differences in industrial structure, and thus in the shape of the job queues, between East and West Germany may have reinforced or moderated some of these tendencies. The FRG was much more on its way to becoming a service society than the GDR.[2] (See Appendix A for industrial distributions of East and West Germany from 1950 to 1998.) With industrial and occupational restructuring, the relative number of traditionally male jobs declined and the share of traditionally female jobs expanded (Rubery, Smith, Fagan & Grimshaw, 1998). Employers would not be able to go as far down labor queues (shaped by union requirements, apprenticeships, and gendered preferences) for the male jobs, such that men would retain dominance over these jobs. One might expect to see concentration of women in relatively few occupations, especially the middle white collar and lower services positions (Gottschall, 1989).

The move to a service economy was much slower in the GDR. In 1989, the industrial structure of East Germany resembled West Germany's in 1965, with a large proportion of agricultural and manufacturing jobs. While the changes were not as dramatic as in the West, the expansion of the service sector concentrated women in female jobs to a greater extent than in the FRG. That is, women may have been concentrated in fewer occupations overall in the FRG, but female occupations may have been even more segregated in the GDR. With the post-War labor shortages and the relatively greater number of "male" jobs, though, women may have been more likely to be in what in the FRG were predominantly male occupations. Further, in the GDR, women may have filled jobs male guest workers took in the West.[3] Therefore, we expect, again, more integration in blue collar and perhaps lower service occupations in the East.

Education and Vocational Training

Changes in occupational demand were met to a large extent by changes in the distribution of vocational credentials. The two German states shared important institutional traditions with respect to vocational training and higher education. Extremely tight linkages between the educational and occupational system, especially when selection of a vocation takes place early, such as was true in the FRG and GDR, are particularly likely to result in sex-typed choices (Buchmann & Charles, 1995). In the absence of economic crisis, given the nature of the German educational system, much of the change in the gender composition of jobs came about through the vocational training of new labor force entrants (Quack et al., 1992). Credentials were highly gender segregated in both Germanies, with a small number of degrees out of bounds for women because of protective considerations (such as in mining). In the GDR, the state attempted to plan for occupational needs by setting up quotas leading to restricted choices. The path from credentials to jobs was somewhat tighter in the East than the West (Solga & Konietzka, 1999).[4] From the mid-1970s on, there was a process of occupational resegregation, preceded by increasing sex segregation in education and vocational training. Women and men earned the same levels of vocational credentials, including higher qualifications (such as university and college degrees), but there was increasing differentiation by gender in content of training. These trends led to the feminization of technical college degrees (which were needed for teaching, nursing, and some business occupations), while men continued to receive training for "male" jobs (such as crafts apprenticeships and male-dominated majors at university).

Thus, labor queues were increasingly differentiated by gender. In addition to increasing demand in the tertiary sector and vocational channeling (sometimes based on assumptions about women's use of family benefits), explanations for this resegregation in the East included socialization in family and school, unlawful behavior of enterprises that disadvantaged women, and technology policy that put women on the periphery, with access mainly to routinized, lower-level computerized jobs (Nickel, 1993). At the same time, the proportion of women in the East earning crafts and trades credentials was still higher than in the West, 45% compared with 17% in 1989 (Schober, 1994).

Before unification, then, based on the two countries' social, economic, and political contexts, we expect to see in the GDR as compared with the FRG a higher overall level of segregation, greater segregation of predominately women's occupations, but somewhat more integration of predominately male jobs, and a greater range of jobs for women. Despite less selectivity into the labor force, more extensive benefits for employed mothers, and resegregation of vocational training, we may still see, as Chang (2000) predicts, somewhat greater integration of administrative, managerial, and professional occupations in the East than in the West, given the ideology of gender equality, increased concentration of women in the tertiary sector, and women's greater employment continuity.

After Unification

After unification, the East experienced radical industrial restructuring and labor market crisis. Mothers of young children lost much of the support they had had under state socialism and were confronted with new difficulties in reconciling work for the family and on the job (Rudd, 2000). Pressures on both the demand and supply sides reduced the relative number of women workers and may have affected the types of jobs women and men held in the East. There were, of course, changes during the post-unification decade in the West, but they were much less dramatic, continuing many previous trends.

Consistent with its Marxist ideology, practically there had been no unemployment in the GDR, with resulting overstaffing of some jobs. Firms were often inefficiently managed because they lacked strong incentives to contain costs. As a consequence of the sudden exposure to market competition, there was a drastic, rapid reduction of jobs in East Germany between 1990 and 1995. At the end of 1989 there were 9.6 million people employed, at the end of 1995, only 6.4 million. Since then the number of employment opportunities seems to have been relatively stable. As can be seen in Appendix A, while West Germany showed very little change in its basic industrial structure, there was a marked shift in the East between 1989 and 1991. The East experienced a remarkable, though mainly passive move to a service economy. Job loss took place mainly in the primary and secondary sectors whereas the number of jobs in the tertiary sector remained relatively stable. Within the service industries, areas expanded that were underdeveloped under state socialism, such as financial services and insurance, while other parts shrank, including public administration and transportation (Goedicke, 2002).

The restructuring of the East German labor market has not been gender neutral (Nickel, 1999). Since 1990, East German women's unemployment has been higher and longer than men's. In 1998, 23% of East German women and 17% of East German men were unemployed, while this was true for 8% of West German women or men (Statistisches Bundesamt, 1999a).[5] At the beginning of the transformation, women lost jobs across all industries, independent of expected labor demand or the previous degree of gender segregation. This process has come to an end. By 1998, women's industrial distribution was much the same in East and West Germany, with the exception that women in East Germany had a relatively higher share in services (Statistisches Bundesamt, 1999a).

Soon after unification, some social scientists had argued that the high degree of sex segregation within industries and occupations would limit the extent of open gender competition for jobs in East Germany. There might even be an advantage for highly qualified women, particularly those in public services, which had stronger job protection (Nickel, 1993). By now, however, sociologists' views on changes in gender segregation have become more pessimistic. East Germany has enduring economic stagnation and a service sector that is not expected to generate new jobs, because of the lack of a manufacturing base (Kratzer, 1997). There is an increasing competition between women and men for jobs (Beckmann & Engelbrech, 1999). While social scientists have debated the broad outlines of gender redefinition of jobs (e.g. Maier, 1991), very few make explicit claims about specific changes in occupational gender segregation.

Keeping the economic situation and changes in family policy in mind,what changes do we expect in the East/West differences in occupational sex segregation by the end of the first decade after unification? It is not clear how the *overall level* of segregation changed. We expect, however, to see some convergence in *patterns* of occupational sex segregation in the East and West. With loss of employment in manufacturing, where many jobs were dominated by men, we expect to see "male" jobs becoming more male, as employers go down labor queues a shorter distance than before. This may be true to a greater extent in the East, where there may have been more integration in these jobs previously. Increased competition between women and men for jobs, fewer women in the work force, and a breakdown of industries (such as textiles and food processing) with high concentrations of women may have led to "female" occupations becoming somewhat more integrated. Again, this may be true to a greater extent in the East. In the 1990s, many formerly predominantly women's occupations, such as in banking and insurance, became more attractive to East German men, both because of men's high unemployment and also because of the rising status of some of these occupations under the new regime, raising these occupations in men's job queues (Rubery et al., 1998).[6] At the same time, we may find women in the East concentrated in relatively fewer apprenticeships and occupations than before and thus more like West Germans in range of jobs.[7] In addition, in some cases job distributions, with possibly gendered requirements and preferences, were imported directly to the East when firms moved establishments from the West. One would not expect full convergence of occupational gender patterns between East and West, however, because of remaining differences in economic structure as well as the continuing influence of the decades before unification.

DATA AND METHODS

Data

We have the most detailed information available on the distribution of women and men across occupations from the 1987 FRG and 1981 GDR population censuses, the last censuses before unification,[8] and the 1998 German micro-census, a 1% population survey on central population and labor market characteristics. These surveys include non-citizens and non-German speakers. The original occupational categories in the three census surveys are not fully comparable. The FRG census used 328 3-digit occupational titles (Klassifizierung der Berufe, Ausgabe 1975 [Statistisches Bundesamt, 1990, pp. 8–9]), while the GDR census employed much more detailed occupational categories (575 4-digit occupational titles) (Solga, 1993). Occupations in the 1998 micro-census were coded according to yet another system, with 369 3-digit occupational classifications (Statistisches Bundesamt, 1999b).

It is a challenge in itself to choose comparable categories that cover the range of occupations without collapsing too much and eliminating distinct intra-country differences (Charles & Grusky, forthcoming). Most cross-national comparisons of occupational sex segregation use very broad categories because of the difficulty of making different occupational schemes substantively and computationally similar. We have recoded all three data sets to 116 comparable standard 1988 ISCO codes (International Labour Organisation, 1990), with up to 95 categories present in any particular year and country.[9] The ISCO codes are based on type of tasks and skill levels of jobs. As the first digit of the code increases, the average skill required decreases. As well, this classification scheme pays special attention to providing enough detail to distinguish predominately male from predominately female job clusters (International Labour Organisation, 1990).

Detail of occupational codes is important in assessing both the level and patterns of occupational segregation. The finer the job categories, usually the more segregation found (Bielby & Baron, 1986). If different countries or regions have different numbers of occupational categories, that alone could lead to finding different overall levels of segregation. Further, greater occupational detail enables one to get closer to a picture of how the job structure varies by gender across countries. There is much occupational and job segregation that we miss, even with fairly detailed codes. Further, even the same occupation may have had different characteristics between the East and West, given differences in technology, work rules, hierarchy, and rewards, and may have changed over time in both countries. Our results probably underestimate differences and over-estimate similarities.

Measuring Occupational Segregation

Because there is no agreement on how to measure occupational sex segregation, we will be using both the well-know Duncan index of dissimilarity (weighted and unweighted) and a log-linear index of association to measure overall gender segregation levels (Grusky & Charles, 1998; see also Weeden, 1998; Watts, 1998a, b). Each measure has its limitations. The index of dissimilarity, D, is calculated as:

$$0.5 \times \left(\sum_{i=1}^{n} \left| \frac{W_i}{W} - \frac{M_i}{M} \right| \right) \times 100 \qquad (1)$$

where n = the number of occupations, W_i = the number of women in occupation i, W = the total number of employed women, M_i = the number of men in occupation i, and M = the total number of employed men. It ranges from 0 (complete integration) to 100 (complete segregation) and compares the occupational distribution of women with that of men. Its value gives the percentage of women (or men) who would need to be in another occupational category for the occupational distributions of women and men to be the same.

In this form, the segregation index is affected by the relative size of occupations, with large occupations having more weight. As discussed above, expansion of occupations traditionally filled by women may increase segregation if women who would be employed elsewhere or would not be employed move into these positions. On the other hand, expansion of predominately male occupations may decrease segregation if the supply of men is not adequate to provide new workers needed. Differences in occupational distributions and change in these distributions could affect comparisons using D. Therefore, we also use a weighted index of segregation, SD =

$$0.5 \times \left(\sum_{i=1}^{n} \left| \frac{W_i}{T_i} \Big/ P_w - \frac{M_i}{T_i} \Big/ P_m \right| \right) \times 100 \qquad (2)$$

where W_i and M_i are as before, T_i is the total number of people in occupation i, P_w is the proportion of women among all the employed ($\Sigma\ (W_i/T_i)$), and P_m is the proportion of men ($\Sigma\ (M_i/T_i)$). Again, this ranges from 0 to 100, but now gives the percentage of women (or men) who would have to change occupations for the occupational distributions to be the same by gender – if all occupations were the same size.

Growth or decline in the proportion of the labor force that is women (or men) may affect D and SD. For example, if expansion of "female" occupations draws previously non-employed women into the work force, the index of dissimilarity would increase, even without a redistribution of existing workers. To overcome these problems, Charles and Grusky (1995) introduced a "margins-free" measure of the association between occupations and gender, based on the sex ratios within occupations, rather than the distribution over occupations:

$$\ln(A) = \left\{ \frac{1}{n} \times \sum_{i=1}^{n} \left[\ln(W_i/M_i) - \left(\frac{1}{n} \times \sum_{i=1}^{n} \ln(W_i/M_i) \right) \right]^2 \right\}^{\frac{1}{2}} \qquad (3)$$

in other words, the square root of average squared deviations of the occupations' (logged) sex ratio from the overall logged sex ratio. In unlogged form, A gives the factor by which women (or men) are over-represented in occupational categories, on average. Here, perfect integration is when the (logged) sex ratio is the same *within* every occupation. (See Charles & Grusky, forthcoming; Weeden, 1998, for use of this index.)

Each index summarizes occupational gender segregation in one number similar to an average. We will also look at the shape of the overall occupational distributions, using the distribution of occupations and workers across occupations' percentage of men. To examine what Charles and Grusky (forthcoming) call the "occupational-specific contours" of segregation – the patterns within particular groups of occupations – we will go on to compare the gender makeup of specific occupational categories for the East and West at the two times.

RESULTS

Levels of Segregation

Table 1 shows the indices for overall segregation. In 1981, the two indices of dissimilarity (D and SD) comparing differences in the distribution of women with that of men indicate just about the same level of segregation in the two countries. The Charles-Grusky measure (A), which takes into account country differences in both occupational size and gender composition of employment, shows greater segregation in the East: Women (or men) were over-represented

Table 1. Overall Occupational Sex Segregation in East and West Germany, 1980s and 1998.

A. Using All Available Occupations

	N of occupations	D	Size-standardized D	A × 10
GDR 1981	83	49.9	50.5	62.5
FRG 1987	89	49.3	49.9	52.6
East Germany 1998	84	60.0	47.7	52.3
West Germany 1998	95	53.8	46.3	49.0

B. Using Only Occupations Available for Both Countries for a Given Year

	N of occupations	D	Size-standardized D	A × 10
GDR 1981	81	49.7	50.1	60.9
FRG 1987	81	51.7	50.8	54.4
East Germany 1998	84	60.0	47.7	52.3
West Germany 1998	84	53.7	50.3	50 4

in the average GDR occupation by a factor of 6, while one gender or the other was over-represented in the average FRG occupation by a factor of 5. This is consistent with our prediction that occupational gender segregation would be greater in the East before unification because of statistical discrimination and "channeling" in education and jobs, less selectivity of women into the labor force, and a smaller service sector.

In 1998, the level of occupational segregation (especially after controlling for at least occupational size) is about the same between the two regions: In both parts of Germany, about 50% of either women or men would need to change occupational categories for the occupational distributions to be the same (assuming equal occupation size, SD), and women or men were overrepresented in the average occupation by a factor of 5 (A). This provides initial evidence for a trend toward convergence between the two parts of Germany.

Occupational and Worker Gender Segregation Distributions

Figure 1A shows how the distribution of occupations by percentage men differed between the East and the West in the 1980s, and Figure 2A gives the

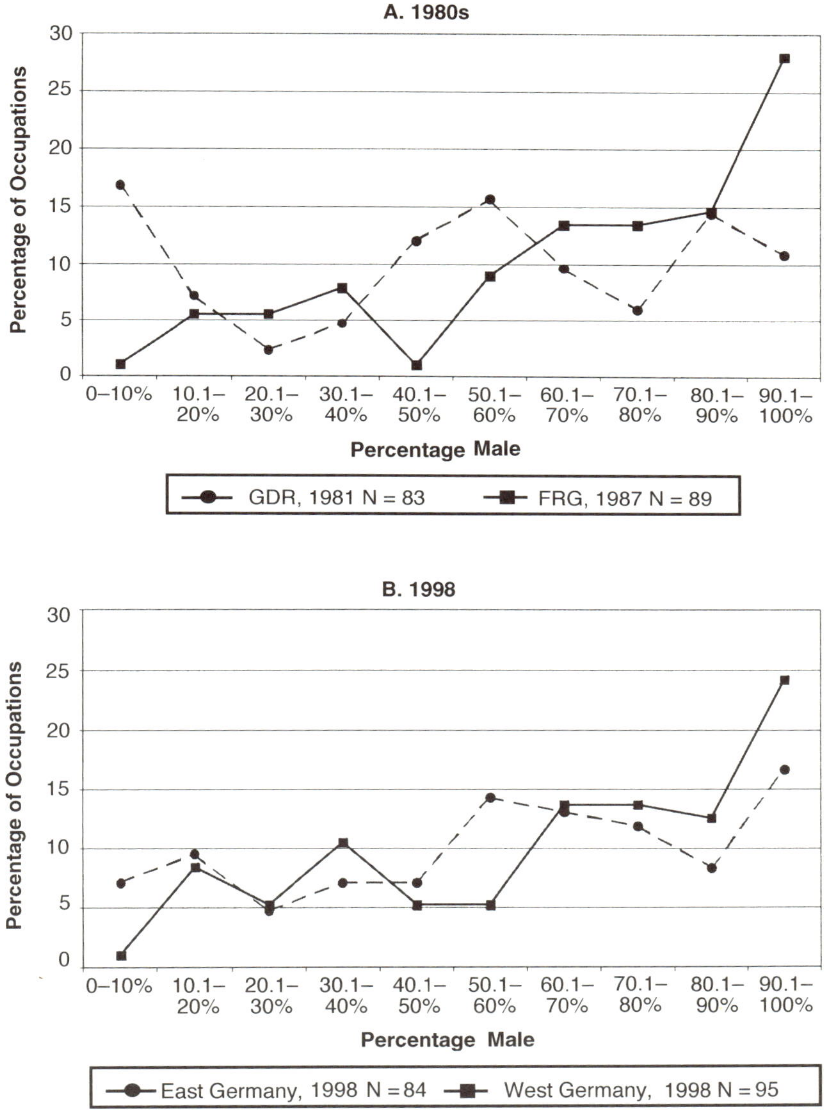

Fig. 1. Distribution of Occupations Across Deciles of Percentage Male in Occupational Categories in East and West Germany, 1980s and 1998 (3-digit ISCO88 Occupational Categories).

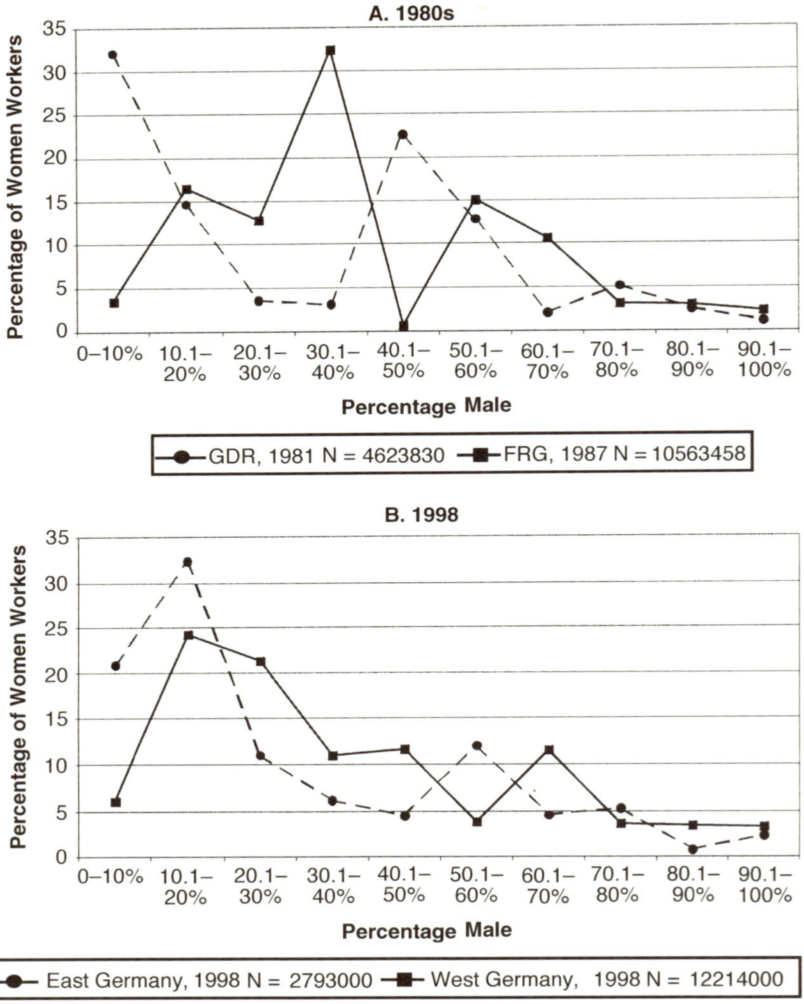

Fig. 2. Distribution of Women Workers Across Deciles of Percentage Male in Occupational Categories in East and West Germany, 1980s and 1998 (3-digit ISCO88 Occupational Categories).

difference for women workers over occupations with varying levels of percent male. (See also Appendix B, parts A and B.) Before unification, over 15% of GDR occupational categories were no more than 10% men, and over 30% of East German women workers were in such categories. In the FRG, fewer than 5% of occupations were so overwhelmingly female, and fewer than 5% of women workers were in such gender-segregated occupations. This is consistent with our prediction that in the East, women would be more overrepresented in "women's" occupations. At the same time, there were relatively more occupational categories that were mixed and fewer that were almost totally male in the East than in the West, again consistent with the idea that "male" occupations were not as heavily segregated in the GDR, perhaps because of greater labor needs, a smaller range of protective legislation, relatively few male guest workers, and a smaller service sector. Higher relative numbers of West German women, however, were in occupations 60% or more men.

By 1998, there was an amazing degree of convergence, as Figs 1B and 2B show. Rather than one country's distribution over degrees of sex segregation being the mirror image of the other, the shapes of the distributions were almost the same. (See also Appendix B, parts A and C.) There are hints of the former patterns: Somewhat more occupational categories in the East were almost entirely female or mixed almost equally and more East German women were in such occupations, while relatively more occupational categories in the West were overwhelmingly male and a somewhat greater proportion of women were in these categories. But contrasts are much muted. There was more change overall in the East than the West. Jobs were more concentrated at the "male" extreme in 1998 than in 1981 for the East – over 15% of occupational categories were 90% or more male in 1998, compared with just over 10% in 1981 – while they were less concentrated at the "female" end of the distribution. The proportion of occupational categories that were almost entirely occupied by women remained fairly stable in the West, while the relative number of occupations 90% or more male decreased. Women workers in the East were less concentrated in extremely female occupations eight years after unification, while men were more concentrated in occupations over 90% male. Shifts at the extremes among West German workers were considerably smaller.

Occupational Concentration

What sorts of differences in specific occupations were behind these general trends in occupational gender segregation? We first look at occupations in which women were concentrated. Table 2 lists the 5 detailed occupations

Table 2. Women Workers' Occupational Concentration in East and West Germany, 1980s and 1998.

A. Top 5 3-digit Occupations Employing the Most Women in the 1980s (and Percentage Male)

	GDR 1981	FRG 1987
1	Senior government officials (46.3% male)	Administrative associate professionals (39.4% male)
2	Shop salespersons and demonstrators (9.8%)	Shop salespersons and demonstrators (20.0%)
3	Building caretakers and cleaners (14.6%)	Manufacturing laborers (57.8%)
4	Administrative associate professionals (8.8%)	Secretaries and keyboard-operating clerks (30.0%)
5	Cashiers, tellers, and related clerks (8.6%)	Building caretakers and cleaners (35.1%)
% in top occupation	15.4	20.2
% in top 5	37.4	45.0
% in top 10	55.2	63.2

B. Top 5 3-digit Occupations Employing the Most Women in 1998 (and Percentage Male)

	East Germany	West Germany
1	Secretaries and keyboard operating clerks (14.3%)	Secretaries and keyboard-operating clerks (22.8%)
2	Shop salespersons and demonstrators (18.0%)	Shop salespersons and demonstrators (18.8%)
3	Library, mail, and related clerks (14.6%)	Personal care and related workers (6.8%)
4	Primary and pre-primary teaching professionals (8.5%)	Customs, tax, and related government associate professionals (44.9%)
5	Nursing and midwifery professionals (8.2%)	Building caretakers and cleaners (28.9%)
% in top occupation	9.8	13.2
% in top 5	38.0	37.0
% in top 10	55.7	54.8

employing the most women in the East and the West for each decade. There is considerable overlap of lists from the two countries/regions. Middle white-collar or lower service occupations make up four of the five top categories in both the FRG and GDR in the 1980s. The two differences are "senior government officials" (consisting mainly of administrative and assistant jobs within the political system) as the leading employer of women in the GDR and "manufacturing laborers" as the third occupation in the FRG. Concentration of women in government administration fits Chang's (2000) description of economy-centered countries. The presence of "manufacturing labor" as a top employer of women in the West, but not the East, may seem to contradict the generalization that blue collar occupations were more integrated in the GDR. Actually, while this category is one of the largest for West German women, it was more integrated in the East (42% male). Not surprising given our finding that women in the GDR were in more heavily female occupations, the top occupations in the East generally had a greater proportion of women than the top occupations for the West. Overall, 37% of East German women and 45% of West German women were in just 5 occupations, and over half in just 10. There is some evidence here for a greater range of occupations available to women in the East, but the differences are not great.

By 1998, the degree of women's occupational concentration was almost the same for the East and the West. Again, there is overlap of the top five occupations: In each country, three out of the five are lower-white collar. In the West, the remaining two occupations are lower-level service jobs. In the East, they include predominantly women's professions for which credentials required had been higher in the GDR than the FRG (primary school teachers being the exception).

Occupation-specific Comparisons

What about women's relative representation across all occupational categories? Figures 3A and 3B show percentage male across 2-digit ISCO88 categories for the East and the West in the 1980s and in 1998. (See also Appendix C.) The comparison between East and West Germany based on the 2-digit codes serves as an initial overview. To get a clearer picture of changes that have occurred between the 1980s and 1998, we then refer to the more detailed occupational levels. In discussing the results we focus on differences in percentage male across occupations of at least 10 percentage points.

As we already saw, many East German women were in government positions. In the 1980s, East German women were generally better represented than West German women in running the government, usually in lower-level

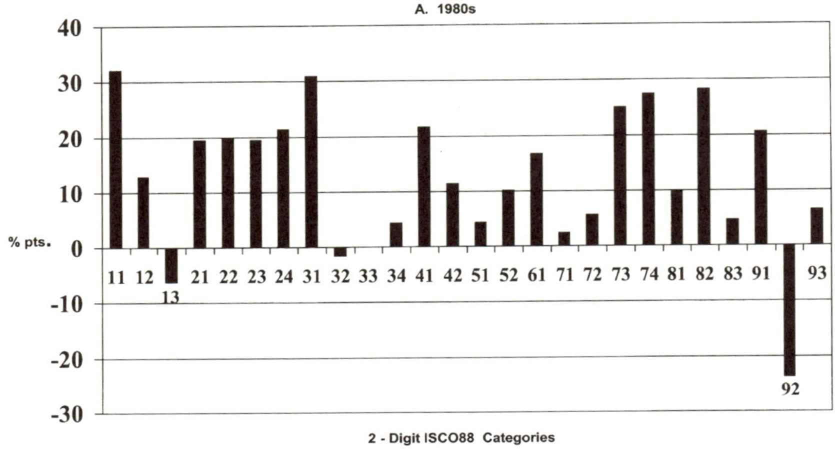

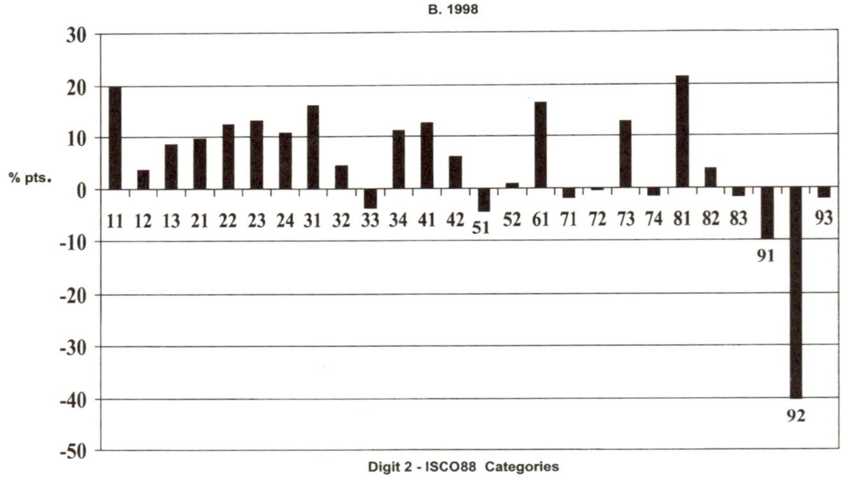

Fig. 3. Differences between West and East Germany in Percentage Male Across Broad Occupational Categories, 1980s and 1998 (2-digit ISCO88 Occupational Categories, % male West Germany – % male East Germany).

(See Appendix C for definition of occupational codes).

positions. The "legislators and senior officials" category (11) was 78.5% male in the West and 46.4% male in the East. (In both countries, legislators (a very small category) were male: 94% in the West and 73% in the East.) East German women were somewhat greater proportions of management, as well. Across all legislative, senior official, and managerial occupations, men were 70% in the West and a small majority, 55%, in the East. Consistent with what Chang (2000) predicted, one could say women in the GDR had greater access to at least some positions of authority, although the meaning of this authority may have differed between the countries.

Again consistent with Chang's scheme, women in the East were a greater proportion of professionals, even those in math and science (21), and technicians (31), where women are less likely to be found in most countries (Rubery & Fagan, 1995). As well, and as we expected, while most operatives, craftspeople, and lower-level service workers (category 91, "sales and services elementary occupations") were men in the West, in the East, women were proportionately or over-represented in these categories. Printing, textiles, and leather-goods trades, as well as chemical-production operatives (73, 74, 82), were essentially women's occupations in the East. On the other hand, though East German women were relatively more likely to be skilled agricultural workers, those in the West had a higher likelihood of being agricultural laborers, perhaps because of the presence of family farms.

At the same time, "women's occupations" tended to be more female in the East, in white collar and service occupations. While almost a third of preschool and primary teachers (23) were men in the West, only about 10% in the East were. Not only nursing professionals but also medical doctors (22) tended to be dominated by women to a larger extent in the East than in the West. Also many clerical, customer service, and sales positions (41, 42, 52) were filled almost entirely by women in the former GDR. This is what we saw in the distribution of occupations by percentage male – more integration among "male" occupations in the East, but more segregation among "female" occupations.[10] This basic pattern was still evident in the first micro-census for the unified Germany taken in 1991 (Statistiches Bundesamt, 1993).

As Figure 3 shows, a decade after unification, we see fewer occupations with large differences in percentage male between the East and West, and differences are smaller in general (with agriculture an exception). (See also Appendix C, part B.) What underlies the tendency toward convergence in the gendered distribution of occupations between the regions? Following Gatta and Roos (2000), we distinguish "masculinizing" and "feminizing" occupations to grasp the nature of this change. (See Table 3.)

Table 3. Differences in Percentage Male of Selected Occupations between the 1980s and 1998 in East and West Germany.

	East Germany	West Germany
Masculinizing Occupations[a]	Production and operations department managers (122) Life science professionals (221) Social science and related professionals (244) Life science technicians and related associate professionals (321) Nursing and midwifery associate professionals (323) Social work associate professionals (346) Numerical clerks (412) Protective service workers (516) Precision workers in metal and related materials (731) Printing and related trades workers (734) Chemical-processing-plant operators (815) Printing-, binding- and paper-products machine operators (825) Locomotive-engine drivers and related workers (831) Street vendors and related workers (911) Building caretakers, window and related cleaners (914) Agricultural, fishery and related laborers (921) Mining and construction laborers (931) Transport laborers and freight handlers (933)	Business professionals (241) Life science technicians and related associate professionals (321) Nursing and midwifery associate professionals (323) Social work associate professionals (346) Pelt, leather and shoemaking trades workers (744) Wood-processing- and paper-making-plant operators (814) Chemical-processing-plant operators (815)
Feminizing Occupations[b]	Other department managers (123) Secondary education teaching professionals (232) Travel attendants and related workers (511) Other personal service workers (514)	Legislators (111) Secondary education teaching professionals (232) Primary and pre-primary teaching professionals (233) Legal professionals (242) Business services agents and trade brokers (342)

Table 3. Continued.

East Germany	West Germany
	Administrative associate professionals (343) Library, mail and related clerks (414) Travel attendants and related workers (511) Printing and related trades workers (734) Chemical-products machine operators (822) Assemblers (828) Street vendors and related workers (911)

[a] ISCO88 3-digit occupations in which the percentage male increased by at least 10% points from the 1980s to 1998.
[b] ISCO88 3-digit occupations in which the percentage male decreased by at least 10% points from the 1980s to 1998.

The most noticeable pattern in Table 3 is that relatively more occupations in East Germany have a tendency toward "masculinization" as compared to "feminization" whereas in West Germany it is the other way around. In that way West Germany seems to embody the more stable society with predictable influences of increasing demands within the service sector and women's higher qualifications on women's inroads into previously male domains. The "masculinizing" occupations in the East include occupations from the full range of the skill hierarchy, from managers to laborers, while the "feminizing" occupations are those that are already likely to have a substantial proportion of women. In the West, occupations gaining relatively more men are mainly middle level white collar and blue collar, while those becoming more female go from legislators to vendors, with the majority upper or middle white collar. Again, this shows the tendency toward convergence between East and West, with greater movement in the East, where the social, political, and economic changes have been much greater.

CONCLUSIONS

Social scientists, journalists, and the general population had contradictory assumptions about the extent and pattern of occupational gender segregation in the former East Germany and thus of changes with unification. For any given country at any particular time, there are a large number of demographic, ideological, social, political, and economic factors interacting to affect gendered labor queues and job queues, making it easier to explain contrasts and change after the fact than to make predictions beforehand. Nevertheless, we developed hypotheses about the nature and change in occupational sex segregation in the East and the West before and after 1989. We considered the influences of differences in official gender ideology, labor needs, family policies, industrial structure, and vocational training, along with using Chang's typology based on the combination of legal support for workplace equality and state support for working parents. We were able to contrast a state socialist and capitalist state and then see to what extent a former state socialist country took on the appearance of the capitalist society with the fall of the communist regime. Our predictions concerned overall level of occupational gender segregation, the shape of this segregation across occupations, the occupational concentration of women workers, and gender composition of specific occupational categories.

In the GDR, women expected to be both producers and reproducers, with men mainly producers. Official policy and, to some extent, vocational and occupational channeling took this into account. As well, the GDR moved more slowly than the West toward a service economy. In the FRG, more women chose between motherhood and full-time employment, a choice conditioned and reinforced by family-relevant policies and less pressing labor needs. We predicted that in the GDR compared with the FRG, there would be a higher level of overall segregation, greater segregation of predominately women's occupations, somewhat greater integration of "men's" jobs, and a greater range of occupations open to women. In particular, in the East we expected to see relatively greater representation of women in administrative, managerial, and professional occupations, and in crafts and production jobs. With the erosion of supports for mothers, economic crisis, and the transformation of some jobs after unification, we hypothesized that the gendered division of labor in the East would become more similar to that in the West, not only in terms of women's employment rates, but also in their occupational location.

Using census data for the FRG in 1987, GDR in 1981, and micro-census data for both parts of Germany in 1998, we found support for most of these predictions. By the end of the 20th century, the occupational sex segregation regime in the eastern part of Germany was much more like a "traditional-family" than an "economy-centered" country. Although we were focusing on how differences in institutional contexts affected occupational gender composition, we need to keep in mind that the labor market was highly sex segregated in both countries at both times, even as measured by 3-digit occupational codes rather than by more detailed occupations or jobs.

In this process of transformation, one could consider East German women the losers, in terms of both employment opportunity in general and in specific occupations. In the East, women were hit harder than men by the dramatic reduction in jobs that occurred with reunification and by restructuring of the economy. In the West, women gained more employment than men in the expanding service sector, while women in the East lost jobs relative to men even here. There were more feminizing occupations in the West, more that became increasingly male in the East. Preliminary examination using finer occupational codes shows that over the 1990s, many of the service economy jobs in which West German women increased their representation (e.g. physician, judge, financial official, dental technician, legal representative) had been integrated or predominantly male at the beginning of the decade. In the East, jobs that increased in proportion male (e.g. social worker, librarian, bank employee, cook, tax consultant, technician) had been integrated or woman dominated at unification (Goedicke & Trappe, 2001).

The comparison of the state socialist society of the GDR with the market society of the FRG, and the changes with unification, took advantage of a natural experiment in which at least some traditions and institutions were the same and where one government literally took over another. Concentrating on these two countries, we have been able to give a fairly detailed account of the transformation especially of the East. An extension of this research would be to make comparisons with other countries before and after they made the transition from a planned to a capitalist economy.

Another take on the process of occupational segregation is to look at correlates and outcomes of occupational sex segregation in the two Germanies using life course data. A problem with looking at cross-sections of the occupational structure, as we have here, is that they combine birth cohorts who attained their vocational training, formed families, and sought employment (or not) at different times, in different economic, social, and political contexts. By following a more narrow range of cohorts across their early work lives, one can see how occupational segregation occurs and is maintained. For example, the human capital explanation of gender segregation emphasizes differences between women and men in their family roles (Becker, 1991; Polachek, 1981). Was family status associated with gender composition of occupations to a greater extent in the GDR, where employment was almost universal, compared with the FRG, where relatively fewer women were employed? What about for men, who are also concentrated in occupations dominated by their own gender? Our analyses of young adults' work and family histories before reunification suggests that the answer is that there was no association of family configuration and gender type of occupation in either country (Trappe & Rosenfeld, 2001).

In the U.S., Jerry Jacobs (1989) talks of revolving doors, as individuals move back and forth across occupations with different sex types, but the overall distribution remains stable and the flow is strong back to a gender-typical job. Was stability of occupational sex segregation maintained by such mobility or by immobility in the GDR and FRG, where any occupational change was less common than in the U.S.? Our results show that there was at least some "revolving door" mobility.

What was happening in the period between unification and the end of the century still needs to be filled in at both the macro and the individual lifecourse levels. Given our results from the pre-unification period, it is unlikely that changes in family formation processes that occurred with unification would be reflected in the occupational structure's gender division of labor, although we might find that they affect and are affected by employment per se. At least some of the change in the nature of occupational gender segregation especially in the East, however, may have come about through individuals' entering or leaving gender-typical occupations. Overall, we would not expect occupational gender segregation to decrease rapidly in the future, in either part of Germany. In Germany, there is a fairly direct path between type of education and job. Vocational training and subjects studied in higher education are still very gender typed. For example, in 1998, 54% of female apprentices and 37% of male apprentices were concentrated in the top ten vocational areas for their gender. Those rankings have been relatively stable over the years, with the top apprenticeship for women being office administrator and for men vehicle mechanic (Bundesministerium für Bildung und Forschung, 2000). Vocational training and the relationship between training and occupational career are topics to which we need to pay attention in order to understand gender segregation in the unified Germany.

Gender differences are rarely only that. Women's jobs usually pay less than men's, and occupational sex segregation helps account for income, benefits, and opportunity inequality by gender. There is not always a one-to-one correspondence, however, between the distribution of jobs by gender and the gender distribution of rewards. Change in one can occur without change in the other. As Reskin (1988) argues, those with power may change the rules about how rewards are allocated when job distributions change, while continuing to use a gendered job structure to justify these rules. Without job-focused equal opportunity and affirmative action policies *and* policies that help parents simultaneously care for a family and earn a living without being caught in gender stereotypes, we may not see rapid progress in labor market gender equality. We will therefore also want to study the consequences of occupational sex segregation and its change in different types of societies.

NOTES

1. During this time period especially, East German women were encouraged to enter "male" fields because of the shortage of men workers. To rebuild the country, heavy manufacturing was considered particularly important (Trappe, 1996).

2. In the FRG, however, the service sector was smaller than in other Western societies, in part at least because many services were still provided within the family to a greater extent than elsewhere (Quack et al., 1992).

3. In West Germany, migration had a significant impact on employment rates over recent years. In 1975, the proportion of migrants among all non-self employed reached 12%, its historical peak, and was still 9.3% in 1995. During the 1970s and 1980s the labor force participation of migrant men (56.9% in 1989) was about twice as high as that of migrant women (30.9%). In 1975, two-thirds of employed male and female guest workers were in manufacturing industries and one-third was in construction, trade, transportation, and services. Already before 1995, migrants were more concentrated in services than West German citizens (Münz et al., 1997).

4. Gender inequalities in the vocational system and in the system of higher education were transferred into the occupational system in the GDR, but not reinforced as was the case in the FRG. In West Germany, even if women had the same kind of training as men, they were more likely to be placed at lower level jobs within the same occupation (Solga & Konietzka, 2000).

5. From 1989 to 1998, women's labor force participation rate (which includes the unemployed) in the East decreased to 73.5%. West German women's labor force participation increased slightly during the period, to 60.5% in 1998. The figure for men in both parts of the country was 80.2% (Statistisches Bundesamt, 1999a).

6. Change has taken place along the dimensions of professionalization, job satisfaction and other rewards, mobility chances, and job security in whole occupational fields during the East German transformation (see Nickel & Schenk, 1994, on financial services, and Rabe-Kleeberg, 1999, on pre-primary education). Some occupations were upgraded while others were downgraded. Under the Unification Treaty, the vast majority of GDR qualifications kept their formal value. It was still necessary for people in particular occupations to get additional training after unification, with consequences for pay, social status, and work conditions. (For example, primary school teachers in the GDR needed only a technical college degree, in the FRG, a university degree. In contrast, pre-primary school teachers in the GDR were also required to have a technical college degree, while those in the FRG had a vocational degree.)

7. After unification, the protective laws in the old FRG were no longer in force. Women could get training in almost all the recognized occupations (except two in mining), and almost all occupations were open to them. Still, in 1995 about 75% of women with vocational credentials were concentrated in only 20 occupations, mainly in services (Helwig, 1997).

8. The difference in years between 1981 and 1987 is unavoidable. It should not, however, greatly affect our comparisons of the pre-unification period. Again, Appendix

A shows relatively stable differences in industrial distributions between the countries in the 1980s, with a distinct change after 1989.

9. Some occupations were missing at both times in East and West Germany (e.g. 324 – "traditional medicine practitioners and faith healers"), and some occupations were not present for both countries for both periods partly because of system-specific reasons (e.g. 341 – "finance and sales associate professionals" in the former GDR) and partly because of the smaller numbers in the micro-census (e.g. 234 – "special education teaching professionals").

10. We had speculated that women would be better represented in blue-collar and lower-level service occupations in the East partly because guest workers were likely to meet demand in these occupations in the West. While we know foreign percentage in an occupational category from the 1987 FRG census, we are not able to disaggregate this by gender. Preliminary results, though, suggest that our speculation may be correct. The "top 5 male-dominated" occupations for foreigners in the FRG were much more "feminized" in the East than in the West. For example, "locomotive-engine drivers and related workers," one of the large employers of foreign workers in the FRG in the late 1980s, was 2.5% women in the West, but 33.4% women in the GDR in 1981.

ACKNOWLEDGMENTS

We would like to thank Jennifer Carpenter, Stephanie Moller, and Annett Wilde for their research assistance and Ivy Kennelly and Angelika von Wahl for their comments.

REFERENCES

Becker, G. S. (1991). *A Treatise on the Family*. Enlarged Edition. Cambridge, MA: Harvard University Press.

Beckmann, P. (1996). Introduction: New Approaches to the Analysis of Occupational Segregation by Gender. In: P. Beckmann (Ed.), *Gender Specific Occupational Segregation* (pp. 1–15). Nürnberg: IAB BeitrAB 188.

Beckmann, P., & Engelbrech, G. (1999). Beschäftigungsentwicklung und -perspektiven ostdeutscher Frauen in den 90er Jahren. (Employment Development and Employment Prospects of East German Women in the 90s.) In: *Die arbeitsmarkt- und beschäftigungspolitische Herausforderung in Ostdeutschland* (*The Challenge for Labor Market and Employment Policies in East Germany*) (pp. 203–226). Nürnberg: IAB BeitrAB 223.

Berghahn, S., & Fritzsche, A. (1991). *Frauenrecht in Ost- und Westdeutschland: Bilanz, Ausblick* (*Women's Rights in East and West Germany: Situation, Outlook*). Berlin: Basisdruck Verlag.

Bielby, W. T., & Baron, J. N. (1986). Men and Women at Work: Sex Segregation and Statistical Discrimination. *American Journal of Sociology, 91*, 759–799.

Blossfeld, H.-P., & Rohwer, G. (1997). Part-Time Work in Germany. In: H.-P. Blossfeld & C. Hakin (Eds), *Between Equalisation and Marginalisation: Women Working Part-Time in Europe and the United States of America* (pp. 164–190). New York: Oxford University Press.

Buchmann, M., & Charles, M. (1995). Organizational and Institutional Factors in the Process of Gender Stratification. *International Journal of Sociology, 25*, 66–95.

Bundesministerium für Bildung und Forschung (Federal Ministry for Education and Research) (Ed.) (2000). *Berufsbildungsbericht* (*Report on Vocational Education/Training*). Bonn.

Chang, M. L. (2000). The Evolution of Sex Segregation Regimes. *American Journal of Sociology, 105*, 1658–1701.

Charles, M., & Grusky, D. B. (1995). Models for Describing the Underlying Structure of Sex Segregation. *American Journal of Sociology, 100*, 931–971.

Charles, M., & Grusky, D. B. (Forthcoming). *Sex Segregation in Comparative Perspective*. Stanford: Stanford University Press.

Gatta, M. L., & Roos, P. A. (2000). Occupational Integration and Gender Equity. Paper presented at the annual meeting of the American Sociological Association, Washington D.C., August.

Geißler, R. (1992). *Die Sozialstruktur Deutschlands: Ein Studienbuch zur sozialstrukturellen Entwicklung im geteilten und vereinten Deutschland* (*The Social Structure of Germany: A Book to Study the Social Structural Development in the Separated and in the Unified Germany*). Opladen: Westdeutscher Verlag.

Goedicke, A. (2002). *Beschäftigungschancen und Betriebszugehörigkeit. Die Folgen betrieblichen Wandels für ostdeusche Erwerbstätige nach 1989* (*Employment Opportunities and Firm Affiliation. The Consequences of Organizational Restructuring for East German Employees after 1989*). Wiesbaden: Westdeutscher Verlag.

Goedicke, A., & Trappe, H. (2001). Young Women's Early Occupational Careers in East and West Germany: How Are They Shaped By Gender-Segregated Labour Markets? Paper presented at European Societies or European Society? EuroConference on European Welfare States and Changing Life Courses. Kerkrade, Netherlands, 6–10 October.

Gornick, J. C. (1999). Gender Equality in the Labor Market: Women's Employment and Earnings. In: D. Sainsbury (Ed.), *Gender Policy Regimes and Welfare States* (pp. 117–146). Oxford, U.K.: Oxford University Press.

Gornick, J. C., Meyers, M. K., & Ross, K. E. (1997). Supporting the Employment of Mothers: Policy Variation across Fourteen Welfare States. *Journal of European Social Policy, 7*, 45–70.

Gottschall, K. (1989). Frauenerwerbsarbeit und Tertiarisierung. Zur Erosion und Rekonstruktion geschlechtsspezifischer Arbeitsteilung in der Dienstleistungsgesellschaft (Women's Employment and the Development of the Tertiary Sector. On the Erosion and Reconstruction of a Gender Specific Division of Labor in the Service Economy). In: Autorinnengemeinschaft (Ed.), *Arbeitsmarkt und Frauenerwerbsarbeit* (*The Labor Market and Women's Employment*) (pp. 26–54). SAMF Arbeitspapier 1989–16.

Grusky, D. B., & Charles, M. (1998). The Past, Present, and Future of Sex Segregation Methodology. *Demography, 35*, 497–504.

Helwig, G. (1997). Frauen in Deutschland: Auf dem Weg zur Gleichstellung. (Women in Germany: On their Way to Equity.) *Informationen zur politischen Bildung* (*Information for Political Education*), *254*, 16–26.

International Labor Organisation (1990). *International Standard Classification of Occupations: ISCO-88*. Geneva: International Labour Office.

Jacobs, J. A. (1989). *Revolving Doors: Sex Segregation and Women's Careers*. Stanford: Stanford University Press.

Jacobs, J. A., & Lim, S. T. (1995). Trends in Occupational and Industrial Sex Segregation in 56 Countries, 1960–1980. In: J. Jacobs (Ed.), *Gender Inequality at Work* (pp. 259–293). Thousand Oaks, CA: Sage.

Kratzer, N. (1997). Sektoraler Wandel der ostdeutschen Arbeitsplatzstruktur: Empirische Befunde zu einem erwarteten Modernisierungspfad. (Sectoral Change of East Germany's Employment Structure: Empirical Evidence for an Expected Path of Modernization.) In: S. Schenk (Ed.), *Ostdeutsche Erwerbsverläufe zwischen Kontinuität und Wandel (East German Work Histories between Continuity and Change)* (pp. 59–112). Opladen: Leske + Budrich.

Maier, F. (1991). Erwerbstätigkeit von Frauen – Geschlechtsspezifische Umbrüche im Arbeitsmarkt und Beschäftigungssystem (Women's Employment – Gender Specific Change in the Labor Market and the Employment System). In: A. Westphal et al. (Eds), *Wirtschaftspolitische Konsequenzen der deutschen Vereinigung* (*Political and Economic Consequences of the German Unification*) (pp. 295–318). Frankfurt/New York: Campus.

Münz, R., Seifert, W., & Ulrich, R. (1997). *Zuwanderung nach Deutschland: Strukturen, Wirkungen, Perspektiven* (*Migration to Germany: Structures, Effects, Perspectives*). Frankfurt/New York: Campus.

Nickel, H. M. (1993). Mitgestalterinnen des Sozialismus – Frauenarbeit in der DDR (Co-designers of Socialism – Women's Work in the GDR). In: G. Helwig & H. M. Nickel (Eds), *Frauen in Deutschland 1945–1992* (*Women in Germany 1945–1992*) (pp. 233–256). Berlin: Akademie Verlag.

Nickel, H. M. (1999). Lebenschancen von Frauen in Ostdeutschland: Risiken und Optionen der Neuformierung von Frauenerwerbsarbeit (Women's Life Chances in East Germany: Risks and Options for the Reformation of Women's Employment). In: W. Glazer & I. Ostner (Eds), *Deutschland im Wandel: Sozialstrukturelle Analysen* (*Germany in Changing Times: Social Structural Analyses*) (pp. 255–264). Opladen: Leske + Budrich.

Nickel, H. M., & Schenk, S. (1994). Prozesse geschlechtsspezifischer Differenzierung im Erwerbssystem (Process of Gender Specific Differentiation in the Employment System). In: H. M. Nickel et al. (Eds), *Erwerbsarbeit und Beschäftigung im Umbruch* (*Work and Employment under Restructuring*). Berlin: Akademie Verlag.

Ostner, I. (1993). Slow Motion: Women, Work and the Family in Germany. In: J. Lewis (Ed.), *Women and Social Policies in Europe: Work, Family and the State* (pp. 92–115). Aldershot, Hants, England: Edward Elgar.

Polachek, S. (1981). Occupational Self-selection: A Human Capital Approach to Sex Differences in Ocupational Structure. *Review of Economics and Statistics*, *58*, 60–69.

Quack, S., Maier, F., & Schuldt, K. (1992). Berufliche Segregation in der BRD und der ehemaligen DDR: 1980–1989. (Occupational Segregation in the FRG and the Former GDR: 1980–1989.) Bericht fur die EG-Kommission (Report for the EG-Commission), Generaldirektorat V, Gleichstellungsstelle.

Rabe-Kleeberg, U. (1999). Wie aus Berufen für Frauen Frauenberufe werden: Ein Beitrag zur Transformation der Geschlechterverhältnisse. (How Occupations for Women Turn into Women's Occupations: A Contribution to the Transformation of Gender Relations.) In: H. M. Nickel (Ed.), *Transformation – Unternehmensorganisation – Geschlecterforschung* (*Transformation – Firm Restructuring – Gender Studies* (pp. 93–107). Opladen: Leske + Budrich.

Reskin, B. F. (1988). Bringing the Men Back In: Sex Differentiation and the Devaluation of Women's Work. *Gender and Society*, *2*, 58–81.

Reskin, B. F. (1991). Labor Markets as Queues: A Structural Approach to Changing Occupational Sex Composition. In: J. Huber (Ed.), *Macro-micro Linkages in Sociology* (pp. 170–192). Newbury Park, CA: Sage.

Reskin, B. F., & Roos, P. (1990). *Job Queues, Gender Queues*. Philadelphia, PA: Temple University Press.

Rosenfeld, R. A., Van Buren, M. E., & Kalleberg, A. L. (1998). Gender Differences in Supervisory Authority: Variation among Advanced Industrialized Democracies. *Social Science Research, 27*, 23–49.

Rubery, J., & Fagan, C. (1995). Gender Segregation in Societal Context. *Work, Employment, and Society, 9*, 213–240.

Rubery, J., Smith, M., Fagan, C., & Grimshaw, D. (1998). *Women and European Employment*. London and New York: Routledge.

Rudd, E. (2000). Reconceptualizing Gender in Postsocialist Transformation. *Gender and Society, 14*, 517–539.

Schober, K. (1994). Junge Frauen beim Übergang vom Bildungs- ins Beschäftigungssystem: die Lage in den neuen Bundesländern (Young Women's Transition from Education to Work: The Situation in the New States of Germany). In: P. Beckmann & G. Endelbrech (Eds), *Arbeitsmarkt für Frauen 2000 – Ein Schritt vor oder ein Schritt zurück? (The Labor Market for Women 2000 – One Step Forward or Two Steps Back?)* (pp. 523–566). Nürnberg: IAB BeitrAB 179.

Solga, H. (1993). Systematik der beruflichen Tätigkeiten und Ausbildungen in der DDR (A Systematization of Occupational and Vocational Titles in the GDR) *Arbeitsbericht 2/1993*. Berlin: Max-Planck-Institut für Bildungsforschung, Forschungsbereich Bildung, Arbeit und Gesellschaftliche Entwicklung (Max Planck Institute for Human Development, Center for Sociology and the Study of the Life Course).

Solga, H., & Konietzka, D. (1999). Occupational Matching and Social Stratification: Theoretical Insights and Empirical Observations Taken from a German-German Comparison. *European Sociological Review, 15*, 25–47.

Solga, H., & Konietzka, D. (2000). Das Berufsprinzip des deutschen Arbeitsmarktes: Ein geschlechtsneutraler Allokationsmechanismus? (The Occupational Principle of the German Labor Market: A Gender Neutral Mechanism of Allocation?) *Schweizerische Zeitschrift für Soziologie (Swiss Journal of Sociology), 26*, 111–147.

Sørensen, A., & Trappe, H. (1995). Frauen und Männer: Gleichberechtigung – Gleichstellung – Gleichheit? (Women and Men: Equal Rights – Equality – Equity?) In: J. Huinink et al. (Eds), *Kollektiv und Eigensinn: Lebensverläufe in der DDR und danach (Collectivism and Obstinacy: Life Courses in the GDR and Thereafter)* (pp. 189–222). Berlin: Akademie Verlag.

Statistisches Amt der DDR (Ed.) (1990). *Statistisches Jahrbuch der DDR '90 (Statistical Yearbook of the GDR '90)*. Berlin: Rudolf Haufe Verlag.

Statistisches Bundesamt (Ed.) (1990). *Bevölkerung und Erwerbstätigkeit. Volkszählung vom 25. Mai 1987 (Population and Employment. Population Census of May 25, 1987), Fachserie 1, Heft 10 Erwerbstätige, Teil 1: Sozio-ökonomische und berufliche Gliederung, Schulausbildung (Employees, Vol. 1: Socio-economic and Occupational Structure, Schooling)*. Stuttgart: Metzler-Poeschel.

Statistisches Bundesamt (Ed.) (1993). *Bevölkerung und Erwerbstätigkeit (Population and Employment), Fachserie 1, Reihe 4.1.2 Beruf, Ausbildung und Arbeitsbedingungen der Erwerbstätigen 1991 (Ergebnisse des Mikrozensus) (Occupation, Vocational Training and Working Conditions of Employees 1991 – Results of the Micro Census)*. Stuttgart: Metzler-Poeschel.

Statistisches Bundesamt (Ed.) (1997). *Datenreport 1997: Zahlen und Fakten über die Bundesrepublik Deutschland (Data Report 1997: Figures and Facts about the Federal Republic of Germany)*. Bonn:Bundeszentrale für politische Bildung (Federal Agency for Political Education).

Statistisches Bundesamt (Ed.) (1999a). *Bevölkerung und Erwerbstätigkeit (Population and Employment), Fachserie 1, Reihe 4.1.1 Stand und Entwicklung der Erwerbstätigkeit 1998 (Ergebnisse des Mikrozensus) (Situation and Development of Employment 1998 – Results of the Micro Census).* Stuttgart: Metzler-Poeschel.

Statistisches Bundesamt (Ed.) (1999b). *Bevölkerung und Erwerbstätigkeit (Population and Employment), Fachserie 1, Reihe 4.1.2 Beruf, Ausbildung und Arbeitsbedingungen der Erwerbstätigen 1998 (Ergebnisse des Mikrozensus) (Occupations, Vocational Training and Working Conditions of Employees 1998 – Results of the Micro Census).* Stuttgart: Metzler-Poeschel.

Statistisches Bundesamt (Ed.) (1999c). *Datenreport 1999: Zahlen und Fakten über die Bundesrepublik Deutschland (Data Report 1999: Figures and Facts about the Federal Republic of Germany).* Bonn: Bundeszentrale für politische Bildung (Federal Agency for Political Education).

Trappe, H. (1996). Work and Family in Women's Lives in the German Democratic Republic. *Work and Occupations, 23*, 354–377.

Trappe, H., & Rosenfeld, R. A. (1998). Gender Inequality at Work in the Early Adult Lifecourse. *European Sociological Review, 14*, 1–26.

Trappe, H., & Rosenfeld, R. A. (2001). Occupational Sex Segregation and Family Formation: A Comparison of Pre-Unification East and West Germany. Presented at the annual meeting of the American Sociological Association, Anaheim, CA, August.

Uunk, W., Mach, B., & Mayer, K. U. (1998). Job Shift Patterns in the Former German Democratic Republic and the Federal Republic of Germany: Convergence, System Contrast or Institutional Variation? *Arbeitsbericht 1/1998.* Berlin: Max-Planck-Institut für Bildungsforschung, Forschungsbereich Bildung, Arbeit und Gesellschaftliche Entwicklung (Max Planck Institute for Human Development, Center for Sociology and the Study of the Life Course).

von Wahl, A. (1999). *Gleichstellungsregime: Berufliche Gleichstellung von Frauen in den USA und in der Bundesrepublik Deutschland* (*Equality Regime: Employment Equality of Women in the USA and the Federal Republic of Germany*). Opladen: Leske + Budrich.

Watts, M. (1998a). Occupational Gender Segregation: Index Measurement and Econometric Modeling. *Demography, 35*, 489–496.

Watts, M. (1998b). The Analysis of Sex Segregation: When Is Index Measurement Not Index Measurement? *Demography, 35*, 505–508.

Weeden, K. A. (1998). Revisiting Occupational Sex Segregation in the United States, 1910: Results from a Log-linear Approach. *Demography, 35*, 475–487.

APPENDIX A
Industrial Distributions of East and West Germany (% Employment by Sector)

Country	Sector	1950	1960	1970	1980	1989	1991	1995	1998
West Germany	primary	25	13	9	5	4	3	3	3
	secondary	43	49	49	45	41	41	36	34
	tertiary	33	38	42	49	55	56	61	63
	total*	101	100	100	99	100	100	100	100
East Germany	primary	31	17	13	11	11	7	4	4
	secondary	42	49	51	52	50	42	36	32
	tertiary	27	34	36	38	40	51	60	64
	total*	100	100	100	101	101	100	100	100

* Totals differ from 100 because of rounding.

Sources: Geißler, 1992; Statistisches Bundesamt, 1997, 1999c. Appendix A.

APPENDIX B

Distribution of Occupations and Workers across Percentage Male in Occupational Categories in East and West Germany, 1980s and 1998.

		% Male in 3-Digit ISCO88 Occupational Category										
		0–10	10.1–20	20.1–30	30.1–40	40.1–50	50.1–60	60.1–70	70.1–80	80.1–90	90.1–100	Total*
A. % of Occupations Across Deciles of Percentage Male in Occupational Category												
GDR 1981	*N* = 83	16.87	7.23	2.41	4.82	12.05	15.66	9.64	6.02	14.46	10.84	100.00
FRG 1987	*N* = 89	1.12	5.62	5.62	7.87	1.12	8.99	13.48	13.48	14.61	28.09	100.00
E.G. 1998	*N* = 84	7.14	9.52	4.76	7.14	7.14	14.29	13.10	11.90	8.33	16.67	99.99
W.G. 1998	*N* = 95	1.05	8.42	5.26	10.53	5.26	5.26	13.68	13.68	12.63	24.21	99.98
B. 1980s % of Workers Across Deciles of Percentage Male in Occupational Category												
GDR 1981	% women workers, *N* = 4623830	32.13	14.71	3.61	3.09	22.6	12.88	2.11	5.15	2.58	1.15	100.01
	% men workers, *N* = 4739267	2.53	2.24	1.17	1.78	18.55	16.07	3.65	12.58	14.83	26.61	100.01
FRG 1987	% women workers, *N* = 10563458	3.47	16.47	12.83	32.41	0.72	15.07	10.60	3.14	2.98	2.32	100.01
	% men workers, *N* = 15937719	0.17	2.34	3.06	12.71	0.42	12.91	13.41	6.33	10.09	38.56	100.00

APPENDIX B
Continued.

		% Male in 3-Digit ISCO88 Occupational Category										
		0–10	10.1–20	20.1–30	30.1–40	40.1–50	50.1–60	60.1–70	70.1–80	80.1–90	90.1–100	Total*
C. 1998 % of Workers Across Deciles of Percentage Male in Occupational Category												
E.G.	% women workers, $N = 2793000$	20.87	32.33	11.03	6.19	4.51	12.03	4.58	5.30	0.79	2.36	99.99
	% men workers, $N = 3407000$	1.53	4.90	3.43	2.73	3.11	11.68	6.28	13.94	3.70	48.69	99.99
W.G.	% women workers, $N = 12214000$	6.08	24.28	21.26	10.96	11.66	3.87	11.49	3.64	3.47	3.28	99.99
	% men workers, $N = 16529000$	0.33	3.87	5.26	4.18	7.00	3.78	14.77	8.42	12.20	40.20	100.01

* Totals differ from 100% because of rounding.

APPENDIX C

Differences between East and West Germany in Percentage Male across Broad Occupational Categories for the 1980s and 1998.

A. 1980s

ISCO88 Categories (2-digit code)	% Male in Occupational Categories		
	West Germany 1987	East Germany 1981	West-East Diff. % male
Legislators and senior officials (11)	78.5	46.4	32.1
Corporate managers (12)	84.8	71.9	12.9
General managers (13)	56.4	62.7	–6.3
Physical, mathematical, and engineering science professionals (21)	92.9	73.4	19.5
Life science and health professionals (except nursing) (22)	36.1	16.4	19.7
Teaching professionals (23)	45.2	25.7	19.5
Other professionals (24)	63.2	41.9	21.3
Physical and engineering science associate professionals (31)	80.1	49.1	31.0
Life science and health associate professionals (32) (includes nurses)	14.2	15.8	–1.6
Teaching associate professionals (33)	–	2.5	–
Other associate professionals (34)	45.8	41.4	4.4
Office clerks (41)	44.7	23.0	21.7
Customer service clerks (42)	20.0	8.6	11.4
Personal and protective services workers (51)	38.9	34.5	4.4
Models, salespersons, and demonstrators (52)	20.0	9.8	10.2
Market-oriented skilled agriculture and fishery workers (61)	68.4	51.7	16.7
Extraction and building trades workers (71)	98.5	96.0	2.5
Metal, machinery, and related trades (72)	96.1	90.4	5.7
Precision, handicraft, printing, and related workers (73)	71.6	46.6	25.0
Wood-treaters, cabinet-makers, and related trades workers (including food processing and textile trades) (74)	67.9	40.5	27.4
Stationary-plant and related operators (81)	84.5	74.7	9.8
Machine operators and assemblers (82)	74.9	46.6	28.3
Drivers and mobile plant operators (83)	96.8	92.1	4.7
Sales and services elementary occupations (e.g., messengers, domestic helpers) (91)	31.2	10.6	20.6
Agriculture, fishery, and related laborers (92)	21.9	45.6	–23.7
Mining, construction, manufacturing, and transport laborers (93)	62.3	55.8	6.5
(*N* employed)	(26,501,177)	(9,363,097)	

APPENDIX C. *Continued.*

B. 1998

ISCO88 Categories (2-digit code)	% Male in Occupational Categories		
	West Germany 1998	East Germany 1998	West-East Diff. % male
Legislators and senior officials (11)	73.6	53.8	19.8
Corporate managers (12)	81.6	78.1	3.5
General managers (13)	61.8	53.2	8.6
Physical, mathematical, and engineering science professionals (21)	87.0	77.3	9.7
Life science and health professionals (except nursing) (22)	34.5	22.2	12.3
Teaching professionals (23)	37.7	24.6	13.1
Other professionals (24)	64.9	54.2	10.7
Physical and engineering science associate professionals (31)	75.3	59.2	16.1
Life science and health associate professionals (32) (includes nurses)	33.5	29.1	4.4
Teaching associate professionals (33)	57.8	61.5	–3.7
Other associate professionals (34)	48.7	37.6	11.1
Office clerks (41)	34.0	21.4	12.6
Customer service clerks (42)	18.7	12.8	5.9
Personal and protective services workers (51)	37.4	41.9	–4.5
Models, salespersons, and demonstrators (52)	18.8	18.0	0.8
Market-oriented skilled agriculture and fishery workers (61)	70.0	53.6	16.4
Extraction and building trades workers (71)	94.8	96.7	–1.9
Metal, machinery, and related trades (72)	95.7	96.1	–0.4
Precision, handicraft, printing, and related workers (73)	68.3	55.6	12.7
Wood-treaters, cabinet-makers, and related trades workers (including food processing and textile trades) (74)	75.7	77.2	–1.5
Stationary-plant and related operators (81)	92.8	71.4	21.4
Machine operators and assemblers (82)	78.8	75.3	3.5
Drivers and mobile plant operators (83)	94.9	96.7	–1.8
Sales and services elementary occupations (e.g., messengers, domestic helpers) (91)	33.3	43.3	–10.0
Agriculture, fishery, and related laborers (92)	28.9	69.2	–40.3
Mining, construction, manufacturing, and transport laborers (93)	66.1	68.3	–2.2
(*N* employed)	(28,743,000)	(6,200,000)	

INTERCITY VARIATION IN GENDER INEQUALITIES IN CHINA: ANALYSIS OF A 1995 NATIONAL SURVEY

Xiaoling Shu and Yanjie Bian

ABSTRACT

Recent research portrays a mixed picture of the impact of post-1978 economic reforms on gender inequality in China. We analyze a 1995 national survey of urban China (10,967 individuals in 55 cities) and city-level data compiled from Chinese statistical yearbooks to show intercity covariations between an index of marketization and a set of indicators of gender inequality in the labor markets. Our analysis shows gender gaps in human capital, political capital, labor market placement, and work earnings. Most of these gender inequalities remain constant across cities of varying degrees of product, labor, and capital marketization. To the extent that the amount of gender inequality is correlated with marketization, this association is a non-monotonic one, indicating a nonlinear, accumulative marketization process. Major changes have taken place in the most marketized cities, where the gender disparity in affiliation with the state sector has diminished and gender-based occupational segregation has been on the rise.

INTRODUCTION

Recent research portrays a mixed picture of the impact of post-1978 economic reforms on gender inequality in China. One observation is that the growth of

The Future of Market Transition, Volume 19, pages 269–309.

ISBN: 0-7623-0835-4

market economies created off-farm employment opportunities for rural women, narrowed the gender gap in household income contribution, and enhanced women's relative status to men's (Entwisle et al., 1995; Matthews & Nee, 2000; Michelson & Parish, 2000). Another observation, mostly from the cities, is that as markets eroded the power of the state both as employer and advocator of women's rights, labor market discrimination against female workers re-emerged in hiring/layoffs, job placement, promotion, and wage determination in both state and non-state sectors, lowering the economic status of women relative to men (Honig & Hershatter, 1988; Ran, 1988; Robinson, 1985; Wu, 1995; Lee, 1995; Honig, 2000; Hershatter, 2000). Evidence from rural China also shows that men are leading the expansion of family businesses while women are left behind to specialize in agriculture (Entwisle et al., 1995). Discrimination from the family may also have risen (Davis, 1995; Entwisle et al., 1995; Michelson & Parish, 2000). Yet a third observation is that despite changes brought by state policy shifts and especially economic reforms, gender gaps in earnings and other work statuses in the cities have remained stable from the 1950s to the 1990s (Bian & Logan, 1996; Bian, Logan & Shu, 2000; Zhou, Tuma & Moen, 1996, 1997).

All three assessments about the trends of gender inequality have some merit. In his critical review of recent scholarship on China's gender inequalities, Whyte (2000) identifies several areas in which controversies may lie. For instance, the realms in which research attention is focused differ, so assessments about women's relative statuses in work and non-work lives or about rural and urban women may lead to very different conclusions. Research conducted in the same realm but with different indicators and measures can also lead to different conclusions because even if the researchers have the same conceptual goals behind their diverse research tools, these indicators and measures may mean different things. Finally, controversies lie in the different data sources used, especially when researchers collect their data from different locations, in different time periods, or with different designs. Given China's tremendous regional variations in socioeconomic development and pace of reform, this last problem is particularly severe. Whyte's suggestion is constructive: Serious scholarly work that assesses the impact of reforms on gender inequality must carefully identify a realm of research, utilize a well-defined set of indicators and measures, and rely on comparable and systematic data.

Inspired by Whyte's suggestion, we examine in this paper intercity variation in gender inequalities in the labor markets by analyzing national data from the 1995 Chinese Household Income Project (CHIP). We focus on four sets of indicators and measures of labor market inequality available from the data:

human capital, political capital, labor market placement, and work earnings. Although these four do not exhaust all sources of labor market inequality, they are the most important aspects of work statuses of women and men as informed by an established gender and work literature (see a review by Marini, 1989) and by the research of Chinese social stratification (see a review by Bian, 2002). Because these indicators and measures were defined within a single survey project and data collection in multiple locations followed a uniform set of procedures, the data lend us a fairly high-quality assessment about measured gender inequalities at a national level.

Because of known inter-region and intercity variations in pace of reforms (Nee, 1996; Parish & Michelson, 1996; Xie & Hannum, 1996), Chinese cities conceivably will vary in level of marketization – the extent to which commodities are processed through product markets, people are matched to jobs through labor markets, and investment finances are allocated through capital markets. If, among the cities included in the 1995 CHIP data, level of marketization is associated negatively with degree of gender inequalities measured, this would be systematic evidence for the proposition that market transition reduces gender inequality in a big country like China (Nee & Matthews, 1996). If the association is positive, it lends support for the alternative argument that markets increase gender inequalities. If the results show no association or a curve-linear association, then additional careful studies into the causes of these patterns are needed. Our statistical analyses that follow will not in any way offer theoretical interpretations of any of these possible results but only present carefully documented quantitative patterns that may imply clues to such interpretations.

DATA AND MEASURES

Individual-Level Data and Measures

The individual level data are from the urban portion of the 1995 CHIP. Through a multistage sampling procedure, this project selected 11 province-level administrative units (out of a total of 31). These were Beijing, Shanxi, Liaoning, Jiangsu, Anhu, Henan, Hubei, Guangdong, Yunnan, Gangsu, and Sichuan. Then 69 cities and towns (out of a total of 226) were selected. The sample contains 21,696 individuals from 6,931 households. These household surveys collected information on all household members. Because we have no reliable macrolevel data for 14 county-headquarters, 1,174 individuals in the non-agricultural labor force were excluded from this analysis. Under the assumption that within-household clustering is negligible (Shu & Bian, 2001), we treat all wage-earning household members, ages 18–60, as independent observations for this analysis.

In addition to age of wage earners, we measured gender inequality in four areas: human capital, political capital, labor market placement, and work earnings. The two measures of human capital are a continuous variable of years of schooling and a dichotomous variable of college education. In previous studies, these measures have shown consistent, positive effects on attainment of political capital, favorable labor market placements, and wage attainments in urban workplaces (Lin & Bian, 1991; Walder, 1992, 1995; Bian, 1994; Bian & Logan, 1996; Zhou et al., 1996, 1997). We use Communist party membership as the measure of political capital. Recent studies show that even in the reform era Communist party membership is carefully screened for political loyalty, and membership increases opportunities for mobility into elite classes (Walder et al., 2000; Bian, Shu & Logan, 2001; Li & Walder, 2001), although its impact on wage attainment is less consistent from one study to another (see a review by Nee & Matthews, 1996).

Labor market placement is measured by placement in work sectors, occupations, and industries. Three work sectors are the state, the collective, and the new sector. The contrast between state and collective sectors entails an analogy of core and peripheral sectors in advanced capitalist economies (Walder, 1986; Lin & Bian, 1991), and its changing structure in the reform era is complicated by the booming, more prosperous new sector, which is largely independent of state control and heterogeneous in property-rights arrangements. It encompasses private businesses, joint ventures, foreign investment, township enterprises, and other hybrid forms of ownership. The new-sector variable is constructed from respondents' reports about their work-unit sector, employment status, and occupations. Because of the undersampling of employees in private enterprises and individual entrepreneurs (*geitihu*), individuals in these new forms of ownership are substantially under-represented in this sample[1] (China State Statistical Bureau, 1998).

Informed by recent studies on urban classes (Davis, 1995, 2000), we identified five occupational categories: owners and operators of private businesses, professional and technical workers, cadres and managers of government agencies and state firms, office clerks, and skilled and unskilled workers. Finally, we identified five industries: manufacturing; mining, construction, and transportation; commerce, real estate, finance, and service; education, culture, and public health; and party and government agencies. We identify these industries based on the social and economic rankings of the industries and the documented gender disparity in industry segregation, e.g. women are more likely to be employed in sales, service, and education, while men are more likely employed in heavy industry (Whyte, 1984). A crude industry classification was used in the data collection, which does not afford for careful analysis of within industry heterogeneity.

Work earnings are difficult to measure precisely because of institutional uncertainties on the legitimacy of some sources of earnings. From the CHIP data, we identified three sources of compensation workers earn at the workplace: regular salary, bonus and subsidies, and earnings from private businesses. The annual earnings were calculated as the sum of total salary (bonuses, subsidies, and stipends for temporarily laid-off workers) and earnings from private businesses including earnings as owners of private enterprises and operators of private businesses.

City-Level Data and Measures

The city-level data was compiled from the China Statistical Yearbooks and the Statistical Yearbooks of selected cities for 1995.[2] In Table 1, we compare the 1995 CHIP urban sample with China-wide statistics by the Central Place Hierarchy[3] – a ranking of cities based on the levels of their socioeconomic development (Skinner, Henderson & Yuan, 2000).

Although higher-level cities were oversampled, the distribution of sampled individuals in the non-agricultural labor force is consistent with the national distribution across the Central-Place Hierarchy. Five of 10 apex metropolises and six of 20 central metropolises were included in our sample. However, only 16 of 225 greater cities and 11 of 768 local cities were included, indicating that these lower-level cities are under-represented in the city sample. The distribution of city residents across the Central-Place Hierarchy is more consistent with the national distribution, with residents of regional cities and of greater cities slightly overrepresented and residents of local cities slightly underrepresented. Similarly, the distribution of individuals in the non-agricultural labor force is also very similar to the national statistics, with individuals of regional cities and of greater cities slightly overrepresented and individuals of local cities slightly underrepresented. Thus the 1995 CHIP sample is fairly representative of the Chinese urban labor force.

In the city-level data we compiled, three variables were used to measure degree of marketization. Marketization of the commodity market is measured by the percentage of industrial output by nonstate enterprises out of the total industrial output. Marketization of the labor market is measured by the percentage of employees in nonstate firms out of the total number of workers. And marketization of the capital market is measured by the percentage of foreign investment out of the total investment in the city.

Table 1. Comparing the 1995 CHIP Urban Sample with China-wide Statistics, by Central-Place Hierachy.[a]

	CHIP			CHINA		
	Number of Cities	Percent of Sampled City Residents	Percent of Sampled Labor Force	Number of Cities	Percent of Total City Residents	Percent of Total Labor Force
Apex Metropolis	5	23.68	24.39	10	22.50	20.24
Central Metropolis	6	15.87	14.77	20	14.31	15.02
Regional City	17	24.73	24.46	66	19.06	19.90
Greater City	16	24.98	25.48	225	21.31	21.11
Local City	11	10.72	10.91	768	22.83	23.73
Total Number	55	19,522	10,967	1,149	168,060,000	91,493,900

[a] Skinner and colleagues (2000) identified eight urban hierarchal levels using detailed socioeconomic data from a one-percent household sample from China's 1990 population census. The 1995 CHIP sample, excluding the county headquarters, contains cities at the top five levels in the Central-Place Hierarchy.

Table 2 presents city-level variables used in the analysis and the correlations among these variables. On average, in these 55 cities in 1995, less than 45% of industrial commodities were produced by non-state sector, 36% of the nonagricultural labor force were in new and collective enterprises and business, and less than 4% of total investment were from foreign investment. The average GDP per capita was 10,494.96 yuan.

We further reduce the three indicators of marketization in commodity market, labor market, and capital market into one latent construct. This latent construct can be identified using confirmatory factor analysis as described by the following equation:

$$y = \Lambda_y \eta + \varepsilon$$

Where y is a vector of the three observed indicators, Λ_y is a matrix of parameters linking the latent construct, η to the observed indicators, and ε is a vector of error terms. The model assumes that each indicator is a function of the underlying latent construct and an error term that is independent of the latent construct (Jöreskog & Sörbom, 1988, 1993). The fit statistics for this one-factor confirmatory factor analysis model ($\chi^2 = 0.9$, $df = 1$, $GFI = 1.00$, $RMR = 0.031$, and $BIC = -1.32$) indicate that this model fits our data well. The factor scores generated from this analysis were then used to construct a composite measure of marketization. This standardized measure of marketization has a mean of 0 and a standard deviation of 1, with negative values for lower degrees of marketization and positive values for higher degrees of marketization.

The three indicators of marketization are fairly highly correlated with one another (from 0.47 to 0.68), and this results in a composite measure of marketization that has strong associations with all three indicators, as evident in the high correlations among them (from 0.80 to 0.90). In contrast, the composite measure of marketization is only moderately associated (0.42) with economic development level as measured by GDP per capita.

We divide the cities into four groups based on their scores on the index of marketization. The distribution of cities on this marketization index is highly skewed, with the majority of cities having scores less than 0.5. Because our interest is in the relationship between marketization and gender inequality, we use this index both as a continuous variable and a categorical variable by differentiating the cities into four groups. Cities with scores less than -0.5 are the "least marketized cities" – 16 cities are in this group containing 38% of the individual wage earners ("respondents") in the sample. Cities with scores between -0.5 and less than 0.5 are "marketized cities"; 27 such cities account for 49% of the total respondents. Seven cities have scores between 0.5 and 1.5 and these are characterized as "highly marketized cities" containing 8% of the

Table 2. Descriptive Statistics and Correlations among City-level Variables Used in the Analysis, for 1995 ($N=55$).

	Descriptive Statistics		Correlations			
	Mean	Std. Dev.	Commodity Market	Labor Market	Capital Market	GDP Per Capita
INDEX OF MARKETIZATION	0.00	1.00	0.90***	0.85***	0.80***	0.42***
Commodity Market	44.53	23.04		0.68***	0.61***	0.40***
Labor Market	36.07	13.83			0.47***	0.21
Capital Market	3.43	6.04				0.38***
GDP Per Capita	10,494.96	11,192.32				

*** $P < 0.001$.

respondents. The remaining five cities score higher than 1.5 on the index of marketization and are characterized as the "most marketized cities" with 5% of the respondents.

ANALYSIS

Describing Gender Gaps

Table 3 describes gender gap in human capital, political capital, labor market placement, and work earnings. Among the eighteen measures we examined, a gender gap is found in all but three variables. The average age of the men in the non-agricultural labor force is more than two years older than that of the women. Gender gap in education remains. On the average, men have close to one year more schooling than women, and 12% more men have college or some college education than women. Gender gap in political capital is also marked. Compared with women, 17% more men are Communist Party members. The percentage of men who are cadres and managers is 10% higher than women, while the percentage of women who are clerical workers and workers are 3% and 7% higher than men, respectively. Men and women are equally as likely to be owners and managers of private businesses and to be professionals. Gender gap in sector placement is also visible, with 9% more men in the state sector and 9% more women in the collective sector, but there is no gender difference in placement in the new sector. Gender difference in industry placement also remains with men more likely to be employed in the manufacturing industry; in mining, construction, and transportation industry; and in party and government agencies, and women more likely to be employed in commerce, real estate, finance, and in education, culture, and research.

Marketization and Gender Gaps in Human and Political Capitals

Figure 1 displays measured gender inequalities across cities grouped into four levels of marketization. On the whole, men have more education than women do regardless of level of marketization. Men on average have 0.5 to 2.0 more years of schooling than women, and 10% to 20% more men than women have attained some college education. These difference margins vary across levels of marketization, and in the case of number of years of education this difference appears to increase with marketization. With regard to college education, the gender disparity appears to have a concave association with marketization, with the highly marketized cities having the largest gap. For both men and women, years of schooling and the proportion of college educated decline with

Table 3. Descriptive Statistics of Individual-level Variables Used in the Analysis, by Gender.

	Total ($N = 10{,}967$)		Women ($N = 5{,}225$)		Men ($N = 5{,}742$)		Gender Gap
	Mean	Std. Dev.	Mean	Std. Dev.	Mean	Std. Dev.	t
AGE	38.66	9.55	37.35	8.83	39.84	10.01	13.85***
EDUCATION							
Year of Schooling	10.79	2.94	10.46	2.84	11.09	2.99	11.23***
College and Some College	0.28	0.45	0.22	0.41	0.34	0.47	13.10***
CCP MEMBER	0.24	0.43	0.15	0.36	0.32	0.47	21.92***
SECTOR							
State	0.81	0.39	0.76	0.42	0.85	0.35	11.90***
Collective	0.15	0.36	0.20	0.40	0.11	0.31	–12.26***
New Sector	0.04	0.20	0.05	0.21	0.04	0.20	–1.14
OCCUPATION							
Owners & Operators (Private)	0.02	0.12	0.01	0.12	0.02	0.13	0.78
Professionals	0.23	0.42	0.24	0.42	0.22	0.42	–1.42
Cadres and Managers (State)	0.11	0.32	0.06	0.23	0.16	0.37	17.85***
Clerical Workers	0.20	0.40	0.21	0.41	0.18	0.38	–4.12***
Skilled and Unskilled Workers	0.44	0.50	0.48	0.50	0.41	0.49	–6.70***
INDUSTRY							
Manufacturing	0.42	0.49	0.41	0.49	0.43	0.50	2.61**
Mining, Construction, Transportation	0.09	0.28	0.07	0.26	0.10	0.30	5.01***
Commerce, Real Estate, Finance	0.19	0.39	0.22	0.42	0.16	0.37	–7.85***
Education, Culture, Research	0.14	0.34	0.16	0.36	0.12	0.33	–5.23***
Party and Government Agency	0.10	0.30	0.08	0.28	0.12	0.32	6.26***
EARNINGS	6,300.51	3,804.40	5,731.89	3,487.04	6,809.43	3,999.83	14.84***

*** $P < 0.001$ ** $P < 0.01$ * $P < 0.05$.

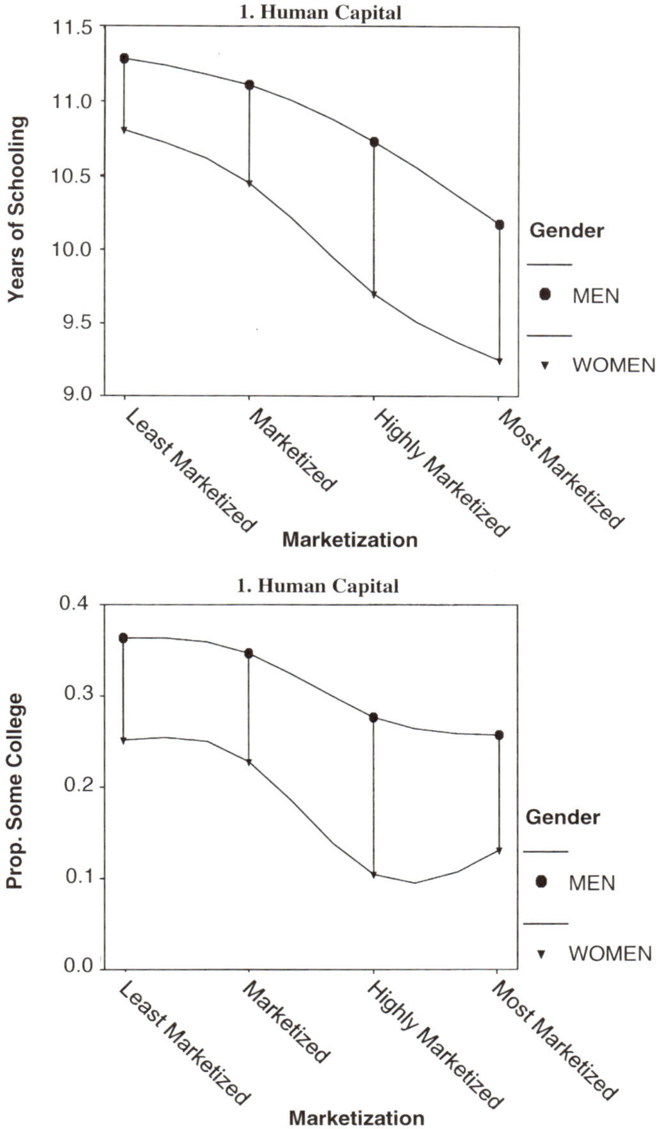

Fig. 1. Effect of Marketization on Human Capital, Political Capital, Placement in the Labor Force, and Earnings, by Gender.

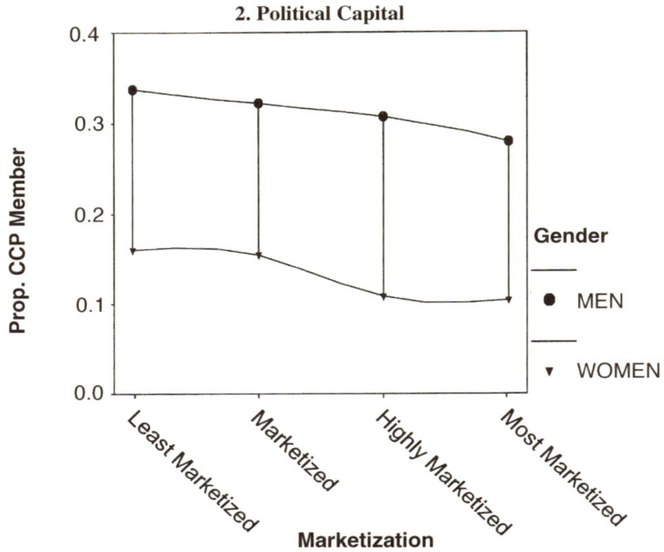

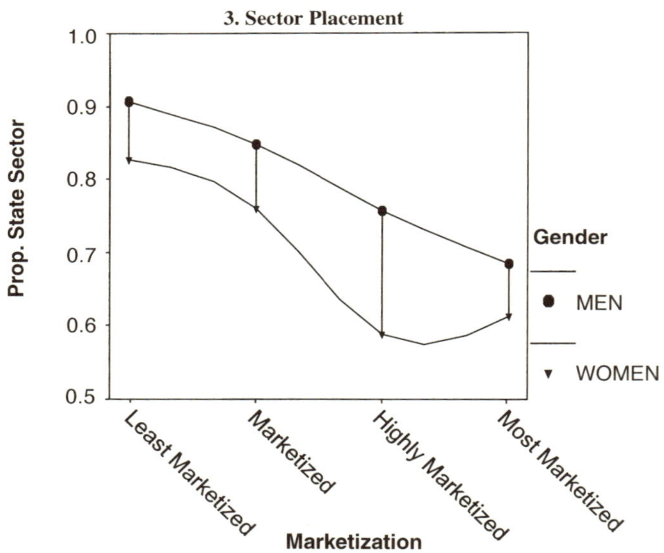

Fig. 1. Continued.

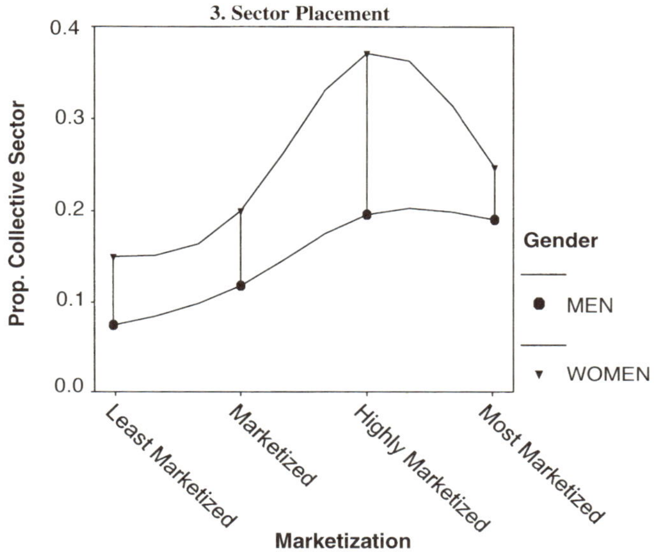

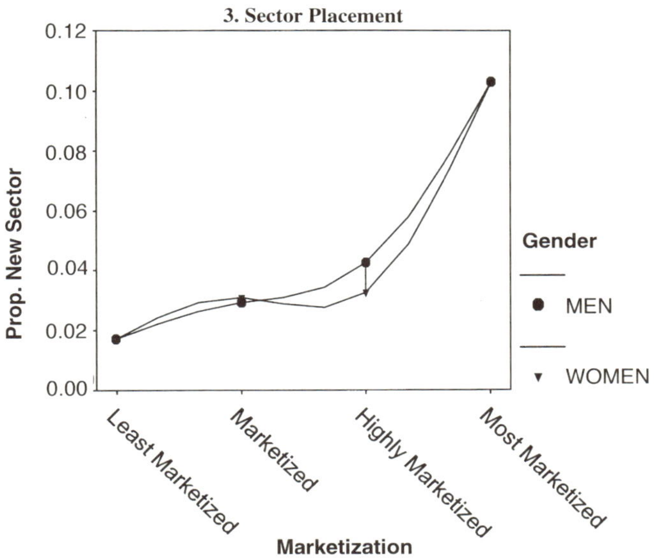

Fig. 1. Continued.

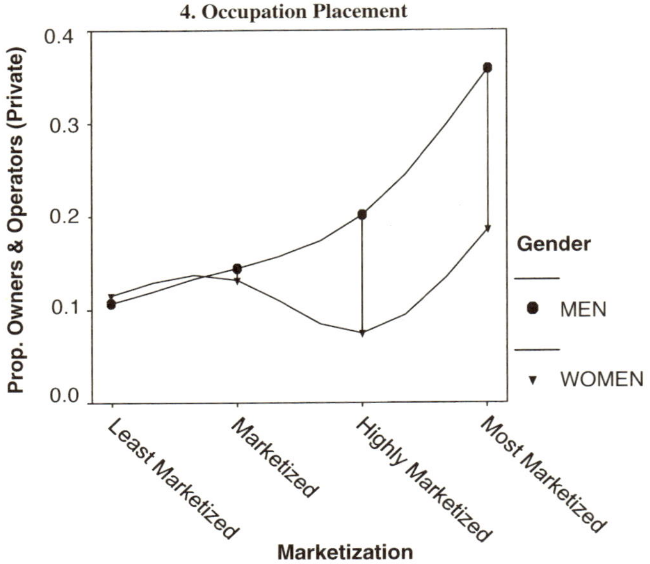

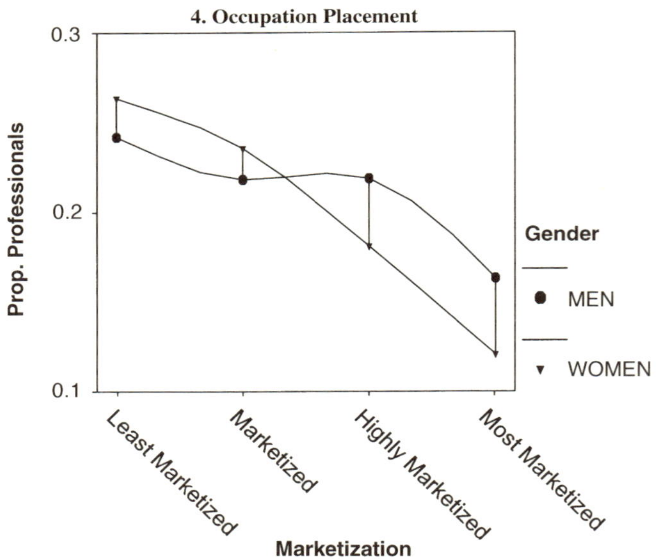

Fig. 1. Continued.

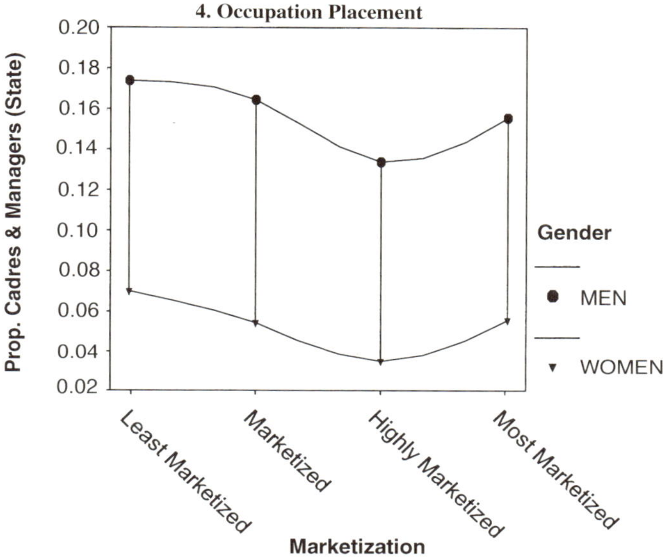

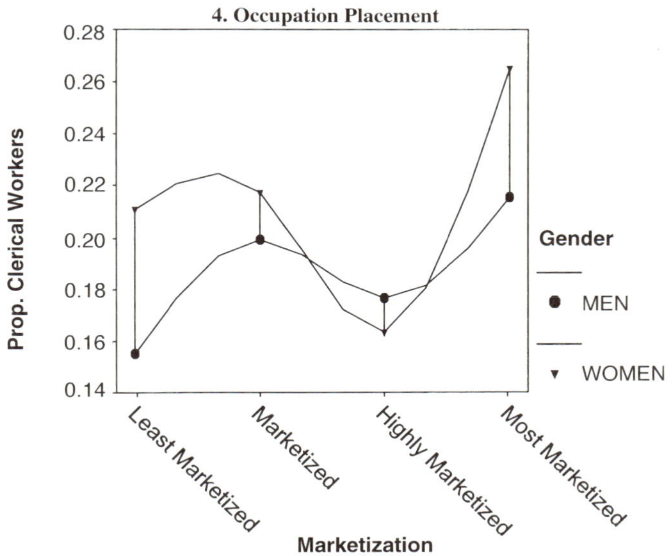

Fig. 1. Continued.

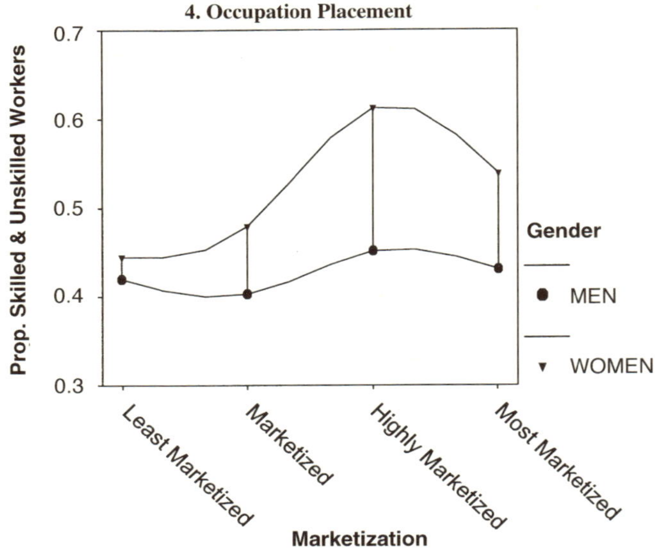

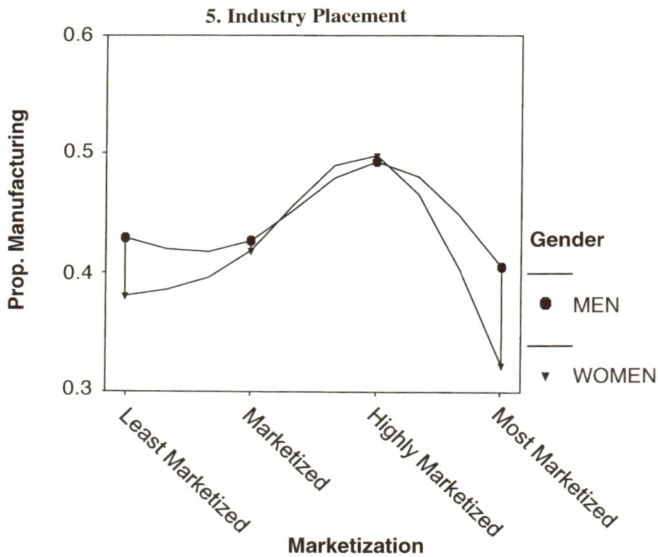

Fig. 1. Continued.

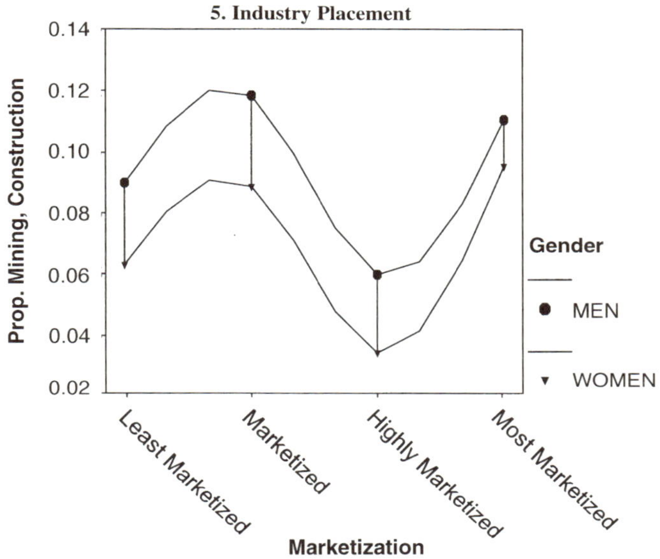

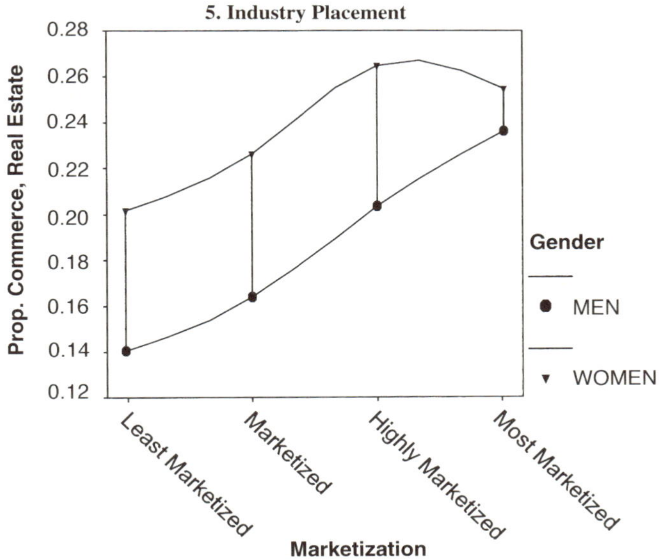

Fig. 1. Continued.

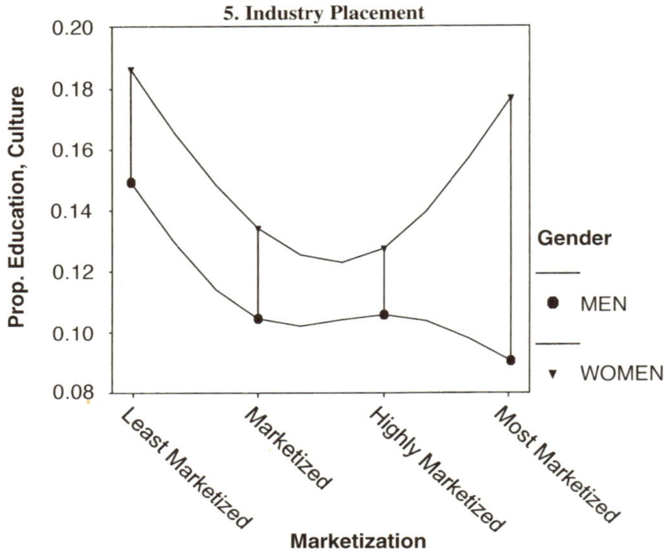

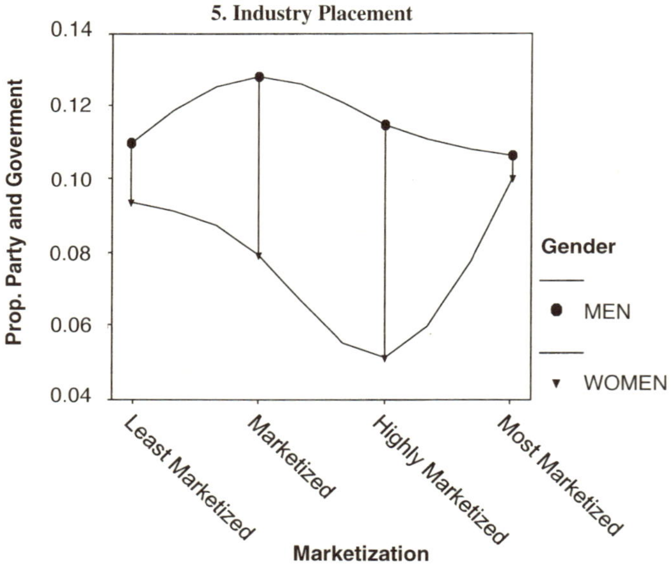

Fig. 1. Continued.

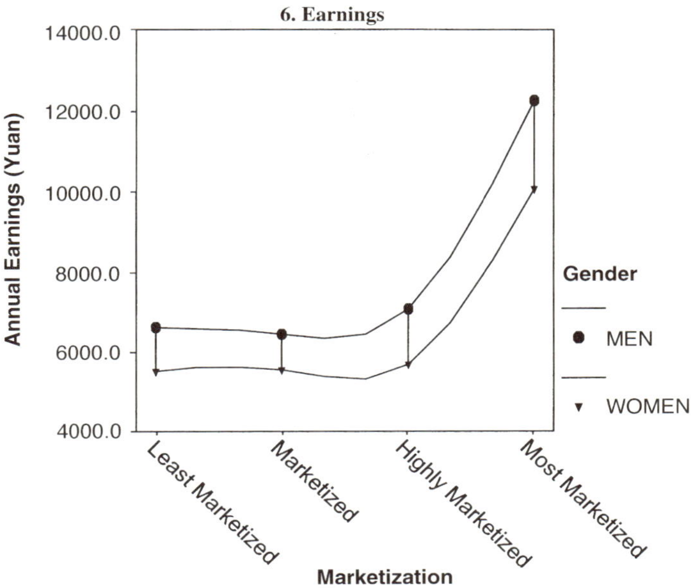

Fig. 1. Continued.

marketization. In the Chinese context, the more marketized cities have been expanding their manufacturing and service sectors, thus having large numbers of low-educated workers in construction and service sectors. This may have caused the observed negative association between education and marketization across cities.

Gender difference in Communist party membership has a 20% margin favoring men, and this differential does not vary by level of marketization. For both men and women, the proportion of party members slightly declines with marketization.

Marketization and Gender Gaps in Labor Market Placements

Gender differences in sector placement are marked across all levels of marketization. There were 8% to 20% more men in the state sector and 8% to 20% more women in the collective sector, and these gender differentials are largest in highly marketized cities. Because the collective sector is still less attractive than the state sector (Bian & Li, 2000), this finding points to the poorer sector placement of women with marketization. In the most highly marketized cities, the state sector starts to lose its relative advantage over the nonstate sectors making the state sector not as desirable,[4] allowing more women to move into this sector. Nevertheless, no gender difference is found in employment in the new sector, which is true in all levels of marketization even though significantly more people are getting jobs in the new sector in more marketized cities (from less than 2% in the least marketized cities to 10% in the most marketized cities). Because the new sector contains market opportunities per se, this particular finding indicates that market growth does not necessarily discriminate against or favor women in new sector jobs. However, because our data do not provide a representative sample of the new sector, we are unsure about the extent to which this finding can be generalized.

Gender disparity was found in two of the five occupations we examined. There were 10% more men in state cadres and manager positions than women, a pattern that is consistent across all levels of marketization. The proportion of people who are cadres and managers of state agencies and enterprises remain constant across all levels of marketization. This indicates that market growth has not eroded the size of the state elite nor the gender gap in the state elite. On the contrary, 3% to 20% more women were workers, and this gender gap increases with marketization and decreases at the high end of marketization. Considering that the average earnings ratio between workers and cadres decreased from 70% to 50% in the most marketized cities, gender gap resulting from occupation-based earnings differentials is likely to increase with marketization. Gender gap in owning and managing private businesses also grows with marketization, although this gender gap is not statistically significant. With marketization, the proportion of people in professional jobs decreases for both men and women, but the decline is faster for women than for men.

Overall, the pattern of occupational placement with marketization indicates that marketization has a larger impact on women's occupational placement than on men's as evidenced by a larger variation in women's occupation distribution across the four groups of cities. Although with marketization, there have been a decrease in the proportion employed in professional jobs and an increase in the proportion in skilled and unskilled worker jobs, the sizes of both changes are larger for women than for men. Increasing marketization usually is accompanied by the expansion of manufacturing and service sector jobs in the Chinese context. Considering that the ratio in earnings between workers and professionals declined from 79% to 64% in the most marketized cities, we derive that this occupational shift has a profound implication for gender disparity in earnings.

Gender gaps also exist in industry placement in every industry except manufacturing. Men were more likely to be in mining, construction, transportation, and party and government agencies, while women were more likely to be in commerce, real estate, finance, and education, cultural, research, and technology. Among the five industries, only in the commerce, real estate, and finance industry does the proportion of employees linearly increase with marketization. This increase is faster for men than for women, indicating that with marketization, men are moving at a faster pace into market-connected industries than women are. The proportion of people in party and government agencies decreases with marketization, with those in the highly marketized cities having the lowest proportion. Again, this decrease is faster for men than for women. Gender gap in mining, construction, transportation, in commerce, real estate, and finance (except the most marketized cities), and in education, culture, research, technology, and public health (again except the most marketized cities) remains constant with marketization. Gender gap in party and government agencies increases with marketization but then almost disappears in the most marketized cities.

Marketization and Gender Gap in Work Earnings

The size of the gender gap in earnings is independent of the process of marketization. While the average earnings rose from about 6,200 yuan to more than 11,000 yuan in the most marketized cities, gender gap in earnings increased at a similar pace from about 1,100 yuan to about 2,000 yuan in the most marketized cities. Although the average annual earnings in the most marketized cities is double the amount of earnings in the least marketized cities (5,538 yuan vs. 10,083 yuan for women, and 6,648 yuan vs. 12,277 yuan for men), women's earnings in all four groups of cities remain within 81% to 86% of men's.

Interactive Effects of Marketization and Gender

Marked gender difference is found in labor cohort composition, as illustrated in Figure 2. Compared with women, men in the older labor cohorts (entry in 1958–1960 and earlier) account for 32% of the male labor force, and women in this same cohorts account for only 20% of the female labor force. Much of this gender difference is due to the policy of a five-year earlier retirement age for women than men. Because this cohort difference may affect the previously described gender inequalities, we present estimates of the effects of gender, marketization, and the interactive effect of gender and marketization on

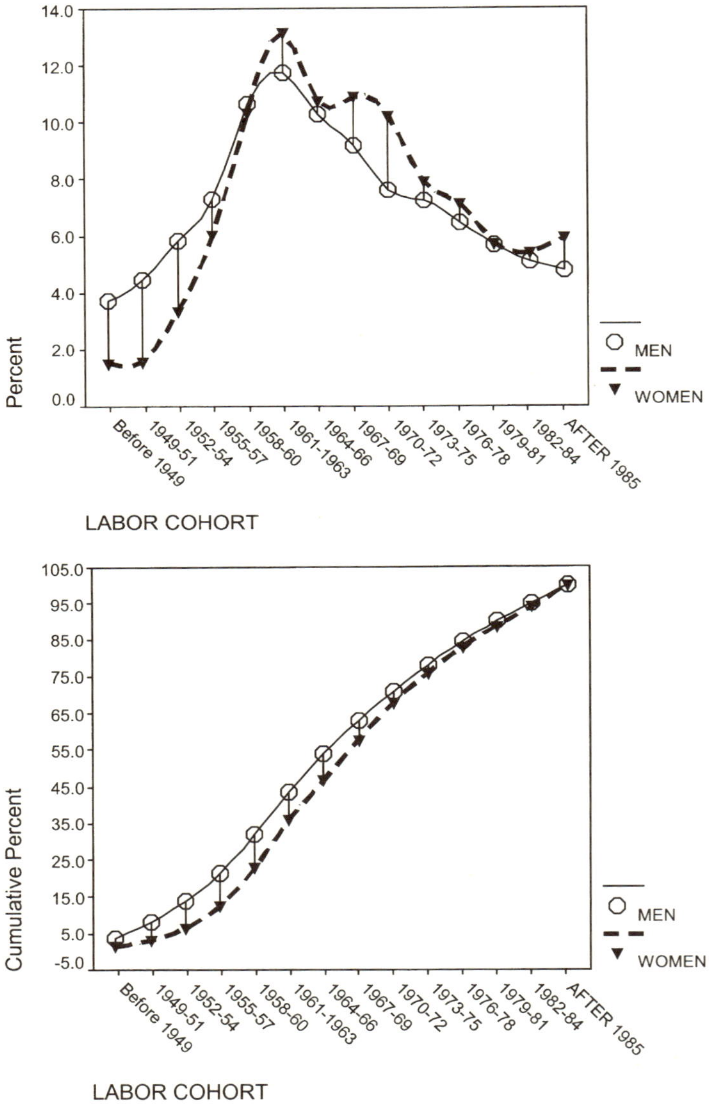

Fig. 2. Gender Difference in Labor Cohort Composition.

the various measures of gender inequality, controlling for cohort effects in Table 4.

Our results confirm a consistent gender gap in human capital, political capital, labor-market placements, and work earnings. With labor cohorts and marketization controlled for, on the average, women have 0.72 fewer years of education, and the odds of having college or some college education are only 52% of the odds for men. These gender gaps are largest in highly marketized cities where women have 1.26 fewer years of education and where the odds for women having a college education decrease to less than 27% of that for men. The odds for a woman to be a Communist party member are only 39% of that for a man, and there is no intercity variation in this gender gap.

Gender gap exists on two of the three sector placements. The odds for a woman to be in the state sector are 50% of that for a man or the same characteristics, but her odds of being in the collective sector are 2.20-fold that for a comparable man. There is no gender difference in employment in the new sector. These gender gaps do not vary by degree of marketization.

Gender difference is found in four of the five occupational placements. Women are slightly more likely to be in professional occupations but their odds of being cadres and managers of state organizations are only 38% of that for men. There is no gender difference in being in clerical occupations, except in the highest marketized cities, where the odds for women are 42% times higher than that for men. Women in middle-degree marketized cities were more likely to be workers (odds between women and men are 1.25 times in low-marketization cities and 1.77 in high-marketized cities). There is no gender difference in being owners and mangers of private businesses. Gender gaps in being clerical workers and workers are nonlinearly associated with degree of marketization, with women being more likely to be clerical workers at the middle range of marketization and more likely to be workers at the two extremes of marketization.

Gender gap is also found in four of the five industry-placements. The odds for being in manufacturing for women are 81% of that for men, although this gender gap disappears in low-marketization cities. Women are less likely to be in mining, construction, and transportation industry (70% of men's odds ratio), but more likely to be in commerce, real estate, and finance industry (1.52-fold men's odds ratio) and education, culture, research, technical service, and public health (1.36-fold men's odds ratio). In cities of low degree of marketization, the odds for women to be in party and government agency were 30% lower than that for men, and this gap widens to 49% in cities of high degree of marketization. No gender difference is found in cities at the two extremes of

Table 4. OLS and Logistic Regression Estimates of the Effects of Gender and Marketization on Human Capital, Political Capital, Placement in the Labor Force, and Log Earnings (1995 CHIP, $N = 10{,}967$).

DEPENDENT VARIABLES	Female	Female × Marketization			Marketization		
		Low	High	Highest	Low	High	Highest
HUMAN CAPITAL							
Year of Schooling	–0.72***	–0.16	–0.54**	–0.40	–0.19***	–0.63***	–1.05***
	(0.04)	(0.11)	(0.20)	(0.26)	(0.08)	(0.14)	(0.18)
College	–0.65***	–0.04	–0.67**	–0.22	–0.07	–0.44	–0.51
	(0.08)	(0.11)	(0.23)	(0.28)	(0.07)	(0.13)	(0.17)
POLITICAL CAPITAL							
Communist Party	–0.95***	0.02	–0.33	–0.22	–0.10	–0.13	–0.34*
	(0.08)	(0.11)	(0.21)	(0.28)	(0.06)	(0.12)	(0.15)
SECTOR							
State	–0.70***	0.13	–0.11	0.42	–0.57***	–1.12***	–1.52***
	(0.10)	(0.12)	(0.18)	(0.22)	(0.09)	(0.14)	(0.16)
Collective	0.79***	–0.16	0.13	–0.49	0.53***	1.11***	1.09***
	(0.11)	(0.13)	(0.19)	(0.25)	(0.10)	(0.15)	(0.18)
New Sector	0.10	0.07	–0.40	–0.00	0.43**	0.75**	1.73***
	(0.19)	(0.24)	(0.38)	(0.34)	(0.17)	(0.25)	(0.23)
OCCUPATION							
Owners & Operators (Private)	0.22	–0.28	–1.15	–0.81	0.39	0.73	1.30**
	(0.31)	(0.39)	(0.74)	(0.68)	(0.27)	(0.40)	(0.41)
Professionals	0.14*	–0.04	–0.36	–0.49	–0.11	–0.11	–0.47**
	(0.07)	(0.10)	(0.19)	(0.28)	(0.07)	(0.13)	(0.18)
Cadres and Managers (State)	–0.98***	–0.24	–0.41	–0.10	–0.08	–0.27	–0.17
	(0.11)	(0.15)	(0.33)	(0.36)	(0.08)	(0.15)	(0.19)
Clerical Workers	0.35***	–0.25*	–0.47*	–0.07	0.31***	0.14	0.40***
	(0.08)	(0.11)	(0.20)	(0.24)	(0.08)	(0.14)	(0.17)
Skilled and Unskilled Workers	0.07	0.22*	0.57***	0.34	–0.09	0.10	0.05
	(0.07)	(0.09)	(0.16)	(0.20)	(0.06)	(0.11)	(0.14)

Table 4a. Continued.

DEPENDENT VARIABLES	Female	Female × Marketization			Marketization		
		Low	High	Highest	Low	High	Highest
INDUSTRY							
Manufacturing	–0.21**	0.18*	0.23	–0.16	–0.02	0.26	–0.10
	(0.07)	(0.09)	(0.15)	(0.20)	(0.06)	(0.11)	(0.14)
Mining, Construction, Transportation	–0.35**	0.02	–0.22	0.15	0.32**	–0.41	0.25
	(0.12)	(0.15)	(0.36)	(0.33)	(0.10)	(0.21)	(0.22)
Commerce, Real Estate, Finance	0.42***	–0.03	–0.11	–0.33	0.16	0.43	0.61
	(0.08)	(0.11)	(0.18)	(0.23)	(0.08)	(0.13)	(0.16)
Education, Culture, Research	0.31***	0.00	–0.06	0.48	–0.36***	–0.35*	–0.53*
	(0.09)	(0.12)	(0.23)	(0.30)	(0.09)	(0.17)	(0.23)
Party and Government Agency	–0.19	–0.35*	–0.67*	0.15	0.16	0.00	–0.03
	(0.11)	(0.14)	(0.29)	(0.32)	(0.09)	(0.17)	(0.22)
LOG EARNINGS	–0.20***	0.04	–0.04	0.05	–0.05**	0.07*	0.54***
	(0.02)	(0.03)	(0.05)	(0.06)	(0.02)	(0.03)	(0.04)

The constant terms and a series of dummy variables indicating labor cohorts are not reported. For these estimates, see the Appendix.
The two omitted dummy variables in this analysis are: the Lowest Marketization category in Female × Marketization, and the Lowest Marketization category in Marketization.
*** $P < 0.001$ ** $P < 0.01$ * $P < 0.05$.

marketization. With the exception of this last industry, there is no association between gender gap in industry placement and marketization.

Women's income was approximately 20% less than men, and this earnings gender gap is consistent across levels of marketization indicating a persistent gender gap in earnings independent of the market transition process.

A Hierarchical Model

To consider the combined effects of macro- and microlevel influences on gender inequality, we estimated a series of multilevel models (Bryk & Raudenbush, 1992; Goldstein, 1987). These models have two components. The basic microlevel equation is:

$$LC_{ij} = \beta_{0j} + \sum_{1}^{K} \beta_{kj} IC_{kij} + \varepsilon_{ij} \qquad \text{(B1.0)}$$

Where LC_{ij} represents one measure of labor force characteristics for individual *i* in *j*th community when the response variable is a continuous variable, LC_{ij} represents the log odds of being in a category in a logit hierarchical model when the response variable is a dichotomous variable, IC_{kij} represents this individual's *k*th characteristic that is pertinent to the measure of gender inequality LC_{ij}. The β_k's are microlevel coefficients, the interpretations of which are similar to those for a multiple regression when the response variable is continuous or a logit regression when the response variable is dichotomous.

The microcomponent of the model is applied to each of the communities on which our analysis is based, but we expect the effects of the microlevel variables to vary across communities. This is captured in the second component of the model – the macrocomponent where the microcoefficients are assumed to depend stochastically on macrolevel characteristics. We include two variables at the macrolevel: an index of marketization and a control variable, GDP per capita in 1995 as a measure of economic development level. This macrocomponent of the multilevel model is expressed by the following set of $K + 1$ equations:

$$\beta_{0j} = \alpha_{00} + \gamma_{01} MARKET_j + \gamma_{02} MARKET_j^2 + \gamma_{03} GDP_j + \mu_{0j} \qquad \text{(B2.0)}$$

$$\beta_{1j} = \alpha_{10} + \gamma_{11} MARKET_j + \gamma_{12} MARKET_j^2 + \gamma_{13} GDP_j + \mu_{1j} \qquad \text{(B2.1)}$$

$$\vdots$$

$$\beta_{Kj} = \alpha_{K0} + \gamma_{K1} MARKET_j + \gamma_{K2} MARKET_j^2 + \gamma_{K3} GDP_j + \mu_{kj} \qquad \text{(B2.K)}$$

Where GDP_j is GDP per capita in 1995 in community *j*, and $MARKET_j$ is the degree of marketization in 1995, the γ's are coefficients, and the μ's are macro error terms. The macro error terms (the μ's) are assumed to be normally distributed with a mean of zero, independent and exchangeable across communities and correlated across equations. The micro coefficients β's are dependent quantities in these equations.

The multilevel model expressed in Eqs B1.0 and B2.0 to B2.K is then combined into a single equation for estimation purposes:

$$LC_{ij} = \alpha_{00} + \gamma_{01} MARKET_j + \gamma_{02} MARKET_j^2 + \gamma_{03} GDP_j$$

$$+ \sum_{1}^{K} (\alpha_{k0} + \gamma_{k1} MARKET_j + \gamma_{k2} MARKET_j^2 + \gamma_{k3} GDP_j) * IC_{kij}$$

$$+ \mu_{0j} + \sum_{1}^{K} \mu_{kj} IC_{kij} + \varepsilon_{ij} \qquad \text{(B3.0)}$$

This equation indicates that expressing the micro-slope coefficients as a function of the macro variables is the same as a multilevel specification in which the macro and micro determinants interact. The γ's in Eq. B3.0 generally have the same interpretation as in Eq. B2.0 to B2.2. However, Eq. B3.0 demonstrates that γ_{01}, γ_{02}, and γ_{03} are not only coefficients for the effects of *MARKET*, *MARKET Squared*, and *GDP* on the micro-intercept but are also coefficients for the main effects of the macro variables on the dependent measure. These multilevel models as expressed by Eqs B1.0, B2.0 – B2.K, and B3.0 are "slopes-as-outcomes" models (Bryk & Raudenbush, 1992) estimated by a combination of maximum likelihood, empirical Bayes, and generalized least squares procedures using the Fisher Scoring/EM algorithm for linear hierarchical models, and PQL estimation approach for Benoulli response variables in HLM 5 (Bryk & Raudenbush, 1992).

The estimates of macro- and microlevel influences on human capital, political capital, and placement in the labor force are presented in Table 5. Similar to the results in Table 4, after controlling for these other correlates, gender effect exists for all but two of the 18 measures of inequality. On average, compared with a man of the same age living in the same city, a woman has 0.83 fewer years of education and is less likely to have college or some college education. She is also less likely to be a Communist party member than a man with the same age and education is. Similarly, when comparing a woman to a man of the same age, education, and political status, a woman is less likely to be in the state sector and more likely to be in the collective sector; more likely

Table 5. HLM Estimates of the Effects of Gender, Marketization, and GDP Per Capita on Human Capital, Political Capital, Placement in the Labor Force, and Earnings (1995 CHIP, $N = 10{,}967$).

DEPENDENT VARIABLES	Female	Female × Marketization	Female × Marketization Squared	Marketization	Marketization Squared	Female × GDP ($\times 10^{-4}$)	GDP Per Capita ($\times 10^{-4}$)
HUMAN CAPITAL							
Year of Schooling	–0.83***	–0.25*	0.04	–0.26*	–0.09	0.08	0.16!
	(0.07)	(0.10)	(0.05)	(0.12)	(0.06)	(0.08)	(0.09)
College	–0.73***	–0.15	0.01	–0.17!	–0.02	0.16*	0.08
	(0.07)	(0.09)	(0.05)	(0.10)	(0.05)	(0.07)	(0.07)
POLITICAL CAPITAL							
Communist Party	–0.80***	–0.00	–0.02	–0.02	–0.02	0.07	–0.03
	(0.06)	(0.10)	0.06	(0.08)	(0.04)	(0.08)	(0.06)
SECTOR							
State	–0.39***	0.07	0.02	0.48***	0.07	0.10	0.07
	(0.07)	(0.10)	(0.05)	(0.11)	(0.05)	(0.08)	(0.08)
Collective	0.47***	0.09	–0.02	0.45***	–0.10	0.00	–0.15
	(0.07)	(0.10)	(0.05)	(0.11)	(0.06)	0.08	0.08
New Sector	–0.11*	0.00	0.01	0.34**	–0.06	–0.12	0.09***
	(0.08)	(0.11)	(0.05)	(0.12)	(0.06)	(0.08)	(0.09)

DEPENDENT VARIABLES							
OCCUPATION							
Owners & Operators (Private)	–0.07	–0.23**	0.16***	0.08	–0.00	–0.51***	–0.09*
	(0.05)	(0.08)	(0.03)	(0.05)	(0.02)	(0.07)	(0.04)
Professionals	0.33***	0.01	–0.01	–0.10	–0.00	0.01	–0.04
	(0.05)	(0.06)	(0.04)	(0.07)	(0.03)	(0.05)	(0.03)
Cadres and Managers (State)	–0.57***	–0.07	0.02	–0.05	0.04	0.12	–0.05
	(0.08)	(0.11)	(0.06)	(1.01)	(0.05)	(0.09)	(0.08)
Clerical Workers	0.20***	–0.14*	0.05*	0.10	0.02	0.12!	–0.09*
	(0.05)	(0.07)	(0.03)	(0.08)	(0.03)	(0.06)	(0.04)
Skilled and Unskilled Workers	0.17**	0.13*	–0.08*	–0.04	–0.07*	–0.03	0.14*
	(0.05)	(0.06)	(0.03)	(0.08)	(0.03)	(0.04)	(0.06)
INDUSTRY							
Manufacturing	–0.25***	0.12*	–0.10*	–0.01	–0.04	–0.06	–0.01
	(0.05)	(0.07)	(0.04)	(0.11)	(0.06)	(0.06)	(0.08)
Mining, Construction, Transportation	–0.39***	–0.14*	0.01	–0.13*	0.01	0.13**	0.10**
	(0.04)	(0.06)	(0.03)	(0.06)	(0.04)	(0.05)	(0.03)
Commerce, Real Estate, Finance	0.25***	–0.11	0.01	0.18*	–0.06	–0.10	–0.03
	(0.05)	(0.08)	(0.04)	(0.09)	(0.04)	(0.07)	(0.06)
Education, Culture, Research	0.61***	0.14	0.13*	–0.18	0.01!	–0.04	0.14*
	(0.07)	(0.09)	(0.05	(0.09)	(0.05)	(0.07)	(0.07)
Party and Government Agency	0.01	–0.06	0.09	0.01	0.08	0.26*	–0.31**
	(0.08)	(0.11)	(0.06)	(0.11)	(0.05)	(0.11)	(0.10)

*** $P < 0.001$ ** $P < 0.01$ * $P < 0.05$.

Table 5. Continued.

DEPENDENT VARIABLES	Intercept	Age	Age × Marketization	Age × Marketization Squared	Age × GDP	Education	Education × Marketization	Education × Marketization Squared	Education × GDP	CCP	CCP × Marketization	CCP × Marketization^2	CCP × GDP
HUMAN CAPITAL													
Year of Schooling	10.55***	–0.04***	–0.00	–0.00	0.01								
	(0.09)	(0.00)	(0.01)	(0.00)	(0.01)								
College	–1.11***	–0.01*	–0.00	0.00	0.01**								
	(0.07)	(0.00)	(0.01)	(0.00)	(0.00)								
POLITICAL CAPITAL													
Communist Party Member	–1.32***	0.08***	–0.00	0.00	0.00	0.20***	0.02	0.02	–0.01				
	(0.05)	(0.00)	(0.00)	(0.00)	(0.00)	(0.01)	(0.02)	(0.01)	(0.02)				
POLITICAL CAPITAL													
Communist Party Member	–1.32***	0.08***	–0.00	0.00	0.00	0.20***	0.02	0.02	–0.01				
	(0.05)	(0.00)	(0.00)	(0.00)	(0.00)	(0.01)	(0.02)	(0.01)	(0.02)				
SECTOR													
State	1.57***	0.02***	–0.01*	0.00	0.01*	0.19***	0.01	0.01*	–0.04	0.60***	0.22*	–0.03	0.13
	(0.06)	(0.00)	(0.01)	(0.00)	(0.00)	(0.01)	(0.02)	(0.00)	(0.02)	(0.08)	(0.09)	(0.07)	(0.07)
Collective	–1.81***	–0.00	0.01	–0.00	0.00	–0.18***	0.01	–0.01	0.03	–0.52***	–0.21*	0.05	–0.12
	(0.06)	(0.00)	(0.01)	(0.00)	(0.00)	(0.01)	(0.02)	(0.01)	(0.02)	(0.07)	(0.08)	(0.06)	(0.07)
New Sector	–3.08***	–0.04***	0.02*	–0.01*	–0.02**	–0.07**	–0.05	–0.00	0.04	–0.10	–0.18	0.02	–0.09
	(0.09)	(0.01)	(0.01)	(0.00)	(0.01)	(0.02)	(0.03)	(0.02)	(0.03)	(0.14)	(0.20)	(0.11)	(0.16)

DEPENDENT VARIABLES													
OCCUPATION													
Owners & Operators	−3.84***	0.01***	0.02***	−0.01***	−0.02***	−0.13***	−0.04**	0.01!	0.00	0.47***	−0.48***	0.11**	−0.06
(Private)	(0.04)	(0.00)	(0.00)	(0.00)	(0.00)	(0.01)	(0.01)	(0.01)	(0.01)	(0.07)	(0.09)	(0.04)	(0.08)
Professionals	−1.45***	0.04***	0.01*	0.00	−0.00	0.35***	0.01	0.01!	0.01	−0.47***	0.17	−0.19***	0.14*
	(0.05)	(0.00)	(0.00)	(0.00)	(0.01)	(0.01)	(0.02)	(0.01)	(0.01)	(0.07)	(0.09)	(0.04)	(0.05)
Cadres and Managers	−2.55***	0.04***	0.00	−0.00	0.00	0.10***	−0.03	0.01	−0.01	1.95***	0.12	0.03	0.00
(State)	(0.07)	(0.00)	(0.01)	(0.00)	(0.01)	(0.01)	(0.02)	(0.01)	(0.02)	(0.10)	(0.13)	(0.07)	(0.11)
Clerical Workers	−1.34***	−0.02***	0.00	0.00	0.00	0.03***	0.02	0.01	−0.01	0.28**	−0.10!	0.06	−0.15*
	(0.05)	(0.00)	(0.00)	(0.00)	(0.00)	(0.01)	(0.01)	(0.01)	(0.01)	(0.08)	(0.11)	(0.05)	(0.07)
Skilled and Unskilled	−0.47***	−0.05***	−0.00	−0.00	0.01	−0.38***	0.03	−0.02**	0.02!	−1.27***	−0.10	−0.07	0.10*
Workers	(0.06)	(0.00)	(0.00)	(0.00)	(0.00)	(0.01)	(0.02)	(0.01)	(0.01)	(0.06)	(0.08)	(0.05)	(0.04)
INDUSTRY													
Manufacturing	−0.37***	−0.00	−0.00	0.00	0.00	−0.12***	0.02	−0.01	−0.01	−0.34***	−0.03	−0.03	0.03
	(0.08)	(0.00)	(0.00)	(0.00)	(0.00)	(0.01)	(0.02)	(0.01)	(0.01)	(0.06)	(0.08)	(0.05)	(0.07)
Mining, Construction,	−2.34***	0.00	0.00	−0.00	−0.00*	−0.07***	−0.02	0.01	−0.01	−0.13!	0.11	−0.09*	0.07
Transportation	(0.05)	(0.00)	(0.00)	(0.00)	(0.00)	(0.01)	(0.11)	(0.01)	(0.01)	(0.07)	(0.08)	(0.04)	(0.07)
Commerce, Real Estate,	−1.42***	−0.02***	0.00	−0.00	−0.01*	−0.07***	−0.02	−0.00	0.02	−0.20*	−0.15	0.03	−0.06
Finance	(0.06)	(0.00)	(0.00)	(0.00)	(0.00)	(0.01)	(0.02)	(0.01)	(0.02)	(0.08)	(0.11)	(0.06)	(0.10)
Education, Culture,	−2.03***	0.04***	0.00	0.00	0.00	0.26***	0.03	0.00	−0.03!	−0.27**	−0.05	−0.16*	0.24**
Research	(0.07)	(0.00)	(0.01)	(0.00)	(0.00)	(0.02)	(0.02)	(0.01)	(0.02)	(0.09)	(0.11)	(0.08)	(0.09)
Party and Government	−2.26***	−0.00	−0.00	0.00	0.01	0.15***	0.02	0.02	0.00	1.19***	0.28*	0.04	−0.12
Agency	(0.08)	(0.00)	(0.01)	(0.00)	(0.01)	(0.01)	(0.02)	(0.01)	(0.02)	(0.09)	(0.12)	(0.07)	(0.12)

*** $P < 0.001$ ** $P < 0.01$ * $P < 0.05$.

to be a professional, less likely to be a cadre or a manager of a state organization, more likely to be a clerical worker and a worker; less likely to be in manufacturing industry and mining, construction, transportation industries; and more likely to be in education, culture, research, technical service, and public health.

Most of these gender gaps remain constant across cities of differing degrees of marketization. Few gender gaps covary with marketization. Gender gap in years of education is negatively associated with marketization; the more marketized the city, the larger the gender gap in years of schooling. Gender gap in clerical occupations placement is negatively associated with marketization, while gender gap in mining, construction, and transportation increases with marketization. A curvilinear association is found between marketization and gender gap in three occupational placements: With an increase in marketization, gender gap in placement in owners and managers of private businesses emerges (for cities with a marketization score of 0), with women being less likely to be in this occupation. This gender gap peaks in cities with a marketization score of 0.72 and starts to decrease. There is also a U-shaped association between gender gap in placement in clerical occupations and marketization and a concave association between gender gap in placement in worker occupations and marketization. A curvilinear association is found between marketization and gender gap in being employed in the manufacturing industry. Least marketized cities have the largest gender gap in employment in the manufacturing industry. This gender gap keeps shrinking and disappears in more marketized cities but reemerges in the most marketized cities.

Effects of human and political capital variables on labor-market placements and on wage attainments are highly consistent with the analyses of CHIP data by other researchers (Xie & Hannum, 1996; Hauser & Xie, 2001; Bian & Zhang, in this volume). These effects, self-evident in Table 5 and other tables, are not in our analytic interest here and are thus given no further attention.

Table 6 shows the results from a nonlinear hierarchical model estimating the effects of gender and marketization on earnings after controlling for age, education, political status, labor force placement, and GDP per capita of the city. Compared with a man of the same age, education, political status, placement in the labor force, and living in the same city, a woman makes 9.0% less in annual earnings. There is no intercity variation on this gender disparity. Marketization has not interrupted the existing gender gap in earnings, despite the increase in overall earnings with marketization. The advantage enjoyed by state sector declined with marketization, and the return to owners and operators of private businesses rose exponentially with marketization.

Table 6. HLM Estimates of Macro-, Micro-, and Interactive Effects on Log Earnings (1995 CHIP, $N = 10,967$).

	Main Effect	Marketization	Marketization Squared	GDP
Intercept	8.57***	0.11	0.06	0.04
	(0.03)	(0.04)	(0.02)	(0.03)
Gender	–0.09***	0.04	–0.01	0.01
	(0.01)	(0.02)	(0.01)	(0.02)
Age	0.02***	–0.00	–0.00	0.00
	(0.09)	(0.00)	(0.00)	(0.00)
Education	0.01**	0.00	0.00	–0.00
	(0.00)	(0.00)	(0.00)	(0.00)
CCP Membership	0.09***	0.02	–0.00	0.02
	(0.02)	(0.02)	(0.00)	(0.02)
SECTOR				
State	0.24***	–0.06*	0.02	
	(0.02)	(0.03)	(0.02)	
Collective	–[a]	–	–	
New Sector	0.11	0.14	–0.07	
	(0.08)	(0.10)	(0.05)	
OCCUPATION				
Owners & Operators (Private)	0.03	–0.17	0.12*	
	(0.08)	(0.11)	(0.05)	
Professionals	0.19***	0.03	–0.01	
	(0.02)	(0.03)	(0.02)	
Cadres and Managers (State)	0.19***	0.04	0.02	
	(0.02)	(0.03)	(0.02)	
Clerical Workers	0.00***	0.04	–0.00	
	(0.00)	(0.03)	(0.02)	
Skilled and Unskilled Workers	–	–	–	
INDUSTRY				
Manufacturing	–0.06*			
	(0.03)			
Mining, Construction, Transportation	0.01			
	(0.04)			
Commerce, Real Estate, Finance	–0.07***			
	(0.03)			
Education, Culture, Research	0.02			
	(0.03)			
Party and Government Agency				

*** $P < 0.001$ ** $P < 0.01$ * $P < 0.05$.

[a] Omitted category.

SUMMARY AND DISCUSSION

Our analysis shows that by 1995 Chinese men and women in the cities differ in level of human and political capitals, labor market placements, and work earnings. Compared with a man of the same individual characteristics living in the same city, a woman has fewer years of education and is less likely to have a college education, be a Communist party member, be in the state sector, be a cadre or manager in a state enterprise, and be in manufacturing, mining, construction, and transportation. They are more likely than men are to be a clerical worker or a worker and to be in education, culture, research, technical service, and public health.

This pattern of gender gap in human and political capital and gender segregation in labor force is by and large consistent with prior studies on gender gap in education (Lavely et al., 1990), in political capital (Bian, Shu & Logan, 2001; Lin & Bian, 1991; Zhou, Tuma & Moen, 1996), and in labor force placement (Bian, 1994; Bian & Logan, 1996; Lin & Bian, 1991; Whyte, 1984; Zhou, Tuma & Moen, 1996, 1997). As in the pre-reform era (Whyte, 1984), in 1995 a woman's annual earnings were approximately 14% to19% less than a male counterpart, and this gap shrinks to 9% after controlling for human and political capitals, labor market placement, and city-level variation in development and marketization. A 1993 sample from Tianjin indicates that in 1978, the wage ratio between women and men was 86.8%, and this percentage remained almost unchanged through 1993 (Bian & Logan, 1996, Table 3). A 20-city sample from 1994 shows that women's wages were 81% to 86% of men's wages between 1978 and 1993 (Zhou, 2000), and a comparison of the 1988 and 1995 CHIP data demonstrates that women made 83.9% and 83.8% of men's earnings in 1988 and 1995, respectively (Shu & Bian, 2001).

Most of these gender inequalities remain constant across cities of differing degrees of marketization. We analyzed the intercity variation in gender disparity in human and political capital, labor force placement, and work earnings both by comparing four groups of cities grouped into different levels of marketization and using a series of hierarchical models to estimate the interactive effects between gender and an continuous index of marketization. In all these estimates, we found little evidence for a linear covariation between gender disparity and marketization. Other studies based on the 1988 and 1995 CHIP data did not find a systematic intercity variation in gender disparity in earnings with economic growth (Hauser & Xie, 2001) or with the growth of the ratio of nonstate workers, foreign investment, and manufacturing industry (Bian & Zhang, 2002). These findings support the assertion that within the realm of gender relationship there are relatively separate and autonomous components from the economic domain not readily penetrable by economic forces. The gender relationships appear to operate according to its internal logic not immediately subject to the influences of the growth of the markets.

To the extent that market transition influences gender inequality, the relationship is a nonmonotonic one. In particular, the association between marketization and gender gap in labor force placements is curvilinear; there is a concave association between marketization and gender gap in being owners and managers of private businesses and gender gap in being workers; and there is a U-shaped association between marketization and gender gap in placement in clerical occupations and gender gap in the manufacturing industry.

These changes point to the nonlinear process of marketization where important fundamental changes took place in the most marketized cities. These nonlinear changes reveal the increasing significance of the occupational and industrial placement and the declining importance of sector affiliation in accounting for gender gap in earnings in the most marketized cities. One of the major sources of gender inequalities in pre-reform China and in the less marketized cities remains the segregation of female workers in the collective sector, which provides substantially lower earnings and fringe benefits (Whyte, 1984). However, this ownership-based economic segmentation is less marked in the most marketized cities as evidenced by the much narrower pay disparity between the state sector and the collective sector in these cities. On the other hand, occupation- and industry-based pay differentials have been on the rise in these highly marketized cities. These new patterns of occupational and industrial placement in the most marketized cities indicate that the sources of gender inequalities in the labor force is starting to shift from the sector affiliation to occupational and industrial placement.

Our analyses point to new directions for future research about gender inequalities in China's transitional economy. Necessarily, one must assess and measure the development of product, labor, and capital markets in any locality and time in which data about gender inequalities are collected. In localities where these markets grow slowly and gradually, research should focus on how gender inequalities between the state and nonstate sectors have continued despite the introduction of market forces. In more and increasingly marketized localities, the research tasks should include analyses of how market forces, especially labor markets, maintain gender disparity in the labor force by moving women workers from the disadvantaged collective sector to low-paying jobs. The underlying process for this mobility must be studied to see how it may have sustained the gender gap in labor market opportunities and outcomes. Careful empirical research into both economic and sociological logics of gender relationships in work, domestic spheres, and belief system is needed.

NOTES

1. Among China's 190,930 million urban employees in 1995, 4.6% (2.4% were men and 2.2% were women) worked in nonstate and non-collective firms except private business (*siyin*) and individual entrepreneurs (*geiti*), and 10.7% (sex composition unknown) were individual entrepreneurs or employees in private businesses.

2. Multiple data sources were used to compile the city-level database: Urban Socioeconomic Research Team of Chinese State Statistical Bureau, 1993. *Chinese Urban Statistical Yearbook;* Chinese Statistical Publishing House, Urban Socioeconomic Research Team of Chinese State Statistical Bureau, 1994. *Chinese Urban Statistical Yearbook;* Chinese Statistical Publishing House, Urban Socioeconomic Research Team of Chinese State Statistical Bureau, 1996. *Chinese Urban Statistical Yearbook*; Chinese Statistical Publishing House, Consortium on Chinese Urban Development and Chinese Association of Administration Science, 1996. *Statistical Yearbook of Chinese Cities;* Chinese City Statistical Yearbook Press. *Statistical Yearbook of Beijing 1996; Statistical Yearbook of Liaoning 1996; Statistical Yearbook of Jiansu 1996; Statistical Yearbook of Anhui 1996; Statistical Yearbook of Heinan 1996; Statistical Yearbook of Hubei 1996; Statistical Yearbook of Sichuan 1996; Statistical Yearbook of Yunnan 1996; Statistical Yearbook of Gansu 1996;* Statistical Bureau of Datong, 1995. *Statistical Abstract of Datong*; Statistical Bureau of Changzhi, 1996, *Statistical Yearbook of Changzhi*; Statistical Bureau of Guangzhou, 1996, *Statistical Yearbook of Guangzhou*; Foshan Statistical Yearbook Committee, 1996, *Statistical Yearbook of Foshan*; Guangdong People's Publishing House, Zhangjian Statistical Bureau, *Statistical Yearbook of Zhanjian, 1990–1995*; *Shenzhen Statistical Yearbook 1996*; Chinese Statistical Publishing House, Huizhou Statistical Bureau, 1996, *Huizhou Statistical Yearbook*; Chinese Statistical Publishing House, Zhaoqing Statistical Bureau, 1996, *Zhaoqing Statistical Yearbook*; Shantou Economic Special Zone Yearbook Committee, 1996, *Shantou Economic Special Zone Yearbook.*

3. Skinner and colleagues (2000) identified eight urban hierarchical levels using detailed socioeconomic data from a 1% household sample from China's 1990 population census. The 1995 CHIP sample, excluding the county headquarters, contains cities at the top five levels in the Central-Place Hierarchy.

4. The average earnings in the most marketized cities are 1.49- to 2.24-fold those in less marketized cities. The largest increase took place in the collective sector, making the earning ratio between the collective and the state sector rise from 62% and 74% to 84%.

ACKNOWLEDGMENTS

This is a revised version of a paper presented at the Research Committee 28 of the International Sociological Association 2001 annual conference, August 2001, Berkeley, CA. We thank Bill Skinner for generously providing his data on Central-Place Hierarchy and summary statistics from the 1% Chinese 1990 population census, Zhang Zhanxin for his assistance in compiling city-level data, and Jennifer Gregson for her assistance in data analysis. We also thank editor Kevin Leicht for his helpful comments. Partial support for Xiaoling Shu came from a Faculty Research Grant and an IGA Junior Faculty Research Grant, University of California Davis. Yanjie Bian acknowledges two grants from Hong Kong's Research Grants Committee (HKUST6052/98H, HKUST6007/00H) and a post-doctoral matching grant from the Vice-President Office of the Hong Kong University of Science and Technology, which partially supported the collection and analysis of the data reported in this paper. Direct all correspondence to Xiaoling Shu, Department of Sociology, University of California, Davis, One Shields Avenue, Davis, CA 95616 or send e-mail to xshu@ucdavis.edu.

REFERENCES

Bian, Y. (1994). *Work and inequality in urban China*. Albany: State University of New York Press.

Bian, Y. (2002). Chinese Social Stratification and Social Mobility. *Annual Review of Sociology, 28*, 91–116.

Bian, Y., & Li, Y. (2000). Social Network Capital of Urban Chinese Families. *Hsinghua Sociological Review, 2*, 1–14.

Bian, Y., & Logan, J. R. (1996). Market Transition and the Persistence of Power: The Changing Stratification System in Urban China. *American Sociological Review, 61*, 739–758.

Bian, Y., Logan, J. R., & Shu, X. (2000). Wage and Job Inequalities in the Working Lives of Men and Women in Tianjin. In: B. Entwisle & G. E. Henderson (Eds), *Re-Drawing Boundaries: Work, Households, and Gender in China* (pp. 111–133). Berkeley: University of California Press.

Bian, Y., Shu, X., & Logan, J. R. (2001). Communist Party Membership and Regime Dynamics in China. *Social Forces, 79*, 805–841.

Bian, Y., & Zhang, Z. (2002). Marketization, Segmentation, and Income in Urban China: 1988 and 1995. *Research in Social Stratification and Mobility* (this volume).

China State Statistical Bureau (1998). *China Statistical Yearbook*. Beijing: China Statistical Publishing House.

Davis, D. (1995). Inequality and Stratification in the Nineties. *China Review, 11*, 1–5.

Davis, D. S. (2000). Social Class Transformation in Urban China: Training, Hiring, and Promoting Urban Professionals and Managers after 1949. *Modern China, 26*, 251–275.

Entwisle, B., Henderson, G. E., Short, S. E., Bouma, J., & Fengying, Z. (1995). Gender and Family Businesses in Rural China. *American Sociological Review, 26*, 251–275.

Goldstein, H. I. (1986). *Multilevel Models in Education and Social Research*. London: Oxford University Press.

Hauser, S., & Xie, Y. (2001). Temporal and Regional Variation in Earnings Inequality: Urban China in Transition between 1988 and 1995. Paper presented at the International Sociological Association RC28 Conference, Berkeley, CA.

Hershatter, G. (2000). Local Meanings of Gender and Work in Rural Shaanxi in the 1950s. In: B. Entwisle and G. E. Henderson (Eds), *Redrawing Boundaries: Work, Households, and Gender in China* (pp. 79–96). Berkeley: University of California Press.

Honig, E., & Hershatter, G. (1988). *Personal Voices: Chinese Women in the 1980s*. Stanford, CA: Stanford University Press.

Honig, E. (2000). Iron Girls Revisited: Gender and the Politics of Work in the Cultural Revolution: 1966–76. In: B. Entwisle and G. E. Henderson (Eds), *Redrawing Boundaries: Work, Households, and Gender in China* (pp. 97–110). Berkeley: University of California Press.

Jöreskog, K. G., & Sörbom, D. (1988). *LISREL VII: A Guide to the Program and Applications* (2nd ed.). Chicago: SPSS, Inc.

Jöreskog, K. G., & Sörbom, D. (1993). *LISREL VIII: Structural Equation Modeling with the SIMPLIS Command Language*. Chicago: Scientific Software International, Inc.

Lavely, W., Zhenyu, X., Bohua, L., & Freeman, R. (1990). The Rise in Female Education in China: National and Regional Patterns. *China Quarterly, 121*, 61–93.

Lee, C. K. (1995). Engendering the Worlds of Labor: Women Workers, Labor Markets, and Production Politics in the South China Economic Miracle. *American Sociological Review, 60*, 378–397.

Li, B., & Walder, A. G. (2001). Career Advancement as Party Patronage. Sponsored Mobility into the Chinese Administrative Elite, 1949–1996. *American Journal of Sociology, 106*(5), 1374–1408.

Lin, N., & Bian, Y. (1991). Getting Ahead in Urban China. *American Journal of Sociology, 97*, 657–688.

Marini, M. M. (1989). Sex Differences in Earnings in the United States. *Annual Review of Sociology, 15*, 343–380.

Matthews, R., & Nee, V. (2000). Gender Inequality and Economic Growth in Rural China. *Social Science Research, 29*, 606–632.

Michelson, E., & Parish, W. L. (2000). Gender Differentials in Economic Success: Rural China in 1991. In: B. Entwisle & G. E. Henderson (Eds), *Re-Drawing Boundaries: Work, Households, and Gender in China* (pp. 134–156). Berkeley: University of California Press.

Nee, V. (1996). The Emergence of a Market Society: Changing Mechanisms of Stratification in China. *American Journal of Sociology, 101*, 908–949.

Nee, V., & Matthews, R. (1996). Market Transition and Societal Transformation in Reforming State Socialism. *Annual Review of Sociology, 22*, 401–435.

Parish, W. L., & Michelson, E. (1996). Politics and Markets: Dual Transformations. *American Journal of Sociology, 101*, 1042–1059.

Ran, M. (1988). Women's Employment Challenge. *Beijing Review* (July), 29–30.

Raudenbush, S. W., Bryk, A., Cheong, Y. F., & Congdon, R. (2000). *HLM 5: Hierarchical Linear and Nonlinear Modeling*. Lincolnwood, IL: Scientific Software International, Inc.

Robinson, J. (1985). Of Women and Washing Machines: Employment, Housework, and the Reproduction of Motherhood in Socialist China. *China Quarterly, 101*, 32–57.

Rona-Tas, A. (1994). The First Shall Be Last? Entrepreneurship and Communist Cadres in the Transition from Socialism. *American Journal of Sociology, 100*, 40–69.

Shirk, S. (1993). *The Political Logic of Economic Reform in China*. Berkeley and Los Angeles: University of California Press.

Shu, X., & Bian, Y. (2001). Marketization and Gender Gap in Earnings in Urban China. Paper presented at the American Sociological Association annual meeting, Anaheim, CA.

Skinner, G., Henderson, W. M., & Jianhua, Y. (2000). China's Fertility Transition through Regional Space. *Social Science History, 24*, 613–652.

Stark, D. (1996). Recombinant Property in East European Capitalism. *American Journal of Sociology, 101*, 993–1027.

Walder, A. G. (1986). *Communist Neo-traditionalism. Work and Authority in Chinese Industry.* Berkeley: University of California Press.

Walder, A. G. (1992). Property Rights and Stratification in Socialist Redistributive Economies. *American Sociological Review, 57*, 524–539.

Walder, A. G. (1995). Career Mobility and the Communist Political Order. *American Sociological Review, 60*, 309–328.

Walder, A. G., Li, B., & Treiman, D. (2000). Politics and Life Chances in a State Socialist Regime: Dual Career Paths into the Urban Chinese Elite, 1949 to 1996. *American Sociological Review, 65*, 191–209.

Whyte, K. M. (1984). Sexual Inequality under Socialism: The Chinese Case in Perspective. In: J. L. Watson (Ed.), *Class and Social Stratification in Post-Revolution China*. New York: Cambridge University Press.

Whyte, K. M. (2000). The Perils of Assessing Trends in Gender Inequality in China. Pp. 157–67 In: B. Entwisle & G. E. Henderson (Eds), *Re-Drawing Boundaries: Work, Households, and Gender in China*. Berkeley: University of California Press.

Wu, N. (1995). Employment and Chinese Women. *Beijing Review* (March), 6–12.

Xie, Y., & Hannum, E. (1996). Regional Variation in Earnings Inequality in Reform-Era Urban China. *American Journal of Sociology, 101*, 950–992.

Zhou, X. (2000). Economic Transformation and Income Inequality in Urban China: Evidence from Panel Data. *American Journal of Sociology, 105*, 1135–1174.

Zhou, X., Tuma, N. B., & Moen, P. (1996). Stratification Dynamics under State Socialism: The Case of Urban China: 1949–1993. *Social Forces, 74*, 759–796.

Zhou, X., Tuma, N. B., & Moen, P. (1997). Institutional Change and Job-Shift Patterns in Urban China: 1949 to 1994. *American Sociological Review, 62*, 339–365.

APPENDIX

Table A. Complete OLS and Logistic Regression Estimates for Table 4: the Effects of Labor Cohort on Human Capital, Political Capital, Placement in the Labor Force, and Earnings (1995 CHIP, $N = 10{,}967$).

	Intercept	1949–51	1952–54	1955–57	1958–60	1961–63	1964–66	1967–69	1970–72	1973–75	1976–78	1979–81	1982–84	After 1985
HUMAN CAPITAL														
Year of Education	7.91***	1.73***	2.24***	2.68***	2.59***	2.91***	3.39***	3.77***	3.98***	3.95***	4.53***	4.60***	4.91***	5.84***
	(0.17)	(0.22)	(0.20)	(0.19)	(0.18)	(0.18)	(0.18)	(0.18)	(0.18)	(0.19)	(0.19)	(0.19)	(0.20)	(0.19)
Some College	-3.88***	2.67***	2.95***	3.07***	2.82***	2.99***	3.27***	3.34***	3.40***	3.53***	4.10***	3.96***	4.02***	4.57***
	(0.51)	(0.53)	(0.52)	(0.51)	(0.51)	(0.51)	(0.51)	(0.51)	(0.51)	(0.51)	(0.51)	(0.51)	(0.51)	(0.52)
POLITICAL CAPITAL														
Communist Party	–0.01	0.10	–0.14	–0.25	–0.38**	–0.29*	–0.39**	–0.44**	–0.94***	-1.06***	-1.16***	-1.74***	-1.98***	-2.87
	(0.13)	(0.17)	(0.16)	(0.15)	(0.14)	(0.14)	(0.14)	(0.14)	(0.15)	(0.16)	(0.16)	(0.18)	(0.20)	(0.26)***
SECTOR														
State	2.21***	0.03	0.09	–0.06	0.13	0.07	0.23	0.14	–0.18	0.13	0.20	0.21	0.09	–0.06
	(0.17)	(0.22)	(0.20)	(0.19)	(0.18)	(0.18)	(0.18)	(0.18)	(0.18)	(0.19)	(0.19)	(0.20)	(0.20)	(0.19)
Collective	2.44***	0.10	0.00	0.10	–0.07	–0.04	–0.13	–0.07	0.16	–0.22	–0.35	–0.34	–0.49*	–0.51*
	(0.19)	(0.23)	(0.22)	(0.20)	(0.19)	(0.19)	(0.19)	(0.19)	(0.19)	(0.20)	(0.21)	(0.22)	(0.22)	(0.22)
New	-3.40***	–0.48	–0.57	–0.43	–0.61	–0.48	–0.74*	–0.65	–0.15	–0.03	0.01	–0.16	0.45	0.79*
	(0.30)	(0.42)	(0.38)	(0.34)	(0.33)	(0.32)	(0.34)	(0.33)	(0.32)	(0.32)	(0.33)	(0.34)	(0.32)	(0.31)
OCCUPATION														
Owners & Operators	–4.17***	0.01	–0.54	–0.15	–0.51	–0.40	–0.30	–0.80	–0.45	–0.07	–0.27	-1.82***	-1.06	–0.83
(Private)	(0.46)	(0.56)	(0.58)	(0.50)	(0.50)	(0.48)	(0.48)	(0.52)	(0.51)	(0.49)	(0.52)	(0.82)	(0.65)	(0.61)
Professionals	-1.84***	0.79***	0.92***	0.89***	0.63**	0.62**	0.69***	0.68***	0.46*	0.52**	0.93***	0.78***	0.70**	0.63**
	(0.18)	(0.22)	(0.20)	(0.20)	(0.19)	(0.19)	(0.19)	(0.19)	(0.20)	(0.20)	(0.20)	(0.20)	(0.20)	(0.21)
Cadres and Managers	–0.93***	–0.06	–0.36*	-2.82***	–0.45***	–0.35*	–0.37*	–0.40*	–0.82***	–0.85***	-1.37***	-1.77***	-2.22***	-3.02***
(State)	(0.15)	(0.20)	(0.19)	(0.18)	(0.17)	(0.17)	(0.17)	(0.17)	(0.19)	(0.19)	(0.22)	(0.25)	(0.31)	(0.43)
Clerical Workers	-1.65***	–0.26	–0.17	–0.34	–0.25	–0.25	–0.14	–0.01	0.07	0.07	0.29	0.17	0.22	0.29
	(0.16)	(0.22)	(0.19)	(0.18)	(0.17)	(0.17)	(0.17)	(0.17)	(0.17)	(0.18)	(0.17)	(0.18)	(0.18)	(0.18)
Skilled and Unskilled	–0.33*	–0.31	–0.23	–0.15	0.11	0.07	–0.05	–0.08	0.17	0.12	–0.20	0.15	0.21	0.23
Workers	(0.13)	(0.17)	(0.15)	(0.14)	(0.14)	(0.13)	(0.14)	(0.14)	(0.14)	(0.14)	(0.14)	(0.15)	(0.15)	(0.15)

	Intercept	1949–51	1952–54	1955–57	1958–60	1961–63	1964–66	1967–69	1970–72	1973–75	1976–78	1979–81	1982–84	After 1985
INDUSTRY	–0.57***	0.16	0.31*	0.34*	0.53***	0.53***	0.27	0.28	0.26	0.29	0.10	0.11	0.27	–0.06
	(0.13)	(0.17)	(0.15)	(0.15)	(0.14)	(0.14)	(0.14)	(0.14)	(0.14)	(0.14)	(0.15)	(0.15)	(0.15)	(0.15)
Manufacturing	–2.25***	–0.04	–0.09	–0.05	–0.08	0.11	–0.04	–0.09	0.02	–0.14	–0.35	–0.10	–0.38	–0.31
	(0.21)	(0.27)	(0.25)	(0.24)	(0.22)	(0.22)	(0.22)	(0.23)	(0.23)	(0.24)	(0.25)	(0.25)	(0.26)	(0.26)
Mining, Construction, Transportation	–1.71	–0.53	–0.22	–0.32	–0.23	–0.27	–0.08	–0.05	0.02	0.12	–0.08	–0.08	0.10	0.48
	(0.16)	(0.23)	(0.20)	(0.18)	(0.17)	(0.17)	(0.17)	(0.17)	(0.17)	(0.17)	(0.18)	(0.18)	(0.18)	(0.18)
Commerce, Real Estate, Finance	–2.28***	0.78**	0.96***	0.73**	0.51	0.36	0.59*	0.35	0.29	0.13	0.54*	0.50*	0.60*	0.44
	(0.22)	(0.26)	(0.24)	(0.24)	(0.23)	(0.23)	(0.23)	(0.23)	(0.24)	(0.25)	(0.24)	(0.24)	(0.25)	(0.25)
Education, Culture, Research	–1.66***	–0.14	–0.79**	–0.55**	–0.83***	–0.73***	–0.47*	–0.22	–0.33	–0.22	0.15	–0.04	–0.68**	–0.86***
	(0.17)	(0.23)	(0.24)	(0.21)	(0.20)	(0.19)	(0.19)	(0.19)	(0.20)	(0.20)	(0.19)	(0.20)	(0.23)	(0.24)
LOG EARNINGS	866.41***	8.63	10.82*	14.82**	12.38**	13.00**	12.78**	9.74*	–0.08	–4.70	–10.68*	–24.94***	–27.39***	–44.82***
	(4.07)	(5.24)	(4.81)	(4.55)	(4.34)	(4.29)	(4.34)	(4.36)	(4.42)	(4.49)	(4.55)	(4.66)	(4.72)	(4.73)

The omitted labor cohort is "Before 1949".
*** $P < 0.001$ ** $P < 0.01$ * $P < 0.05$.

PART IV: THEORETICAL AND EMPIRICAL EXPLICATIONS OF MARKET TRANSITION THEORY

FROM CADRE MANAGERS TO PRIVATE ENTREPRENEURS: ENTRY INTO FAMILY BUSINESS IN RURAL CHINA

Litao Zhao

ABSTRACT

How political advantages change in transitional economies remains an unsolved issue. There still needs clearer theoretical formulations linking institutional changes to the reshuffling social structure. I shift the analytic focus from market expansion to property rights, and establish a causal relationship between local government enterprises and cadre advantages. The rapid growth of local public ownership in rural China in the 1980s not only sustains cadre power, but also generates managerial experience for cadres and managers. This type of human capital is highly valuable in an economy where expertise is traditionally concentrated in the urban sector. When cadres apply it to their own businesses, it becomes a new source of advantage. I test this conversion-of-cadre-experience thesis, using nationally representative data collected in China in 1996. Findings confirm this conversion process and show interesting contrasts: Managerial experience acquired through cadreship facilitates entry into businesses with employees, whereas education only facilitates entry into businesses without employees; Cadres with managerial experience

The Future of Market Transition, Volume 19, pages 313–337.

ISBN: 0-7623-0835-4

begin to explore private businesses, whereas other cadres are more likely to be found still in the public sector.

INTRODUCTION

Transition from state socialism provides social scientists rare opportunities to observe grand social changes, from the rise of markets and the growth of private property, to the collapse of the party-state system and the creation of democratic institutions. Recent sociological research on stratification focuses on the institutional change in resource allocation mechanisms, asking whether a shift from plan to market leads to a shift of power and economic advantage from cadres to private entrepreneurs. The erosion-of-cadre-power thesis predicts the decline of political capital and the erosion of cadre income advantages (Nee, 1989). The persistence-of-cadre-power thesis emphasizes the benefits conferred by the public sector and the persistence of cadre advantages (Bian & Logan, 1996; Xie & Hannum, 1996). The conversion-of-cadre-power thesis predicts a transformation of political advantage into new entrepreneurial opportunities (Rona-Tas, 1994).

These different arguments arise in part because they capture different phases and conditions of market transition (Rona-Tas, 1994). In China the erosion-of-cadre-power thesis captures the very beginning of market transition when the commune system has disbanded but collective enterprises have yet to develop (Walder, 2002). The persistence-of-cadre-power thesis describes the urban sector in which market reforms lag behind the rural sector. Potentially it also pertains to rural areas where local government enterprises have prospered. The conversion-of-cadre-power thesis seems to suit Eastern Europe and Russia, where the political system has experienced a fundamental change, and former elites have to lose if they cannot find new lucrative opportunities. Transformation of state socialism is less encompassing in China. Political changes and privatization have never seriously threatened cadre privilege. Cadres therefore feel less pressure to convert their *political power* into *private entrepreneurship*. However, another conversion process may have occurred in which cadres convert their *managerial experience* into private *entrepreneurship*. Rural cadres have long been involved in collective production under state socialism. After the abandonment of the commune system, they have actively participated in building and managing local enterprises. This type of managerial experience is highly valuable in an economy where expertise is traditionally concentrated in the urban sector. When cadres subsequently apply it to their own private businesses, they convert it into new economic advantages. While the persistence-of-cadre-power thesis may still hold – the public sector continues to be the primary source of cadre advantages – there is a growing trend of cadre household entry into private businesses.

UNDERSTANDING MARKET TRANSITION

Market Transition and Institutional Change in Resource Allocation

The redistributive economy of state socialism is widely believed to be the foundation of cadre advantage (Djilas, 1957; Manchin & Szelenyi, 1987).[1] This belief inspires sociologists to look for changes in the stratification system generated by the transition from a planned economy to a market economy. Market transition theory is the first systematic account of the impact of this institutional change (Nee, 1989, 1991). It views the control of resources as the basis of power and advantage. Because market transition promotes the flow of resources from the redistributive system to the market, power is thought to shift from cadres to private entrepreneurs. In the emerging market economy, the value of political capital (cadre position or party membership) declines while that of human capital (education and experience) increases.

Analyses of data collected in 1985 in Fujian, a coastal province in South-East China, lend support to the market transition theory. Village cadres, whether former or current, have no advantage over others in terms of household income. Cadre position, in fact, has a negative effect when entrepreneurs are included in the model. In contrast, entrepreneurs have clear advantages over other groups, although surprisingly it is cadre entrepreneurs, not private entrepreneurs, who have the largest advantage (Nee, 1989, p. 672). The idea of market expansion of markets as a self-reinforcing process and the finding that cadre advantage disappeared quickly in the very early period of market transition invite bold speculations that social inequality rooted in the redistributive economy will soon be reversed (or at least compensated for) by market expansion. However, this may be a premature conclusion. The erosion-of-cadre-power thesis may have captured the very early transition when the commune system is disbanded, and local government enterprises have yet to expand (Walder, 2002). Moreover, private business has a high political risk at that time, which deters cadres from becoming the first private entrepreneurs.

Surprisingly, local cadres adapt to market transition by creating township-and-village enterprises, which become a new source of cadre advantage. Market transition theory soon acknowledges the "persistence" of cadre privilege, but it does not relate it to the legitimate growth of local public ownership. Instead, it sees the lingering cadre advantage as a result of imperfect transition (Nee, 1991). Under partial reform, cadres still control valuable resources. More importantly, they are able to monetize their control of resources through rent-seeking activities. When the market is bounded by political institutions, access to resources depends more on formal positional power and informal personal connections than on rational market principles. As a result, cadre entrepreneurs, who occupy strategic positions in connecting the state sector to the private economy, yield a clear advantage over private entrepreneurs (Nee & Lian, 1994).

Subsequent analyses of national survey data collected in 1989–1990 reveal large net cadre advantages (Nee, 1996). However, this is not seen as a counter evidence to market transition theory. According to Nee, market transition theory only implies "more upward mobility of poor peasants than downward mobility of the rich" (1991, p. 274), or that "*the earnings of many economic actors in society increase at a faster rate than that of political actors*" (1996, p. 916). Because longitudinal data are not available, Nee uses cross-sectional data to test the proposition that political capital is declining with market transition. Two variables are used to gauge the development of market institutions. The variable "production market," measured by the number of private and collective enterprises in the township, gauges "marketization at the local level." The second variable "labor market" – the proportion of village population taking non-farm work outside the village – serves as a measure of the extent of local labor market. The interaction terms of cadre and these contextual variables are believed to measure the effect of market transition on political capital. Nee (1996, p. 930) reports a negative effect of "cadre × production market" on household income, and sees it as an evidence that "the thicker the market environment, the lower the income return for local cadres."

However, the erosion-of-cadre-power thesis is challenged by the persistence-of-cadre-power thesis, which claims that, so far, markets are not a threat to cadre advantages. Bian and Logan (1996) use urban data collected in Tianjin in 1988 and 1993, and analyze income change between 1978 and 1988. Consistent with the prediction of market transition theory, they find a decline in the income gap, but this decreased inequality is accounted for by an egalitarian wage policy that gives salary increases to workers at the low end of pay scale. Therefore the decreased income gap is not due to market transition. What happens in the name of market transition actually serves the purposes of redistribution (Walder, 1990). Moreover, income of Communist Party members and those with high redistributive power increases faster than others. Bian and Logan interpret these results as evidence of the "persistence of power" (p. 755). Xie and Hannum (1996) analyze the impact of economic growth on returns to human capital and political capital in the urban sector. Using data from the 1988 Chinese Household

Income Project, they find no evidence that the faster the economic growth, the greater the returns to education. Neither is it true that returns to party membership decline with economic growth. Instead, they find a negative association of human capital and economic growth.

The persistence-of-cadre-power thesis describes social stratification in the urban sector, in which market reforms lag behind the rural sector. In this sense Nee is right that these findings do not contradict market transition theory, which acknowledges the persistence of cadre power in the "redistributive" sector. But a real challenge presented by the persistence-of-cadre-power thesis is that market transition theory does not specify what is a partial reform and what is a genuine transition. Market transition theory is vague about the process of transition: is it self-reinforcing or is it conditional on other changes? On the one hand, Nee suggests that "the expansion of markets opens up new opportunity structures or niches in which entrepreneurs thrive; their activities, in turn, drive further expansion of markets" (1991, p. 269). If this is what market transition theory implies, the persistence-of-cadre-power would show the theory to be wrong. There is no declining trend for cadre advantages. On the other hand, Nee suggests that "market transition theory does not assume that the direction of change is unidirectional or linear," and "reversals towards greater reliance on central planning" are possible (1991, p. 280). Without further specification of what is (or drives) market transition, any change can be seen as a reversal towards redistribution or a progress towards market, depending on whether it serves to sustain or erode cadre advantage. In this sense market transition theory is impossible to test, if not tautological (Rona-Tas, 1994; Walder, 1996).

The persistence-of-cadre-power thesis gains new support in a recent study of rural household income. Using nationally representative survey data collected in 1996, Walder (2002) finds that cadre household advantages do not change with economic growth or market expansion. In contrast, returns to entrepreneurship decline markedly with the growth of labor market. Market transition (expansion) per se does not seem to have any generic effect once other processes are taken into account – for example, structural changes from an agrarian subsistence economy to an industrializing economy. The persistence-of-cadre-power thesis finally hits the weakest point of market transition theory. If market transition is not a self-reinforcing process, the explanatory power of market transition theory is lost. Market transition is no longer a driving force generating social change, which occurs in an ad hoc manner and has yet to be explained by other factors. This means that a transition from plan to market has no inherent or generic effect on stratification. A more productive approach will therefore look to real changes that directly shape the distribution of economic opportunities.[2]

The Impact of Privatization: Conversion of Political or Human Capital

Research on transitional economies in Eastern Europe and the former Soviet Union offers an alternative account of transition from state socialism. This process is not just understood as a change from plan to market, but a journey from socialism to capitalism. Grand changes extend from the economic sphere to the political and legal system, with a key change being the transformation of state ownership (Rona-Tas, 1994; Stark, 1996; Eyal et al., 1998). Under this circumstance, the conversion-of-cadre-power thesis emerges as a third account of cadre advantages. Redistributing property into private hands deprives former socialist elites of their power base. They have to convert past advantages into new lucrative opportunities if they are to stay on the top. The question is the extent to which political and human capital can be converted.

The "political capitalism" argument emphasizes the convertibility of political capital. Former power elites manipulate the privatization process and transfer state assets into their own hands (Hankiss, 1990; Staniszkis, 1991). These "socialists" lose redistributive power as privatization continues, but they gain economic power by becoming "capitalists." The "managerial capitalism" argument highlights the value of cultural capital, a concept broader than human capital, including not only education and experience, but also insider knowledge of former state-owned enterprises and skills of negotiation with strategic outsiders (Eyal et al., 1998). This argument notes that political change in Hungary blocks the access of former power elites to state assets, and that the post-communist transformation begins with the absence of a propertied class. This peculiar historical contingency gives former technocrats and managers uncontested authority over strategic enterprises, most of which remain under a form of state ownership. These new managers take advantage of the absence of real owners by establishing subcontracting firms of their own, and harnessing transactions between the parent company and their own business. The diffusion of state assets into corporate companies therefore enables former technocrats and managers (but not bureaucrats) to reproduce their advantage in the post-socialist transformation. Cultural capital replaces political capital to be the dominant stratification mechanism.

Rona-Tas (1994) dissolves the contrast between political capital and human capital by arguing that human capital is as important in capitalism as in socialism, and that political capital confers expertise and connections crucial to successful business. He carefully specifies the scope condition under which each capital takes effect. In the traditional sector of household farming, in which production skills are evenly distributed among the farmer population and transactions with other organizations are minimal and simple, both education and cadreship make no difference. In the non-corporate sector, where typical enterprises are small and modestly lucrative, cadres are overrepresented, but this is accounted for by their education. In the dynamic corporate sector, however, both education and cadreship have significant effects on entry into corporate entrepreneurship, making socialist cadres the biggest winner of the transition.

Although it is disputed whether the former communist elite as a whole or only its technocratic faction benefits from early transition, and although it remains to be seen how further privatization will eventually shape the opportunity structure, the conversion thesis shows the legacy of socialism as capitalism emerges. Expertise is concentrated in the state sector, where political organizations are also concentrated. To the extent that building a post-socialist economy needs expertise and social networks, those who have acquired these properties are in a better position to get ahead.

China is different from East European countries in the scope and depth of transformation. But traditionally China has a same concentration of expertise in the state sector and an extensive political network within the party and government system. Building a market economy in China means that technology and expertise flows from state-owned enterprises to township-and-village enterprises, and that political networks are used for economic transactions (Yang, 1995). If we do not focus narrowly on the erosion-of-cadre-power thesis vs. the persistence-of-cadre-power thesis, we may find a conversion process occurring in which rural enterprises "import" advanced technology from the state sector, and use governmental influence over local banks to obtain start-up capital. In this paper, I further ask whether the rural sector has created its own expertise, whether the expertise is concentrated in cadres' hands, and whether cadres are converting the expertise into personal gains by creating their own private businesses.

Local Government Enterprises as a Training Ground: Political Capital Generates Human Capital

Although market transition in China is often described as an institutional change from plan to market, there is a parallel line of analysis that portrays it as a change in property rights (Oi, 1992; Walder, 1995; Walder & Oi, 1999). A primary driving force for change in Rural China is not the expansion of the markets, but the transfer of property rights from the state to local governments, and from government to enterprises and ordinary households. The initial change began with the abolition of the commune system in the late 1970s. Farmlands were evenly distributed among village populations. Households gained income and control rights. Productivity increased and peasants began to move out of agriculture for more lucrative opportunities, which in turn expanded local product and labor markets. This very early stage of transition is probably what the erosion-of-cadre-power thesis captures. The foundation of cadre power was gone, and cadres were not very likely to take advantage of new opportunities – private business was lucrative, but with a high political risk; household farming was labor-intensive and not lucrative. Unwilling to compete with ordinary households either in farming or business, cadres appeared to be losers.

However, the fiscal reform of the mid-1980s quickly changed the institutional landscape of rural China. It transferred property rights over enterprises from the central government to the local governments by allowing local governments to retain a share of profits. Local cadres were quick to respond to this new incentive structure. They created new firms, made important decisions of production and marketing, and carefully monitored managers and workers (Byrd & Gelb, 1990; Oi, 1995; Wong, 1988). Problems of bargaining and soft budget constraints, typical of state ownership, were minimized in local public ownership. Local governments had stronger financial interests in enterprises, and more capacity to monitor them, which accounted for their superior performance over state-owned enterprises (Walder, 1995). Peng (2001) offers a different but complimentary account of why township-and-village enterprises outperform state-owned enterprises. Public firms in a "reforming socialist economy" encounter a new agency problem: How to make managers committed to the financial performance of their enterprises? Intensified market competition mitigates this problem for township-and-village enterprises, but not for state-owned enterprises. While managers of state-owned enterprises can blame "irrational price control, redundant and retired workers, and bureaucratic intervention" for low productivity and money loss, their counterparts in township-and-village enterprises have to blame themselves for any mismanagement (Peng, 2001, p. 1350).

It should be noted that this was not the first time that rural collective enterprises came into existence. In fact they first appeared as early as the 1950s when China launched a large-scale agricultural cooperative movement. Individual handicraft workers were organized into specialized sideline production teams (*fuye zhuanye dui*). But frenetic political mobilizations could not sustain the ambition of industrializing the whole country. Commune and brigade enterprises soon faded away in the early 1960s. They did not gain momentum until the central government decided to speed up agricultural mechanization in 1970. Since then commune and brigade enterprises began to take off. Their output value increased from Y9.25 billion in 1970 to Y49.3

billion in 1978 (Byrd & Lin, 1990, p. 10). Despite their steady growth, these local government enterprises were confined within the rural sector, and were prohibited from competing with state-owned enterprises for inputs and markets.

These restrictions were loosened in the 1980s. Local government enterprises began to compete with state-owned enterprises on the national market, and outperformed them by taking their share of markets and profits. From 1985 to 1996, the share of local government enterprises in gross industrial output grew from 14.6% to 27.8%, while that of state-owned enterprises shrank from 65% to 28.5% (Jefferson & Rawski, 1999, p. 27). Local government enterprises became a sector comparable to that of state-owned enterprises.

What is the implication of prospering rural industry for local cadres? First of all, local public enterprises become a new source of cadre advantage. Their salaries multiply; their influence over household welfare increases; and their authority over community issues grows. Second, cadres acquire managerial experience. The growth of rural enterprises changes the distribution of expertise traditionally concentrated in the urban sector. Millions of people in the countryside have learned industrial production, management, and marketing, and cadres and managers are major beneficiaries. Cadres actively participate in building enterprises from the very beginning, and are intimately involved in decisions on investments, production, hiring and wage determination. Some observers even compare local governments to "holding companies, investment corporations, or headquarters of loosely controlled multidivisional corporations." (Byrd & Lin, 1990, p. 5) Local government enterprises clearly become a training ground for rural cadres. To borrow the language of market transition literature, *political capital* generates *human capital*. They are not just competing sources of advantages. They reinforce each other in a way that makes the advantaged even more advantageous. A key question is: Are cadres willing and able to convert recently acquired human capital into new advantages by creating their own business?

The Utility of Experience Acquired through Cadreship

Cadres often have to make a choice: to stay in the public sector and find non-farm jobs for family members, or to set up a private business and have others (or themselves) manage it. I argue that while many prefer to stay in the public sector, some may pursue a different strategy to enrich themselves. There are several reasons. First, having a private business means exclusive rights over its profits. This may attract some cadres who are prepared to take economic risks.[3] Second, they can choose to hold the office and let family members run the business. This double dipping strategy allows them to enjoy the security provided by the cadre position and the money generated by the business. Third, many cadres have stepped down from their positions. They lose if they fail to convert past advantages into new ones.[4] A fourth reason is related to the hardship that local government enterprises experienced in the 1990s. Intensified market competition drives downward the profit rate of all kinds of enterprises (Naughton, 1995). At the lowest level of the administrative hierarchy, township and village governments had little authority over local branches of the state banks (Che & Qian, 1998), and therefore could not bailout enterprises that began to lose money. Many of them have been observed to go to private persons through outright sale (Kung, 1999). If local government enterprises are transformed into private ownership, the power base of cadres may shrink again. Willingly or unwillingly, the best choice for many cadres is to convert their accumulated advantages into new ones by setting up their own business.

To sum up, a conversion process occurs in which cadres benefit from their power over local public assets, their connections with other cadres, and especially managerial experience acquired through cadreship. Since managerial experience is heavily concentrated in the hands of cadres and managers, cadres with managerial experience will be more likely than others to set up a family business (except managers). Hereafter I refer to cadres with managerial experience as cadre-managers, and their household as cadre-manager household.

Hypothesis 1: Cadre-manager households are more likely to have a business than other households (except manager households).

The size of business matters for the conversion process. Rona-Tas (1994) found that in the traditional farming sector, there is little conversion, whereas in the non-corporate sector, cadres convert their higher education into more income, and in the corporate sector, cadres are able to convert political advantages into corporate entrepreneurship. If cadre-managers decide to convert their managerial experience, does the size make a difference? Are they more likely to be in a larger business than ordinary people? The answer in part depends on the quality of their managerial experience vs. that of others. To be sure, local government enterprises are not the only source of expertise and managerial skills. The prospering private economy becomes ordinary person's training ground. But the quality of experience generated by local government enterprises is fundamentally different from that acquired from private business. The majority of private businesses are small. Most of them are traditional undertakings. Normally they do not require sophisticated skills, nor do they upgrade their owner's expertise to a higher level. In contrast, local government enterprises are much larger. They hire more workers, have more inputs and outputs, and employ more advanced technology. As a result they generate more valuable experience for cadres and managers of local government enterprises.

Table 1 shows the growth and average enterprise size of these two sectors from 1978 to 1992. Although private enterprises grew much faster in number than local government enterprises, their size remained very small. On average they hired no more than 3 workers throughout the whole period. In contrast, a typical local government enterprise had 34 employees by the year of 1992. If the size indicates the quality of experience, cadres and managers of local government enterprises will have an edge over others. This advantage will facilitate their entry into a large business, which usually requires more sophisticated managerial experience.

Hypothesis 2: Cadre-manager families are more likely to have a larger business than other families (except manager families).

DATA, MEASUREMENT AND METHODS

Data

The data are from a life history survey of a nationally representative sample of rural Chinese adults (aged 20–69). The survey, directed by Treiman and Walder, was conducted in 1996. It used a multi-stage sampling procedure and the primary sampling unit was the county-level jurisdiction as defined by the Chinese Census Bureau (Tibet was not in the sampling frame). Through multi-stage sampling procedures, the survey obtained a representative sample of 3003 rural residents. The data set has detailed information about respondents' career histories, household composition, family member's career in certain years (1954, 1963, 1970, 1979, 1989 and 1996 for their parents and grandparents; the year of marriage and 1996 for spouse and spouse's father), family economic activities, and number of employees, which is suitable for testing the conversion-of-cadre-experience hypotheses.

Measurement

Family Business

Respondents were asked about their household economic activities, from growing crops, to agricultural sidelines and non-agricultural sidelines. I define family business as non-agricultural sidelines, coded 1 if the family has one in

Table 1. Number and Size of Township and Village Enterprises (1978–1992).

Year	Number of Enterprises (1) (10,000)		Number of Employees (2) (10,000)		Amount of Product (3) (billion yuan)		Employyes (4) /enterprise (2)/(1)		Product/Enterprises (5) [(3)/(1)]100 (1,000 yuan)	
	Collective	Private	Collective	Private	Collective	Private	Collective	Private	Collective	Private
1978	152.42	–	2826.56	–	49.51	–	18	–	32.48	–
1980	142.46	–	2999.67	–	66.51	–	21	–	44.69	–
1981	133.75	–	2969.56	–	73.97	–	22	–	55.30	–
1982	136.17	–	3112.91	–	84.93	–	23	–	58.10	–
1983	134.64	–	3234.64	–	100.79	–	24	–	74.86	–
1984	186.30	420.22	3982.16	1225.95	145.38	24.40	21	3	78.04	5.81
1985	184.99	1037.47	4327.05	2651.98	207.37	68.14	29	2	139.18	6.57
1986	172.77	1342.54	4541.28	3395.86	255.63	102.70	26	3	148.00	7.65
1987	158.28	1591.82	4718.23	4086.95	335.76	158.79	30	3	212.13	9.98
1988	159.00	1729.16	4893.94	4651.52	473.48	228.29	31	3	297.79	13.20
1989	153.57	1715.06	4720.14	4646.64	558.23	281.66	31	3	363.50	16.42
1990	145.39	1705.05	4592.51	4672.30	625.38	332.73	32	3	430.14	19.51
1991	144.17	1763.71	4767.03	4842.04	771.98	390.19	33	3	535.47	22.12
1992	152.72	1938.90	5175.78	5448.81	1177.66	588.32	34	3	771.12	30.34

Data Source: Yearbook of Chinese Township and Village Enterprises, 1993, pp. 145–147.

Note: Township and village enterprises consist of four types of enterprises: township enterprises (*xiangzhen ban qiye*), village enterprises (*cun ban qiye*), partnership enterprises (*hezuo qiye*), and individually-owned enterprises (*geti qiye*). I combine the first two into collective enterprises, and the last two into private enterprises.

1996. Since non-agricultural sidelines have low barriers to entry, they are widespread in rural China – 640 families out of 3,003 (21%) were involved in non-agricultural activities in 1996.

Size of Family Business

Rural non-agricultural sidelines are usually very small undertakings. Many of them are staffed by members of the household. I use the number of employees to indicate the size of family business. A small business has no employees – the majority of entrepreneur households fall into this category (553 families out of 640). A large business has at least one paid employee. There are 87 such families in the sample.

Types of Household[5]

I distinguish six types of household: (1) Cadre household, which is a household with at least one cadre (whether still in the office or not), but without managers or cadre-managers. In other words, cadres in this category do not have managerial experience. (2) Manager household, a household with at least one manager (whether in the public or private sector, former or current), but without any cadres. Manager is defined broadly to include those in a middle-level or high-level managerial position, or head of a private enterprise (before their own private business, if there is any). (3) Cadre and manager household, a household with at least one cadre and one manager, who are different persons. (4) Cadre manager household, a household with one or more cadres who have acquired managerial experience through cadreship. Cadres in this category managed local government enterprises for more than six months while holding a cadre office at the same time. This is a key independent variable. Because this paper emphasizes the conversion of managerial experience acquired through cadreship into private entrepreneurship, I make a strict distinction between this type of household and the household with both cadres and managers, which may pursue a different strategy to enrich itself. (5) Worker household, a household with at least a worker, but no cadre or manager. (6) Peasant household. This is the residual category and the comparison group.

Human Capital

I use two variables to measure household human capital: education and family business experience before communist takeover. Household education is the average years of education for working members. Past family business experience is a dummy variable, coded 1 if respondent's parents or grandparents ran a business before the communist takeover. This intergenerational experience has been found to have an impact on rural household farming in other settings (Szelenyi, 1988).

Coastal Region
Past studies suggest to take regional variations into account (Xie & Hannum 1996). I use the variable "coastal region" as a control, coded 1 if the family is in a coastal province.

Methods

I use logistic regression models to test the hypothesis of entry into a family business, and multinomial logistic regression models to test the hypothesis of entry into businesses of different sizes. Multinomial logistic regression modeling is an extension of the logistic regression method to dependent variables with three or more categories. The logistic regression model takes the form:

$$Y_i^* = \mathbf{x}_i\beta + \varepsilon_i$$

Where Y_i^* is a latent variable, $\mathbf{x}$ is a vector of covariates, β is a vector of coefficients associated with $\mathbf{x}$, and ε_i is the measurement error. The latent variable Y_i^* is related to the observed dichotomous variable Yi through the measurement equation:

$$Y_i = 1 \quad \text{if} \quad Y_i^* > \tau, \text{ or}$$
$$Y_i = 0 \quad \text{if} \quad Y_i^* \leq \tau$$

where τ is the hypothetical threshold. If Y_i^* exceeds the threshold τ, Y_i is observed. Maximum likelihood method is used to estimate both logistic regression models and multinomial logistic regression models.

RESULTS

A Preliminary Analysis of the Composition of Family Income

The persistence-of-cadre-power thesis would predict that the public sector is the domain where cadres reproduce their advantages. Cadres prefer to stay away from the private sector, which has many uncertainties and risks. They also pull their family members into the public sector, and find highly paid jobs for them. As a result the majority of family income comes from wages and

Table 2. Variable Labels, Definitions, and Descriptive statistics ($N = 3{,}003$).

Variables	Definition	*N*	Mean
Family Business	Non-agricultural family undertaking	640	0.21
Size of family business			
Small family business	Family business without non-family workers	553	0.18
Large family business	Family business with at least one non-family workers	87	0.03
Types of household			
Cadre household	A household with at least one cadre, present or former, but having no manager.	97	0.03
Manager household	A household with at least one manager, whether in a public or private firm, but having no cadres	266	0.09
Cadre and manager household	A household with at least one manager and one cadre, who are not the same person	14	0.01
Cadre-manager household (Managerial experience acquired through cadreship)	A household with at least one cadre who at the same time is (was) a manager.	66	0.02
Worker household	A household with at least one worker, but no cadres or managers	691	0.23
Household education	Average years of schooling for working family members.	3003	5.20
Past family business experience	Parents or grandparents ran a business in 1948.		
Coastal Region	Households living in a coastal province, including Hebei, Liaoning, Jiangsu, Zhejiang, Fujian Shandong, Guangdong and Guangxi.	1251	41.95

Source: The 1996 Chinese Life History Survey.

Table 3. Composition of Household Income by Household Types, 1996.

Household Types	Income from agriculture	Income from non-agricultural business	Income from wages	*N*
Cadre household	3,191	1,865	4,391	97
Manager household	2,484	3,848	6,250	266
Cadre and manager household	2,206	14,956	6,706	14
Cadre manager household	2,746	5,362	5,776	66
Ordinary household	3,346	991	2,620	2,560

Source: The 1996 Chinese Life History Survey.
Note: "Income from agriculture" is based on self-reported income from growing crops and agricultural sidelines; "income from non-agricultural business" includes income from non-agricultural sidelines; and "income from wages" includes income from salaried jobs.

bonuses. The conversion-of-cadre-experience thesis does not necessarily deny this point. But it predicts a trend of converting experience acquired through cadreship into new private business. As a result cadre manager families may have more income from family business than ordinary households, which indicates a new source of advantages for cadre managers.

Table 3 reports different sources of family income by family types. For most elite families, incomes from wage are the primary source of total income. The cadre and manager family is an exception, but there are only 14 such families in the sample. In contrast, agriculture remains the primary source of income for ordinary families. Of special interest here is income from non-agricultural businesses. For the cadre family and the manager family, this type of income is significantly less than income from wages, indicating that many prefer not to run their own business. This result lends support to the persistence-of-cadre-power thesis. But note that their income from non-agricultural businesses is much higher than that of ordinary families, suggesting that private business may be another source of advantages for them, albeit a very small one. For cadre manager families, however, it is a big advantage. Their income from family business not only exceeds that for other families (except the cadre and manager families), but also matches their income from salaried jobs. This is a clear evidence for the conversion-of-cadre-experience thesis.

Entry into Family Business

The first question I asked is whether those advantaged in the public sector are also advantaged in the private sector. Table 4 presents results from a logistic

Table 4. Maximum Likelihood Estimates for Logistic Regression of Family Business on Explanatory Variables ($N = 3{,}003$).

Variables	Model 1	Model 2
Types of Household		
Cadre household	1.71**	1.24
	(0.41)	(0.30)
Manager household	3.14***	2.35***
	(0.44)	(0.34)
Cadre and manager household	4.52***	2.82*
	(2.43)	(1.56)
Cadre-manager household	1.83**	1.15
	(0.51)	(0.33)
Worker household	1.15	0.89
	(0.13)	(0.11)
Human Capital		
Average household education		1.16***
		(0.03)
Past family business experience		1.16
		(0.24)
Coastal region		1.96***
		(0.18)
Likelihood Ratio test: chi2 (Δdf)		88.42***(3)

Source: The 1996 Chinese Life History Survey.
Notes: Reported are odds ratios. Standard errors are in parentheses; * $p < 0.10$; ** $p < 0.05$; *** $p < 0.01$ (two-tailed test).

regression analysis of entry into family business. Model 1 shows the odds ratios of different types of households compared with ordinary peasant households. Model 2 adds two human capital variables and a variable measuring location effect.

Are elite families more likely to have a private business? The answer is a qualified yes, conditional on their amount of education. Without controlling for education, families with cadres and/or managers have a higher rate to enter private business. When education is taken into account, however, the majority of elite families are not more likely than ordinary households to have a business. Model 1 compares the likelihood of entry into private business for various types of family, without any control variables. The results show the overall advantages (or disadvantages) of each type of family, whatever the source is – it could come from political capital, human capital or social capital. Overall, families with one or more managers (including manager families and cadre and manager families) are the most likely ones to have a business. Cadre and manager families are 4.5 times as likely as ordinary peasant families to run a business. But because there are only 14 such families in the sample, I will not focus attention on them in the subsequent analyses. If cadre and manager families are not counted, manager families have the highest chance to enter a private business (3.1 times as likely as ordinary peasant families), suggesting that managerial experience is valuable for entry into private entrepreneurship.

My focus is on two types of cadre families: cadre families (without managerial experience) and cadre-manager families. They also have some advantages over ordinary peasant families, but the magnitude is much smaller (1.7 times for cadre families, and 1.8 times for cadre manager families). However, their advantages disappear when human capital is taken into account. Model 2 shows that controlling for education and past business experience, manager families are the only ones to have an edge over peasant families, suggesting that the advantages of other elite families are accounted for by their higher education and/or familial business history. Meanwhile, education has a strong effect on entry into a business. One more year of schooling increases the likelihood by 16%. If a family averages five more years of education than its neighbor, this family would be 2.4 times as likely to have a business ($1.16^5 = 2.44$).

To sum up, cadre families and cadre-manager families are more likely to run a business, but this is only because they are more educated. The first hypothesis therefore is not supported: Cadres are not converting their managerial experience or political advantages into a private business. What does this suggest? The erosion-of-cadre-power thesis would see it as evidence that political capital is declining and human capital is on the rise. The persistence-of-cadre-power thesis would interpret it as a proof that cadres are not interested in private business insofar as the public sector still sustains cadre privilege. On the other hand, the conversion-of-cadre-experience thesis would suggest that cadres withhold their experience in the sector with a very low entry barrier, but will convert it if the entry barrier is higher. Entry barrier is closely related to the nature of business. In general a business requiring less start-up capital, no advanced technology, and few managerial skills has a lower entry barrier. But exactly because entry into this type of business is not difficult, competition is more intensive and profit rate is much lower. Probably most entrepreneur households in our sample operate their businesses in this sector. By contrast, a business hiring more employees and requiring more inputs has a higher entry barrier. Because competition is less intensive and profit rate is higher, cadre-managers have enough incentive to convert their managerial experience in this sector. I continue to test these possibilities in the following section.

Entry into a Larger Family Business

Family businesses in rural China are extremely small, the majority of which have no employees. In our sample, among 640 business families, only 13.6% have one or more outside workers (87/640 = 13.6%, see Table 2). Having at least one employee seems to be a barrier that so far most business families are not able to overcome. How about cadre families? Can they overcome this barrier with their managerial experience? Results in Table 5 provide a definite answer to this question.

Table 5 presents two models. Model 1 contrasts having no business with having a small business (without any employees). Results of this model are very similar to those reported in Model 2, Table 4, which contrasts having no business with having a business, regardless of size. This is not surprising, since the overwhelming majority of family businesses have no employees. As Model 1 shows, manager families are the only ones to have an advantage over peasant families. Education has a remarkable effect on entry into a small business – an additional year of education increases the chance by 16%. Location matters as well. Other things being equal, people in coastal regions have nearly a double chance to set up a small family business.

Model 2 contrasts entry into a large business vs. a small one. Manager families still have an advantage, but their advantage is exceeded by that of cadre-manager families by a large margin. While the former are 2.2 times as likely as ordinary peasant households to run a business with one or more employees, the latter are 5.4 times as likely compared to peasant households. This is clear evidence that cadre families are converting their managerial experience into private business. For those cadre families without managerial experience, Model 2 shows that they are not more likely than peasant families to establish a large business, suggesting that so far it is *managerial experience acquired through cadreship*, not *political power* per se, that accounts for cadre presence in private business. Two more findings are noteworthy. First, education does not have an impact. Having more years of schooling alone is not sufficient to overcome the entry barrier to a sizeable business. Ordinary households cannot compensate for their lack of managerial experience by more education. Managerial experience and formal education as two main types of human capital are not exchangeable. Second, a worker family has some advantage over a peasant family in entry into a large business, but not a small

Table 5. Maximum Likelihood Estimates for Multinomial Logistic Regression of the Size of Family Business on Explanatory Variables ($N = 3{,}003$).

	Model 1 No employee vs. no business	Model 2 One or more employees vs. no employee
Types of Household		
Cadre household	1.17	1.66
	(0.30)	(0.97)
Manager household	2.11***	2.20**
	(0.32)	(0.70)
Cadre and manager household	1.80	6.96**
	(1.16)	(5.57)
Cadre-manager household	0.81	5.36***
	(0.28)	(2.84)
Worker household	0.84	1.66*
	(0.10)	(0.52)
Human Capital		
Average household education	1.16***	0.99
	(0.03)	(0.06)
Past family business experience	1.20	0.79
	(0.26)	(0.43)
Coastal region	1.87***	1.43
	(0.18)	(0.36)
– 2*loglikelihood	3435.7	3435.7

Source: The 1996 Chinese Life History Survey.
Notes: Reported are odds ratios. Standard errors are in parentheses; * $p < 0.10$; ** $p < 0.05$; *** $p < 0.01$ (two-tailed test).

one, probably because a salaried job is a substitution for a small business, but not a larger one.

How to assess these findings with regard to the competing theses? First, there is limited support for the erosion-of-cadre-power thesis. Education matters for the small business. It seems that more educated families have a chance to compensate for their political weakness, and begin their upward mobility from a small business. But so far there is a limit for the effect of education. When it comes to a large business, the effect of education is gone, which diminishes the hope of ordinary households to develop a small business into a large one. Second, there is qualified support for the persistence-of-cadre-power thesis.

The majority of cadre families (97 out of 177, which is the sum of 97, 14 and 66. See Table 3) are not engaged in any private undertakings. They seem to prefer a salaried job for themselves and their family members. But their stay away from private business is due to their lack of managerial experience. Finally, there is clear evidence for the conversion-of-cadre-experience thesis. Cadre managers are indeed willing to convert their experience into private business, now a new source of advantage for them. Managerial experience, highly valuable in an economy that traditionally concentrates expertise in the urban sector, enables cadre managers to overcome the entry barrier insurmountable for many ordinary households, and adds another title to them – they are not only *cadre managers*, but also *private entrepreneurs*.

DISCUSSION

Economic and social changes have been reflected in academic works. The erosion-of-cadre-power thesis captures a short period in which the old public ownership was dismantled, but the new one had not been created. Ordinary families found new lucrative opportunities in private business, and the better educated began to take off. This peculiar historical contingency led to a decline of political capital and a rise of human capital, which was captured by the erosion-of-power thesis. But history keeps changing. The unexpected growth of public ownership became a new source of cadre advantage, and empirically lent more support to the persistence-of-cadre-power thesis. A potential contribution of this thesis is its skepticism of the decline of political capital. The fall and rise of political capital mirrors the fall and rise of public enterprises. Linking political capital to public ownership therefore reveals the weakness of a central claim of the erosion-of-cadre-power thesis, which regards the decline of political capital as a necessary outcome of transition from plan to market. The diminished political capital observed by the erosion-of-cadre-power thesis is historically contingent on a particular change in public ownership, not inherently determined by transition from plan to market. When public ownership began to grow in the mid-80s, the declining trend of political capital was reversed. What happened in the rural sector later therefore confirms the causal relationship between political capital and public ownership, and casts doubt on the relationship between political capital and "market transition." Market mechanism was allocating more and more resources, but the value of political capital did not decrease further.

Economic and social change continues, however. Intensified market competition in the 1990s presented a new challenge to the local public ownership, and transformed some local government enterprises into shareholding companies or even private properties. This new change directs our attention to the conversion process through which cadre households become private entrepreneurs. Market transition literature has suggested political capital and human capital as two main types of resources that can be converted into entrepreneurship. So far the majority of cadres are still in the public sector, and there is no evidence that political capital has been directly transformed into entrepreneurial opportunities. In contrast, human capital matters for entry into private business. This study examines two types of human capital, education and managerial experience acquired through cadreship, and finds another interesting contrast. Managerial experience acquired through cadreship greatly facilitates entry into larger businesses (with employees), whereas education only facilitates entry into small businesses (without employees). This contrast sheds new light on the role of human capital in generating economic advantages. First, different types of human capital are not always exchangeable. Education increases the likelihood of ordinary families to enter private business, but cannot compensate for their lack of managerial experience, which is crucial for operating a large business. In other words, education alone is not sufficient to upgrade a small business into a larger one. Second, human capital is related to political capital through local government enterprises, which become a training ground for cadres. Although political capital has no direct impact on the conversion process, it indirectly shapes the distribution of entrepreneurial opportunities through managerial experience. Therefore it would be misleading to sever the relationship of political capital and human capital, and see them as competing sources of advantages.

When we focus more attention on historical contingencies, we are more skeptical about inherent mobility regimes, and are likely to see more punctuated social changes. For now, we find the majority of cadres staying comfortably in the public sector. But a conversion process is occurring. Cadres with managerial experience are transforming themselves into private entrepreneurs, and reproducing their advantages in the private sector. What remains to be seen is whether the public sector alone can sustain cadre advantages, whether cadres without managerial experience will be forced into private businesses, and whether those cadres will use political power to compensate for their lack of managerial experience.

NOTES

1. While in general this is true, Walder (2002) cautions against overestimation of the magnitude of cadre advantages in rural China. Mao-era communes served to transfer

agricultural surplus to the urban sector as part of a low-wage industrialization strategy. Local cadres had little redistributive power over this surplus, and therefore income advantages conferred by political positions were unusually small in rural China.

2. Recent research begins to call attention to multiple processes involved in market transition. Zhou (2000) explicitly states that market expansion is only one among many. Political and social forces are often interacting with market institutions to produce what he calls "a co-evolutionary process" between politics and markets. Walder (2002) points out that economic growth is conceptually prior to market transition in explaining income inequality in rural China. What Nee attributes to market transition – higher returns to education – is actually caused by economic development from an agrarian economy to an industrializing economy, a causal link firmly established in past studies of developing economies.

3. It is possible that cadres can reduce economic risks by using their connections with former colleagues to establish relatively secure niches in production or service, or to gain preferential access to subcontracting opportunities and protection.

4. Based on fieldwork in Bin Shen, a neighborhood in Chengdu city, Bruun (1995, p. 191) reports that "retired cadres are numerous in private businesses, usually being the true managers pulling the strings behind registered wives, sons, or daughters-in-law."

5. This coding scheme is based on past experience, since I emphasize the convertibility of managerial experience into private entrepreneurship. Others may classify households differently, for example, using their current occupation instead of their past ones. Although the two coding schemes may use the same label, what they refer to may be different.

ACKNOWLEDGMENTS

I thank Andrew Walder for helpful comments on earlier drafts. I also thank Mark Granovetter, Kevin Leicht, Bobai Li, and Nancy Tuma for their useful comments on an earlier version. An earlier draft was presented at the third graduate students retreat at Yale University, May 12, 2001. I thank participants for their comments and suggestions. Direct correspondence to Litao Zhao, Department of Sociology, Stanford University, Stanford, CA 94305 (ltzhao@stanford.edu).

REFERENCES

Bian, Y., & Logan, J. G. (1996). Market Transition and the Persistence of Power: The Changing Stratification System In Urban China. *American Sociological Review, 61*, 739–758.

Bruun, O. (1995). Political Hierarchy and Private Entrepreneurship in a Chinese Neighborhood. In: A. G. Walder (Ed.), *The Waning of the Communist State: Economic Origins of Political Decline in China and Hungary* (pp. 184–212). Berkeley and Los Angeles: University of California Press.

Byrd, W. A., & Gelb. (1990). Why Industrialize? The Incentives for Rural Community Governments. In: W. A. Byrd & Q. Lin (Eds), *China's Rural Industry: Structure, Development and Reform* (pp. 358–387). New York: Oxford University Press.

Byrd, W. A., & Lin, Q. (1990). China's Rural Industry: An Introduction. In: W. A. Byrd & Q. Lin (Eds), *China's Rural Industry: Structure, Development and Reform* (pp. 1–18). New York: Oxford University Press.

Che, J., & Qian Y. (1998). Institutional Environment, Community Government, and Corporate Governance: Understanding China's Township-Village Enterprises. *The Journal of Law, Economics, and Organization, 14*, 1–23.

Department of Agriculture, PRC (1989). Zhongguo Xiangzhen Qiye Nianjian (*Yearbook of China's Township-and-Village Enterprises*). Beijing: Agricultural Press.

Department of Agriculture, PRC (1993). Zhongguo Xiangzhen Qiye Nianjian (*Yearbook of China's Township-and-Village Enterprises*). Beijing: Agricultural Press.

Djilas, M. (1957). *The New Class: An Analysis of the Communist system of Power*. New York: Praeger.

Eyal, G., Szelenyi, I., & Townsley, E. (1998). *Making Capitalism without Capitalists: Class Formation and Elite Struggles in Post-Communist Central Europe*. New York: Verso.

Hankiss, E. (1990). *East European Alternatives*. Oxford: Clarendon Press.

Jefferson, G. H., & Rawski, T. (1999). Ownership Change in Chinese Industry. In: G. H. Jefferson & I. Singh (Eds), *Enterprise Reform in China: Ownership, Transition, and Performance* (pp. 23–42). New York: Oxford University Press.

Kung, J. K. (1999). The Evolution of Property Rights in Village Enterprises: The Case of Wuxi County. In: J. C. Oi & A. G. Walder (Eds), *Property Rights and Economic Reform in China* (pp. 95–120). Stanford, California: Stanford University Press.

Manchin, R., & Szelenyi, I. (1987). Social Policy under State Socialism: Market, Redistribution, and Social Inequalities in East European Socialist Societies. In: G. Espring-Andersen, M. Rein, & L. Rainwater (Eds), *Stagnation and Renewal in Social Policy* (pp. 102–139). White Plains, New York: Sharpe.

Naughton, B. (1995). *Growing out of the Plan: Chinese Economic Reform: 1978–1993*. Cambridge: Cambridge University Press.

Nee, V. (1989). A Theory of Market Transition: From Redistribution to Markets in State Socialism. *American Sociological Review, 54*, 663–681.

Nee, V. (1991). Social Inequalities in Reforming State Socialism: Between Redistribution and Markets in China. *American Sociological Review, 56*, 267–282.

Nee, V. (1996). The Emergence of a Market Society: Changing Mechanisms of Stratification in China. *American Journal of Sociology, 101*, 908–949.

Nee, V. & Lian, P. (1994). Sleeping with the Enemy: A Dynamic Model of Declining Political Commitment in State Socialism. *Theory and Society, 23*, 253–296.

Oi, J. C. (1992). Fiscal Reform and the Economic Foundations of Local State Corporatism. *World Politics, 45*, 99–126.

Oi, J. C. (1995). The Role of the Local State in China's Transitional Economy. *China Quarterly, 144*, 1132–1149.

Peng, Y. (2001). Chinese Villages and Townships as Industrial Corporations: Ownership, Governance, and Market Discipline. *American Journal of Sociology, 106*, 1338–1370.

Rona-Tas, A. (1994). The First Shall Be the Last? Entrepreneurship and Communist Cadres in the Transition from Socialism. *American Journal of Sociology, 100*, 40–69.

Staniszkis, J. (1991). Political Capitalism in Poland. *East European Politics and Societies, 5*, 127–141.

Stark, D. (1996). Recombinant Property in East European Capitalism. *American Journal of Sociology, 101*, 993–1027.

Szelenyi, I. (1988). *Socialist Entrepreneurs: Embourgeoisement in Rural Hungary*. Madison: University of Wisconsin Press.

Szelenyi, I., & Manchin, R. (1987). Social Policy under State Socialism: Market, Redistribution, and Social Inequalities in East European Socialist Societies. In: G. Espring-Andersen, M. Rein, & L. Rainwater (Eds), *Stagnation and Renewal in Social Policy* (pp. 102–139). Armonk, New York: M. E. Sharpe.

Wong, C. (1988). Interpreting Rural Industrial Growth in the Post-Mao Period. *Journal of Comparative Economics*, *11*, 385–398.

Walder, A. G. (1990). Economic Reform and Income Distribution in Tianjin: 1976–1986. In: D. Davis & E. F. Vogel (Eds), *Chinese Society on the Eve of Tiananmen* (pp. 135–156). Cambridge, MA: Harvard University Press.

Walder, A. G. (1995). Local Governments as Industrial Firms: An Organizational Analysis of China's Transitional Economy. *American Journal of Sociology*, *101*, 263–301.

Walder, A. G. (1996). Markets and Inequality in Transitional Economies: Toward Testable Theories. *American Journal of Sociology*, *101*, 1060–1073.

Walder, A. G. (2002). Markets and Income Inequality in Rural China: Political Advantage in an Expanding Economy. *American Sociological Review*, *67*, 231–253.

Walder, A. G., & Oi, J. C. (1999). Property Rights in the Chinese Economy: Contours of the Process of Change. In: J. C. Oi & A. G. Walder (Eds), *Property Rights and Economic Reform in China* (pp. 1–24). Stanford, California: Stanford University Press.

Xie, Y., & Hannum, E. (1996). Regional Variation in Earnings Inequalities in Reform-Era Urban China. *American Journal of Sociology*, *101*, 950–992.

Yang, M. (1994). Taolun: Zhongguo Xiangzhen Qiye de Qiji Shi Zenyang Chuxian de? [Discussion: How Did the Miracle of China's Township-and-Village Enterprises Come into Existence?]. In: R. Ma, C. H. Huang, H. Wang & M. Yang (Eds), *Jiushi Niandai Zhongguo Xiangzhen Qiye Diaocha* [*An Investigation of China's Township-and-Village Enterprises in the 1990s*] (pp. 436–465). Hongkong: Oxford University Press.

Zhou, X. (2000) Economic Transformation and Income Inequality in Urgan China: Evidence from Panel Data. *American Journal of Sociology*, *105*, 1135–1174.

INSTITUTIONAL TRANSFORMATION AND RETURNS TO EDUCATION IN URBAN CHINA: AN EMPIRICAL ASSESSMENT

Wei Zhao and Xueguang Zhou

ABSTRACT

Patterns of returns to education reflect fundamental principles in which human resources are allocated and rewarded in a society. Major theoretical ideas about institutional transformation in former state socialist societies are centered on changing mechanisms of resource allocation, with direct empirical implications for the changing roles of education in the transformation processes. In this study, we draw a set of hypotheses from these theoretical ideas in the literature and examine changes in returns to education in urban China between 1978 (the beginning of the post-Mao era) and 1993 (15 years into the economic reform). We find significant and substantial increases in returns to education over time, and especially in the non-state sector where market mechanisms prevail. These patterns are consistent with the core arguments developed in market transition theory. There is also evidence on an active role of the state and state policies in promoting the role of education in the same direction. These findings suggest that markets and political processes are interacting in more complicated ways than simply undermining each other.

The Future of Market Transition, Volume 19, pages 339–375.

ISBN: 0-7623-0835-4

INTRODUCTION

In contemporary societies, education has become the most important vehicle for upward mobility and economic well-being. Not surprisingly, social scientists have long been interested in returns to education, and have generated a large and still growing literature (Psacharopoulos, 1994). In particular, returns to education have become an analytical focus for studying allocative mechanisms in different institutional contexts, and scholars have developed alternative conceptualizations of the role of education in these allocative processes. In labor economics, for example, human capital theory treats earnings as reflecting returns to individuals' investment in education as governed by market mechanisms. For sociologists, returns to education provide a research arena to examine barriers, structures, and discriminations in labor markets, and the role of social institutions in mediating education and market outcomes.

Patterns of returns to education also present an ideal research arena to examine and assess changes in mechanisms of resource allocation in the transformation of formal state socialist societies. Important theoretical ideas about these transformation processes are centered on conceptualizations of competing mechanisms of resource allocation, especially regarding the allocation of human resources. Nee's market transition theory, for example, develops explicit arguments about the changing role of education in the transformation of the state socialist economy. Given that educational qualification has been critical in the organization of work and labor markets, patterns of returns to education also allow us to assess the direction and extent of institutional changes in the transformation of state socialism in these societies.

The purpose of this study is to systematically examine the mechanisms under which human resources are allocated and rewarded in urban China, a state socialist economy that has been undergoing fundamental changes in the last two decades. Although education has been included as part of explanatory models in the previous studies, there have been few studies that examined changes in returns to education over time systematically. In this study, we identify the specific channels through which education takes effect and its variations across occupational groups, and across the state and non-state sector. We also contrast returns to education and those to party membership in the transformation processes. Our presentation is organized as follows: We first discuss main theoretical arguments and debates in the literature and, on this basis, derive a set of hypotheses with regard to returns to education. We then explicitly test these hypotheses by comparing changing patterns of returns to education over time between 1978 (the beginning of the post-Mao era) and

1993 (15 years into the economic reform). Our analyses are based on life history data of a national sample of urban residents drawn from 20 cities in China.

MARKET, REDISTRIBUTION, AND ALLOCATION OF HUMAN RESOURCES: THEORETICAL ISSUES

Human capital theory, originated in labor economics, is built on the premise that human resources are allocated through market mechanisms. Individual earnings are results of matching processes between employers and employees. Employers choose and reward those employees whose qualification (educational training) yields the highest productivity for the designated tasks. For potential employees, they will choose jobs that can maximize their human capital investment. Accordingly, human capital plays an important role in determining one's economic rewards in a market economy, where factors of production are allocated through competitive market transactions (Becker 1964). In essence, this model posits that education is an individual investment in human capital. Like other forms of capital investment, investment in human capital can only be sustained if the returns exceed the cost of the investment. In this light, returns to education are interpreted as yields accrued to the investment that individuals made in acquiring formal education and training. In particular, the wage model proposed by Mincer (1974) has been widely used to examine returns to education in earnings. As Willis (1986, p. 526) put it:

> As an empirical tool, the Mincer earnings function has been one of the great success stories of modern labor economics. It has been used in hundreds of studies using data from virtually every historical period and country for which suitable data exist. The results of these studies reveal important empirical regularities in educational wage differentials and the life cycle patterns of earnings . . .

Specifically, there are two components in the conventional human capital model. The first component is education, often measured in years of schooling, which is expected to yield positive returns (e.g. higher earnings). The second is on-the-job training, which is another form of human capital. So long as workers gain experience on the jobs they perform, their skills and experience increase their productivity. Therefore, human capital accumulated on the job should also yield positive returns. The lack of a precise measure of on-the-job training often leads researchers to use the duration in the labor force as a proxy for on-the-job training. Because of the life cycle factors in productivity, it is often expected that returns to work experience increase at a decreasing rate, following an inversed U-shape.

Sociologists have long examined the role and limitations of human capital theory in explaining patterns of social stratification and mobility. The importance of education has been developed in the earlier status attainment model (Blau & Duncan, 1967) and is recognized in intergenerational mobility over time (Hout, 1984). Moreover, sociologists have argued that the existence of social institutions – labor market structures, discriminations, and social norms – introduces mechanisms of labor force participation different from those derived from the human capital model. Nevertheless, a large number of studies have shown empirical results that are consistent with the Mincerian model, suggesting that the human capital model has considerable explanatory power in market economies.

In contrast, the human capital arguments are ill-fitted to explain the role of education in state socialist economies, which is organized on principles qualitatively different from those in a market economy. Under state socialism, the state and state policies ultimately determine the allocation of resources in production and consumption areas. All resources, including human resources, are subject to "redistribution" through central planning, which follows a political logic rather than a market logic. Decision making is centralized in the hands of the state apparatus and implemented through bureaucracies rather than based on individual choices in response to price signals.

Several distinctive characteristics emerge with regard to the principles of human resource allocation under state socialism. First, the political logic of redistribution emphasizes the importance of political loyalty over competence. For example, several studies have revealed the common practice of rewarding political capital such as party membership rather than competence as indicated by formal education levels in China in the Mao era (Lee, 1991; Walder, 1986). Second, because a large proportion of resources are allocated through work organizations, economic rewards are often tied not to individual attributes (such as educational qualifications) but to work organizations. The socialist regime effectively creates a hierarchy of work organizations that determine the allocation of human resources in a redistributive economy (Bian, 1994; Lin & Bian, 1991; Walder, 1986, 1992; Zhou, Tuma & Moen, 1997). As a result, we expect that the role of education is significantly different from that in market economies (Xie & Hannum, 1996).

However, this does not necessarily mean that education is not important in upward mobility and allocation of economic rewards. Konrad and Szelényi (1979) developed the early arguments that the communist state has successfully incorporated intellectuals into the ruling class and rewarded them accordingly in East European societies. This incorporation implies that returns to education are determined in ways somewhat parallel to those in a market economy. The role of education in China may reflect a more complicated picture. Walder and his associates (Walder, 1995; Walder, Li & Treiman, 2000) have developed a "dual career path" model to explain two distinctive elite (cadre/professional) trajectories in China. Walder argues that the selection processes under state socialism involve both political loyalty and educational qualification. A dual career path is developed for different kinds of elite positions, with two underlying processes: the first one is a political screening process, and the second is a process of political incorporation. In this model, education is most important for entry into professional positions, which have "high occupational prestige but little authority and fewer material privileges" (Walder, 1995, p. 309). The more desirable career in the redistributive economy is the line of administrative positions. Although higher education, and especially college education, significantly increases the rate of becoming a cadre, political credentials are more important determinant of entry into the administrative positions. In other words, professional occupation only requires human capital, while administrative occupation requires both human capital and political capital (Walder, 1995; Dickson & Rublee, 2000).

To sum up, the role of education reflects distinctive institutional logics in different societies. The nature of centralized planning and the lack of labor markets in China raise questions about the realism of allocating human resources and developing reward schedules comparable to those in a market economy. Logically, we should expect that returns to education in these two types of economies differ in significant ways.

Recognition of these distinctive mechanisms of human resource allocation provides an important empirical basis for assessing the direction and changes in the transformation of state socialist economies. Nee's (1989, 1991, 1996; Nee & Matthews, 1996) market transition theory emphasizes the importance of market mechanisms in the processes of institutional changes in former state socialist societies. Market transition theory is centered on the premise that markets and state socialist redistribution represent two fundamentally different logics of resource allocation. The emergence of market economies in former state socialist societies competes with and undermines the redistributive economy. Nee (1989) argues: "A fundamental change in the processes of socioeconomic attainment occurs in the transition from redistribution to markets, involving not only a reduction in the relative transfers of surplus from producers to redistributors but changes in opportunity structures and incentives resulting from market reforms" (p. 678), and that "the expanding private/hybrid sector and entrepreneurship create new opportunity structures where economic activities are governed by market principles and are largely beyond the control of the state" (Cao & Nee, 2000, p. 1183). As a result, patterns of resource allocation, especially in the area of human resources, should be governed by and reflect these market mechanisms and fundamental institutional changes.

Nee's market transition theory has stimulated a lively debate on the mechanisms and processes of institutional changes and empirical research (Bian & Logan, 1996; Gerber & Hout, 1998; Raymo & Xie, 2000; Rona-Tas, 1994; Stark, 1996; Xie & Hannum, 1996; Walder, 1995; Zhou, 2000a, b). Despite differences in emphases and logics of explanation, in our view researchers largely agree with Nee on the importance of market economies in the processes of transformation. Disagreements are centered on the relationships between market mechanisms and other mechanisms of resource allocation, especially with regard to the role of the state in the reform processes. In Nee's early formulation, markets and redistribution are seen as antithetical to each other. The rise of the former implies the decline of the latter. His critics, on the other hand, have emphasized the coexistence and continuing importance of the state and redistributive institutions in resource allocation in China's economic transformation (Bian & Logan, 1996; Parish & Michelson, 1996; Gutherie, 1997; Walder, 1995). Zhou (2000a) argued that markets and politics not only coexist in the transformation processes but also coevolve in response to each other. That is, both are transformed to such an extent that it is no longer meaningful to treat them as discrete and antithetical categories in empirical studies. In this framework, the coexistence of markets and politics is no longer conceptualized as a transitional phenomenon in a "partial reform." Rather, their coexistence and interaction patterns shape new institutional forms and stratification orders. This line of arguments predicts that both markets and politics exert influence on resource allocation and the emergence of new institutional forms. As a result, a more complicated picture of institutional changes emerges that defies a single logic of explanation. The cumulative evidence in recent years is still consistent with Bian and Logan's assessment (1996, p. 756): "The trend, perhaps, is in the direction of market transition, but the overall situation remains mixed."

Recognizing multiple processes involved in the transformation of the state socialist economy, our approach in this study is to focus on alternative mechanisms underlying institutional changes and consider their implications for returns to education. In our conceptualization, these mechanisms may coexist and compete with, or mutually reinforce, each other. The increasing importance of one mechanism does not necessarily imply the decreasing role of other mechanisms. We see interactions between these multiple processes as a co-evolutionary process in that the interplay between politics and markets may lead to the transformation of, and co-adaptation to, each other in the processes of institutional changes.

INSTITUTIONAL CHANGES AND RETURNS TO EDUCATION: HYPOTHESES

Based on the theoretical ideas discussed above, we now develop a set of hypotheses on the mechanisms of institutional changes and their effects on returns to education in the transformation of state socialism in urban China. In particular, we motivate our considerations in comparison of returns to education over time, across occupational groups, and across sectors of different governance structures.

Changes in Returns to Education over Time

The increasing role of market mechanisms in the allocation of human resources, as elaborated in Nee's market transition theory, affects returns to education in two ways. First, relative to the central planning processes, market mechanisms can make better utilization of human resources; as a result, it tends to yield higher returns to education than those in a redistributive economy. Thus Nee (1989, p. 674) predicted: "The transition to a market-like economy should result in higher returns to human capital characteristics." Secondly, the rise of the market economy may compete with state socialist redistributive institutions and undermine its monopoly rents in economic sectors. As a result, market mechanisms may create new opportunities outside of the traditional state sector and attract more educated and more able employees, which, in turn, affect rates of returns to education.

We agree with this line of argument and think that the emergence of market economies in urban China has indeed fundamentally changed the ways in which resources are allocated in the last two decades. But this is not the whole story. We argue that the salience of human capital in the reform era cannot be completely attributed to the emergence of a market economy. Instead, state policy plays an important role in increasing returns to education in recent years. Evidence shows that, since the early 1980s, the state has adopted explicit policies that aggressively emphasize educational credential as one of the most important criteria in obtaining political and positional power even before market reform in the urban areas took place. As a result, educational credentials greatly improved individuals' chances of becoming party members and promotion in the reform era (Bian, 1994; Lee, 1991; Walder, 1995; Walder, Li & Treiman, 2000; Dickson & Rublee, 2000; Zhou, 1995, 2001). These new policies were not anomalies for state socialist societies. As students of state socialism have observed, the socialist states in East European countries have emphasized, to various extents, the importance of education and competence in order to carry out its central planning of the economy (see Walder, 1995 for related discussion). Therefore, both the advance of market mechanisms and changes in state policies in the reform era lead us to predict that:

> *Hypothesis 1*: There is a significant increase in returns to education over time in the transformation of state socialism.

Returns to Human Capital vs. Political Capital

A more direct contrast between political and market mechanisms is with respect to the relative importance of political vs. human capital. If the market logic and the political logic of redistribution are fundamentally incompatible, as posited in market transition theory, we would expect opposite changes in returns to these two types of capital in the reform era. That is, the increasing role of human capital is associated with the prevalence of market mechanisms, which in turn should diminish returns to political capital.

On the other hand, there are alternative arguments that point to the coexistence of both in the processes of institutional changes. One explanation is the power persistence arguments (Bian & Logan, 1996) that emphasize the continuing role of the state and redistributive institutions in resource allocation and the sustained importance of political capital. We also argue that markets and politics may coevolve in that increasing competitions for talents in the private sector may have induced corresponding increases in returns to education in the state sector, or vice versa. In this light, political and market processes interact in ways that are not necessarily undermining each other. In addition, the advance of markets may also have changed political selection processes, making them merit-based as indicated by the increasing importance of education in the recruitment of party membership and promotion. In this view, then, returns to education may be mediated by the continuing importance of political capital even in the reform era.

> *Hypothesis 2*: If markets and politics coevolve with each other, we should observe that both human capital and political capital have persistent and significant effects on economic rewards over time.

Returns to Education and Occupational Status

If returns to education reflect different logics of resource allocation, we should also observe distinctive patterns of returns to education across different occupational groups. As we noted before, in a redistributive economy, resource allocation is decided by central authorities in accordance with their political and developmental priorities. Those occupations that are close to the central authorities (e.g. administrators) tend to receive higher economic benefits compared with those who are peripheral in the redistributive economy. Along with the expansion of the market economy, alternative principles of resource allocation have emerged, with implications for different patterns of economic rewards. For instance, Cao and Nee (2000, pp. 1175–1176) predict "a decline of the advantage of redistributive power and other forms of political capital *relative* to nonstate economic actors who posses market power" and "new opportunities centered on market activities, for example, entrepreneurship." The empirical evidence of the advantages of entrepreneurs in the previous studies shows support of this line of arguments (Gerber & Hout, 1998; Rona-Tas, 1994; Zhou, 2000a). But these studies also find evidence of the persisting advantages of redistributive positions such as cadre occupations and state firms. Walder (1995) finds that administrators have the most advantageous positions and extensive benefits (see also Bian & Logan, 1996; Rona-Tas, 1994; Zhou, 2000a). Based on cohort analyses, Dickson and Rublee (2000) find that, compared with college education, cadre position brings even higher returns to both regular wage and total income in two cohort groups younger than 40 years old.

What are the implications of these arguments on returns to education? If market mechanisms are effective in allocating resources, we expect to find significant, higher rates of returns to education in those occupations that are close to markets. On the other hand, if state policies also contribute to the increasing role of education, we should expect a similar trend of increasing returns to education in those occupations and organizations that are close to the state. The recognition of the active role of the state leads us to predict that:

Hypothesis 3: There is a parallel increase in returns to education between those occupations and organizations that are close to markets and those that are close to political authorities in the reform era.

Returns to Education across Sectors

In the discussions above, we have proposed to compare and contrast the role of the two alternative mechanisms, markets and politics, along several dimensions – over time, in comparison with returns to human and political capital, and across types of occupations. Perhaps the most direct contrast between the roles of the state and markets is between the state and nonstate sectors (Zang, 2001). As is well known, there has been long a coexistence of a state sector and a nonstate sector in the Chinese economy (Bian, 1994; Lin & Bian, 1991; Zhou, Tuma & Moen, 1997). The state sector includes state firms, public organizations, and government agencies. These organizations are under much stronger influence of state policies than those outside of the state sector. The non-state sector is consisted of private firms, joint venture firms, hybrid firms, as well as collective firms. These types of firms are market-oriented, and they are less affected by regulatory or redistributive policies of the state. Therefore, these two sectors may have developed distinctive channels of resource allocation and reward structures. Evidence shows that there are noticeable income differences across types of work organizations in the reform era. For example, Zhou (2000a) finds that organizations in the state sector (government agencies, public organizations, and state firms) had significant, higher income than those in collective firms and this pattern has not changed in the reform era. At the same time, private/hybrid firms show significant increases in income during the reform process.

What are the implications of these sectoral differences for returns to education? Market transition theory predicts that the emergence of market institutions leads to "higher returns to human capital than under a centrally planned economy" (Cao & Nee, 2000, pp. 1175–1176). In an interesting study of sectoral differences, Zang (2001) advocated this line of argument and found noticeable differences in returns to education in one city in Guangdong Province. This argument implies that the specific channels that affect returns to education may be fundamentally different between a state sector and a nonstate sector. But given the strong advocacy of educational qualification in state personnel policies since the 1980s, we expect that the state sector also witness an increase in returns to education that parallel those in the nonstate sector. That is, competitions from the private sector in recruitment for talents may have forced those organizations in the state sector to increase returns to education and to replicate the practice adopted in the private sector (or vice versa). Therefore, we develop the following hypothesis:

Hypothesis 4: The coevolutionary arguments predict that the competition and diffusion processes lead to parallel patterns of returns to education between the state sector and the non-state sector.

RESEARCH DESIGN

Data

The data used in our study is based on a sample of urban residents drawn from 20 cities through a stratified sampling scheme in 1993 and 1994. First, six provinces were selected, each representing a conventional geographical region in China. Second, within each province, the capital city of the province was chosen to represent large cities (population above 1 million) in that province; and a medium-size city (population between 200,000 and 1 million) and a small city (population below 200,000) were randomly selected based on the 1990 *Yearbook of Chinese Cities* (State Statistics Bureau, 1990). In addition, this data also included Beijing, the political center, and Shanghai, the largest industrial city. Third, within each targeted city, a systematic sampling procedure was used to select every *n*th block and the *n*th household within each selected block. The sample size in each city was proportional to the population of that size of a city in the province. Finally, in each household, a respondent aged 25–65 was chosen based on a random-number table. The data set included a total of 4,600 individuals. Using a pretested questionnaire, we collected information on the life histories of the respondents with regard to their educational experience, experiences in the labor force, and their job characteristics. In addition, we also asked information about their income in specific years. In our analysis, we excluded the information of the respondents after they have retired since their income or labor force behavior could be different from the period when they were still in the labor force.

We collected retrospective information on the respondents' personal income in selected years. For this study, we analyze the respective income data in two specific years: 1978 and 1993. 1978 is the year at the beginning of the economic reform. The characteristics of this year reflected more the legacies of the radical policies of the Cultural Revolution than those of the economic reform. 1993 is the latest year in which we have complete data in our sample. By 1993, China had been 15 years into the economic reform, which allows us to assess the impacts of institutional changes on returns to education in urban China.

Dependent Variable

Income

Our dependent variables are logarithms of both basic and total (monthly) income. "Basic income" refers to the fixed income based on the official salary/wage system. Total income reflects the respondent's basic salary and wage, as well as bonuses, and any additional income gained by the respondent.[1]

Independent Variables

Education

For comparative purpose, we use a standard formula to convert educational levels into "years of schooling." Specifically, we use the following conversion formula: elementary school = 6 years of schooling; junior high = 9 years of schooling; senior high school = 12 years of schooling; junior college = 14 years of schooling; college = 16 years of college; post-graduate degree = 18 years of schooling. Given the fluctuations in China's educational system in the past, this is only an approximation.

Labor Force Duration

We follow the convention and use the following formula to capture one's work experience: labor force duration = age – years of schooling – 6. We use both the first and the second order effects of "labor force duration" to capture the potential life cycle factors in returns to experience.

Occupational Groups

We distinguish the following occupational groups: (1) top managers – heads of the workplace; (2) mid-level managers in a workplace; (3) low-level managers in a workplace; (4) high-rank professionals; (4) low-rank professionals; (5) workers (including clerks, service workers, skilled and unskilled workers); (6) private entrepreneurs.[2] "Workers" are used as the reference category in our analyses. Information with regard to managerial positions in the workplace is based on respondents' self-reported top, mid-, or low-level managerial positions in his/her work organizations. The category of high-rank professionals includes those who are at the rank of "engineer" or above. Low-rank professionals include assistant engineers or technicians.

The State and Non-state Sector

In some analyses, we estimate returns to education for the state and nonstate sectors separately. We include the following types of organization in the state sector: (1) government agencies; (2) public organizations; (3) state firms. The nonstate sector includes collective firms, hybrid firms, joint ventures, and private firms.

For control purpose, we include a dummy variable (female = 1) to capture the gender effect. We also include a set of indicator variables for the 20 cities from which the data was drawn. Table 1 reports the descriptive statistics of the covariates.

Models and Methods

To examine returns to education with respect to income, we begin with the standard human capital model in economics. That is, we first estimate a

Table 1. Descriptive Statistics for Variables Used in the Analysis.

	1978	1993		
	Total	Total	State Sector	Non-state Sector
Total income, inflation adjusted (monthly)	57.7	111.4	111.5	111.2
Basic income, inflation adjusted (monthly)	48.9	51.8	50.8	54.3
Female	46.5	41.4	38.9	47.3
Year of schooling	9.1	10.7	11.1	9.7
Labor force duration	17.9	22.4	22.4	22.5
Occupations[1]				
Top manager	3.4	4.8	4.3	6.0
Midlevel manager	6.2	8.8	10.6	4.7
Low-level manager	10.9	13.3	15.4	8.4
Professional (engineer or above)	3.5	7.6	9.5	3.1
Technician	15.4	14.1	15.9	10.2
Private entrepreneur	0.4	3.5	–	11.2
Worker (including clerk)	66.6	58.8	56.4	64.0
Type of work organization				
Government agency	8.6	10.1	14.6	
Public organization	11.1	12.6	18.1	
Central government firm	51.9	46.8	67.4	
Collective firm	25.6	22.0		72.0
Hybrid firm	1.7	2.6		8.4
Joint Venture	0.1	0.9		2.9
Private firm	1.0	5.1		16.7
N	2,705	3,678	2,555	1,123

Note: Income, labor force duration, year of schooling, and total *N* refer to the means of these variables. All other numbers in the table refer to percentages in the designated category.

[1] Percentages in the occupational categories do not add up to unity because there are overlaps between administrative positions and professional positions. That is, a respondent can be in a managerial position and also be a professional.

Mincerian model in which the logarithm of income is regressed on years of schooling and work experience as follows:

$$\ln Y = \beta_1 + \beta_2 (S) + \beta_3 (\exp) + \beta_4 (\exp)^2 + \varepsilon$$

where "S" indicates "year of schooling" and "exp" indicates experience as measured by "labor force experience."

For further analysis, we then extend the Mincerian model to incorporate information on occupation and workplace locations in the model. In addition, we also include interactions between "year of schooling" and the occupation variables to identify and assess the specific channels that are effective in returns to education. For our research purpose, we will compare statistical models across time (1978 vs. 1993), between sectors (state sector vs. non-state sector), and for different types of income (basic income and total income).

RESULTS

One major finding from the previous studies is that, as Xie and Hannum (1996) pointed out, returns to education in China are low compared with other developing or state socialist societies. They are also noticeably lower than those in market economies.[3] This may in part reflect the allocative principles of the redistributive economy and in part the unique egalitarian policies adopted in Mao's era. This is the starting point of our study.

To set up the context for our study, we first briefly review the empirical findings on returns to education in the previous studies. Although studies of patterns of educational attainment are relatively few (Hannum, 1999; Hannum & Xie, 1994; Zhou, Moen & Tuma, 1998), many studies have examined returns to education in China. Table 2 reports selected findings on returns to education over the last two decades. We only focus on studies in the *urban areas* for the ease of comparison. We note that these studies use different samples, different covariates in their models, and at times different model specifications. Therefore, these estimates are not directly comparable. We summarize these findings as an intuitive device to capture the general patterns.

Table 2 shows, first of all, that there have been a wide range of estimates for the rates of returns to education among these studies. These variations are in part due to the inclusion of different control variables, different model specifications, and different samples at different times. Few studies in Table 2 developed their model specification on the basis of the conventional Micerian human capital model. As a result, these results are not directly comparable with the studies of returns to education in other societies. Most studies included education variables as part of the explanatory models, but did not examine the specific channels through which education takes effect in earnings distribution. Despite the fact that almost all empirical studies of income have included education as part of the causal explanations, there is a lack of sustained attention to the role of education as an analytical focus and there is little accumulation of evidence in this area. We hope that our analyses reported below fill some gaps in the literature.

Table 2. Empirical Studies of Returns of Income to Education in Urban China.

Study	Sample/year	Dependent Variable: ln(income)	Education Variable	Coefficient
Byron & Manaloto (1990)	Nanjing, 1986	Income	Years of Schooling	0.0374***
Walder (1990)	Tianjin, 1986	Salary	Years of schooling	0.087***
		Total income	Years of schooling	0.067*
Peng (1992)	Six cities, 1986	Income	Junior high	−0.011
			Senior high	0.000
			College	0.090*
Walder (1995)	Tianjin, 1986	Salary	High school	0.006
			College	0.089***
		Total Income	High school	0.001
			College	0.039
Xie & Hannum (1996)	National sample, 1988	Total income	Years of schooling	0.029*** (for male)
				0.050*** (for female)
Bian & Logan (1996)	Tianjin, 1988 and 1993	Salary[a]	Education[b]	0.26***
		Total income[a]	Education[b]	0.26***

Table 2. Continued.

Study	Sample/year	Dependent Variable: ln(income)	Education Variable	Coefficient
Dickson & Rublee (2000)	National sample, 1988	Salary	High school	0.007
			College	0.096***
		Total income	High school	0.021***
			College	0.091***
Raymo & Xie (2000)	National sample, 1992	Postretirement income	Years of schooling	0.015***
Zhou (2000a)	National sample, 1993, 1978	Total income	Junior high	0.11***
			Senior high	0.18***
			College	0.17***
		Total income	Junior high	0.04
			High school	0.03
			College	0.07*

[a] The dependent variable in Bian and Logan (1996) is the difference between 1978 and 1988 nominal incomes.

[b] In Bian and Logan's (1996) study, education is measured with an ordinal scale: (1) elementary school and lower; (2) middle school; (3) high school and vocational school; and (4) college and higher.

* $p < 0.1$; ** $p < 0.05$, *** $p < 0.01$.

Changes in Returns to Education over Time

We first present some descriptive information about the average total income for different age groups and at different educational levels. Figures 1 and 2 display the age-wage profiles of urban residents in our sample by educational levels. Compared with the patterns in the United States (see Willis, 1986, p. 530 for a basis of comparison), the Chinese patterns show some striking differences.

Figure 1 shows the mean total income at different educational levels over the respondents' life cycle in 1978, the year at the end of the Cultural Revolution. Because our sample is restricted to those aged 25–65 in 1994, the age range of our sample in 1978 is between 25 and 50. As one can see, those at the college level experienced an increasing trend with age. Those at the senior high level experienced the most fluctuation. For senior high school graduates, the wage for the 25–30 group started at a level even lower than junior high school graduates. This may be due to the impact of the send-down episode, since a large proportion of senior high school graduates were sent to the countryside and returned only recently. The group aged 35–40 experienced income stagnation and slight decline, compared with the group aged 30–35. In contrast, those with junior high or elementary school education showed a general pattern of increasing wage with age.

The pattern changed substantially by 1993, 15 years into the economic reform era (see Fig. 2). Those at the college level had a higher return to their education before 35 than those between 35 and 45, whose average income in fact declined. The 50–55 group appeared to have the largest return. Returns to education for those at senior high level were relatively stable over the entire age range. Both junior high and elementary school graduates experienced greater variations in income across age groups. For the former, the peak of their income is at ages of 50–55, whereas for the latter, the peak of income is at 45–50.

Fluctuations in the age-wage profiles shown in these two figures may partly result from relatively small numbers of cases in our sample. But some of these patterns can be readily explained by changing historical contexts. For instance, the fluctuation of senior high school graduates in 1978 can be directly attributed to the disruptive state policies during the Cultural Revolution period in which 17 million high school graduates were sent to the countryside. Also, the fluctuation of college graduates in 1993 (Fig. 2) shows that the economic reform has disrupted the life course and created opportunities especially for younger generations of college graduates. Clearly, these patterns cannot be adequately explained by a human capital model.

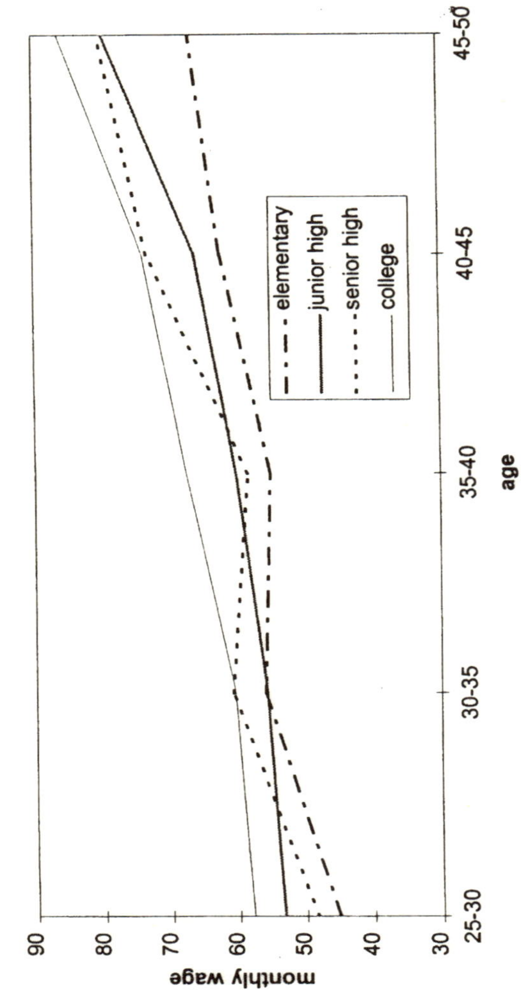

Fig. 1. Age-wage Profiles of Urban Residents by Educational Level, 1978.

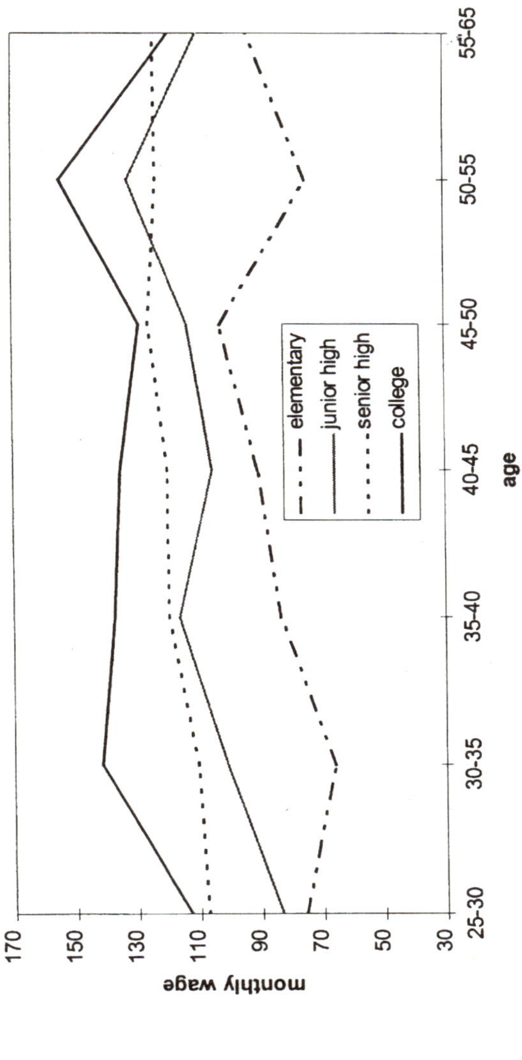

Fig. 2. Age-wage Profiles of Urban Residents by Educational Level, 1993.

We now turn to the OLS regression estimates of the determinants of the wage equation in 1978 and 1993 (see Table 3). We estimated three models for each year. Model 1 for each year is the conventional human capital model. Model 2 incorporates occupational variables in the model. Model 3 adds the interaction terms between year of schooling and occupational status. In our exploratory analyses, we experimented with different functional specifications of education (dummy variables, interactions, and spline functions), none of these alternative specifications shows systematic and significant effects, after including "year of schooling" in the model. Therefore, we only report the results using "year of schooling" variable in the model.

First consider direct returns to education as measured by the coefficient for "year of schooling." In 1978, the rate of return to each year of schooling was about 2.8% (exp[0.028] = 1.028). In 1993, the rate increased to be about 3.7%. Clearly there was a noticeable increase in returns to education in the 15 years of economic transformation in urban China. Although the coefficients for "year of schooling" are markedly different between the two years, our formal test of the quality of coefficients between the two shows that the differences between the two coefficients are only marginally significant (F-statistic = 3.1, $p < 0.08$).[4] It is noticeable that returns to education are relatively low compared with findings in other societies (Cf. Table A2 in Psacharopoulos, 1994, p. 1342). This rate appears to be even not as high as those in the USSR before the collapse of the Soviet Union (see Zhou & Suhomlinova, 2000).

In Model 2 and Model 3, we further examine the specific channels through which education takes effect by including interactions between year of schooling and occupation. First note that, for both years, the inclusion of occupational variables (in Model 2) leads to a downward change in the direct returns to education (coefficients for "year of schooling" in Model 2 for two years as 1978 and 1993). This means that returns to education are confounded with, and partially captured by, one's occupational status. In 1978, the role of education was mainly captured by the direct measure of year of schooling and the role of occupational locations (Model 2). As Model 3 indicates, there is no systematic evidence of variations in returns to education across occupations, as indicated by the interaction terms between occupations and year of schooling, except for lower returns to education to midlevel managers, compared to those to workers (the reference category). The reported R^2 between the two models indicate that there is no improvement in model fit between Model 3 and Model 2.

These patterns have changed in the 15 years of economic reform in China. By 1993, new patterns had emerged. We first consider the role of occupations in Model 2. Adding the set of occupational categories in Model 2 significantly

Table 3. OLS Regression Estimates of Returns to Education in 1978 and 1993.

	1978			1993		
	Model 1	Model 2	Model 3	Model 1	Model 2	Model 3
Intercept	3.222***	3.283***	3.269***	3.966***	4.020***	3.956***
Female	-0.177***	-0.161***	-0.159***	-0.200***	-0.186***	-0.183***
Year of schooling	0.028***	0.022***	0.023***	0.036***	0.028***	0.035***
Labor force duration	0.042***	0.039***	0.040***	0.017***	0.016***	0.015***
LF duration-squared/100	-0.054***	-0.053***	-0.055***	-0.024***	-0.024***	-0.023***
Occupations						
Top manager		0.181***	0.159		0.259***	0.387**
Midlevel manager		0.165***	0.423***		0.133***	0.479***
Low-level manager		0.085***	0.162*		0.041	0.293***
High-rank professional		0.040	-0.252		0.022	0.511***
Low-rank professional		-0.014	-0.076		0.075***	0.281**
Private entrepreneur		–	–		0.531***	-0.267*

Table 3. Continued.

	1978			1993		
	Model 1	Model 2	Model 3	Model 1	Model 2	Model 3
Top manager*schooling			0.002			– 0.012
Mid manager*schooling			– 0.024**			– 0.029***
Low manager*schooling			– 0.007			– 0.022**
High prof*schooling			0.022			– 0.035**
Low prof*schooling			0.005			– 0.017*
Entrepreneur*schooling			–			0.087***
Adj-R^2	0.26	0.27	0.27	0.38	0.41	0.42
N	2,567	2,567	2,567	3,600	3,600	3,600

Note: " 'Worker' is the reference category for occupation", "collective firm" for type of work organization.
In all the models, a set of 19 dummy variables are included to indicate the specific cities in which the data are drawn. All coefficients reported in the table are after controlling for these city ariations.
* $p < 0.10$; ** $p < 0.05$; *** $p < 0.01$.

increases the model fit. The direct effect of education (the coefficient associated with year of schooling) had increased, compared with the same model for 1978. Managerial as well as professional positions all contribute significantly to increases in one's income.

In Model 3, the interactions between year of schooling and occupational status show somewhat surprising patterns. Except for top manager positions, all interaction effects with respect to managerial and professional status show negative effects. That is, returns to education in these positions are lower than those for workers, controlling for the main effects of education and occupational status. In contrast, private entrepreneurs, on average, have lower income than those in collective firms, but there are increasing returns to education for this group, which contribute to the overall higher income level for this group (as shown in Model 2). How do we explain these patterns? One plausible explanation is that, in the reform era, income allocation in formal organizations is mainly based on positional power or official titles associated with positions. Because of the demography of promotions in the past years, many positions were occupied by those in the earlier cohorts with less educational credentials, and younger and more educated employees were still waiting along the promotion ladders. As a result, we observe the negative interaction effects, after controlling for returns to these positions. Private entrepreneurs were free from these organizational constraints and, as a result, they directly captured all the benefits in returns to education.

Finally, it is instructive to compare the general patterns of returns to human capital across the two years. Both education and work experience are major factors in the conventional human capital model. In the 15 years of economic reform in China, patterns of returns to human capital have changed significantly. To illustrate the changing patterns, we plotted the rates of change in returns to year of schooling and to work experience in Fig. 3, based on the parameter estimates in Model 1 for the two years.

As indicated by the two straight lines in Fig. 3, there has been a noticeable increase in the rate of returns to year of schooling between 1978 and 1993. More dramatic changes are observed for returns to work experiences. There was a sharp decline in returns to work experience between 1978 and 1993. The peak year for returns to work experience also changed from nearly 40 years (about 55 years old) in the labor force to about 30 years (on average 48 years old) in the labor force. Over time, we see a gradual shift from an emphasis on seniority (work experience) to formal education, in the process of institutional changes in China. An alternative and plausible interpretation about work experience is that, based on the egalitarian policies of the Mao era, seniority was used as the main criterion in the distribution of economic

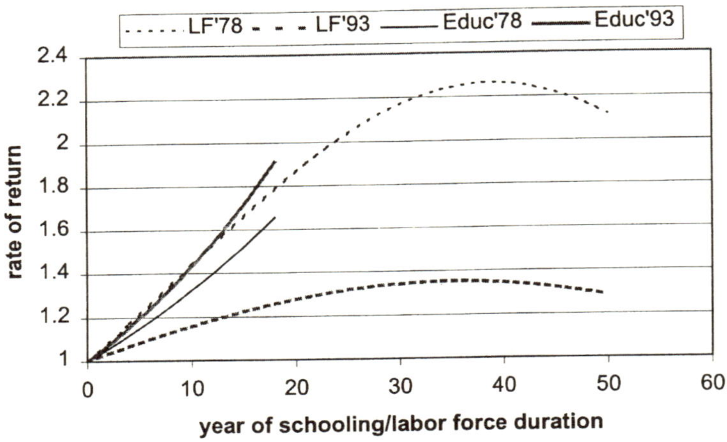

Fig. 3. Rates of Returns to Education and Work Experience.

rewards. This criterion gave away to educational qualification in the reform era. In either case, it is obvious that changes in returns to human capital are remarkable across these two historical contexts.

Comparing with patterns of returns to education in other societies, our findings revealed several unique features of the distribution of economic rewards in urban China: First, returns to education in urban China were markedly lower than in other parts of the world. This is consistent with the view that human resource allocation in a redistributive economy differs significantly than that in a market economy. Recent changes in economic reform have not yet fundamentally changed this pattern. Second, there was a noticeable increase in returns to education between 1978 and 1993, as consistent with H1. This trend, however, cannot be construed as solely driven by market mechanisms, as we discussed before. The increasing returns to administrative positions and especially to professional positions in 1993 suggest that market mechanisms have indeed played a major role in inducing higher returns to those positions that involve ability and productivity. However, the interaction terms in Model 3 show that returns to occupational positions are not necessarily congruent with the effects of education. As we noted before, this pattern may result from the institutional legacy of a mismatch between positions and educational credentials in the past. The positive returns to education for private entrepreneurs are the strongest evidence in support of market transition theory. Thus, the empirical evidence with regard to H3 is mixed. We will revisit this hypothesis in the analyses of sectoral differences later.

Comparison of Returns to Education and Communist Party Membership

Theoretical ideas about returns to education in the literature are often discussed in comparison with political capital, as measured by Communist Party membership. These ideas are formulated in our second hypothesis. We now examine and compare returns to education and to communist party membership.[5] We estimated models that are identical to those reported in Table 2 except that we added the party membership variable. The results are reported in Table 4.

As one can see in Table 4, adding "party membership" in the model did not change the effects of other covariates in any significant way, despite the fact the new analyses omitted 20% of the sample due to missing values in party membership information. The main finding in this set of analyses is that returns to party membership, in Model 1, were stable between the two years. In 1978, being a party member increased one's income by about 11% (exp[0.101] = 1.11). The same rate of returns was observed in 1993. When occupation and the interactions between occupation and education were controlled for, as in Models 2 and 3, returns to party membership appeared to have increased between 1978 and 1993. But our test of equality of coefficients shows that the apparent changes in the corresponding coefficients are not statistically significant at $p < 0.05$. In other words, there were no significant changes in returns to party membership in all three models between the two years. One may argue that, relative to the increasing returns to education over this period of time, returns to party membership has declined. We agree with this argument. But the persistent importance of political capital in the face of significant institutional changes over time also suggests that the political logic and corresponding state policies may not necessarily compete with market mechanisms as in a zero-sum game. In this scenario, an individual may benefit from both human capital and political capital. Therefore, our tentative conclusion is that, although returns to education have increased in the reform era, the importance of political capital has not diminished.

Returns to Education across State and Non-state Sectors

A major area of contention in market transition debates is about the role of education in the allocation of human capital. To address this issue in a more direct way, we now examine returns to education in the state and non-state sector. Specifically, we treat governmental agencies, public organizations, and state firms as belonging to the state sector, and collective firms, hybrid firms, joint ventures and private firms as part of the non-state sector. Work organizations in the state sector tend to be more sensitive to changes in state policies and administrative fiat, whereas organizations in the non-state sector

Table 4. OLS Regression Estimates of Returns to Education in 1978 and 1993 (Party Membership Included).

	1978			1993		
	Model 1	Model 2	Model 3	Model 1	Model 2	Model 3
Intercept	3.244***	3.310***	3.287***	3.987***	4.029***	3.961***
Female	-0.180***	-0.167***	-0.165***	-0.192***	-0.190***	-0.188***
Year of schooling	0.024***	0.018***	0.019***	0.034***	0.027***	0.034***
Labor force duration	0.043***	0.041***	0.042***	0.015***	0.015***	0.015***
LF duration-squared/100	-0.060***	-0.057***	-0.060***	-0.022***	-0.023***	-0.022***
Party Memebrship	0.101***	0.053**	0.051*	0.101***	0.066**	0.057**
Occupations						
Top manager		0.135**	0.099		0.231***	0.380**
Midlevel manager		0.166***	0.456***		0.111***	0.455***
Low-level manager		0.119***	0.157		0.042	0.188
High-rank professional		0.066	-0.325		0.038	0.611***
Low-rank professional		-0.003	-0.008		0.084***	0.254**
Private entrepreneur		–	–		0.516***	-0.211*

	1978			1993		
	Model 1	Model 2	Model 3	Model 1	Model 2	Model 3
Top manager*schooling			0.003			– 0.013
Mid manager*schooling			– 0.026**			– 0.028**
Low manager*schooling			– 0.004			– 0.013
High prof*schooling			0.029			– 0.041***
Low prof*schooling			– 0.001			– 0.015*
Entrepreneur*schooling			–			0.079***
Adj-R^2	0.28	0.29	0.29	0.42	0.44	0.44
N	2,075	2,075	2,075	2,755	2,755	2,755

Note: " 'Worker' is the reference category for occupation", "collective firm" for type of work organization.

In all the models, a set of 19 dummy variables are included to indicate the specific cities in which the data are drawn. All coefficients reported in the table are after controlling for these city variations.

* $p < 0.10$; ** $p < 0.05$; *** $p < 0.01$.

are more subjective to market mechanisms in the allocation of human capital as well as other types of capital. By examining returns to education in these two distinctive sectors, we can uncover if there are distinctive patterns of returns to education between the two areas. However, we hasten to add that this dichotomous categorization is only an approximation. Even within the state sector, work organizations face various extents of market competition. Similarly, firms in the non-state sector also vary in their relations to the political authority. For this comparison, we focus on the patterns in the year of 1993 only. This is because there were fewer private, joint venture or hybrid firms in the non-state sector in 1978, making it impractical to compare the state and non-state sectors.

We estimated OLS models for returns to education in the two sectors separately. In this set of analyses, we estimated models similar to those reported in Table 3 except that we also included indicator variables for different types of work organizations within each sector. The parameter estimates are reported in the first panel of Table 5.[6] In terms of total income, there is a noticeable and large discrepancy in returns to education between the state and the non-state sector. Controlling for other covariates in the models, one additional year of schooling contributes to 1.9% ($\exp[0.019] = 1.019$) of the total income for employees in the state sector, but the rate is 5.7% in the non-state sector. Test of equality of coefficients indicates that this discrepancy is statistically significant (F-statistic = 12.3, $p < 0.01$). This difference is very large, suggesting that returns to education are significantly higher in the non-state sector where the principles of human resource allocation are more governed by market mechanisms. This is consistent with the core prediction in market transition theory.

A closer look at the effects of other covariates shows that, in the state sector, total income is affected by other mechanisms as indicated by the significant effects of managerial positions as well as the high-rank professional position. In contrast, only top managers in the non-state sector receive higher income than the reference category of workers. In the state sector, the interaction terms between these positions and schooling show lower rates of returns to education, compared with those for workers, after controlling for the effects of positions. There is little evidence of the interaction effects in the nonstate sector. This is further evidence in support of our previous speculation that there is a "mismatch" between education and positional power (administrative and professional ranks) in formal organizations. Such organizational factors are especially prevalent in the state sector in which large, formal organizations are concentrated. Even if education plays an important role in these organizations,

Table 5. OLS Regression Estimates of Returns to Education in 1993, by Sector.

	Total Income		Basic Income	
	State sector	Non-State sector	State sector	Non-State sector
Intercept	4.023***	3.684***	2.880***	3.175***
Female	-0.120***	-0.230***	-0.101***	-0.122***
Year of schooling	0.019***	0.056***	0.026***	0.023**
Labor force duration	0.018***	0.019***	0.029***	0.012
LF duration-squared/100	-0.026***	-0.029**	-0.033***	-0.013
Occupations				
Top manager	0.344*	0.696**	0.478**	0.575*
Midlevel manager	0.390***	0.378	0.251*	0.789*
Low-level manager	0.327***	-0.097	0.452***	0.058
High-rank professional	0.384**	0.292	0.436**	0.642
Low-rank professional	0.204	0.514**	0.068	0.005
Top manager* schooling	-0.006	-0.047*	-0.025*	-0.026
Mid manager* schooling	-0.022**	-0.024	-0.010	-0.056
Low manager* schooling	-0.023***	-0.012	-0.033***	-0.001
High prof* schooling	-0.027**	-0.013	-0.025*	-0.046
Low prof* schooling	-0.012	-0.040*	-0.004	0.005

Table 5. Continued.

	Total Income		Basic Income	
	State sector	Non-State sector	State sector	Non-State sector
Type of work organization				
Government agency	−0.068		−0.141	
Public organization	−0.012		−0.279**	
Hybrid firm		−0.112		−0.201
Joint venture		0.727		−0.010
Private firm		0.294*		0.686***
Government*schooling	0.013		0.006	
Public orgn*schooling	0.006		0.015	
Hybrid firm*schooling		0.042**		0.070***
Joint venture*schooling		−0.035		0.032
Private firm*schooling		0.036**		0.009
Adj-R^2	0.39	0.51	0.30	0.29
N	2,526	1,073	2,387	898

Note: " 'Worker' is the reference category for occupation for both sectors". "State firm" is the reference category for type of work organization in the state sector, and "collective firm" for type of work organization.

In all the models, a set of 19 dummy variables are included to indicate the specific cities in which the data are drawn. All coefficients reported in the table are after controlling for these city variations.

* $p < 0.10$; ** $p < 0.05$; *** $p < 0.01$.

mere demographic factors may considerably delay the timing of a favorable match between positions and educational credentials.

The finding that there is a low return to education in the state sector is striking and troublesome. Given the aggressive state policies in emphasizing educational credentials since the 1980s, does this finding imply that these policies were merely symbolic or ineffective at all? To further explore this issue, we conducted additional analyses and examined the determinants of *basic income*. In China, basic income is largely determined by the administrative system and reflects the principles of human resource allocation and rewards in the corresponding state policies. In contrast, bonus, which constitutes an increasingly large proportion of one's total income captures performances by one's workplace and is less related to state policies. Generally, compared with regular salary, total income (including bonus and subsidy) or bonus and subsidy share are poorly explained by the conventional models, and are less closely associated with education (Bian & Logan, 1996; Dickson & Rublee, 2000; Xie & Hannum, 1996; Walder, 1990). Therefore, to assess the role of the state policies in returns to education, it is more instructive to consider the determinants of basic income.

Indeed, the story in the determinants of basic income is quite different. The determinants of basic income reported in the second panel of Table 5 show that, in terms of basic income, returns to education are comparable between the state and the non-state sector. (The test of equality of coefficient shows that there is no statistically discernible difference between the two.) This finding provides indirect evidence that, as far as basic income is concerned, the role of education is comparable between the state sector and the non-state sector, after controlling for other covariates in the models. In other words, both markets and state policies promote the role of education in the reform era and both exert influence to increase returns to education.

To sum up, there is strong evidence in support of the main arguments in market transition theory that returns to education are significantly higher in those organizations that are more governed by market mechanisms. Comparisons of returns to basic income partially support our argument that the state and state policies also actively promote the role of education. It appears that the noticeable differences in returns to education in the state and non-state sectors can be attributed to the increasing role of firms in determining their wages and benefits within their firms, which are largely governed by market mechanisms. We interpret the evidence to suggest that, as far as returns to education are concerned, both market mechanisms and state policies exert effects in the same direction. These trends may result from interactions and co-adaptation between the two. For instance, benefits of the welfare program in the state sector (e.g.

housing) may have induced the non-state sector to increase returns to education to attract able employees away from the state sector.

DISCUSSION AND CONCLUSION

In this study, we take returns to education as an analytical focus to examine multiple mechanisms underlying institutional changes and to assess the direction and pace of changes in urban China in a 15-year time span, between 1978 and 1993. We estimated returns to education in urban China in terms of both the direct path of wage determination, and the specific channels through which the role of education takes effect, such as occupational status and sectoral differences. The main findings show that returns to education have indeed increased substantially in the reform era and the increase is especially salient in the non-state sector where market mechanisms prevail. Among occupational groups, returns to education increase especially with entrepreneurial status. These findings render support to the main predications derived from Nee's market transition theory.

We also want to call attention to the complexities and subtleties of institutional changes when interpreting the findings in our study. First, returns to education are only part of the human capital model. Work experience is another important component in the conventional human capital model. As Fig. 3 shows, there is a higher return to work experience in 1978 than in 1993. Parameter estimates in Table 5 also indicates that there is a higher rate of return to work experience in the state sector than in the non-state sector. There are many factors that may contribute to these patterns. If returns to seniority reflected egalitarian policies of the state in the Mao era, then the decline of such returns shows evidence of shifting from political mechanisms to market mechanisms. An alternative interpretation is based on the self-selection processes. That is, those with more work experience tend to stay in the state sector, whereas those who are more educationally qualified tend to move to the nonstate sector where returns to education are more competitive. Seen in this light, the patterns associated with the effects of work experience and education may indicate two distinctive and parallel returns to human capital, in which market mechanisms reward only the component of formal education. This is an important empirical issue. Unfortunately we cannot reach a definitive conclusion given the information in our data.

Second, to understand returns to education in China, one needs to consider multiple redistributive channels and the role of education in access to these channels. In a market economy, economic rewards are much more transparent, often in the form of monetary rewards (wage rate). In a redistributive economy, a large proportion of resources is redistributed by state institutions (occupations and organizations). Therefore, it is important to examine how educational credentials facilitate or inhibit one's access to these institutions. Indeed, as we have shown elsewhere, education has played an important role in entry into, job shifts across, and promotion within, administrative and professional positions and these patterns are especially prevalent in the state sector (Zhou, 2001; Zhou, Tuma & Moen, 1997). Other studies also show similar patterns (Walder, 1995; Walder, Li & Treiman, 2000). Returns to education in the state sector are also indirectly captured by returns to these administrative and professional positions. In this light, there are good reasons to speculate that the analytical focus on returns to education in earnings in our study underestimates the importance of education in one's economic benefits. This is especially true for employees in the state sector.

Finally, several findings also point to the persistence of the political logic and state policies in resource allocation. Returns to party membership did not decline over the 15-year time span. As far as basic income is concerned, where the influence of state policies is most effective, returns to education are comparable to those in the non-state sector. As we noted before, the significant returns to administrative/professional positions in the state sector may be in part attributed to the role of education. Therefore, the evidence does suggest an active role of state policies in the direction of promoting the importance of education in allocating and rewarding human resources.

These qualifications notwithstanding, we want to emphasize the main finding that, despite the still marked low returns to education in urban China, recent institutional changes have caused and are reflected in increasing returns to education. We believe that this trend has been continuing since 1993. At the same time, the continuing significance of political capital and occupational status associated with positions indicate that the state and state policies also contribute positively to the increasing role of education in the allocation of human resources in the presence of market expansion. As we discussed before, we suspect that there is a mismatch between education and administrative/ professional positions, as indicated by the negative interaction effects between the two. This was due to demographic factors in promoting more educated personnel into higher administrative/professional ranks. If this "mismatch" hypothesis is valid, we should observe more positive returns to education through these positions in more recent years as educational credentials and the occupancy of administrative/professional positions are better aligned over time. Such delayed effects of state policies were not captured in our data, which ended in 1993.

Given these considerations, we find it more instructive to consider the interactions between markets and politics in a coevolutionary framework. These different mechanisms may compete with each other; but at a different level they may also mutually adapt to and reinforce each other. For example, it is not difficult to imagine that the competition for able employees in the non-state sector causes the flow of talents from the state sector to the non-state sector after the job barriers have disappeared. However, it is plausible that organizations in the state sector may adjust their own incentive structures to retain employees and to attract able employees from other organizations. We suspect that the high salaries in the non-state sector partly result from inter-sector competition, especially in response to the presence of significant latent benefits in the state sector (e.g. housing, medical and labor insurance). In this process, the role of competition from the non-state sector induces changes in allocative mechanisms in the state sector. This scenario suggests that the interactions between the two sectors are likely to induce institutional changes in both rather than one undermining the other. This line of reasoning is consistent with the empirical patterns revealed in this study. In this sense, it is useful for us to move away from treating political and market processes as fundamentally incompatible and to appreciate more complicated interactions between the two and their consequences for the emergence of new institutional forms and new stratification orders.

NOTES

1. In labor economics, wage rate or weekly wage is often used because these wage rates measure more precisely productivity-related rewards. In the Chinese context, since most urban employees are full-time workers, monthly wage serves the same purpose well.

2. The categories of "managers" in this study differ from the categories of "high-rank" or "low-rank" cadres in our previous studies (e.g. Zhou, 2000a) that were based on the official national administrative ranking system. We made these adjustments because, in the analysis of sectoral differences, the official ranking system applies only to the state sector, making it infeasible to compare with the non-state sector in our study.

3. For instance, using the 1960 census data, Mincer (1974) estimated a return of 10% for each additional year of schooling.

4. Although the coefficients for the same variables across subsamples (e.g. for 'year of schooling') may differ, this discrepancy may be due to either genuine changes over time or sampling variability between the two subsamples. Therefore, one needs to conduct formal test of equality of coefficient to ascertain that the observed differences between the two coefficients are not caused by sampling variability.

5. Because party membership information is missing in six cities in our data (about 20% of the sample), we estimated separate statistical models for the analyses in which party membership variable was included.

6. We also estimated a model with party membership included in the model. The inclusion of party membership does not affect the effects of other covariates significantly. Party membership contributes significantly to income in the state sector but its effect is not statistically significant in the non-state sector. This is largely due to the fact that there are relatively fewer party members in the non-state sector and they tended to be concentrated in the low-pay collective firms.

ACKNOWLEDGMENTS

An earlier version of this study was presented at a conference on "Educational Reform in China" at Harvard University and at the RC-28 Conference at Berkeley in the summer of 2001. We thank Emily Hannum, Kevin Leicht, Donald Treiman, Yu Xie, and participants at these meetings for their helpful comments. This research is supported by a grant from the National Science Foundation (SBR-9413540), an ASA/NSF fund for the advancement of the discipline, and a Spencer Fellowship. We are grateful to the Department of Sociology at Fudan University and the People's University, the Institute of Sociology at Tianjin Academy of Social Sciences and, in particular, Weida Fan, Qiang Li, Yunkang Pan, and Xizhe Peng for their assistance in data collection.
Direct communication to Wei Zhao, Department of Sociology, Duke University, NC 27708, or via email to wzhao@soc.duke.edu.

REFERENCES

Becker, G. S. (1964). *Human Capital: A Theoretical and Empirical Analysis, with Special Reference to Education*. New York: Columbia University Press.

Bian, Y. (1994). *Work and Inequality in Urban China*. Albany, NY: State University of New York Press.

Bian, Y., & Logan, J. R. (1996). Market Transition and the Persistence of Power: The Changing Stratification System in Urban China. *American Sociological Review*, *61*, 739–758.

Blau, P. M., & Duncan, O. D. (1967). *The American Occupational Structure*. New York, NY: Wiley.

Byron, R. P., & Manaloto, E. Q. (1990). Returns to Education in China. *Economic Development and Cultural Change*, *38*, 783–796.

Cao, Y., & Nee, V. G. (2000). Comment: Controversies and Evidence in the Market Transition Debate. *American Journal of Sociology*, *105*, 1175–1189.

Dickson, B. J., & Rublee, M. R. (2000). Membership Has Its Privileges: The Socioeconomic Characteristics of Communist Party Members in Urban China. *Comparative Political Studies*, *33*, 87–112.

Gerber, T., & Hout, M. (1998). More Shock than Therapy: Market Transition, Employment, and Income in Russia: 1991–1995. *American Journal of Sociology*, *104*, 1–50.

Guthrie, D. (1997). Between Markets and Politics: Organizational Responses to Reform in China. *American Journal of Sociology, 102*, 1258–1304.

Hannum, E. (1999). Political Change and the Urban-Rural Gap in Basic Education in China: 1949–1990. *Comparative Education Review, 43*, 193–211.

Hannum, E., & Xie, Y. (1994). Trends in Educational Gender Inequality in China: 1949–1985. *Research in Social Stratification and Mobility, 13*, 73–98.

Hout, M. (1988). More Universalism, Less Structural Mobility: The American Occupational Structure in the 1980s. *American Journal of Sociology, 93*, 1358–1400.

Konrad, G., & Szelényi, I. (1979). *The Intellectuals on the Road to Class Power.* New York: Harcourt, Brace, Jovanovich.

Lee, H. (1991). *From Revolutionary Cadres to Party Technocrats in Socialist China.* Berkeley, CA: University of California Press.

Li, T., & Zhang, J. (1998). Returns to Education under Collective and Household Farming in China. *Journal of Development Economics, 56*, 307–335.

Lin, N., & Bian, Y. (1991). Getting Ahead in Urban China. *American Journal of Sociology, 97*, 657–688.

Mincer, J. (1974). *Schooling, Experience and Earnings.* New York, NY: Columbia University Press.

Nee, V. (1989). A Theory of Market Transition: From Redistribution to Markets in State Socialism. *American Sociological Review, 54*, 663–681.

Nee, V. (1991). Social Inequalities in Reforming State Socialism: Between Redistribution and Markets in State Socialism. *American Sociological Review, 56*, 267–282.

Nee, V. (1996). The Emergence of a Market Society: Changing Mechanisms of Stratification in China. *American Journal of Sociology, 101*, 908–949.

Nee, V., & Matthews, R. (1996). Market Transition and Societal Transformation in Reforming State Socialism. *Annual Review of Sociology, 22*, 401–435.

Parish, W. L., & Michelson, E. (1996). Politics and Markets: Dual Transformations. *American Journal of Sociology, 101*, 1042–1059.

Peng, Y. (1992). Wage Determination in Rural and Urban China: A Comparison of Public and Private Industrial Sectors. *American Sociological Review, 57*, 198–213.

Psacharopoulos, G. (1994). Returns to Investment in Education: A Global Update. *World Development, 22*, 1325–1343.

Raymo, J. M., & Xie, Y. (2000). Income of the Urban Elderly in Postreform China: Political Capital, Human Capital, and the State. *Social Science Research, 29*, 1–24.

Rona-Tas, A. (1994). 'The First Shall Be Last?' Entrepreneurship and Communist Cadres in the Transition from Socialism. *American Journal of Sociology, 100*, 40–69.

Stark, D. (1996). Recombinant Property in East European Capitalism. *American Journal of Sociology, 101*, 993–1027.

State Statistical Bureau, PRC (SSB) (1990). *Yearbook of Chinese Cities.* Beijing, China: China Statistical Publishing House.

Walder, A. G. (1986). *Communist Neo-Traditionalism: Work and Authority in Chinese Industry.* Berkeley and Los Angeles: University of California Press.

Walder, A. G. (1990). Economic Reform and Income Distribution in Tianjin: 1976–1986. In: D. Davis & E. F. Vogel (Eds), *Chinese Society on the Eve of Tiananmen* (pp. 135–156). Cambridge, MA: Harvard University Press.

Walder, A. G. (1992). Property Rights and Stratification in Socialist Redistributive Economies. *American Sociological Review, 57*, 524–539.

Walder, A. G. (1995). Career Mobility and the Communist Political Order. *American Sociological Review, 60*, 309–328.

Walder, A. G., Li, B., & Treiman, D. J. (2000). Political And Life Chances in a State Socialist Regime: Career Paths into the Urban Chinese Elite: 1949 to 1996. *American Sociological Review, 65*, 191–209.

Willis, R. J. (1986). Wage Determinants: A Survey and Reinterpretation of Human Capital Earnings Functions. In: O. Ashenfelter & R. Layard (Eds), *Handbook of Labor Economics* (Vol. 1, Chap. 10). Amsterdam: Elsevier Science Publishers BV.

Xie, Y., & Hannum, E. (1996). Regional Variation in Earnings Inequality in Reform-Era Urban China. *American Journal of Sociology, 101*, 950–992.

Zang, X. (2001). Labor Market Segmentation and Income Inequality in Urban China. *Sociological Quarterly* (forthcoming).

Zhou, X. (1995). Partial Reform and the Chinese Bureaucracy in the Post-Mao Era. *Comparative Politics Studies, 28*, 440–468.

Zhou, X. (2000a). Economic Transformation and Income Inequality in Urban China: Evidence from Panel Data. *American Journal of Sociology, 105*, 1135–1174.

Zhou, X. (2000b). Reply: Beyond the debate and toward substantive institutional analysis. *American Journal of Sociology, 105*, 1189–1195.

Zhou, X. (2001). Political Dynamics and Bureaucratic Career Patterns in the People's Republic of China: 1949–1994. *Comparative Political Studies, 34*, 1036–1062.

Zhou, X., Moen, P., & Tuma, N. B. (1998). Educational Stratification in Urban China: 1949–1994. *Sociology of Education, 71*, 199–222.

Zhou, X., & Suhomlinova, O. (2000). Redistribution under State Socialism: A USSR and PRC Comparison. *Research in Social Stratification and Mobility, 18*, 163–204.

Zhou, X., Tuma, N. B., & Moen, P. (1997). Institutional Change and Job-Shift Patterns in Urban China: 1949 to 1994. *American Sociological Review, 62*, 339–365.

MARKETIZATION AND INCOME DISTRIBUTION IN URBAN CHINA, 1988 AND 1995

Yanjie Bian and Zhanxin Zhang

ABSTRACT

Marketization is both a central and a controversial term in the ongoing debate about the socioeconomic consequences of market reforms in China and elsewhere. We present a view that China's course of marketization has been an interactive process of market growth and state transformation. We quantitatively measure intercity variation in labor and capital marketization and examine income returns to positional power and human capital with national survey data from the 1988 and 1995 Chinese Household Income Projects. Our analyses show that over the seven-year period: (1) income differential increases between workers in the monopoly and open sectors; (2) income returns to such positional power as Communist party membership and cadre status increases; (3) income returns to human capital as measured by education and professional competence increase; and (4) 1995 income returns to measures of positional power and human capital are significantly higher in cities where labor and capital markets are more developed.

INTRODUCTION

Marketization is both a central and a controversial term in the ongoing debate about the socioeconomic consequences of market reforms in China and

The Future of Market Transition, Volume 19, pages 377–415.

ISBN: 0-7623-0835-4

elsewhere (Nee, 1989, 1991, 1996; Walder, 1994, 1996; Rona-Tas, 1994; Lin, 1995; Bian & Logan, 1996; Parish & Michelson, 1996; Szelényi & Kostello, 1996; Xie & Hannum, 1996; Gerber & Hout, 1998; Zhoum 2000). While no one disputes that "market" has emerged, grown, and been a driving force for societal transformations in China, there is noted disagreement as to how to define and measure market forces and exactly what implications the process of marketization may and may not have (see reviews by Nee & Matthews, 1996; Nee & Cao, 1999). So far, marketization has been explicitly or implicitly equated to passage of time (Nee, 1989, 1991; Bian & Logan, 1996; Gerber & Hout, 1998; Zhou, 2000), approximated by economic growth (Xie & Hannum, 1996), or indicated by distinctive groupings of localities that are nominally evaluated into different modes of market exchange (Nee, 1996; Parish & Michelson, 1996). These inconsistent operationalizations of marketization are in part the reason for controversial empirical analyses and conflicting theoretical conclusions (see reviews in Szelényi & Kostello, 1996; Nee & Matthews, 1996; Cao & Nee, 2000).

Capitalizing on both aggregate statistics and two comparable national sampling household surveys of urban China – 1988 and 1995 Chinese Household Income Project (henceforth CHIP) – we measure *level of marketization* and examine its impact on income distribution among wage earners. We proceed with two analytical strategies. First, because of the tremendous growth of product, labor, and capital markets after 1992, we use multiple regression models to conduct a trend analysis comparing 1988 and 1995 CHIP surveys for two sets of determinants of income distribution: (1) individual-level variables that measure a wage earner's gender, age, education, and party membership; and (2) structural variables that measure a wage earner's position in the occupational and economic structures. Second, given China's vast regional variation in pace of reforms and socioeconomic developments, we quantitatively measure level of marketization across 55 cities, taking into account intercity variation in labor markets, capital markets, and economic growth. The impact on income determination of these city-level measures is then estimated in hierarchical linear models using the 1995 CHIP data. Our analyses are guided by a view that China's course of marketization has been an interactive process of market growth and state transformation.

THREE PERSPECTIVES ON MARKETIZATION

The market transition debate offers a number of themes about the nature and consequences of China's marketization, which can be grouped into three theoretically distinctive perspectives: (1) Marketization is the process through which the mode of resource allocation is shifted from redistribution to market domination; (2) Marketization is a dual transformation of political and economic institutions; and (3) Marketization is a process of property rights reassignments.

Nee (1989, 1991, 1996) has made a bold statement for the first perspective. In his theory of market transition (1989), Nee refers to markets as a qualitatively different mode of resource allocation from that of redistribution in state socialism and to marketization as the increasing proportion of mutual voluntary exchanges between economic transactors. Under state redistribution, argues Nee, "surplus is appropriated from producers through the non-market trade of labor and commodities and redistributed by administrative processes," benefiting those with redistributive power (i.e. cadres) "since redistributors tend to favor their own" (p. 678). In contrast, in market economy "a greater share of the surplus is retained by direct producers" (p. 666). Therefore "the transition from redistribution to markets involves a transfer of power [control over resources] favoring direct producers relative to redistributors" (p. 667). Nee identifies some important corresponding changes in stratification mechanisms: increasing returns to entrepreneurship and human capital and decreasing returns to positional power of redistributors. In his further statement, Nee is more cautious about the pace and incompleteness of China's reforms (1991) and more assertive about *relative* change in income returns between political power and entrepreneurial and human capital (1996). Nevertheless, Nee is consistent in his argument that marketization is a "societal force" and the decisive source of transformation (Nee & Cao, 1999; Cao & Nee, 2000).

While Nee regards market as the agent of change, his critics argue that politics, too, is an undeniable source of transformation (Walder, 1995; Bian & Logan, 1996; Parish & Michelson, 1996; Zhou, 2000). For these researchers, "pure" marketization never occurred in China because marketization itself has been a dual transformation of political and economic institutions. For example, local governments surprisingly have become central players of market-oriented economies and have been seen as primary sources of economic change and growth (Walder, 1995). Market reform has been found to be subject to a political logic of control and stability (Shirk, 1993), producing coexistent hierarchical and market mechanisms in income distribution that gives rise to the persistence of political power (Bian & Logan, 1996). The growth of economic markets has been accompanied by and led to "political markets" – bargaining between interest groups active in emerging market economies. This dual transformation protects vested interests and maintains the old order (Parish & Michelson, 1996). To Zhou (2000), the expansion of markets has *not* been a self-evolving process, but is associated with political interests, producing a co-evolutionary transformation governed by two mechanisms simultaneously: market forces that compete against and undermine the redistributive economy and interest politics that influences market development through establishing, enforcing, and changing institutional arrangements.

Recognizing the institutional complexities and variations of China's emerging economic order, Walder (1994, 1996; Walder & Oi, 1999) proposed that marketization be redefined in reference to property rights reassignments. "The shift to market allocation per se has no inherent consequences for the allocation of power and income" (1996, p. 1061), but the arrangements and enforcement of property rights in productive assets do. Walder provides a pair of scenarios to illustrate his argument. When rural households are reassigned the rights to use land, to claim residual income from crops, and to lease out their land for rents, this marketization process benefits ordinary peasants and reduces the power of village cadres, resulting in a destratified distribution of income. If, however, productive assets are not easily dividable, as in industry, those rights – control, income, and transfer – over industrial properties are likely to be reassigned from state bureaucracies to local governments (villages, townships, and urban districts) and enterprises. During this kind of marketization process, local officials and enterprise managers rather than "direct producers" gain power and collect rewards. Walder contends that these two different processes of marketization imply that the changing order of stratification can be in multiple directions, contingent upon concrete "property rights regimes" that are both confined to and vary widely across organizations and communities (see case studies in Oi & Walder, 1999).

A MARKET-STATE INTERACTION VIEW

Our argument is that China's economic transition has been an interactive process of market growth and state transformation. Building on the views of market-hierarchy coexistence (Bian & Logan, 1996), dual transformation of economic and political markets (Parish & Michelson, 1996), and market-politics coevolution (Zhou, 2000), we emphasize two features of China's market and state interactive process. First, marketization is a multifaceted, historical process of market expansion and penetration into product, labor, and capital markets. Thus, we can take analysis from a conceptual abstraction and characterization to the operational levels that allow for a quantitative assessment of the impacts of kinds of market growth on income distribution. Second, along the growth of different kinds of markets, the Communist party-state transforms itself in order to protect its interest and retain its influence in the growing market economies. Therefore, we must examine the specific ways in which state transformation occurred and the consequences on income distribution. Guided by this market-state interaction view, our overall prediction is that under a growing economy such as China's, there will be a pattern of parallel increases: the increasing income returns to human capital because of growing market mechanisms and the increasing income returns to positional power because of the continuing influence of the Communist party-state in the economy. The aggregate result is increasing inequality in income distribution.

Marketization as a Multifaceted, Historical Process

Commenting on the market transition debate, Szelényi and Kostello (1996) offer a typology about three types of "market penetration" into the socialist redistributive economy. The first is penetration of market forces into local commodity markets, the periphery of the redistributive economy. This type of market penetration is not conceivably subjected to politics because elites never were producers or sellers of the commodities processed in these markets. The second type is penetration of legalized private economic activities into scale production, creating a "socialist mixed economy." This mixed economy is highly influenced by political elites who, with reduced risks and increasing profitability of entrepreneurship, are central economic players in the expanded market activities. The third type of market penetration occurs when the entire state sector is privatized. Szelényi and Kostello assessed that this last change occurred in East Europe after 1989 but had not appeared in China by 1996.

Implied in this typology is the view that marketization is a multifaceted, historical process in which kinds of markets grow through different historical trajectories. This view applies to China, where local commodity markets emerged in cities in the early 1980s when the state began to allow sales of agricultural products and food items by peasants and urban peddlers in what were termed "agricultural trade markets" (*nong mao shichang*). The success of these markets led to their quick spread to urban neighborhoods; the steady growth of private stores, shops, vendors, restaurants, and other service outlets; and, in the end, the diminished role of state plans in an open-price market for consumer goods and industrial products throughout Chinese cities. By the mid-1990s, "the Chinese economy has been transformed from a typical planned one into one in which the market plays a major role in resource allocation" (Lin, Cai & Li, 1996, p. 3). In the *product market*, Nee's version of marketization meets Walder's specifications: sellers all have a bundle of property rights; they control their assets, process sales, and retain after-tax earnings.

Labor markets, on the other hand, took a long, bumpy road to "grow out of the plan" (Naughton, 1995). Under Mao, urban workers were assigned jobs, and no one had private rights for choosing or switching between occupations or places of work (Walder, 1986; Davis, 1990; Bian, 1994). This bureaucratic control and allocation of labor was little affected in the 1980s when labor markets were given limited room to grow in forms of self-employment and employment in the revived domestic and foreign private sector (Gold, 1990). "Expert markets" were created to facilitate job mobility of a small number of professionals and technicians (Davis, 1990). These changes, though small, paved the way to the rise of labor markets after 1992, when labor control policies were finally relaxed to allow job searches and job switching at free will (Bian, 1999). Consequently, peasant labor entered the cities, surplus workers left the state sector, either by force or choice, and new-entry job seekers flooded labor markets (Yuan & Fang, 1998; Ma, 2001). Since 1995, stagnated state-owned enterprises have not done much hiring, but fast growing non-state economies have become the main employers absorbing labor supply in all cities, particularly those in coastal areas.

If the labor market grew slowly, capital markets lagged behind. In the 1980s, capital flow was subject to a state-tailored investment process (Walder, 1992), bank loan allocations and interest were bureaucratically coordinated (Shirk, 1993). There were a few breakthroughs: informal credit and loan markets quietly emerged in some areas (Liu, 1992) and foreign investments began to take a role in coastal developmental zones (Lardy, 1989). The new wave of reforms since 1992 sparked more lively capital flow: stock exchange markets opened in Shanghai and Shenzhen, foreign investments grew rapidly throughout coastal regions (Cheng, 1996), and informal credit and loan markets became much more active (Lardy, 1998, p. 126). These developments were not without government restrictions, however. The banking system, although experiencing change, still hindered the entire reform (Lardy, 1998), stock market securities issuing was limited to state enterprises, and the stock market operated under comprehensive government monitoring. On the whole, capital market was born but grew under the shadow of government bureaucracies, thus it was subject to political bargaining and rent seeking by officials (Lin, Cai & Li, 1996, pp. 203–208).

Marketization with State Transformation

While gradually losing its "traditional" redistributive character, the Chinese party-state has adjusted and shifted its role in the economy in three meaningful ways. First, in response to rapid marketization in all economic spheres, the state substantially modified its functions in order to intervene in the growing market economies. Reflecting this change is the slogan that the state government changed its administrative functions "from direct regulation and control" (through state planning and government organs of industrial ministries) to "indirect regulation and control" (through central banks and market regulations). Substantial changes occurred in the 1990s when the central state restructured government administration and reallocated state officials at both central and local levels. During this restructuring, the central government's industrial ministries, which were in charge of economic production, were either closed or transformed into economic companies.

Second, in response to market penetration, the state has maintained close control over industries vital to the political interests of Communist rule. From the early 1980s to the mid-1990s, industries that gradually opened to market penetration were commerce, service, construction, and manufacturing. Other industries that provide nationalized products and services (e.g. postal and telecommunication, railroad transportation, electric power), exercise macro economic coordination (e.g. banking and finance), or play key roles in political and ideological control (e.g. education, mass media, "social mass organizations") remained highly restricted to state operations. Consequently, by the late 1980s China's industries became divided into two sectors: a state monopoly sector that is exclusively operated by state organizations and retains monopoly profits and an "open sector" that allows for competition between and among state and non-state entities.

Finally, through a process of "inside privatization" (He, 1998), the state gradually devolved executive rights over state properties to enterprise-level cadres. The devolvement went through several forms, from a factory director responsibility system, to a performance-based contract system, and to the latest development of a managers-as-shareholders system (Naughton, 1995; Oi & Walder, 1999). As a result, these cadres obtained income rights and earnings from their positional power. Much of this positional power lies in the entrepreneurial ability and managerial competence of incumbent cadres because they must continue proving their ability to manage their enterprises to earn profits in an increasing competitive economy. Even within the state monopoly sector, generating profits has become a criterion for evaluating incumbent cadres (Lin & Zhang, 1999). However, cadres are nevertheless nominated, screened, and appointed by their party authorities and government jurisdictions, thus ensuring the continuation of party clientelism (Wank, 1999): In competition for a profitable post, rank-and-file cadres must first ensure and maintain their political loyalties to appointing authorities, which makes it inadequate to treat administrative expertise as a pure form of human capital as argued elsewhere (Cao & Nee, 2000, p. 807). But reform-era cadres do differ from pre-reform redistributors. Whereas pre-reform redistributors maintained their income privileges merely because of their positions in the party-state apparatus, reform-era cadres must actively make use of the authority they hold to "earn" income one way or another. To be sure, "old-fashioned" redistributors are becoming increasingly irrelevant in reform-era China.

Empirical Implications for Income Distribution: Research Hypotheses

When labor markets were absent or limited, income returns for education did not vary between more marketized and less marketized regions in the 1980s (Xie & Hannum, 1996; Parish & Michelson, 1996).[1] The growth of labor markets after 1992 implies that greater bargaining resources are conferred by individuals' labor rights for compensation. This means, as Nee's market transition theory predicts, increasing returns for such human capital as entrepreneurship ability, professional competence, and higher education. But the growth of labor markets did not necessarily limit the power of Communist party members and, more important, cadres – party officials, state administrators, and state enterprise managers. First, in "internal" labor markets within organizations, party members may secure advantageous positions and cadres control the labor of others and exercise income rights over state properties. In "external" labor markets, party and state cadres extract lucrative gains through "moonlighting jobs" because of their positional power and social-political connections. These scenarios suggest that:

Hypothesis 1: The more developed the labor market, the higher the returns to such human capital as education, professional competence, and entrepreneurship.

Hypothesis 2: The more developed labor market will also increase the returns to such positional power as Communist party membership and cadre status.

The expansion of capital markets, mostly driven by foreign investments, leads to a more complex property arrangements and organizational forms, valuing entrepreneurship, professional training, and technical competence. Thus, the greater the capital market, the greater the returns to entrepreneurial and professional abilities. The emergence of capital markets has reduced bureaucratic allocation of finances and in so doing, undermined the redistributive power of cadres. Yet it also provides opportunities for administrative and economic elites to engage in rent seeking, self-serving funds appropriation, and other lucrative activities to capture "unproductive income" (Lin, 2000).

Because of these new sources of power resulting from the expansion of capital market, the development of capital markets is likely to increase income returns to the positional power of cadres. Thus:

> *Hypothesis 3*: The growth of capital markets tends to increase income returns to education, professional competence, and entrepreneurship.

> *Hypothesis 4*: The growth of capital markets also tends to increase income returns to Communist party membership and cadre status.

During marketization, the power and privileges of economic organizations have been historically restructured. Economic organizations in the monopolized sector, all under the institutional umbrella of "state ownership," were largely contained in the redistributive framework in the 1980s, having high dependence on government control and limited ways of generating income outside the plan. But after1992 the situation changed significantly. Enterprises in the monopoly sector began to produce high-profit margins because of their monopoly in fast-growing product markets, and administrative agencies, because of their regulatory power, began to create and collect rents from the economic entities under their jurisdiction (Lin & Zhang, 1999; Duckett, 2001). These profits and rents largely translate into monetary and non-monetary incomes for administrators, managers, and ordinary employees, maintaining income privileges in the monopoly sector.

State enterprises in the open sector are in a completely different situation. Without state protection many of these enterprises cannot survive the market competition brought by fast-growing non-state entities. In the 1980s, non-state actors, mostly household businesses and small firms, were in initial stages of development, and state organizations were protected by the redistributive policies of the government in the provision of raw materials, financial subsidies, investment capitals, and bank loans (Wong, Heady & Woo, 1995; Cheng, 1996; Lardy, 1998). These favorable policies enabled state enterprises to retain relatively high profits and wage levels. During the wave of economic reforms after 1992, the redistributive provisions of economic resources to state organizations were discontinued when the central government hardened the budgets for state enterprises (Hua, 1997). Market competition became "fairer" in the open sector industries, but it was also intensified as non-state actors, now sizable firms with both foreign and domestic investments, became the new sources of economic growth. These two forces – decline of redistributive protection and growth of nonstate actors – combined to weaken the economic position of state enterprises in the open sector after 1992. These statements lead to our final set of hypotheses:

Hypothesis 5: Post-1992 reforms resulted in economic segmentation of industries in which state-run organizations in the monopoly sector began to maintain a high level of income relative to that of state-run organizations in the open sector.

Hypothesis 6: As a new, competitive force, nonstate organizations maintain a high income level relative to that of state organizations in the open sector, but they may not produce higher income relative to state organizations in the monopoly sector after 1992.

Hypothesis 7: Lacking both state protection and market competitiveness, urban collective enterprises tend to provide the lowest income for their workers.

RESEARCH DESIGN

Data and Analytic Strategies

The 1988 and 1995 CHIP surveys were designed and conducted by a group of economists from the Chinese Academy of Social Sciences, with the academic and financial assistance of their foreign collaborators. The CHIP surveys had separate samples for urban and rural China, but in this paper we focus on the urban samples only. The sampling was based on the frame of the State Statistical Bureau's national annual survey of household economics. Although this frame included all 31 province-level units, the CHIP included China's capital, Beijing, and nine provinces – Anhui, Gansu, Guangdong, Henan, Hubei, Jiangsu, Liaoning, Shanxi, Yunnan in its sample; in 1995 Sichuan province was added, despite the fact that the 1995 survey was financially constrained to sample fewer households. Notably, Shanghai and Tianjin, which have been much studied by U.S.-based sociologists, were not included. Nevertheless the CHIP's 11 provincial units provide good coverage of regions with varying paces of reforms and different levels of development (Wang & Hu, 1999). In each of the lower levels (cities, city districts, neighborhoods, and households), sampling units were first arranged according to average income, and then a systematic sampling procedure was used to select every unit with a fixed interval. Information about all wage earners of each sampled household was collected.[2]

Included in the 1988 and 1995 CHIP surveys are 55 cities and a few county seats. A county seat is the town in which the county's government offices, industries, and commercial and public services are located. County seats are in the lowest level of a hierarchical geo-administrative urban structure; higher levels are, in ascending order, county-level cities, prefectural cities, provincial cities, and central-administered cities. Because aggregate statistics about county seats are not available from the sources of data available to us, we excluded the seven county seats from the 1988 data and the 14 county seats from the 1995 data.

Of the 55 cities under study, 35 cities were common and 20 were different between the two CHIP surveys (see Appendix A). The 35 common cities are mostly large cities at the provincial and prefectural levels. The 20 distinct cities come from the lower levels (with the exception for Chengdu), and excluding them would reduce the representativeness of the data. On the other hand, the 20 distinct cities in the 1988 sample are comparable to those in the 1995 sample, as revealed in an analysis (not shown) of mean differences of the main variables (gender, age, education, and aggregate characteristics). Therefore, we include all 55 cities in our analysis. In total our analysis includes 16,887 wage earners in the 1988 data and 11,044 wage earners in the 1995 data. These respondents, who report valid information on income and other relevant variables, are aged 16 to 69 years, as of the year of the survey.

We take two steps to study marketization and its impact on income determination. First, under the assumption that the processes of marketization and income determination are homogeneous across cities, we use multiple regression models to conduct a trend analysis at the national level comparing income determinants estimated from the 1988 and 1995 CHIP surveys. Next, within the 1995 CHIP data, we take regional heterogeneity into account and estimate hierarchical linear models about how individual-level determinants vary with city-level measures of marketization. For city-level measures for the sampled cities, we use relevant aggregate statistics obtained from various official sources around 1988 and 1995 (see Appendix B for more detailed information).

Dependent Variable: Wage Earner's Income

We analyze *total yearly income* earned from all paid jobs of the respondent. We do not differentiate "base salary" and "other income" from total income for two reasons. First, although these two components were once common for state and collective employees, they were not typical for those working in private firms or who were self-employed. Second, many respondents in the 1995 survey reported their total income and did not provide information for the two components. Thus, yearly total income seems to be the most reliable and appropriate measure for our analysis. The logarithm transformation of income allows for a percent difference interpretation about regression coefficients, as well as for meaningful comparison between 1988 and 1995.

Measures of Wage Earner's Individual Characteristics

Our key variables are positional power and human capital. *Positional power* is measured by Communist party membership (1 = member, 0 = non-member), which captures an individual's political affiliation and connection, and by cadre status (1 = cadre, 0 = non-cadre), whether or not one heads his/her working organization or work unit. Most, but not all, cadres are party members and cadres' positional power is associated with their office authority and extended political influence. This measure of cadre status does not apply to private businesses, domestic or foreign.[3]

Human capital is measured by education level: elementary school or lower, middle school, high school, vocational school, and college or higher. Middle school is the median level among the respondents and is used as the contrast group in multivariate analyses. Vocational school, college, or a higher level indicates either occupation-specific training or a human resource investment leading to a professional career, and we therefore give more attention to these levels in our analysis. In addition, we use a dummy variable of one's working in a professional job (1 = professional, 0 = not) as an indicator of competence-based human capital. This variable is one of the occupational dummies, to be described shortly.

We include in our analysis several other common stratification variables, mainly as statistical controls, to estimate "net" effects of our main explanatory variables in OLS and multilevel models. Gender (male = 1, female = 0) is used to capture gender income gap, which has been well documented in western sociological literature (Marini, 1989) and in the growing research on China's recent gender transformation (Entwisle et al., 1995; Lee, 1995; Entwisle & Henderson, 2000). Age and age squares are included as a proxy to work experience. Although age as a proxy to work experience may be interpreted as a form of human capital, alternative interpretations are possible because of a strong seniority rule operating in Chinese bureaucracies (Davis-Friendman, 1985). Another control variable is the respondent's employment status, whether having long-term, full-time employment (= 1) or employment as a migrant peasant labor, laid-off worker getting reemployed with a short-term contact, or a job of temporary nature (= 0). Finally, cities are used as dummy variables in a trend analysis based on regression models.

Measures of Wage Earner's Structural Characteristics

Two sets of dummy variables are used to measure a wage earner's structural characteristics: occupation and economic sector of a wage earner's primary job.

Confined to the datasets, the set of *occupational dummies* includes cadre, professional, entrepreneur, clerical workers, and manual workers. Based on self-reports, respondents are recognized as entrepreneurs when they identify themselves as "an owner or manager of a private business" (the 1988 CHIP definition) or "an owner or manager of a household business or private company" (the 1995 CHIP definition). This inconsistency in defining entrepreneur between the two surveys analysed in this paper causes analytic and interpretative problems, which will be described later.

Our theme of "marketization with state transformation" calls for an innovative effort to measure China's *economic segmentation*, and here we briefly present the result of this extensive effort. Since 1979, the central government of China – the People's Congress, the State Council, and ministries – has issued new laws and administrative directives to regulate economic activities. Our in-depth analyses of these documents, supplemented by consistent quantitative evidence, support the conclusion that a four-sector economy had gradually formed in China by 1993 (Appendix C). Confined to the workplace in which the respondent had his/her main job at the time of the survey, we identify the following four economic sectors: Monopoly sector (all government agencies and state-run organizations in industries of public and political goods and services); Open sector, state (state-run organizations in commerce, service, construction, and manufacturing industries); Open sector, collectives (urban collective enterprises operating in the open sector industries); and Open sector, private firms (new firms emerging after 1980, including foreign and joint-adventure corporations, domestic private firms, household businesses and self-employment, and hybrid economic organizations with ambivalent property arrangements). These various private/semiprivate forms of economic organization operate in the open sector industries.

City-Level Measures: Level of Marketization

Previous researchers have attempted to measure intercity differences in pace of reforms and breadth and depth of marketization. Qualitative approaches to assigning localities into regions of distinctive resource allocation mode require extensive local knowledge, causing disputes that led to controversial empirical analyses and conflicting theoretical conclusions (Nee, 1996; Parish & Michelson, 1996). Xie and Hannum (1996) took a quantitative approach, but their industrial growth is seen as an invalid measure of marketization (Nee, 1996; Szelényi & Kostello, 1996; Walder, 1996). Confined to the available aggregate data, we attempt to quantify marketization as follows:

Labor marketization is measured by the ratio of non-agricultural labor in non-state sectors over the state sector, using 1995 year-end official statistics. Although state-sector workers may well exercise labor rights to bargain for high compensation within organizations, and state enterprise managers may well exercise rights to lay off workers, workers with full employment or a primary job in a non-state sector have more power to exercise *private* labor rights and to receive more immediate impacts of *external* labor markets.

Capital marketization is measured, in 1995, by the ratio of foreign investments to the city's total investments in fixed assets. Alternative measures would combine foreign and domestic private investments or count the capital flow that is free of bureaucratic influences, but neither of these is available from our data sources. When a city attracts more foreign investments, the city's economy is apt to be more global, more subject to international standards of market developments, and to generate more competition in product and labor markets within the city. Because of these market-spreading effects (Wang & Hu, 1999), foreign capital flows into a city are anticipated to boost domestic capital markets in the city and raise the level of economic competition in general. In this sense, our measure of foreign investment ratio is indicative of a city's level of capital marketization.

Industrial growth was previously used to operationalize economic growth and proxy marketization (Xie & Hannum, 1996) but is barely correlated with any of the above measures of marketization (see Appendix B). While marketization speeds up industrial growth (or more broadly, economic development), this effect varies with resource endowments, policy implementation, and developmental strategies (Wang & Hu, 1999). Because these factors differ tremendously among cities, industrial growth may not be a valid measure of marketization. Our application of this measure here is strictly for statistical comparisons with the measures of labor and capital marketization included in our analysis. The specific procedure of this measurement follows Xie and Hannum's formula (p. 963, Eq. 6), but is confined to the growth rate from 1992 to 1995.

TREND ANALYSIS: COMPARING 1988 AND 1995 DATA

Trend in Degree of Income Inequality

Table 1 presents coefficients of variation, a measure similar to gini coefficient that indicates the degree of inequality. As can be seen, nominal yearly income increases from 1,929 yuan in 1988 to 6,839 yuan in 1995, indicating a growth margin of 254% over the seven-year period. When adjusted to the constant

Table 1. Mean, Standard Deviation, and Coefficient of Variation for Total Yearly Income, Urban CHIP: 1988 and 1995.

Total Yearly Income	1988	1995
As reported in the surveys		
Mean	1929.57	6839.53
Standard Deviation (S.D.)	1121.23	4675.91
S.D./mean	0.58	0.68
*Adjusted with 1978 = 100**		
Mean	1019.43	1531.11
Standard Deviation (S.D.)	554.77	968.91
S.D./mean	0.54	0.63
Number of cases	16887	11044

* Adjusted by the Consumer Price Indexes of the sampled provinces as reported in *China's Statistical Yearbook* (1996, p. 255).

yuan value of 1978, the beginning year of reforms, the growth rate is 50%, implying a substantial increase in living standards in urban China from 1988 to 1995. Inequality, on the other hand, increases by a 9% to 10% margin, which is a very large increase in income inequality across seven years, making urban China among the most unequal societies in Asia (Khan & Riskin, 1998). It confirms earlier reports of increasing inequality trends based on a single city (Bian & Logan, 1996) and on a national level (Wang & Hu, 1999).

With the assumptions that labor and capital markets grew significantly from 1988 to 1995 and that levels of marketization were constant across cities, we use ordinary-least-square models to first estimate the effects of respondents' individual characteristics on the logarithm of respondents' total yearly income, and second to estimate the effects of structural characteristics in the full model (see Appendix D for descriptive details of all variables included in the model). Because our purpose is to compare *relative* change in these effects between 1988 and 1995, the logarithm transformation of income meets our needs. The estimated results are presented in Table 2.

Individual Characteristics Effects

Model I shows that with gender, party membership, and education being constant, age effects are positive and nonlinear (age squared has a negative coefficient) in both 1988 and 1995 and little change is observed between the

Table 2. Unstandardized OLS Coefficients from the Regression of Logarithm Total Yearly Income on Seleceted Independent Variables, 1988 and 1995.

	Model I			Model II		
Independent Variables	1988	1995		1988	1995	
Individual Characteristics						
Age	0.079***	0.084***		0.072***	0.076***	
Age squared	− 0.001***	− 0.001***		− 0.001***	− 0.001***	
Gender (male = 1)	0.117***	0.127***		0.101***	0.116***	
Party membership (= 1)	0.093***	0.121***	>	0.068***	0.081***	
Education						
(middle school as contrast)						
Elementary school or lower	− 0.128***	− 0.206***	<	− 0.096***	− 0.142***	<
High school	0.028***	0.101***	>	0.010	0.055***	>
Vocational school	0.061***	0.207***	>	0.013	0.093***	>
College or higher	0.097***	0.275***	>	0.040***	0.131***	>
Structural Characteristics						
Occupation						
(worker as contrast)						
Cadre				0.087***	0.131***	>
Professional				0.073***	0.127***	>
Entrepreneur				0.327***	0.007	<
Clerical Staff				0.028***	0.068***	
Economic Sector						
(collective as contrast)						
Monopoly, state-run				0.102***	0.255***	>
Open, state enterprises				0.124***	0.175***	>
Private firm				0.075*	0.348***	>
Unspecified firm				− 0.061**	0.087***	>
Control Variables						
Permanent employment						
(= 1, others = 0)				0.306***	0.293***	
Cities						
(54, Beijing as contrast)	not presented	not presented		not presented	not presented	
Constant	5.696***	6.759***		5.455***	6.530***	
R-square	0.442	0.396		0.473	0.436	
Adjusted R-Square	0.440	0.393		0.471	0.432	
Number of cases	16887	11044		16887	11044	

Notes:

1. T-tests for statistically significant differences in coefficients are noted by " > " for 1995 higher than 1988 and " < " otherwise (two-tailed tests, $p < 0.05$).
2. Significant levels for coefficients: * $p < 0.05$; ** $p < 0.01$; *** $p < 0.001$ (two-tailed tests).

two years. When effects of age, party membership, and education are held constant, men's income advantage over women is 12.4% in 1988 ($e^{0.117} = 1.124$), and this gap increases to 13.5% in 1995 ($e^{0.127} = 1.135$). The 1.1% increase in gender income gap over the seven-year span is statistically insignificant and is similar to earlier findings from the city of Tianjin (Bian, Logan & Shu, 2000) and inconsistent with a hypothesis of decreasing gender inequality with marketization that was proposed by considering rural women's increasing opportunities for nonagricultural jobs (Nee & Matthews, 1996; Matthews & Nee, 2000). Note that the CHIP surveys did not adequately sample migrated peasant labor in the cities, and the survey results reported here are mostly about city residents with a permanent household registration.

Model I's results on the effects of party membership and education are obtained to show increasing income returns to political and human capital with marketization. With statistical controls of age, gender, and education, party membership's coefficient is positive in both 1988 and 1995, and its magnitude is significantly larger in 1995. Compared to nonmembers, party members' income is 9.7% higher in 1988 and 12.9% higher in 1995 ($e^{0.093}$ and $e^{0.121}$, respectively). This is accompanied by a similar trend in increasing income returns to education. Compared to those with middle-school education, respondents with an elementary-school education or lower were paid relatively less in 1995 than in 1988, from 87.9% ($e^{-0.128}$) of the income for a person with middle-school education to 71.6% ($e^{-0.206}$), revealing a 16.3% slide over the seven years. Respondents with a higher education than middle school, on the other hand, all enjoyed an impressive relative increase in income; those with vocational and college and above education, the two levels of education that by and large indicate occupation-specific training and thus productive human capital, had the largest increases from a moderate 6.3% ($e^{0.061}$) and 10.2% ($e^{0.097}$) margin in 1988 to a huge 23.0% ($e^{0.207}$) and 31.7% ($e^{0.275}$) advantage in 1995. Under the assumption that labor and capital markets grew considerably from 1988 to 1995, the parallel increases in income returns to higher education and party membership lend partial support for Hypotheses 1–4.

Structural Characteristics Effects

Model II incorporates two sets of structural variables – occupation and economic sector. Compared to manual workers, cadres and professionals make higher income in both 1988 and 1995, and these two groups enjoy similar and statistically significant relative increases over the seven years: Cadre's relative increase is from 9.1% to 14.0% ($e^{0.087}$ to $e^{0.131}$) and professional's from 7.6% to

13.5%% ($e^{0.073}$ to $e^{0.127}$). Cadre status is a measure of positional power and the occupation of professional is a measure of competence-based human capital. Thus, the parallel increases in income returns to both cadres and professionals provide further evidence supporting Hypotheses 1–4.

The occupation of entrepreneur, whose relative income growth with marketization is in the core for testing the theory of market transition, is unfortunately inconsistently measured in the 1988 and 1995 CHIP surveys. In Table 2, this grouping shows the highest income relative to all other occupational groupings in 1988, but its income advantage surprisingly is nil in 1995. This result must be considered jointly with the effect of "private firm," a variable in a set of dummies for economic sector. There were 634 respondents, or 3.75%, in the 1988 sample who worked in private firms, and one third (211 respondents) of these chose the precoded response category of "owner of a private business," which is termed "entrepreneur" in Table 2. The proportion of private sector workers increased considerably in the 1995 sample (10.31%), and 1/7 of them (147) chose the reworded response category of "owners of *household* and private businesses." It is widely known that household business owners earn significantly less than private business owners, but we have no way of differentiating between these two groups in the 1995 data. It should also be noted that the relative growth of new sector employment between 1988 and 1995 was primarily due to growth of the nonowner workforce. In 1995, this workforce was occupationally more diversified, no longer concentrated in low-paying jobs, but dispersed to professional and technical jobs in the upper levels of the income hierarchy. This was the main reason for the observed increase in income returns for new sector workers from 1988 to 1995.

The set of dummies for economic sector is designed to test Hypotheses 5–7 concerning change in income differentials with marketization. Compared to collective workers' income, income for state workers in the monopoly sector grew from a moderate advantage of 10.7% ($e^{0.102}$) to a significantly larger margin of 29.0% ($e^{0.225}$). State workers in the open sector also had a relative increase but the growth margin is smaller, and workers in private firms had the highest relative income growth from a 7.8% ($e^{0.075}$) advantage over collective workers in 1988 to a 41.6% ($e^{0.348}$) advantage in 1995. Comparing state workers in the monopoly and in the open sectors, their relative income levels are reversed, indicating that workers in the monopoly sector benefited more from the course of marketization from 1988 to 1995, whereas collective-sector workers' income became relatively worse. On the whole, these findings lend strong support for Hypotheses 5 to 7.

REGIONAL VARIATION ANALYSIS: MULTILEVEL MODELS

Our trend analysis assumes homogeneity about levels of marketization across cities. Adopting a more realistic assumption of heterogeneity, we use hierarchical linear models to assess the extent to which income returns to individual-level variables vary with city-level measures of marketization. Before presenting our results, we make three technical notes. First, we estimate a uniform model for which we enter only one city-level measure each time. Merging multiple measures with high intercorrelations to construct a composite index is possible, but as a first step, separate treatments may help us explore the empirical complexities to which our theoretical discussion has been made reference. Second, because 1988 and 1995 data generate similar results overall, we focus on the 1995 data below. Third, as in the trend analysis, our first model considers variables of individual characteristics and our second, full model incorporates variables of structural characteristics. Our interpretations focus on the macro-micro interactions between city-level measures of marketization and individual-level measures of human capital and positional power. Table 3 presents the macro-micro interactive coefficients estimated from hierarchical linear models (see full results and technical details in Appendix E).

Labor Marketization Effects

The city-level measure of labor marketization is the ratio of nonstate workers over state workers. Model I shows that in cities with a higher degree of labor marketization, income returns to vocational school and higher levels of education – our measure of human capital – are significantly greater. Although less statistical significant, income returns to party membership – a measure of positional power – are also greater. Model II incorporates two additional measures of human capital and positional power – occupation as a professional or as a cadre. In this model, both positions are rewarded significantly higher levels of income in cities with a higher degree of labor marketization. Because professionals tend to have higher levels of education and nearly all cadres are party members, the variables of professional and cadre reflect some indirect effects of education and party membership on income. Quantitatively, when a city's ratio of nonstate vs. state workers increases by 1%, with the same qualifications and working in the same job, a professional will increase his/her income by 1.7% ($e^{0.017}$) and a cadre by 2.5% ($e^{0.025}$). In real-life context, these margins are 50% to 70% or even higher when one compares an inland city with large numbers of state jobs to a coastal city with plenty of employment

Table 3. Estimated Micro-Macro Interactive Coefficients of the Multilevel Models for Logarithm Total Yearly Income, 1995.

City-level Variable	Ratio of Non-state vs. State Labor Model I	Ratio of Non-state vs. State Labor Model II	Ratio of Foreign Investment Model I	Ratio of Foreign Investment Model II	Growth Rate of Manufacturing Industry Model I	Growth Rate of Manufacturing Industry Model II
(MICRO-MACRO INTERACTIVE COEFFICIENTS)						
Intercept	0.059**	0.063*	3.343***	3.586***	0.164	0.133
Individual Characteristics						
Age	0.005***	0.004*	0.154**	0.081	0.045*	0.057***
Age squared	0.000***	− 0.000**	− 0.002***	− 0.001*	− 0.001**	− 0.001***
Gender (male = 1)	− 0.002	− 0.000	− 0.103	− 0.013	− 0.077	− 0.066
Party membership (= 1)	0.010‡	− 0.002	0.570**	0.112	0.065	− 0.028
Elementary school or lower	− 0.002	− 0.017*	− 0.470	− 0.400	− 0.060	− 0.058
High school	− 0.001	− 0.003	− 0.042	− 0.047	− 0.116	− 0.085
Vocational school	0.026*	0.010	0.517	− 0.110	0.060	0.069
College or higher	0.023**	0.008	0.558	0.179	0.014	0.030
Structural Characteristics						
Occupation (worker as contrast)						
Cadre		0.025**		1.275***		0.174‡
Professional		0.017*		0.486‡		0.125*
Entrepreneur		0.006		0.614		0.031
Clerical staff		0.028***		0.691**		0.099

City-level Variable	Ratio of Non-state vs. State Labor		Ratio of Foreign Investment		Growth Rate of Manufacturing Industry	
	Model I	Model II	Model I	Model II	Model I	Model II
Economic Sector (collective as contrast)						
Monopoly, state-run		− 0.010		− 0.525*		− 0.061
Open, state-run		− 0.012		− 0.691*		− 0.021
Private firm		− 0.027		− 0.207		0.208
Unspecified		− 0.015		− 0.257		0.229
Permanent employment (= 1, others = 0)		0.006		0.087		− 0.020

Notes:
1. Full model estimates are reported in Appendix E.
2. Statistical significance: ‡ $p < 0.10$; * $p < 0.05$; ** $p < 0.01$; *** $p < 0.001$ (two-tailed tests).

opportunities in the fast growing non-state sectors. In the latter cities, labor markets operate in their own rights and workers bargain for higher compensation based on their human and positional resources. In Table 2, one may be unsure about whether or not the growth of labor markets was responsible for the increasing income returns to measures of human capital and positional power from 1988 to 1995. The results of multilevel models in Table 3 remove any doubt and present us with a clearer set of findings: Income returns to measures of human capital and positional power increase with level of labor marketization, supporting Hypotheses 1 and 2 about the impacts of growing labor markets.

Capital Marketization Effects

While a fully reliable measure is unavailable, our measure of the extent of foreign capital investments is a valid indicator of China's capital marketization in the cities. Model I shows that in cities where there are more foreign investments, party members have a greater payoff. Although the coefficients for vocational school and college education are positive and large in magnitude, they are statistically insignificant. Model II, however, shows that income returns to cadre status and professional position increase significantly in cities that have attracted more foreign investments. It also shows that clerical workers – whose technical skills may be more appreciated in a more financiallymarketized economy – get significantly higher income in cities with more foreign capital investments. On the whole, the findings pertaining to the increasing income returns to party membership, cadre status, and professional position with capital marketization are an impressive set of evidence supporting Hypotheses 3 and 4.

Industrial Growth Effects

Industrial growth, as a proxy to marketization, does not alter income returns to party membership or education (Model I) but does increase income returns to cadre status and professional occupation (Model II). Quantitatively, when cities generate a 1% industrial growth margin, their cadres' and professionals' incomes increase by 19.0% ($e^{0.174}$) and 13.3% ($e^{0.125}$), respectively. These large income returns are understandable if in fast-developing cities the labor and capital markets provide an opportunity structure most favorably for cadres and professionals.

CONCLUSION AND DISCUSSION

Contentions about the socioeconomic consequences of market-oriented reforms in China and elsewhere have concentrated on the impact of marketization and evolving politics on income distribution. In this study we revisited these issues from a market-state interaction viewpoint. Starting with the position that markets and politics are interrelated (Bian & Logan, 1996; Parish & Michelson, 1996; Zhou, 2000), we focused our attention on two features of this market-state interactive process. The first is marketization as a multifaceted, historical process in which product, labor, and capital markets grew through different historical trajectories and may have had different implications on income distribution. The second is the corresponding transformation of the state, which is reflected in the role transformation from a redistributive state to a regulative state, in the formation of a state monopoly sector and in the conversion of state properties to cadres' control and income rights through an "inside privatization." Thus, growing market forces do not undermine cadres' power and privileges; rather, the course of marketization is conducive for cadres as well as entrepreneurs and professionals. Our overall prediction, therefore, is that the market-state interactive process in a growing economy results in parallel increases in income returns to both positional power and human capital, causing income inequality to grow.

Our measure of income inequality – coefficient of variation – indeed shows an increasing trend of income inequality among wage earners in the CHIP surveys between 1988 and 1995. Our trend analysis comparing these two comparable cross-sectional samples largely confirms earlier findings about increasing income returns to education and professional competence. Although income return for entrepreneurs did not grow between 1988 and 1995, the survey designs of CHIP data are not entirely adequate for testing Nee's hypothesis about entrepreneurship. With regard to the controversies about income returns to positional power, income advantages maintained and grew for Communist party members compared to nonmembers and for cadres compared to non-cadres. While our trend analysis is confirmatory, the national sampling data give us a solid empirical grounding for an overall assessment of changes in income distribution from 1988 to 1995 in urban China as a whole.

We also take the quantitative approach first advocated by Xie and Hannum (1996) to measure level of marketization across cities, but we note that Xie and Hannum used industrial growth as a proxy to marketization, which was criticized to be an invalid measure (Nee, 1996; Walder, 1996). Much of these findings were confirmed in multilevel models estimated to assess the effects of city-level measures of marketization on income returns to positional power and human capital. We found our labor market and capital market measures useful in assessing impacts of marketization on income distribution. Most notable is the finding that income returns for two forms of positional power and political influence – Communist party membership and cadre status – are all increasing with the growing degrees of labor markets or capital markets. The growth of these markets also widens income inequalities between wage earners with higher and lower levels of human capital: a professional would earn significantly more in cities where labor markets, as stimulated by growing proportions of labor in nonstate sectors, and capital markets, as indexed by the extent of foreign capital investments, are more developed, and wage earners with vocational and college educations have significantly higher income returns in cities where labor market is more developed. These findings go beyond the abstract characterization of marketization to allow us to observe and assess more specifically the impacts of different kinds of market developments on income distribution at a national level.

Apart from the concerns about positional power and human capital, we also analyzed the effects of economic segmentation. Here economic segmentation between a state monopoly sector and open sectors was the result of state transformation from a redistributive state with entire control over urban economy to an intervening state with monopoly over a few industries of vital strategic important to the party-state. We found that with other things being equal, workers in the state monopoly sector increased their income level significantly from 1988 to 1995, those state workers in the open sector had a significant relative decline in income compared to workers in the state monopoly sector, and those in new, non-state firms increased their income steadily. These findings suggest that while market competition undermines income privileges of state enterprises in the open sector, such a force is prevented from entering into the monopoly sector in which state workers are better off in 1995 than in 1988.

Thus, attention to the segmented industrial structure gives us a concrete angle to examine the impacts of state and politics on income inequality. Zhou's (2000) co-evolutionary model points to a dual logic of market competition and interest politics in reform and stratification processes. While this characterization of dual transformation may fit any society, an important task is to specify *how* politics evolves in a postsocialist transitional society. Our approach to economic segmentation focuses on the state as a political-economic actor and helps us identify two aspects of an integrated process of state transformation along with marketization: the decline of state redistribution and the rise of state intervention. The decline of state redistribution is triggered by the opening of production to market competition, causing unprotected state workers in the open sector to become the victims of reforms. The rise of state intervention is signified by state regulative power, exercising macro economic control and industrial restructuring. In the resulting monopoly sector, income advantages no longer come from state redistribution but from the reassignment of exclusive productive and income rights to state-run organizations in certain product markets.

By identifying the income advantages of cadres with positional power and state employees in monopoly sector, our study shed light on a central issue of the market transition debate – the evolution of politics with the course of marketization. While state officials' redistributive power is shrinking, cadres' positional power is strengthened by increasing control and income rights over state properties and by state monopoly over vital and profitable industries. These cadre privileges are different from pre-reform redistributors. Whereas pre-reform redistributors benefited from their political position through hierarchical arrangements alone, reform-era cadres work in an increasing competitive market environment and must capitalize on the authority they hold by "earning" their income one way or another.

This "power capitalization" perspective, along with our analyses, leads to the conclusion that income distribution is a phenomenon of the changing political economy. This conclusion concurs with North's (1981, p. 20) wisdom that the "existence of a state is essential for economic growth" and "man-made decline," and is in variance with the vision that the future of transitional economies is a convergent "market society" in which market alone anchors production and distribution. We believe that politics should not be equated to the old, pre-existing order; rather, new political mechanisms and processes grow and evolve in response to and facilitate the process of marketization. The Chinese state has always been a genuine part of the country's marketization process; by the mid-1990s its state power reconfiguration had coevolved with market developments and its state intervention, in place of state redistribution, had direct impacts on economic segmentation and income inequality. Since in no modern economic system do markets entirely replace governments (Wolf, 1993), predicting *continued decline* of political privileges under a Communist state is to expect a little too much of marketization.

Our analyses, based on data collected in 1988 and 1995, offer no definite prediction about patterns of income distribution in urban China in the first years of the twenty-first century. China is evolving on both political and economic fronts. Yet, our focus on China's changing political economy calls for special research attention to macro-micro linkages between marketization and industrial restructuring on the one hand, and stratification dynamics among organizations and individuals on the other. At macro-levels, it is necessary to broadly examine the changing institutional arrangements, not only about ownership and governance structures of economic organization but also about industrial policies of the state that specify rules, preferences, and strategies governing market developments and economic segmentation. At "meso" levels, we must explore the ways in which such macro-structural forces impact the power, profitability, and income-generating capacities of organizations and communities, which are property-rights regimes. At micro-individual levels, and within and across property rights regimes, we then specify the rise and decline of bargaining resources of social groups and individuals and the resulting patterns of distribution of opportunity and compensation.

NOTES

1. We do not propose any hypothesis about the impact of product markets for income distribution because we cannot obtain a good city-level measure of this market from the aggregate statistics available. Our anticipation is that the emergence of small commodity markets in the 1980s which benefited petty entrepreneurs and family businesses but later growth of product markets after 1992 gives these players no such benefits.
2. Consult Griffin and Zhao (1992) and Khan and Riskin (1998) for details about the sampling procedures.
3. The cadre variable, along with entrepreneur and professional variables, are from a series of occupational categories available from the data. Other dummies included in the analysis are clerical workers and manual workers.

ACKNOWLEDGMENTS

Direct correspondence to Yanjie Bian, Division of Social Science, Hong Kong University of Science and Technology, Clearwater Bay, Kowloon, Hong Kong (sobian@ust.hk). The work reported in this paper was supported by grants from the Hong Kong Universities Grants Committee (HKUST6052/98H, HKUST6007/00H) and from the School of Humanities and Social Science (DAG98/99.001, DAG99/00.003) and a Postdoctoral Fellowship from the Vice-President for Academic Affairs of the Hong Kong University of Science and Technology. An earlier version was presented at the international conference on "Money, Growth, and Distribution," Academia Sinica, Taipei, September 6, 2001; the Department of Sociology, Tunghai University, Taichung, September 8, 2001; and the Division of Social Science, Hong Kong University of Science and Technology, Hong Kong, November 19, 2001. We thank Qiyuan Cui and Shi Li for technical assistance with the CHIP surveys and city-level statistics, and Jay Chen, Deborah Davis, Tony Tam, Xiaoling Shu, Tim Zhu, and *RSSM* editor Kevin Leicht, and an anonymous review for helpful comments.

REFERENCES

Bian, Y. (1994). *Work and Inequality in Urban China.* Albany, New York: State University of New York Press.

Bian, Y. (1999). Getting a Job Through a Web of *Guanxi* in China. In: B. Wellman (Ed.), *Networks in the Global Village* (pp. 225–278). Boulder, Co.: Westview.

Bian, Y., & Logan, J. R. (1996). Market Transition and the Persistence of Power: The Changing Stratification System in Urban China. *American Sociological Review, 61*, 739–758.

Bian, Y., Logan, J. R., & Shu, X. (2000). Wage and Job Inequalities in the Working Careers of Men and Women in Tianjin. In: B. Entwisle & G. E. Henderson (Eds), *Re-Drawing Boundaries: Work, Household, and Gender in China* (pp. 111–133). Berkeley, California: University of California Press.

Cao, Y., & Nee, V. (2000). Comment: Controversies and Evidence in the Market Transition Debate. *American Journal of Sociology, 105*, 1175–1188.

Cheng, X. (1996). Fanrong Conghe Erlai? – Zhongguo Jingji Xianzhuang he Qushi de Fenxi (Where Does Prosperity Come From? – An Assessment of the Present Status and Prospects of China's Economy). *Dangdai Zhongguo Yanjiu* (*Modern China Studies*), *54*(3), 18–61.

Davis, D. (1990). Urban Job Mobility. In: D. Davis & E. F. Vogel (Eds), *Chinese Society on the Eve of Tiananmen* (pp. 85–108). Cambridge, Massachusetts: Harvard University Press.

Davis-Friedmann, D. (1985). Intergenerational Inequalities and the Chinese Revolution. *Modern China, 11*, 177–201.

Duckett, J. (2001). Bureaucrats in Business, Chinese-Style: The Lessons of Market Reform and State Entrepreneurialism in the People's Republic of China. *World Development, 29*, 23–37.

Entwisle, B., & Henerson, G. E. (Eds) (2000). *Re-Drawing Boundaries: Work, Household, and Gender in China.* Berkeley, California: University of California Press.

Entwisle, B., Henerson, G. E., Short, S. E., Bouma, J. E., & Feng-ying, Z. (1995). Gender and Family Businesses in Rural China. *American Sociological Review, 60*, 36–57.

Gerber, T. P., & Hout, M. (1998). More Shock than Therapy: Market Transition, Employment, and Income in Russia, 1991–1995. *American Journal of Sociology, 104*, 1–50.

Gold, T. B. (1990). Urban Private Business and Social Change. In: D. Davis & E. F. Vogel (Eds), *Chinese Society on the Eve of Tiananmen* (pp. 157–178). Cambridge, Massachusetts: Harvard University Press.

Griffin, K., & Zhao, R. (1992). *Chinese Household Income Project, 1988 (MRDF).* New York, NY: Hunter College Academic Computing Services (Producer). Distributed by Inter-University Consortium for Political and Social Research, Ann Arbor, Mich.

State Statistical Bureau of China (Ed.) (1996). *Statistical Yearbook of China, 1996.* Beijing: Zhongguo Tongji Chubanshe (Chinese Statistical Press).

He, Q. (1998). Xiandaihua de Xianjing (*Pitfalls of Modernization: Economic and Social Problems in Contemporary China*). Beijing: Jinri Zhongguo Chubanshe (Today's China Press).

Hua, E. (1997). *Zhongguo Jingji de Ruanzhuolu* (The Soft-Landing of China's Economy). Beijing: Zhongguo Caizheng Jingji Chubanshe (Chinese Financial Press).

Khan, A. R., & Riskin, C. (1998). Income Inequality an Its Distribution and Growth of Household Income, 1988 to 1995. *The China Quarterly, 154*, 221–253.

Lardy, N. R. (1989). Dilemmas in the Pattern of Resource Allocation in China: 1978–1985. In: V. Nee & D. Stark (Eds), *Remaking the Economic Institutions of Socialism* (pp. 278–305). Stanford, California: Stanford University Press.

Lardy, N. R. (1998). *China's Unfinished Economic Revolution.* Washington D. C.: Brookings Institute Press.

Lee, C. K. (1995). Engendering the Worlds of Labor: Women Workers, Labor Markets, and Production Politics in the South China Economic Miracle. *American Sociological Review, 60*, 378–397.

Lin, J. Y., Cai, F., & Li, Z. (1996). *The China Miracle: Development Strategy and Economic Reform.* Hong Kong: The Chinese University Press.

Lin, N. (1995). Local Market Socialism: Local Corporatism in Action in Rural China. *Theory and Society, 24*, 301–354.

Lin, Y. (2000). Pitfalls of Modernization: Economic and Social Problems in Contemporary China. *Contemporary Sociology, 29*, 608–613.

Lin, Y., & Zhang, Z. (1999). Backyard Profit Centers: The Private Assets of Public Agencies. In: J. Oi & A. Walder (Eds), *Property Rights and Economic Reform in China* (pp. 203–225). Stanford, California: Stanford University Press.

Liu, Y. (1992). Reform from Below: The Private Economy and Local Politics in the Rural Industrialization of Wenzhou. *China Quarterly, 130*:, 293–316.

Ma, Z. (2001). Urban Labour-Force Experience as a Determinant of Rural Occupation Change: Evidence from Recent Urban-Rural Return Migration in China. *Environment and Planning A, 33*:, 237–255.

Marini, M. M. (1989). Sex Differences in Earnings in the United States. *Annual Review of Sociology, 15*, 343–380.

Matthews, R., & Nee, V. (2000). Gender Inequality and Economic Growth in Rural China. *Social Science Research, 29*, 606–632.

Naughton, B. (1995). *Growing Out of the Plan: Chinese Economic Reform: 1978–1993.* New York: Oxford University Press.

Nee, V. (1989). A Theory of Market Transition: From Redistribution to Market in State Socialism. *American Sociology Review, 54*, 663–681.

Nee, V. (1991). Social Inequalities in Reforming State Socialism: Between Redistribution and Markets in State Socialism. *American Sociological Review, 56*, 267–282.

Nee, V. (1996). The Emergence of a Market Society: Changing Mechanisms of Stratification in China. *American Journal of Sociology, 101*, 908–949.

Nee, V., & Matthews, R. (1996). Market Transition and Societal Transformation in Reforming State Socialism. *Annual Review of Sociology, 22*, 401–435.

Nee, V., & Cao, Y. (1999). Path Dependent Societal Transformation: Stratification in Hybrid Mixed Economy. *Theory and Society, 28*, 799–834.

North, D. C. (1981). *Structure and Change in Economic History.* New York: W. W. Norton & Company.

Oi, J. C., & Walder, A. G. (Eds) (1999). *Property Rights and Economic Reform in China*. Stanford, California: Stanford University Press.

Parish, W. L., & Michelson, E. (1996). Politics and Markets: Dual Transformations. *American Journal of Sociology, 101*, 1042–1059.

Rona-Tas, A. (1994). The First Shall be Last? Entrepreneurship and Communist Cadres in the Transition from Socialism. *American Journal of Sociology, 100*, 40–69.

Shirk, S. (1993). *The Political Logic of Economic Reform in China.* Berkeley and Los Angeles, California: University of California Press.

Szelényi, I., & Kostello, E. (1996). The Market Transition Debate: Toward a Synthesis? *American Journal of Sociology, 101*, 1082–1096.

Walder, A. G. (1986). *Communist Neo-Traditionalism: Work and Authority in Chinese Industry.* Berkeley, California: University of California Press.

Walder, A. G. (1992). Property Rights and Stratification in Socialist Redistributive Economies. *American Sociology Review, 57*, 524–539.

Walder, A. G. (1994). Evolving Property Rights and Their Political Consequences. In: D. S. G. Goodman & B. Hooper (Eds), *China's Quiet Revolution: New Interactions Between State and Society* (pp. 3–18). New York: St. Martin's Press.

Walder, A. G. (1995). Local Governments as Industrial Firms: An Organizational Analysis of China's Transitional Economy. *American Journal of Sociology, 101*, 1060–1073.

Walder, A. G. (1996). Markets and Inequality in Transitional Economies: Toward Testable Theories. *American Journal of Sociology, 101*, 1060–1073.

Walder, A. G., & Oi, J. C. (1999). Property rights in the Chinese Economy: Contours of the Process of China. In: J. C. Oi & A. G. Walder (Eds), *Property Rights and Economic Reform in China* (pp. 1–24). Stanford, California: Stanford University Press.

Wank, D. L. (1999). *Commodifying Communism: Business, Trust, and Politics in a Chinese City.* New York: Cambridge University Press.

Wang, S., & Hu, A. (1999). *The Political Economy of Uneven Development: The Case of China.* Armonk, New York: M. E. Sharpe.

Wolf, C., Jr. (1993). *Markets or Governments: Choosing between Imperfect Alternatives.* Cambridge, MA: The MIT Press.

Wong, C. P. W., Heady, C., & Woo, W. T. (1995). *Fiscal Management and Economic Reform in the People's Republic of China.* Hong Kong: Oxford University Press.

Xie, Y., & Hannum, E. (1996). Regional Variation in Earnings Inequality in Reform-Era Urban China. *American Journal of Sociology, 101*, 950–992.

Yuan, Z., & Fang, Y. (1998). *Zhongguo Jiuye Zhidu de Bianqian* (*Changes in China's Employment*). Taiyuan, China: Shanxi Jingji Chubanshe (Shanxi Economy Press).

Zhou, X. (2000). Economic Transformation and Income Inequality in Urban China: Evidence from a Panel Data. *American Journal of Sociology, 105*, 1135–1174.

APPENDIX

Appendix A. Cities and Sample Sizes Included in 1988 and 1995 Urban CHIP.

Cities Included in 1988 and 1995			Different Cities Sampled in 1988 and 1995			
	Sample size in		1988		1995	
City	1988	1995	City	Sample Size	City	Sample Size
Beijing	65	879	Jincheng	225	Yixing	87
Taiyuan	406	313	Yuncheng	196	Suqiang	100
Datong	378	172	Dandong	192	Taixing	79
Yangquan	230	204	Huaiyin	122	Bozhou	93
Changzhi	208	187	Yancheng	94	Huixian	92
Shenyang	630	623	Yangzhou	309	Xiangfan	186
Dalian	642	338	Anqing	227	Jingsha	170
Jinzhou	387	165	Fuyang	109	Macheng	107
Nanjing	542	350	Huangshan	88	Tianmen	103
Wuxi	465	152	Luoyang	403	Honghu	82
Xuzhou	365	148	Anyang	325	Shunde	113
Changzhou	178	174	Zhumadian	133	Chengdu	366
Nantong	204	193	Nanyang	125	Luzhou	334
Hefei	449	180	Shiyan	202	Zigong	181
Huainan	409	164	Shashi	219	Leshan	182
Wuhu	211	168	Xiaogan	206	Guangyuan	188
Bangbu	194	171	Shaoguan	199	Wanxian	176
Zhengzhou	406	137	Shantou	111	Xuanwei	90
Kaifeng	21	176	Qujing	82	Pingliang	177
Pingdingshan	204	207	Yuxi	195	Wuwei	176
Xinxiang	302	147				
Wuhan	692	474				

Cities Included in 1988 and 1995			Different Cities Sampled in 1988 and 1995			
	Sample size in		1988		1995	
City	1988	1995	City	Sample Size	City	Sample Size
Huanshi	204	179				
Guangzhou	608	366				
Shenzhen	216	89				
Foshan	333	96				
Zhanjiang	205	97				
Huizhou	233	94				
Zhouqing	222	95				
Kunming	594	193				
Tongchuan	155	173				
Gejiu	205	155				
Dali	195	197				
Baoshan	193	178				
Lanzhou	1184	328				
N of cities	30	30		20		20

Appendix B. Correlations, Means, and Standard Deviations of City-Level Measures, 1995.

Cities Included in 1988 and 1995	(1)	(2)	(3)	(4)	(5)	(6)
(1) Non-state vs. state labor ratio	1.000					
(2) Ratio of foreign investment	0.752**	1.000				
(3) Government investment in infrastructures	0.119	0.191	1.000			
(4) Growth rate of manufacturing industry	0.341*	0.227‡	−0.006	1.000		
(5) Ratio of non-state output value	0.659**	0.605**	0.226‡	0.583**	1.000	
(6) Per capita GDP	0.251‡	0.384**	0.107	0.166	0.402**	1.000
Mean	*2.424*	*0.034*	*0.060*	*0.656*	*0.445*	*1.050*
Median	*1.621*	*0.017*	*0.039*	*0.595*	*0.392*	*0.854*
Minimum	*0.520*	*0.000*	*0.000*	*0.230*	*0.100*	*0.150*
Maximum	*13.300*	*0.360*	*0.420*	*1.320*	*0.940*	*8.020*
Standard Deviation	*2.097*	*0.060*	*0.080*	*0.232*	*0.230*	*1.119*

Notes:

Statistical significance: ‡ $p < 0.10$; * $p < 0.05$; ** $p < 0.01$ (two-tailed tests).

Main data sources: Chinese Urban Statistical Yearbook (Chinese Statistical Press, 1996).

Supplement data sources: Local statistical yearbooks for some of the 55 cities under study.

Appendix C. Categorization of Industries into Monopoly and Open Sectors.

1995 CHIP Codes	INDUSTRY *State Statistics Codes (1995)*	*Documentary evidence*[1]	*Non-state-state labor ratio*[2]	*% of the labor force*[2]	*Assignments of Industries in CHIP Data*[3,4]
Industry 1	Farming, Forestry, Animal Husbandry, and Fishery	Open	0.52	52.9	Open
Industry 2	Manufacturing	Open	2.11	15.7	Quite open
	Electricity, Gas and Water Production and Supply	Monopoly	0.10	0.4	
Industry 3	Mining and Quarrying	Open	1.03	1.5	Quite open
	Geological Prospecting and Water Conservancy	Monopoly	0	0.2	
Industry 4	Construction	Open	3.24	5.3	Open
Industry 5	Railways	Monopoly	0	3.1	Considerably monopolistic
	Air Transportation	Monopoly	0		
	Highways, Waterways, and other Transportation	Open	3.48		
	Postal and Telecommunications	Monopoly	0		
Industry 6	Wholesale and Retail Trade, Restaurants, and Storage	Open	2.41	6.9	Open
Industry 7	Real Estate	Monopoly	0	0.1	Considerably monopolistic
	Public Facilities Services	Monopoly	0.11	1.1	
	Residential Services and other Services	Open	2.97		
Industry 8	Health Care, Sports, and Social Welfare	Monopoly	0.02	0.7	Monopolistic
Industry 9	Education, Culture and Arts, Radio, Film and Television	Monopoly	0.01	2.4	Monopolistic
Industry 10	Scientific Research and Polytechnical Services	Monopoly	0.08	0.3	Monopolistic
Industry 11	Financial Inter-mediation and Insurance	Monopoly	0	0.4	Monopolistic
Industry 12	Government Agencies, Party Agencies, and Social Organizations	Monopoly	0	1.7	Monopolistic
Industry 13	Others	Considerably Monopoly	0.22	7.2	Considerably monopolistic

Appendix C. Continued.

Notes:

1. "Documentary Evidence" includes laws and government regulations regarding permissions and restrictions for new organizations entering industries, through which the open/monopolistic feature of all industries in state staistics can be identified. For general industrial restrictions for domestic private firms and individuals, see "*Zhonghua renmin gongheguo siying qiye zanxing guanli tiaoli* (Provisional regulations of People's Republic of China regarding administration of private firm". *Renmin ribao* (People's daily), June 29, 1988. Also see "*Chengxiang geti gongshanghu guanli zanxing tiaoli* (Provisional Regulations regarding administration of individual industrial and commercial household). *Renmin ribao* (People's daily), August 19, 1987. For general industrial restrictions, see "*Waishang Touzi Chanyie Zhidao Mulu* (Guiding Directory of Industries for Foreign Investment)", *Renmin ribao* (People's daily), Jan. 7, 1998. For restrictions regarding enter into some special industries, see "*Zhonghua Renmin Gongheguo Tielufa* (Railways Law of People's Republic of China)", *Renmin ribao* (People's daily), Sept. 9, 1990; "*Zhonghua Renmin Gongheguo Youzhengfa* (Postal Law of People's Republic of China)", *Renmin ribao* (People's daily), Dec. 4, 1986; "*Congshi fangkai jingying dianxin yewu shenpi guanli zanxing banfa* (Temporary provisions concerning examination and approval of doing businesses in opened telecommunication services)", Guojia jihua weiyuanhui 1994; "*Zhonghua renmin gongheguo waizi jingrong jigou guanli tiaoli* (Regulations of People's Republic of China regarding administration on foreign financial institutions), *Renmin ribao* (People's daily), Feb. 25, 1994; "*Zhonghua renmin gongheguo yihang guanli zanxing tiaoli* (Provisional regulations of People's Republic of China regarding bank administration), *Renmin ribao* (People's daily), Jan. 17, 1986.
2. Ratios of non-state over state labor within industries as reported in *Zhongguo Tongji Nianjian* (China Statistical Yearbook, 1996). Nonstate labor here includes workers in all non-state, newly emerged firms.
3. The term "monopolistic industry" emphasizes the nature of exclusive rights of production by state organizations in an industry. Competition between state organizations exists in monopolistic industries. For example, state railroad companies compete with state airline corporations in transportation industry. Such competition, however, is bureaucratically coordinated by the state.
4. Considering the quantitative evidence, we label mixed industries either "quite open" or "considerably monopolistic". For simplicity, however, we classify these industries along with others into "open" and "monopolistic" sectors. Because industries 5 and 7 are small (3.1% and 1.2% of the total labor force, respectively), this simplification should not result in serious bias. Industry 13 contains economic supervision agencies, formerly state organs; it is therefore recognized as "considerably monopolistic" and classified in the monopoly sector.

Appendix D. Means and Standard Deviations of Variables Included in the OLS Regression as Reported in Table 2.

Variable	1988		1995	
	Mean	S.D.	Mean	S.D.
Dependent Variable				
Logarithm	7.4583	0.4631	8.6532	0.6265
Individual Characteristics				
Age	37.1568	10.5034	38.9287	9.8290
Age squared	1490.9427	804.9287	1612.0475	778.5916
Gender (male = 1)	0.5228	0.4995	0.5245	0.4994
Party membership (= 1)	0.2309	0.4215	0.2427	0.4287
Elementary school or lower	0.1244	0.3301	0.0539	0.2258
Middle school	0.3843	0.4864	0.3031	0.4596
High school	0.2476	0.4316	0.2412	0.4278
Vocational school	0.1067	0.3087	0.1655	0.3717
College or higher	0.1311	0.3375	0.2363	0.4248
Structural characteristics				
Occupational group				
Cadre	0.0635	0.2439	0.1116	0.3148
Professional	0.1578	0.3646	0.2234	0.4165
Entrepeneur	0.0152	0.1111	0.0133	0.1146
Clerical Staff	0.2272	0.4190	0.1893	0.3918
Worker and others	0.5390	0.4985	0.4624	0.4986

Appendix D. Continued.

Variable	1988 Mean	1988 S.D.	1995 Mean	1995 S.D.
Economic Sector				
Monopoly, state agency & organization	0.2920	0.4547	0.3071	0.4613
Open, state enterprises	0.4721	0.4992	0.4509	0.4976
Open, collectives	0.1984	0.3988	0.1485	0.3556
Private firm	0.0200	0.1401	0.0359	0.1859
Unspecified firm	0.0175	0.1312	0.0576	0.2330
Control Variable				
Permanent employment status (= 1)	0.9655	0.1826	0.9225	0.2674
Cities (55, Beijing as the contrast)	See Appendix A		See Appendix A	

Appendix E. Full Results for Table 3's Multilevel Models for Logarithm Yearly Income.

City-Level Variable	Ratio of Non-state vs. State Labor		Ratio of Foreign Investment		Growth Rate of Manufacturing Industry	
	Model I	Model II	Model I	Model II	Model I	Model II
(MICROLEVEL COEFFICIENTS)						
Intercept	8.277***	7.847***	8.308***	7.875***	8.317***	7.907***
Individual Characteristics						
Age	0.073***	0.067***	0.078***	0.072***	0.056***	0.041***
Age squared	−0.001***	−0.001***	−0.001***	−0.001***	−.000**	−0.000*
Gender (male = 1)	0.133***	0.116***	0.133***	0.115***	0.177**	0.155**
Party membership (= 1)	0.102***	0.084***	0.108***	0.076***	0.082*	0.092*
Elementary school or lower	−0.146**	−0.084*	−0.167***	−0.110***	−0.149‡	−0.092
High school	0.104***	0.066**	0.105***	0.061**	0.176**	0.114*
Vocational school	0.169***	0.083*	0.206***	0.099***	0.186**	0.062
College or higher	0.234***	0.111***	0.264***	0.125***	0.273***	0.114‡
Structural Characteristics						
Occupation (worker as contrast)						
Cadre		0.077**		0.091***		0.022
Professional		0.111***		0.132***		0.068‡
Entrepreneur		−0.006		−0.006		−0.013
Clerical staff		0.004		0.043*		0.004

Appendix E. Continued.

	Ratio of Non-state vs. State Labor		Ratio of Foreign Investment		Growth Rate of Manufacturing Industry	
City-Level Variable	Model I	Model II	Model I	Model II	Model I	Model II
Economic Sector (collective as contrast)						
Monopoly, state-run		0.297***		0.292***		0.312***
Open, state-run		0.205***		0.197***		0.189**
Private firm		0.370***		0.307***		0.178
Unspecified		0.098*		0.073‡		-0.076
Permanent employment (= 1, others = 0)		0.264***		0.277***		0.299*
(MICRO-MACRO INTERACTIVE COEFFICIENTS)						
Intercept	0.059**	0.063*	3.343***	3.586***	0.164	0.133
Individual Characteristics Age	0.005***	0.004*	0.154**	0.081	0.045*	0.057***
Age squared	0.000***	-0.000**	-0.002***	-0.001*	-0.001**	-0.001***
Gender (male = 1)	-0.002	-0.000	-0.103	-0.013	-0.077	-0.066
Party membership (= 1)	0.010‡	-0.002	0.570**	0.112	0.065	-0.028
Elementary school or lower	-0.002	-0.017*	-0.470	-0.400	-0.060	-0.058
High school	-0.001	-0.003	-0.042	-0.047	-0.116	-0.085
Vocational school	0.026*	0.010	0.517	-0.110	0.060	0.069
College or higher	0.023**	0.008	0.558	0.179	0.014	0.030

City-Level Variable	Ratio of Non-state vs. State Labor		Ratio of Foreign Investment		Growth Rate of Manufacturing Industry	
	Model I	Model II	Model I	Model II	Model I	Model II
Structural Characteristics						
Occupation (worker as contrast)						
Cadre		0.025**		1.275***		0.174‡
Professional		0.017*		0.486‡		0.125*
Entrepreneur		0.006		0.614		0.031
Clerical staff		0.028***		0.691**		0.099
Economic Sector (collective as contrast)						
Monopoly, state-run		−0.010		−0.525		−0.061
Open, state-run		−0.012		−0.691*		−0.021
Private firm		−0.027		−0.207		0.208
Unspecified		−0.015		0.257		0.229
Permanent employment (= 1, others = 0)		0.006		0.087		−0.020

Notes: Statistical significance: ‡ $p < 0.10$; * $p < 0.05$; ** $p < 0.001$ (two-tailed tests).